Intelligent Complex Adaptive Systems

Ang Yang
CSIRO Land and Water, Australia

Yin Shan
Medicare Australia

T0325046

IGI PUBLISHING

Hershey • New York

Acquisition Editor: Kristin Klinger
Senior Managing Editor: Jennifer Neidig
Managing Editor: Sara Reed
Development Editor: Kristin Roth
Copy Editor: Larissa Vinci
Typesetter: Amanda Appicello
Cover Design: Lisa Tosheff
Printed at: Yurchak Printing Inc.

Published in the United States of America by
        IGI Publishing (an imprint of IGI Global)
        701 E. Chocolate Avenue
        Hershey PA 17033
        Tel: 717-533-8845
        Fax: 717-533-8661
        E-mail: cust@igi-global.com
        Web site: http://www.igi-global.com

and in the United Kingdom by
        IGI Publishing (an imprint of IGI Global)
        3 Henrietta Street
        Covent Garden
        London WC2E 8LU
        Tel: 44 20 7240 0856
        Fax: 44 20 7379 0609
        Web site: http://www.eurospanonline.com

Intelligent complex adaptive systems / Ang Yang and Yin Shan, editors.
     p. cm.
  Companion volume to: Applications of complex adaptive systems.
  Summary: "This book explores the foundation, history, and theory of intelligent adaptive systems, providing a fundamental resource on topics such as the emergence of intelligent adaptive systems in social sciences, biologically inspired artificial social systems, sensory information processing, as well as the conceptual and methodological issues and approaches to intelligent adaptive systems"--Provided by publisher.
  Includes bibliographical references and index.
  ISBN-13: 978-1-59904-717-1 (hardcover)
  ISBN-13: 978-1-59904-719-5 (ebook)
  1. Functionalism (Social sciences) 2. System analysis. 3. Biocomplexity--Simulation methods. 4. Social systems--Simulation methods. 5. Economics--Methodology. 6. Organizational sociology--Simulation methods. 7. Modularity (Engineering) 8. Modularity (Psychology) 9. Self-organizaing systems. 10. Adaptive control systems. I. Yang, Ang. II. Shan, Yin.
  HM484.I57 2008
  300.1'1--dc22
                              2007032059

British Cataloguing in Publication Data
A Cataloguing in Publication record for this book is available from the British Library.

Intelligent Complex Adaptive Systems

Table of Contents

Section I
General Theories

Section II
Important Concepts

Section III
Computing Perspectives

Section IV
Social Science Perspectives

Foreword

I don't believe in the existence of a complex systems theory as such and, so far, I'm still referring to complex systems science (CSS) in order to describe my research endeavours. In my view, the latter is constituted, up until now, by a bundle of loosely connected methods and theories aiming to observe— from contrasted standpoints—these fascinating objects of research called complex adaptive systems. Nearly 40 years after Von Bertalanffy's *General System Theory* (1968) and Jacques Monod's *Chance and Necessity* (1971), it is fair to look back and to try to assess how much remains to be said about these complex adaptive systems. After all, Prigogine's *Order out of Chaos* (1984) already demonstrated that future wasn't entirely predictable in a history-contingent world. Nearly at the same period, Maturana and Varela's *Tree of Knowledge* (1987) questioned the closure of biological systems and proposed a challenging theory of autopoieitic systems, oddly left aside by CSS's mainstream research. Later on, Holland's *Hidden Order* (1996) set out the terminology associated with and the characteristics of complex adaptive systems, still in use nowadays. More recently, Watts's *Six Degrees* (2004) epitomized current assumptions of network theorists asserting that a system's structure and organization—most of the time—dictate its functional properties. What remains from these influential contributions are a heterogeneous corpus of partly conflicting theories and a disparate set of tools and methods. Furthermore, too often complex systems science lends itself to criticism when it trades its artificial complex adaptive systems for natural (i.e., actual) ones.

Computer-based simulations, regardless of their expected accuracy, aren't the reality, there are just metaphoric representations; *"the world as it might be, not the world as it is"* according to Holland himself.

So, yes, much remains to be said about complex adaptive systems (CAS). Altogether, we need to better our understanding of natural CAS and to improve analytical capacities of artificial CAS. Both aspects need to be dealt with cautiously in order to avoid ill-fated circularities that have sometimes characterized research out of in-vitro simulations or artificial society experiments. It is indeed an understated challenge to design a computer metaphor that describes a given reality independently of the hypothetical processes to be tested. Flawed designs often result in logical tautologies whereby the model always verifies the assumptions. Another challenge consists in the reconciliation between system-wide and individual-centred representations of CAS. This task is anything but trivial as technical limitations and epistemological differences have contributed to the divide. Technically, latest hybrid simulation platforms provide the means to couple agent-based modelling with dynamical systems modelling or network-oriented simulations. But epistemological differences on internationality, for example, need to be dealt with in a same way biology has progressively dealt with the tension between Lamarckism and Darwinism on evolution.

In this context, the present *ouvrage* comes at its time. The carefully selected chapters cover the latest theoretical developments on natural CAS and innovative ways to improve the analytical capacities of artificial CAS. Traditional concepts of complex systems science are re-visited: what is emergence? Can we explain the emergence of creativity in natural CAS? How does emergent specialization improve artificial CAS's design? Likewise, essential characteristics of social CAS are scrutinized: How do information flows influence the complexity of social systems? Can we propose a robust ontological foundation for social simulations? Finally, this book invites us into an interdisciplinary journey through biological evolution, neo-classical economics, system thinking and social sciences, using CSS as its Arian's thread. Intelligent complex adaptive systems (ICAS) will emerge from this interdisciplinary cross-fertilization combined with technological advances. They will provide powerful analytical capacities, supported by a reunified and holistic vision on complex adaptive systems. They will help us to build what I will have to call, finally, a complex systems theory.

Pascal Perez
Associate Professor, Research School of Pacific & Asian Studies, Australian National University

Preface

Our world is a large, integrated system of systems. These systems, whether they are ecological, social, or financial, are complex and constantly adapt to their environment. Many of them are essential for our very existence. Being so complex, and because of the intensive interactions among the system components, they cannot be fully understood by isolating their components or applying simple cause and effect reasoning. These systems, however, can be examined by looking for patterns within their behaviour. Intelligent complex adaptive systems (ICAS) research uses systemic inquiry to build multi-disciplinary representations of reality to study such complex systems.

Because the use of ICAS is prevalent across a number of disciplines, papers describing ICAS theory and applications are scattered through different journals and conference proceedings. It is, therefore, important to have a book that broadly covers the state-of-art in this highly evolving area. There has been a strong interest among researchers regarding the publication of this book. Forty-nine submissions were received. All papers went through rigid peer review by at least three reviewers and only 23 were accepted for publication, an acceptance rate of just under 50%. Because of size constraints, these papers are published two volumes. This book focuses on the theoretical side of ICAS while its sister book *Applications of Intelligent Complex Adaptive Systems* emphasises the techniques and applications. These two volumes cover a broad spectrum of ICAS research from discussion of general theory and foundations to more practical studies of ICAS in various artificial and natural systems. It is important to highlight that a significant portion of contributions come from the social sciences. This will, we believe, provide readers of these books with extremely valuable diverse views of ICAS, and also clearly demonstrates the wide applicability of ICAS theories.

Intelligent Complex Adaptive Systems

The study of ICAS draws richly from foundations in several disciplines, perhaps explaining in part why ICAS research is so active and productive. These diverse fields that contributed to the formation of ICAS included the genetic algorithm (Holland, 1975) and cellular automata (Gardner, 1970, von Neumann, 1966) in computer sciences, evolution and predator-prey models (Lotka, 1925) in biology, and game theory (von Neumann & Morgenstern, 1944) in economics.

Researchers of ICAS are interested in various questions, but these can be summarised as to how to describe complex systems, and how to describe the interactions within these systems that give rise to patterns. Thus, although researchers from different backgrounds may have very different approaches to the study of ICAS, it is the unique properties of ICAS systems, such as nonlinearity, emergence, adaptivity and modularity that form the centre of inquiries. Many of these properties will be thoroughly explored in these two volumes. It is the complexity of ICAS systems which means that although a variety of techniques which have been employed to study ICAS, computer simulations have become important and widely used. These simulations involve several important computing techniques that may interest readers of these books.

- Evolutionary computation (EC) is a highly active field of research inspired by natural evolution. Essentially, EC models the dynamics of a population of distinctive entities such as chromosomes in genetic algorithms or programs in genetic programming. Thus, while EC has been used as a simplified model to study ICAS, it is also an ICAS itself having wide applicability for solving scientific and engineering problems.

- Cellular automata (CA), and related techniques such as Boolean networks, are common techniques in ICAS. The behaviour of entities that respond to the environment is defined as rules or other forms. Each entity can interact with adjacent ones. The topology of adjacency can be defined in various ways depending on the focus of the research. CA and related techniques have been widely used to study important properties of ICAS such as emergence.

- Multi-agent systems (MAS) are systems composed of several autonomous agents. These agents may use a belief-desire-intention model or other mechanisms to guide their behaviour, respond to the environment, or communicate and interact with other agents. The concept of MAS model can be directly applied to study a number of ICAS systems. More often, a computer simulation of MAS is used to understand corresponding ICAS.

ICAS research has applications across numerous disciplines. As we are surrounded by complex systems, and indeed are ourselves a complex system, applications are everywhere. In this preface, we have no intention of providing a compete list of applications of ICAS, although some of the chapters do survey ICAS applications in a particular field, but we do wish to highlight the following subjects that are covered by this book and its sister volume.

Because human society is a complex system, comprising a large number of autonomous individuals and entities that are connected by various layers of networks, it has been the one of the major fields of applications of ICAS research. As explained in a number of excellent chapters, significant research has been conducted into how disease, information, belief, language, and innovation propagate and diffuse in society.

Economics and finance are also the focuses of applied ICAS research. The economic and financial interactions among the entities of modern society, either at individual or institutional level, are vital to its existence. ICAS has been used to study these interactions and to understand the dynamics that underpin them.

Management can also been understood and further explored with ICAS concepts and methodologies that provide both a novel perspective and an exciting new set of tools. Besides applications to general management, these two books also have chapters dedicated to specific management applications such as military transformation.

And finally, ICAS has been widely used in science and engineering. Complex systems exist almost everywhere in the natural world, from the complex dynamics of the weather to important ecological systems. ICAS plays an important role in understanding these systems. Furthermore, it is well known that the robustness and reliability of an ICAS system is partially due to the fact that there is usually no centralised control system. This idea has been explored in solving engineering problems.

Audience

Researchers working in the field of ICAS and related fields such as machine learning, artificial intelligence, multi-agent systems, economy, finance, management, international relations, and other social sciences should find this book an indispensable state-of-art reference. Because of its comprehensive coverage, the book can also be used as complementary readings at the postgraduate level.

Organisation

The diversity of backgrounds within ICAS research provides the deep well of intellectual resources, which has allowed ICAS research to continue thriving. This diversity of backgrounds leads to a blurring of boundaries when categorising ICAS studies, a feature that should be seen as one of the unique characteristics of this field of research and one that need not be regarded as a problem. In organising a book, however, divisions are necessary. Thus, our organisation of this book into four sections on general theories, importance concepts, and perspectives in computing and the social sciences is only meant to provide the audience with a simple reference to make the book more accessible. The interdisciplinary nature of ICAS means that many articles might fit into multiple sections.

Two chapters in the general theories section seek the core of complex adaptive systems (CAS) and provide an alternative top-down method called "method of systems potential" rather than conventional "agent-based modelling" to study CAS. The first chapter by Wallis seeks to identify the core of CAS theory. To achieve this, it introduces innovative methods for measuring and advancing the validity of a theory by understanding the structure of theory. Two studies of CAS theory are presented. These show how the outer belt of loosely connected concepts support the evolution of a theory while, in contrast, the robust core of a theory, consisting of co-causal propositions, supports validity and testability. The tools presented in this chapter may be used to support the purposeful evolution of theory by improving the validity of ICAS theory.

In the second chapter by Pushnoi et al. emergent properties of CAS are explored by means of "agent-based modelling" (ABM) and compared to results from method of systems potential (MSP) modelling. MSP describes CAS as a holistic system whereas ABM-methodology considers CAS as set of interacting agents. The authors argue that MSP is a top-down approach, which supplements the bottom-up modelling by ABM. Both ABM and MSP exhibit similar macroscopic properties such as punctuated equilibrium, sudden jumps in macro-indices, cyclical dynamics, superposition of deterministic and stochastic patterns in dynamics, fractal properties of structure and dynamics, and SOC-phenomenon. ABM demonstrates these properties via simulations of the different models whereas MSP derives these phenomena analytically.

In the second section of this book on important concepts, two chapters seek to understand modularity, hierarchy, complexity, and emergence in the context of ICAS. Cornforth et al. provide an in-depth discussion of modularity, ubiquitous in CAS. Modules are clusters of components that interact with their environment as a single unit and, when they occur at different levels, form a hierarchy. Modularity occurs widely in natural and artificial systems, in the latter where it is used to simplify design, provide fault tolerance and solve difficult problems by decomposition. Modular and hierarchic structures simplify analysis of complex systems by reducing long-range connections, thus constraining groups of components to act as a single component. Network theory, widely used to understand modularity and hierarchy, can make predictions about certain properties of systems such as the effects of critical phase changes in connectivity.

In the study by Standish, investigation of important concepts in CAS is continued. The term *complexity* is used informally both as a quality and as a quantity. As a quality, complexity relates to our ability to understand a system or object—we understand simple systems, but not complex ones. On another level, *complexity* is used as a quantity when we talk about something being more complicated than another. This chapter explores the formalisation of both meanings of complexity during the latter half of the twentieth century.

The third section of this book features four chapters on the use of modern computing techniques to study the emergence of creativity, emergent specialisation, information bottleneck to central processing in adaptive systems and the role of barriers to information flows in the robustness of complex systems.

Creativity has been a difficult concept to define and its exact relationship with intelligence remains to be explained. In the first of the four chapters on computing techniques, Thórisson presents a theory of natural creativity and its relation to certain features of intelligence and cognitive faculties. To test the theory, the author employs simulated worlds of varying complexity that are inhabited by creatures with a genetically evolving mental model. Plan-making strategies are compared between creatures in each world. This shows that creative behaviours are governed by the world's structural coherence and complexity. The theoretical framework presented in this chapter may serve as a foundation and tool to improve our understanding of natural creativity and to help develop creative artificially intelligent systems.

Nilsson contributes the second study on computing perspectives, considering sensory information bottlenecks in adaptive systems. Such bottlenecks are an inevitable consequence when a complex system adapts by increasing its information input. Input and output bottlenecks are due to geometrical limits that arise because the area available for connections from an external surface always exceeds the area available for connections to an internal surface. Processing of the additional information faces an internal bottleneck. As more elements increase the size of a processor, its interface surface increases more slowly than its volume. Such bottlenecks had to be overcome before complex life forms could evolve. Based on mapping studies, it is generally agreed that sensory inputs to the brain are organized as convergent-divergent networks. However, no one has previously explained how such networks can conserve the location and magnitude of any particular stimulus. The solution to a convergent-divergent network that overcomes bottleneck problems turns out to be surprisingly simple and yet restricted.

In the current information age, a high premium is placed on the widespread availability of information, and access to as much information as possible is often cited as a key to making effective decisions. While it would be foolish to deny the central role that information flow has in effective decision making processes, in the chapter by Richardson, the equally important role of barriers to information flows in the robustness of complex systems are explored. The analysis demonstrates that, for simple Boolean networks, a complex system's ability to filter out certain information flows is essential if the system is not to be beholden to every external signal. The reduction of information is as important as the availability of information.

Specialisation is observable in many complex adaptive systems and is thought to be a fundamental mechanism for achieving optimal efficiency. In the final chapter on computing perspectives, Nitschke et al. present a survey of collective behaviour systems designed using biologically inspired principles in which specialization emerges as a result of system dynamics, and where emergent specialization is used as a problem solver or means to increase task performance. The authors argue for developing design methodologies and principles that facilitate emergent specialization in collective behaviour systems.

In this book's final section, three chapters provide insight into emergence in multi-agent systems in the social sciences, and the application of ICAS theories in international relations and economic systems. Dessalles et al. provide a survey of concept of emergence from both a conceptual and a formal perspective, and discuss the notions of downward/backward causation and weak/strong emergence. They pay particular attention to the formal definitions introduced by Müller and Bonabeau, which are operative in multi-agent frameworks and are derived from both cognitive and social points of view.

In the second social sciences chapter, Alker provides a study on ontological reflections on peace and war. Responding to a question by Hiroharu Seki about Hiroshima ontologies, the author reviews thinking about the ontological primitives appropriate for event-data making, accessing high-performance knowledge bases, and modelling ICAS used by researchers on war and peace. It cautions against "Cliocide," defined as of the "silencing" or symbolic killing of collective historical-political or historical-disciplinary identities and identifying practices by historical or discipline deficient "scientific" coding practices. He proposes that more intelligent multi-agent models in the "complex, adaptive systems" tradition of the Santa Fe Institute should include the socially shared memories of nations and international societies, including their identity-redefining traumas and their relational/migrational/ ecological histories of community-building success and failure. Historicity in an ontologically distinctive sense of the "time ordered self-understandings of a continuing human society" is still a challenge for the computationally oriented literature on war and peace.

In the final chapter of this book, Potts et al. discuss a classic allocation problem. The substitution relation between two primary carriers of complex rules—agents and institutions—is a function of the relative costs of embedding rules in these carriers, all subject to the constraint of maintaining overall system complexity. This generic model is called the allocation of complexity, which they propose as a bridge between neoclassical and complexity economics.

Conclusion

This book and its sister volume bring together prominent ICAS researchers from around the globe who provide us with a valuable diverse set of views on ICAS. Their work covers a wide spectrum of cutting-edge ICAS research, from theory to applications in various fields such as computing and social sciences, and provides both comprehensive surveys on some topics and in-depth discussions on others. This offers us a glimpse of the rapidly progressing and extremely active field that is ICAS research. More importantly, because of the interdisciplinary background of the contributors, these books should facilitate communications between researchers from these different fields and thus help to further enhance ICAS research. Thus, we hope that these books may help to raise the profile of the contribution that complex adaptive systems can make toward better understanding of the various critical systems around us. In doing so, this work should encourage both further research into this area and also the practical implementation of the results derived from this area.

References

Gardner, M. (1970). Mathematical games: The fantastic combinations of John Conway's new solitaire game "life." *Scientific American, 223*(October 1970), 120-123.

Holland, J. H. (1975). *Adaptation in natural and artificial systems.* Ann Arbor, MI: University of Michigan Press.

Lotka, A. J. (1925). *The elements of physical biology.* Baltimore, MD: Williams & Williams Co.

Von Neumann, J. (1966). Theory of self-reproducing automata. In A. W. Burks (ed.), *Lectures on the theory and organization of complicated automata.* Champaign, IL: University of Illinois Press.

Von Neumann, J. & Morgenstern, O. (1944). *Theory of games and economic behaviour.* Princeton, NJ: Princeton University Press.

Ying Shan, Ang Yang
Canberra, Australia
June 2007

Section I

General Theories

Chapter I

From Reductive to Robust:
Seeking the Core of Complex Adaptive Systems Theory

Steven E. Wallis, Independent Consultant, USA

Abstract

This chapter seeks to identify the core of complex adaptive systems (CAS) theory. To achieve this end, this chapter introduces innovative methods for measuring and advancing the validity of a theory by understanding the structure of theory. Two studies of CAS theory are presented that show how the outer belt of atomistic and loosely connected concepts support the evolution of a theory; while, in contrast, the robust core of theory, consisting of co-causal propositions, supports the validity and testability of a theory. Each may be seen as being derived from differing epistemologies. It is hoped that the tools presented in this chapter will be used to support the purposeful evolution of theory by improving the validity of intelligent complex adaptive systems (ICAS) theory.

What is the Core of CAS Theory?

Where other chapters in this book may use intelligent complex adaptive systems (ICAS) theory as a framework to understand our world, we strive in this chapter to understand theory, itself. Through this process, the reader will gain a new perspective on the theory that is applied elsewhere in this book. To gain some perspective on ICAS, we will study the literature of complex adaptive systems (CAS) as developed in the field of organizational theory. As such, this chapter may be of interest to those discussing organizational theory and organizational change, multi-agent systems, learning methods, simulation models, and evolutionary games.

CAS theory originated in the natural sciences as a tool for understanding non-linear dynamics (Kauffman, 1995) and has gained popularity in organizational studies through the efforts of many authors (i.e., Axelrod & Cohen, 2000; Brown & Eisenhardt, 1998; Gleick, 1987; Stacey, 1996; Wheatley, 1992). As CAS expanded into this discipline, every author seems to have placed a personal mark by revising CAS for interpretation and publication. Indeed, in researching the literature, 20 concise, yet different, definition/descriptions of CAS theory were found.

Within these 20 definitions, "component concepts" were identified. For example, Bennet & Bennet (2004) note (in part) that a CAS is composed of a large number of self-organizing components. The concepts of "self-organization" and "large number of components" may be seen as conceptual components of CAS theory as described by those authors. These conceptual components might also be thought of as the authors' "propositions." It is important to note that among the 20 definitions, no two contained the same combination of component concepts. This raises a serious question: When we talk about CAS theory, are we really talking about the "same thing?" After all, if one author states that a CAS may be understood through concepts "a, b, and c" while another author states that the relevant concepts are "c, e, and f," there may be some conceptual overlap but there are also inherent contradictions.

In the social sciences, this issue has been of concern for decades. In one attempt to make sense of the issue, theory has been described as consisting of a "hard core" of unchanging assumptions, surrounded by a more changeable "protective belt" (Lakatos, 1970). When a theory is challenged, a theorist may rise to defend it with a new proposition that changes the belt, but presumably leaves the core intact. Phelan (2001) suggests that complexity theory has its "hard-core assumptions;" however, among the 20 definitions discussed here, there is no one concept that is held in common by all of the authors. If there is no concept, or set of concepts, held in common, where then is the core of CAS theory? Motivated by this apparent lack of commonality, we seek to identify the core of CAS theory.

A Chinese proverb states, "The beginning of wisdom is to call things by their right names." (Unknown, 2006, p. 1). The difficulty of engaging in conversations with imprecise definitions was famously illustrated when Plato called man a "featherless biped." He was forced to add, "with broad flat nails" in response to Digenes, who arrived with a plucked bird, proclaiming "Here is Plato's man." (Bartlett, 1992, p. 77). We may speculatively ask if it was the atomistic nature of Plato's definition that left it so open to misinterpretation. In short, we must wonder how we can know what we are talking about, if the name keeps changing. In contrast to Plato's rapidly evolving definition, Newton's laws (e.g., F=ma) have proved effective, and unchanged, for centuries.

As scholars, of course, we are continually engaged in the discovery (or social construction, depending on your view) of understandings and definitions. And yet, we need some level of shared understanding of existing concepts, so we may communicate effectively as we work to understand new concepts. In short, as scholars, we might see the increasing clarity and stability of our definitions as an indicator of "progress" in a given field. We dig the clay, form it into paving stones, place them in front of us, and walk on them to find more clay. In this chapter, we will suggest some tools for identifying the milestones along our shared road.

Central to the exploration presented in this chapter, we must ask, "Is it possible to ascertain the legitimacy of a theory through its structure?" Dubin (1978) suggests that there are four levels of efficacy in theory; and these levels do reflect the structure of the theory. They are: (1) presence /absence (what concepts are contained within a theory). (2) Directionality (what are the causal concepts and what are the emergent concepts within the theory). (3) Co-variation (how several concepts might impel change in one another). (4) Rate of change (to what quantity do each of the elements within the theory effect one another). Parson and Shills note four similar levels of systemization of theory—moving toward increasing "levels of systemization" (Friedman, 2003, p. 518). Reflecting the validity of these assertions, Newton's formulae might be seen as residing at the highest level because it is possible to identify quantitative changes in one aspect (e.g., force) from changes in other aspects (e.g., mass & acceleration). Such a high level of understanding has been long sought in the social sciences but has, as yet, remained elusive. One goal of this chapter is to advance CAS theory along this scale—and identify how further advances might be enabled for similar forms of theory.

To find the core of a theory, two studies are presented in this chapter. One study is based on content analysis (essentially, looking at the words used by the authors as reasonable representations of the concepts that they are conveying). The second study uses a more traditional narrative analysis. The first study is a reductive look at CAS theory—focusing on the axiomatic propositions of the authors. This method will be seen as adding to the outer belt. The second study focuses on the relational propositions of CAS theory. This method suggests that there is a core to CAS theory. However, it also shows that the core (based on the current state of CAS theory) has only a limited internal integrity. A path for developing a more robust CAS theory is then suggested. The process of developing a robust theory is expected to provide great benefits to scholars (based on the successful use of Newton's robust formulae).

Due to limitations of space, the studies in this chapter will be focused on the level of "concept" (with concepts presented as they are named by the authors and as they may be generally understood by most readers) and theory (as a collection of concepts). These studies will generally avoid the sub-concept level of interpretation and what might be called a post-theory level of application and testing.

The next section includes a relatively linear and reductive analysis of the concepts of CAS theory. This process might be seen as a thought experiment—a cognitive construction that represents the creation of new definitions in an ad-hoc manner.

A Reductive Study of CAS Theory

In this section, we engage in the development of new theory where theory might be seen as a collection of concepts. This process identifies the range of concepts in CAS theory and develops new versions of that theory. The new versions of CAS theory created here may be seen as newly evolved definitions. Although such definitions may be tentatively used to identify various perspectives of CAS theory, they may also be seen as adding to the outer belt of theory rather than clarifying the core.

We begin with a review of literature. Searches of the ProQuest database yielded nearly 100 articles in academic journals where CAS theory was discussed in the context of a human organization. Within those articles, 13 were found to contain concise (less than one page) definitions of CASs. Additionally, those journals (and other sources) suggested other scholarly publications. Promising books were reviewed and seven additional concise definitions were found. In all, this study (although not exhaustive) found 20 relatively concise definitions of CASs. Concise definitions were used so that the study could cover as much ground as possible. It is also assumed that a concise definition includes the most important aspects of each author's version of the theory. It is also expected that a sample of this size will provide a sufficient representation of the body of theory.

Although the authors' definitions are not listed for reasons of space, this study uses concise definitions from Ashmos, Huonker, and McDaniel (1998), Axelrod et al. (2000), Bennet et al. (2004), Brown et al. (1998), Chiva-Gomez (2003), Daneke (1999), Dent (2003), Harder, Robertson, & Woodward (2004), Hunt & Ropo (2003), Lichtenstein (2000), McDaniel, Jordan, & Fleeman, (2003), McGrath (1997), McKelvey (2004), Moss (2001), Olson & Eoyang (2001), Pascale (1999), Shakun (2001), Stacey (1996), Tower (2002), Yellowthunder & Ward (2003).

In the process previously described, the study deconstructed each definition into the authors' propositions, or component concepts. For example, Daneke describes a CAS as, "A simulation approach that studies the coevolution of a set of interacting agents that have alternative sets of behavioral rules" (Daneke, 1999, p. 223). The concepts describing the CAS here would be coevolution, interaction, agents, and rules. While another reader might develop a different list, it is expected that such lists would be substantively similar to the one developed here where a total of 26 concepts were identified, consisting of:

Agent, non-linear/unpredictable, levels, co-evolutionary, adaptive, agents evolve, far from equilibrium/edge of chaos, self-organizing, many agents, interrelated/interacting, goal seeking, decision-making, emergence/surprise happens, act in rules/context of other agents and environment, simple rules, permeable boundaries, evolves toward fitness, boundary testing, iterative process, agents are semi-autonomous, evaluate effectiveness of decisions/ results, self-defining, identity, morality, irreversible, time.

This list might be seen as representing the whole of CAS theory from an atomistic perspective. It should be noted that at this "survey" stage, no component appears to be more "important" than another and no component seems to be closer to the core than any other.

Of the 20 publications, three could clearly be seen as the "most cited" (each having been cited by hundreds instead of tens, or fewer). Between them, there are six concepts used by at least two of the three, including:

Co-evolutionary, many agents, interrelated/interacting, goal seeking, emergence/surprise happens, simple rules.

This focus on what might be considered the "authoritative" versions essentially creates a new definition of CAS theory built on the shared conceptual components of the authors. However, it should be noted that this new definition has lost some conceptual breadth when compared to the whole body of CAS theory. Moving from one form of popularity to another, the following is a list of those six concepts that seemed most popular among the 20 definitions:

Non-linear/unpredictable, co-evolutionary, many agents, interrelated/interacting, goal seeking, emergence surprise happens.

Again, a new definition of CAS theory has been created with a new focus. Again, the conceptual components have shifted—both in comparison to the whole body of CAS concepts and in comparison to the authoritative version.

Additionally, while most authors identified themselves as scholars, others identified themselves as scholar-practitioners. Those whose affiliations were uncertain were left out of this ad-hoc, demonstrative study. The five concepts most commonly described by those authors who identified themselves as scholars were:

Non-linear/unpredictable, self-organizing, many agents, interrelated/interacting, emergence/surprise happens.

Among those who identified themselves as scholar-practitioners, the four most popular concepts used were:

Non-linear/unpredictable, many agents, interrelated/interacting, goal seeking.

There are obvious limitations to this ad-hoc study. However, a number of insights and benefits become apparent here. First, that this study creates a comprehensive view of the concepts within a body of theory. Of course, in this study, that view is limited to the level of the concepts, rather than delving deeper, which is another possible level of exploration. Second, that each group of concepts suggests those specific concepts that might be most appropriate for a given application or area of research. In a sense, each group of concepts might be viewed as a "school of thought" for CAS theory within its specific venue. Importantly, this brief study essentially began with 20 definitions and generated four more. The number of theories in the outer belt was easily increased, yet we do not seem to have increased our understanding of the core. Our lack of core insight may be related to the form of analysis, or the type of data used. Importantly, we approached the data as lists of concepts and rearranged them into new lists. Each attempt to identify a new perspective resulted in a new list. As with the broader survey (the first list), each subsequent list has no discernible core.

The analysis presented in this section has served to demonstrate some strengths and weaknesses of a reductive form of study. In the next section, we look at alternative approaches to the ordering of conceptual components and, in the section following, we apply those ordering ideas to clarify the structure of CAS theory.

Looking at the Structure of Theory

Drawing on Southerland, Weick (1989) discusses theory as, "an ordered set of assertions" (p. 517). If a theory is defined (in part) as consisting of ordered assertions, it begs the question of just how well ordered those assertions might be. By "ordered," we might understand those assertions to be arranged alphabetically, by apparent importance, or any number of possible methods. This "disposition of things following one after another" (Webster's, 1989, p. 1013) do not seem to add much to our understanding of theory, however. It is not clear, for example, that a theory might be considered more valid if the assertions are in alphabetical order instead of ordered (for example) by the year each concept was added to the literature. However, based on that simple interpretation of order, there would seem to be no epistemological preference between ordering the assertions by their historical appearance in the literature, by the first letter in the concept, or ordering the assertions by the apparent importance ascribed to them by an author.

By ordered, therefore, it may be that Weick was implying something more significant than a list. A more useful (or at least an alternative) epistemological validity, therefore, might be developed by looking at the assertions or propositions of a theory as being "interrelated," where the propositions might be seen as, "reciprocally or mutually related" (Webster's, 1989, p. 744). With such a view, a body of theory might be seen as a kind of system and, "...any part of the system can only be fully understood in terms of its relationships with the other parts of the whole system." (Harder et al., 2004, p. 83, drawing on Freeman). It seems, therefore, that every concept within a theory would best be understood through other concepts within that body of theory. Significantly, this perspective seems to fit with Dubin's (above) assertion that theories of higher efficacy have explanations and concepts that are co-causal.

To briefly compare and contrast levels of interrelatedness, we might say that the lowest level of relationship may be found in some jumble of random concepts. A higher level of interrelatedness might be seen in a book where an author describes concepts (thus causing each to exist in closer relationship with others). Other authors have used a wide variety of methods for increasing relatedness such as placing them in a list (as above), a flow-chart showing a cycle (e.g., Nonaka, 2005, for social construction), a matrix (e.g., Pepper, 1961, for metaphors), or a combination of lists and flows to create a meta-model (e.g., Slawski, 1990). With each increasing level of relatedness, a given reader might understand a concept in relationship with other concepts, and so find new insights based on the relatedness between concepts. In short, an increasingly systematic relationship might be viewed as having increasing relatedness. One example of a systemic theory may be seen in Wilber's integral theory of human development (e.g., Wilber, 2001). In his theory, Wilber describes four quadrants that represent categorizations of insights from numerous disciplines. Wilber claims that each of these quadrants is co-defined by the others—in essence, that no quadrant can be fully understood except in relation to the other three. This claim suggests a high degree of relatedness.

Another way to look at interrelatedness might be seen in the concept of "reflexive." Hall (1999) suggests that some forms of inquiry represent a "third path" of inquiry that is primarily neither objective, nor subjective; rather it is essentially reflexive, where meaning is created in a socially constructed sense. In contrast to reflexive forms used in the sense of the interaction between individuals, however, the second study of this chapter looks at reflexive analysis in the sense that suggests a relationship within, or between, the concepts of CAS theory.

Combining the idea of relatedness with the idea of theory having a tight core and a loose belt, we might see the concepts in the core as being more closely interrelated than the belt. For example, the above reductive study of CAS produced definitions with low levels of interrelatedness, as might be found in the loosely defined belt of a theory, because the new theories are presented essentially as lists of concepts.

In addition to the concept of relatedness, another important concept for this chapter is that of "robustness." Wallis (2006a) explored a number of interpretations of this term. Following insights developed from Hegel and Nietzsche, Wallis settled on an understanding of robustness that might be familiar to those working in the natural sciences, where a robust theory is one where its dimensions are "co-defined." An example of this would be Newton's law of motion (F=ma) where each aspect (e.g., mass) may be calculated, or understood, in terms of the other two (e.g., force and acceleration).

It is very important to differentiate between theories whose structure might be seen as robust, and theories whose structure might be understood as an ordered list. For example, a list of assertions might be understood as an atomistic form of theory and might be represented abstractly as "A" is true. "B" is true. "C" is true. In contrast, the propositions of a robust theory might be seen as Changes in "A" and "B" will cause predictable changes in "C." Changes in "B" and "C" will cause predictable changes in "A." And, changes in "C" and "A" will cause predictable changes in "B." The interrelatedness of concepts in a robust theory suggests that the theory may be validated from "within" the theory.

In this book and elsewhere (e.g., Richardson, 2006), the concept of robustness is used to describe the stability of a network experiencing external perturbations. A system that is completely unstable would have a robustness of zero, while a perfectly stable system would be assigned a robustness of one. While it could be legitimately argued that no system can have its measure of robustness at the extreme ends of the scale (zero, or one), this chapter will use zero and one as approximations to facilitate discussion.

An understanding of perturbations might be used to determine what might be called the "dynamic robustness" of a system of theory by identifying the ratio of stable concepts to changing concepts. In this two-step process, one first identifies the concepts contained in each form of the theory and assigns each a numerical value based on the component concepts. Next, the ratio between the two (earlier and later) versions of the theory is taken. If the two theories are identical, the robustness will be equal to "unity" (or one). If the two theories have no concepts in common, they will have a robustness of zero. For example, if theory "A" has four distinct concepts (a, b, c, d) and subsequently evolves into theory "B" with four concepts (c, d, e, f,), we may see theory A and B together as having a total of six concepts (a, b, c, d, e, f) with only two concepts held in common (c, d). This relationship suggests that in the process of evolving from theory A to theory B, the theory exhibited a robustness of 0.33 (two divided by six). Of course, such measures might only be considered valid when the concepts themselves are unambiguous. This method may be seen as responding to Hull's (1988) deep discussion on the evolution of theory—and providing a tool to aid in the mapping of that evolution.

If we look at each author's influence on CAS theory as a perturbation, CAS theory may be seen as having a low level of robustness. For example, Yellowthunder et al. (2003) describe a CAS using four concepts drawn from Olson et al. (2001) who used those four in addition to three additional concepts. This change suggests a robustness of 0.57 (the result of four divided by seven). Other times, CAS does not fare even that well. Dent (2003) states that he drew his conceptualization of CAS from Brown et al. (1998). However, between the six concepts listed by Dent and the eight concepts listed by Brown et al., there are only two concepts that clearly overlap. This suggests a low robustness of 0.14 (the result of two divided by fourteen). In contrast, Newton's formula of force (F=ma) may be seen as having a robustness of one as the formula is unchanged in any non-relativistic application. The widespread use of Newton's formula may suggest that theories of greater robustness are more useful (and may have more predictive power) than theories of less robustness.

While low robustness may be seen as enabling "flexibility" (where a theory changes and evolves with rapidity), it may also be seen as an indicator of confusion or uncertainty. It recalls our original question as to the core of CAS theory and suggests that axiomatic, atomistic, or reductive definitions (e.g., theories with concepts that are structured as lists) have shown too much flexibility to provide an adequate representation of the core. In the following section, we analyze the body of CAS theory to identify more robust relationships between the concepts.

Investigating Relational Propositions

In this section, we investigate the relational propositions described by the authors of the above 20 concise definitions to identify the core of CAS theory, where that core may be seen as shifting CAS theory toward Dubin's (1978) second level of theory efficacy (where concepts are directionally causal).

In this process, as with the reductive study, we deconstructed each of the concise definitions into propositions. Rather than use all of the available conceptual components, however, those statements that were essentially axiomatic are left out. For example, Bennet et al. (2004) state, "There are some basic properties common to many complex adaptive systems. Examples are some level of self-organization, nonlinearity, aggregation, diversity, and flow" (p. 26). Those concepts would be considered axiomatic or atomistic. In contrast, their statement that, "The term complex system means a system that consists of many interrelated elements with nonlinear relationships that make them very difficult to understand and predict" (p. 26) may be seen as a relational proposition because nonlinear relationships are seen to cause unpredictability.

Of the few relational propositions, the first is Stacey (1996) who states that agents follow rules (or schemas) in their interactions to improve on their behavior. This proposition shows that there is some relationship between the agents, their schemas, behaviors, and the subsequent improvement in behavior. Many authors echo this same general idea.

Axelrod et al. (2000) note that varied schemas (situational decision-making rules) differentiate, or provide variety, among agents. Agents are also differentiated by geography (differences in physical and conceptual space). These agents interact with one another (and with tools) in an essentially evolutionary process that might be seen as being based on the agent's fit with the environment. In that process, the agents are changed through changes in their schemas. Changes might be seen as increasing or decreasing the similarity of those agents. Similarly, Shakun (2001) states that agents take actions to reach goals. In this conversation, goals may be seen as generally similar to schemas as both seem to have some influence over the actions of the agents.

McDaniel et al. (2003) also suggest that agents interacting over time leads to self-organization. Time may be seen as important, although most authors include it only implicitly. Moss (2001) notes that members (agents) self-organize toward more stable patterns of activity. This may be seen as generally similar to the process of agents interacting to cause self-organizations—with the added idea that the process of self-organizing causes more stable patterns of activity. These stable patterns of activity are a result of common frames of reference, an idea that seems generally similar to rules or schemas as noted above.

Other authors (e.g. Bennet et al., 2004; Hunt et al., 2003) start from generally the same position—that the components (which might be seen as agents) of a CAS interact. However, according to these authors, the interactions lead to uncertainty. Dent (2003) also agrees and adds that the interaction is to find fit. Dent then notes the results of the agentic interactions may be seen as causing change (that may be thought of as a form of uncertainty).

Somewhere between, or combining, these camps, Harder et al. (2004) state that varied agents interact to maintain a system (homeostasis, in their words) rather than create a new system. However, their description of homeostasis is described by terms such as "dynamic equilibrium," "constant change," and "adaptation." Thus, it seems that the authors are suggesting that agents do not change—so much as they enable their CASs to interact, change, and evolve.

Pascale (1999) notes that the process of agents engaged in interaction will lead to more "levels" of organization. This idea of levels might be seen as conceptually similar to Axelrod et al.'s description of the geographic differentiation of agents (physically and/or conceptually). Additionally, it does not seem as though the creation of a new level of organization should be significantly different (within the context of this conversation) than the creation of a "new" system. It simply seems that this particular new organization is one that is already nested in an existing one. A larger difference between Pascale's version and that of other authors is that Pascale states that the agents are "shuffled" by the larger system.

Drawing on Dooley, Olsen & Eoyang (2001) note that agents evolve over time to reach fitness. Again, we may note the explicit surfacing of the temporal aspect of CASs that many authors leave tacit. Also, where most relational statements discuss agents interacting to achieve fitness, these authors might be seen as leaving the step of interaction as tacit. In both versions, however, agents do tend toward fitness.

Finally, Chiva-Gomez (2003) draws on Stacey to note that CASs that are closer to the edge of chaos (EOC) will experience more self-organization. This concept of EOC might be considered synonymous with "bounded in-stability," which Stacey describes as a balance between formal and informal systems. More broadly, EOC might also be described as the boundary be-tween stability and ambiguity. In developing the OEC concept, Stacey (1996) notes Kauffman, Wolfram, Gell-Mann, and Langton among his influences. Seen from the perspective of the present conversation, Kauffman's (1995) description of bounded instability may be understood as occurring where the number of agents approximates the number of interactions. If there are too many agents, and insufficient interactions, chaos reigns. On the other hand, if there are few agents and many interactions, stability prevails. Therefore, it seems reasonable that we may integrate the EOC concept with the other co-causal statements above because the EOC may be understood as a ratio between the number of agents and their interactions.

Generally speaking, there appears to be considerable overlap between many of the previous causal propositions. Specifically, many authors discuss the existence of agents (including parts), schemas (that may be seen as including goals, rules of interactions), interactions (that may include communication, and also implicitly or explicitly assumes the passage of time), and fit (including evolutionary tests of success). Additionally, it may be seen that the fit test is based on the existence of an external environment (although that environment may be seen as one or more other agents). There are a variety of changes that may result from a fit test including adaptation, change in interaction, change in schemas, increasing uncertainty, increasing certainty, self-organization, and the maintenance of existing organization. Also, as change is seen as a "general" result, change may also be seen to alter agents.

Looking at the concepts in their causal relationship, we may define the core of CAS theory as agents, with schemas, interacting over time. The results of those interactions are maximized at the EOC and are subject to a fit test with the environment. The result may be changes in schemas, changes in interactions, the creation or maintenance of larger systems, increased stability and increased instability. Finally, the status of the EOC may be changed by the creation of new agents, schemas, or CASs. This definition is represented graphically in Figure 1.

Each arrow represents causal direction, where one aspect of CAS theory will have an effect on another. As the concept of non-linear dynamics is an important aspect of CAS theory and complexity theory (e.g., Dent & Holt, 2001; Lichtenstein, 2000), it may be worth noting that the relationship between the causal aspects of this definition of CAS theory seems to support the idea of a non-linear or non-deterministic structure. This view is in contrast to an atomistic list of conceptual components.

The presented definition surfaces additional challenging questions. These questions might be seen as stemming from potentially contradictory statements by the authors. For example, Axelrod et al. note that changes occur at

Figure 1. Relationship between causal concepts

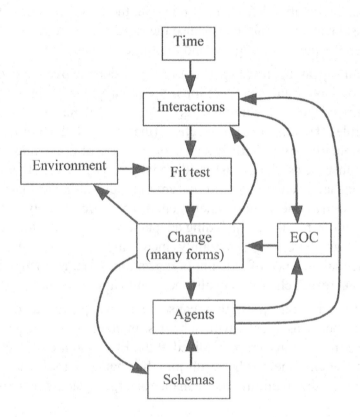

the level of the schema while Moss suggest that change occurs at the level of interactions. These should not, however, be seen as mutually exclusive. Instead, we might ask, "How much change will occur?" Then we might ask, "Where will that change occur?" For example, if a group of individuals self-organize into a corporation to take advantage of a new business opportunity, how much change is seen from the perspective of the business environment (with the inception of a new entity) compared to how much change is seen by the agents (as they organize themselves into new relationships and interactions), and how much change might be seen as occurring at the level of the schema of those individuals?

The structure of this model does not seem to be "perfectly" causal, however, in at least three areas. First, time (along with agents and change) enable the occurrence of interactions. However, nothing seems to "cause" (or alter) time. Therefore, time seems to be seen as an atomistic concept. To become more fully robust, this model should identify what causes (and alters) time or/and its perceived passage. Second, schemas seem to be caused by change, alone. Such a linear relationship would seem to suggest that any change in schemas would create a corresponding change in agents. This relationship would suggest that the concept of schemas might be bypassed. Alternatively, the concept of schemas might be enhanced by adding causal influences. Finally, while the EOC seems to control the "quantity" of change, the variety of possible "forms" of change is still open to interpretation. Similarly, the environment seems to be changed only by change (another linear relationship, like schemas). However, the environment may represent numerous CASs—each with their own nested agents and schemas.

Although this model has left out many component concepts of CAS theory, the closely related nature of the included aspects suggest that it may be a good representative for the core of CAS theory. That is because that causal model more closely meets Dubin's requirement for stage two of efficacy of theory, while the reductive models only reach stage one. In the next section, we compare three models of CAS theory.

Comparisons and Insights

Drawing on Davidson and Layder, Romm (2001) suggests that researchers use "triangulation" (multiple research methods to reduce subjectivity in research). Thus far, we have presented two forms of analysis. A third form of analysis of the same data set may be found in Wallis (2006a) where reflexive dimensional analysis (RDA) was used to understand CAS theory as consisting of five related conceptual dimensions. Developed by Wallis (2006b) from grounded theory and dimensional analysis, RDA is a method for the investigation of a body of theory.

Looking at the broad range of concepts in CAS theory, the previous reductive study has the benefit of including all concepts of the body of CAS theory—presented as a list of atomistic concepts. The RDA version also purports to include all the concepts of CAS theory; however, it presents those concepts as "enfolded" so that concepts not directly represented by the theory might be understood indirectly by combining the dimensions of the theory. For example, the concept of "evolution" (not directly represented) might be understood as "change" over "time" (both of which are directly represented in the model). In contrast to either of the above methods, the causal model leaves out concepts that are considered to be axiomatically atomistic (although those concepts may be seen as still existing in the belt). This suggests some benefits and detriments to each method. Where the atomistic/reductive approach might be more complete, the RDA version might be understood as more abstract (and so has the opportunity to be applied to a wider variety of systems) and more parsimonious (where aspects are related by the minimum number of laws possible, per Dubin).

Comparing the flexibility of these forms of theory (setting aside their common requirement for scholarly justification), it seems that reductive forms enable the easy addition or removal of concepts, essentially adding or removing them from the list. In contrast, forms of theory that are reflexively structured (RDA and causal) are not so easily altered. For example, referring to Figure 1, if we were to remove the concept of interactions, our understanding of other concepts would be imperiled. Time would become "disconnected" from the model, agents would become linearly causal to change (thus eliminating the concept of EOC), and agents would go straight to fit test without interactions (a wholly unsatisfactory description).

In short, it seems that the reductive (and less integrated) forms of theory are more easily changed and therefore may be seen as more easily manipulated or evolved by theorists. That, in turn, suggests that the closer we get to a fully robust form of theory, the more difficult it will become to make further progress. The next few decades, therefore, may see the evolution of competing very-nearly robust theories. Those theories may then be tested (in real world and computer modeling venues). Then too, each version of theory may find its own specific niche (e.g., one model may be applied to organizations, another to individuals, and a third to schemas).

Additionally, the reductive study suggests a technique for identifying which concepts within a general body of theory might be more closely connected with a given focus (e.g., scholarly version of CAS). The RDA and causal versions, in contrast, are both highly integrated so that the researcher is encouraged (almost required) to utilize all of the concepts for any given analysis. In the causal model depicted in Figure 1, for example, a researcher focusing on interactions would be impelled to describe how those interactions are changed by changes in agents, change, and time. Additionally, the causal relationships would suggest that the researcher describe how changes in the interactions aspect altered the EOC and the fit test. In a sense, this creates a road map that might be of benefit to researchers and students alike.

Shifting our focus to the core, we should note that the core concepts of the RDA version of CAS are (atomistically) interactions, agentness, change, levels of difference, and time. The causal version of CAS may be represented as schemas, agents, interactions, time, fit test, change, EOC, and environment. The two models hold in common the concepts of change, interactions, and time. In the RDA version, the schemas, agents, and environment of the causal version might be explained as agentness seen at different levels. Both of these models suffer from understanding time as an atomistic concept. Where time enables change (for example), nothing enables time. This could seem to be a relatively innocuous concept; however, the concept of "flow" (Csikszent-mihalyi, 1991) suggests that the idea of time, especially as a subjective representation of productivity, may be an important area for investigation. The RDA version leaves the idea of agents (and other forms of systems) loosely defined based on the idea that it is the observer who determines what the system "is." The causal version leaves the concept of Levels relatively tacit, seemingly accepting that there are three levels of systems (which may be broadly understood as schemas, agents, and environment). Similarly, there are differences within each causal concept (there are different forms of change, a variety of agents, and schemas include a variety of rules).

In contrast to what might be called the "dynamic" measure of robustness discussed previously in this chapter (where we quantified the level of robustness of a theory as it evolved between authors), we might apply here a more "static" measure of robustness. Static robustness might be applied to quantify the internal integrity of the structure of a body of theory and so provide a point of comparison between the two views of the core. Alternatively, it may be used to differentiate between core and belt concepts within a body of theory. A measure of robustness may be achieved by comparing the total number of aspects within the theory to the number of aspects that are both causal and emergent. On one end of that scale, a theory that simply lists its component concepts, without identifying how the concepts were related to one another would have a robustness of zero. On the other end of the scale, a fully robust theory (e.g., Newton's F=ma) might have three dimensions, each of which is both causal and emergent, and therefore would have a robustness of one (3 / 3 = 1). By "emergent," it is important to note that a given concept must be understood in relation to two or more other concepts, as in Newton's model. If changes in one concept were to be determined directly by only one other concept, that change would be seen as linear, and so adding little to the model. For example, if we were to say that changes in the environment cause changes in the agent that cause changes in the schema, we might as well say that changes in the environment cause changes in the schema. If, on the other hand, there is something about the agent that ameliorates, filters, or accentuates, the changes from the environment, we may then say that the changes in the environment and the effect of the agent result in changes to the schema.

In the previous reductive study, all lists have robustness of zero (e.g., 0 / 29 = 0). In the RDA CAS model, there are a total of five dimensions (agentness, levels, change, time, and interactions). However, of those five, only three are both emergent and causal (agentness, interactions, and levels). Therefore, we might understand this form of the theory as having a static robustness of 0.6 (3 / 5 = 0.6). In contrast, the causal version presented in this chapter contains eight concepts – only five of which may be seen as both causal and emergent providing a robustness of 0.625 (5 / 8 = 0.625). In short, the causal version may be seen as an improvement over the RDA version and this chapter serves as an example of theory-advancement towards a robust core.

Shifting to the relatively non-robust aspects, we see that time appears in the causal model to be atomistic. Schemas and environment are seen as linear/determinant. In the causal model, it seems that the more important area for investigation are the concepts of time, environment, and schema. Understanding how those concepts may be understood as emerging from two or more other concepts within the core should indicate how the model might be rearranged to make sense from a robust perspective. For example, the multiple levels of this model (including schema, agents, and environment) may each be seen, in some sense, as a CAS. That may indicate the opportunity to create a model where each level is represented by that same (simpler) model. Such repetition of simpler models might, in turn, allow the elimination of some redundancies from the model. Indeed, until such an investigation is undertaken, those linear components of an otherwise robust model might be seen as existing somewhere between the belt and the core in an intermediate, or connecting zone.

Finally, based on Dubin's list (where increasing relatedness suggests higher efficacy of theory) and Weick's inference (that propositions should be effectively ordered, or interrelated), it may be suggested that increasing robustness suggests a higher level of epistemological validity of a theory. In general, however, it is important that the causal core may be seen as being derived from a different epistemological validity than the loosely related list of concepts that comprises the belt. Where the belt may find validation from any one of a wide range of research methodologies and points of view, the core finds validation only in the relationship between its own concepts. This is a significant epistemological shift that suggests a rich opportunity for additional study.

Will CAS and/or ICAS Theory Survive?

In this chapter, 20 concise versions of CAS theory were found in the discipline of organizational theory. The conceptual components were identified for each theory and subjected to two forms of analysis. The first, a reductive study, was beneficial in the identification of concepts representing the range of CAS theory, for linking specific concepts within the body to specific uses of the theory, and the creation of additional versions of CAS theory. Each additional definition was seen as adding to the outer belt of the theory rather than clarifying the core. The second study focused on the causal statements found within the body of CAS theory and identified the core of CAS theory by identifying relationships between those concepts. It is suggested that by focusing on causal relationships, we may be able to accelerate the evolution of CAS theory.

This chapter suggests that the flexibility of loosely connected forms of theory may support the spread of that theory through the social sciences. However, the very flexibility that allows CAS theory to grow may also obscure the core. The lack of core, in turn, may limit the effectiveness of that theory in application. Another significant contribution of this chapter is the creation of specific measures of robustness as tools for examining theory. These include measures of dynamic robustness (as an indicator of the evolution and stability of a theory as it passes between authors), and static robustness (a numerical indicator of how well co-defined a theory may be). The more static robustness a theory has, the more it may be considered to be part of the core.

Will CAS theory survive? Or, will it join the 90% of social theory that rises rapidly only to disappear just as quickly (Oberschall, 2000)? This chapter represents a significant step toward a new understanding of theory (in general) and CAS theory (in particular). If CAS theory is to retain its validity and even gain credibility in the face of the next wave of theory (that will, undoubtedly, arrive), it seems that it must develop a robust core. In an important sense, a robust theory might be seen as possessing epistemological justification, not from external testing, but internally, as the understanding of each aspect of the core is tested against the other aspects of the model. Conversations on the structure and construction of theory are likely to continue, and even increase, as our understanding of theory-creation increases. Measures of theory-robustness would seem to provide useful tools for advancing that conversation.

Looking to achieve a more optimal future of CAS theory, investigations should first clarify the causal relationships suggested in this chapter. With a fully robust version of CAS, the next step should be to test that model in the field and through computer modeling to clarify (or deny) relationships suggested by the co-defined aspects. Additionally, the "inter-testability" of the core aspects hints that such a model might be falsifiable in the Popperian sense. For example, if the model pictured in Figure 1 were to experience a change in interactions that did not result in a change in the fit test, the model would be disproved. This would, of course, open the door to improving the model (Popper, 2002). Then too, if everything observable may be explained in terms of the robust aspects, then each application in the field becomes a test of the theory, and we have another opportunity to accelerate the evolution of CAS theory through practice.

This chapter has focused on CAS theory, but what about its close cousin ICAS? While this book may, or may not, contain all concepts related to ICAS theory, it certainly provides a cross-section of that theory. As such, the reader may apply the insights and techniques presented in this chapter as he or she reads other chapters. That way, the reader may identify the full breadth of concepts for ICAS theory. Similarly, within each chapter, the reader may find an emphasis on those concepts specifically related to that particular area of study and so suggest a "school of thought" within ICAS. Finally, the reader may range between the chapters seeking causal relationships between concepts, and so develop a robust model of ICAS theory. Each of these opportunities suggests how the reader might develop an alternative point of view that may be useful for further study and developing new insights.

In conclusion, we have presented three major insights that may support theory development and the progress of ICAS theory. First, a robust form of theory provides the best description of a solid core of a theory and so avoids the growing belt of loose concepts that obscures it. Second, it is possible and desirable to measure a theory's level of robustness and by so doing, to measure the progress of that theory. A corollary here is that measuring the progress of a theory opens the door to advancing that theory in a more rapid and purposeful way. Finally (although less deeply explored), robust theories may provide a path to more effective analysis and application. As the data for developing the core came from the belt, it should be noted that no core is possible without a belt. This suggests that both belt and core, with their separate epistemological justifications, are necessary to the advancement of theory.

Shifting to an evolutionary perspective, CAS might be seen as a recently evolved (and rapidly evolving) "species" of theory—derived from its fecund progenitors in systems theory and complexity theory. As a relatively recent species, it is well adapted to fit its niche as an insight-generator for theorists. Theorists, theory, and this book (as a representative of the conversation) may then be understood as three species—all engaged in a co-evolutionary process. This co-evolutionary process, in turn, suggests the opportunity to improve ourselves by accelerating the evolution of CAS. In the sense of an evolutionary landscape, this book might be seen as a path leading CAS off of the plains (inhabited by herds of "big-belt" theories) and up the slope of Mt. Kilimanjaro.

References

Ashmos, D. P., Huonker, J. W., & Reuben, R., & McDaniel, J. (1998). Participation as a complicating mechanism: The effect of clinical professional and middle manager participation on hospital performance. *Health Care Management Review, 23*(4), 7-20.

Axelrod, R., & Cohen, M. D. (2000). *Harnessing complexity: Organizational implications of a scientific frontier*. New York: Basic Books.

Bartlett, J. (1992). *Familiar quotations: A collection of passages, phrases, and proverbs traced to their sources in ancient and modern literature* (16th ed.). Toronto: Little, Brown.

Bennet, A., & Bennet, D. (2004). *Organizational survival in the new world: The intelligent complex adaptive system*. Burlington, MA: Elsevier.

Brown, S. L., & Eisenhardt, K. M. (1998). *Competing on the edge: Strategy as structured chaos*. Boston: Harvard Business School Press.

Chiva-Gomez, R. (2003). The facilitating factors for organizational learning: Bringing ideas from complex adaptive systems. *Knowledge and Process Management, 10*(2), 99-114.

Csikszentmihalyi, M. (1991). *Flow: The psychology of optimal experience*. New York: Harper Perennial.

Daneke, G., A. (1999). *Systemic choices: Nonlinear dynamics and practical management*. Ann Arbor, MI: The University of Michigan Press.

Dent, E. B. (2003). The complexity science organizational development practitioner. *Organization Development Journal, 21*(2), 82.

Dent, E. B., & Holt, C. G. (2001). CAS in war, bureaucratic machine in peace: The U.S. Air Force example. *Emergence, 3*(3), 90-107.

Dubin, R. (1978). *Theory building* (Revised Edition). New York: The Free Press.

Friedman, K. (2003). Theory construction in design research: Criteria: Approaches, and methods. *Design Studies, 24*(6), 507-522.

Gleick, J. (1987). *Chaos: Making a new science*. New York: Penguin Books.

Hall, J. R. (1999). *Cultures of inquiry: From epistemology to discourse in sociohistorical research*. New York: Cambridge University Press.

Harder, J., Robertson, P. J., & Woodward, H. (2004). The spirit of the new workplace: Breathing life into organizations. *Organization Development Journal, 22*(2), 79-103.

Hull, D. L. (1988). *Science as a process: An evolutionary account of the social and conceptual development of science.* Chicago: University of Chicago Press.

Hunt, J. G. G., & Ropo, A. (2003). Longitudinal organizational research and the third scientific discipline. *Group & Organizational Management, 28*(3), 315-340.

Kauffman, S. (1995). *At home in the universe: The search for laws of self-organization and complexity* (Paperback Edition). New York: Oxford University Press.

Lakatos, I. (1970). Falsification and the methodology of scientific research programmes. In I. Lakatos & A. Musgrave (Eds.), *Criticism and the growth of knowledge* (pp. 91-195), Cambridge University Press.

Lichtenstein, B. M. B. (2000). Emergence as a process of self-organizing: New assumptions and insights from the study of non-linear dynamic systems. *Journal of Organizational Change Management, 13*(6), 526-544.

McDaniel, R. R., Jordan, M. E., & Fleeman, B. F. (2003). Surprise, surprise, surprise! A complexity science view of the unexpected. *Health Care Management Review, 28*(3), 266-277.

McGrath, J. E. (1997). Small group research, that once and future field: An interpretation of the past with an eye to the future. *Group dynamics: Theory, research, and practice, 1*(1), 7-27.

McKelvey, B. (2004). Toward a 0th law of thermodynamics: Order-creation complexity dynamics from physics and biology to bioeconomics. *Journal of Bioeconomics, 6*(1), 65-96.

Moss, M. (2001). Sensemaking, complexity, and organizational knowledge. *Knowledge and Process Management*, 217.

Nonaka, I. (2005). Managing organizational knowledge: Theoretical and methodological foundations. In K. G. Smith & M. A. Hitt (Eds.), *Great minds in management: The process of theory development* (pp. 373-393). New York: Oxford University Press.

Oberschall, A. (2000). Oberschall reviews "theory and progress in social science" by James B. Rule. *Social Forces, 78*(3), 1188-1191.

Olson, E. E., & Eoyang, G. H. (2001). *Facilitating organizational change: Lessons from complexity science*. San Francisco: Jossey-Bass/Pfeiffer.

Pascale, R. T. (1999). Surfing the edge of chaos. *Sloan Management Review, 40*(3), 83.

Pepper, S. C. (1961). *World hypothesis: A study in evidence*. Berkeley, CA: University of California Press.

Phelan, S. E. (2001). What is complexity science, really? *Emergence, 3*(1), 120-136.

Popper, K. (2002). *The logic of scientific discovery* (J. F. Karl Popper, Lan Freed, Trans.). New York: Routledge Classics.

Richardson, K. A. (2006, June). *The role of information "barriers" in complex dynamical systems behavior.* Paper presented at the NESCI, Boston, MA, USA.

Romm, N. R. A. (2001). *Accountability in social research: Issues and debates*. New York: Kluwer Academic/Plenum Publishers.

Shakun, M. F. (2001). Unbounded rationality. *Group Decision and Negotiation, 10*(2), 97-118.

Slawski, C. (1990, July 8-13). *A small group process theory.* Paper presented at the Toward a Just Society for Future Generations—34th Annual Meeting of the International Society for Systems Sciences, Portland, Oregon, USA.

Stacey, R. D. (1996). *Complexity and creativity in organizations*. San Francisco: Berrett-Koehler Publishers.

Tower, D. (2002). Creating the complex adaptive organization: A primer on complex adaptive systems. *OD Practitioner, 34*(3).

Unknown. (2006, 3/6/07). *Quotation*. Retrieved March 3, 2007, 2007, from http://www.quotationsbook.com/quote/27796/

Wallis, S. E. (2006a, July 13, 2006). *A sideways look at systems: Identifying sub-systemic dimensions as a technique for avoiding an hierarchical perspective.* Paper presented at the International Society for the Systems Sciences, Rohnert Park, California.

Wallis, S. E. (2006b). *A study of complex adaptive systems as defined by organizational scholar-practitioners.* Unpublished Theoretical Dissertation, Fielding Graduate University, Santa Barbara.

Webster's. (1989). *Encyclopedic Unabridged Dictionary of the English Language.* Avenel, NJ: Gramercy Books.

Weick, K. E. (1989). Theory construction as disciplined imagination. *Academy of Management Review, 14*(4), 516-531.

Wheatley, M. J. (1992). *Leadership and the new science.* San Francisco: Barrett-Koehler.

Wilber, K. (2001). *A theory of everything: An integral vision for business, politics, science, and spirituality.* Boston, MA: Shambhala.

Yellowthunder, L., & Ward, V. (2003). Designing and implementing organizational change in a complex adaptive system. In G. H. Eoyang (Ed.), *Voices from the field: An introduction to human systems dynamics* (pp. 125-144). Circle Pines, MN: Human Systems Dynamics Institute.

Chapter II

Method of Systems Potential as "Top-Bottom" Technique of the Complex Adaptive Systems Modelling

Grigorii S. Pushnoi, St. Petersburg, Russia

Gordon L. Bonser, California, USA

Abstract

Emergent properties of complex adaptive systems (CAS) are explored by means of "agent-based modelling" (ABM), which are compared with results from modelling on the basis of the method of systems potential (MSP). MSP describes CAS as a holistic system whereas ABM-methodology considers CAS as set of interacting "agents." It is argued that MSP is a "top-bottom" approach, which supplements ABM "bottom-up" modeling of CAS. Adap-

tive principles incorporated into CAS at the level of a holistic system exploit Lamarck's ideas about evolution, while the adaptive rules incorporated in the inner structure of CAS reflect Darwin's ideas. Both ABM and MSP exhibit the same macroscopic properties: (1) "punctuated equilibrium"; (2) sudden jumps in macro-indices; (3) cyclical dynamics; (4) superposition of deterministic and stochastic patterns in dynamics; (5) fractal properties of structure and dynamics; (6) SOC-phenomenon. ABM demonstrates these properties via simulations of the different models whereas MSP derives these phenomena analytically.

Introduction

Traditionally, in modeling the complex adaptive systems (CAS), multi-agent modelling approach (MAM) is used. The complex adaptive system is modelled as a multitude of "agents" interacting with each other in line with certain rules of adaptive behaviour. Setting the rules of the "agents'" adaptive behavior, the researcher has a possibility to trace, using the computer, the behaviour of the system with time. Lately tremendous experience has been gained in the study of macroscopic properties of such systems. As far as these properties cannot be derived from the agents' properties, they are often called the "emergent properties of the system." It has been found that dissimilar MAM-models show the same set of macroscopic emergent properties when being modeled on the computer.

Universal Emergent Properties:

- Punctuated equilibrium.
- Self-organised criticality.
- Superposition of deterministic and stochastic patterns in macroscopic dynamics.
- Discontinuous cycles.
- Catastrophic jumps.
- Self-affine dynamics of macro-indices.
- Power law for avalanche-size distribution.
- Perpetual renewal of configuration.

- Creation of hierarchical fractal-like structure in course of evolution.
- Episodic sudden reconfigurations of CAS-structure.
  (*)

It is notable that the closer the model is to its real prototype, the more precise the intelligent "agents" reproduce the behaviour of real CAS agents, the clearer and more definitely these general macroscopic properties of the models are displayed. This appears to imply that the emergent properties (*) of the system do not depend on its internal structure or on specific features of the "agent's" adaptive behaviour in a specific model, but rather are inherent in CAS as a holistic system. This chapter shall attempt to prove that the emergent properties of CAS may be explained proceeding from general regularities observed in the evolutionary process.

Multi-agent modelling reveals the emergent properties by means of simulation. Within the framework of MAM-platform these properties emerge as unpredictable aggregated macroscopic effects of interaction of a multitude of "agents." Multi-agent modelling is a method of studying CAS on a "bottom-up" basis, starting from the interaction of a multitude of "agents" to revealing the emergent properties of the integral system.

The departure point of our analysis of the integral complex adaptive system is an ensemble of interacting agents. The nature of such systems supposes the existence of some universal *adaptive mechanisms* effective at the level of the integral system. The existence of simple and universal mechanisms of adaptation acting at the level of integral systems has been a subject of discourse with many authors.

Gell-Mann (1994, p. 17), Holland (1995), Arthur, Durlanf, and Lane (1997, pp. 2-3), and McMillan (2004, p. 103) all note that the system is adaptive if it (1) is permanently renewed at all levels, (2) organises a multi-level hierarchical structure within itself, (3) draws information from the surrounding environment, (4) uses this information in its adaptive activity, and (5) adjusts itself proceeding from the efficiency of resultant gain. One may say that CAS accumulates the useful adaptive experience through the process of adaptive activity and applies the gained experience as a means of continued survival.

It is assumed for this analysis that some universal rules of evolution can be formulated in respect to integral systems. These rules describe the aggregate macroscopic effect of agent's interactions within the system under consideration. This approach will be called the **"method of systems potential"** **(MSP)**.

These adaptive mechanisms are effective at the level of the integral system. They may therefore be called *macroscopic* mechanisms of adaptation. They are working in any CAS. Therefore they may be called *universal* mechanisms of adaptation. As far as any CAS comprises a multitude of smaller-scale complex adaptive systems (modules or agents), the *universal macroscopic adaptive mechanisms* (**UMAM**) function in each of these CA-sub-systems. Thus, UMAM function at different levels of CAS, within each of its sub-systems.

The effect of UMAM within CAS may be formalised within the framework of some logical and mathematical scheme. The key notions are:

1. *"Adaptive potential of the system"*: The aggregated ability of CAS to adequately respond to the challenges of the external world,

2. *"Conditions for realisation of adaptive potential"*: The aggregate factors contributing to (or preventing) the exploitation (employment) of the "adaptive potential,"

3. *"Efficiency of CAS"*: The relationship between the exploited "adaptive potential" and the accumulated one.

"Adaptive potential" and "conditions of realisation" are fundamental terms of MSP. These values describe the global steady state of CAS as ensembles of interacting agents. They play the role of "thermodynamic" potentials for these ensembles. "Adaptive potential" and "conditions for its realisation" are two constituents of "useful experience" accumulated in a CAS.

If the adaptive abilities of an agent are greater, the fitness of this agent is greater. "Adaptive potential" of CAS as a whole is the measurement of aggregated adaptive abilities of whole agents within the ensemble. The fitness of each agent is dependent upon both features of agent itself and from inter-agent interactions. "Adaptive potential" is accumulating within the operative memory and functions of agents via learning and training. Mutations fix accumulated "potential" as information coded in the genetic structure.

So long as any CAS consists of complex adaptive sub-systems, the definition of "adaptive potential" of comprehensive CAS depends upon the definition of the "adaptive potential" of sub-systems (modules or agents). The lowest level of real CAS structure is unknown, but we can define "adaptive potential" of CAS under consideration as the sum of "adaptive potentials" of its sub-systems, additionally taking into account inter-sub-systems interaction.

The term "conditions of realisation" is the second "thermodynamic potential" of ensembles of interacting agents. Each agent is limited in it's choice of adaptive behaviour. Interaction with other agents and the influence of environment restrict the region of adaptive search for each agent in its fitness landscape. Its adaptive rules leads to some local peak in the fitness landscape, although other higher peaks in his fitness landscape can exist as a rule. Restrictions in behaviour of agents produced via the sum of agent-agent interactions are working as conditions contributing to (or preventing) the search for optimal (highest) peak within the fitness landscape. "Conditions of realisation" characterises at the macroscopic level of CAS the aggregate effects of agent interactions on the success of an agent's adaptive search.

"Adaptive potential" is exploited in full if each agent is positioned at the top of the attractive fitness peak in its fitness landscape. It can be said that "adaptive potential" is exploited partially if some agents are not positioned on these peaks. Efficiency of adaptive search within an ensemble of interacting agents can be described at the macroscopic level as being exploited per an available "adaptive potential" ratio.

MSP postulates three universal macroscopic adaptive mechanisms (UMAM) of CAS work:

1. The accumulation of useful experience ("adaptive potential" and "conditions of realisation") in CAS takes place driven by the adaptive search of agents within an ensemble. This is the process of learning, training and fixation of useful experience via mutations. Mathematically this process can be described as reinforcing feedback process: "**MSP-potentials**" ("adaptive potential" and "conditions of realisation") → "**adaptive activity**" (adaptive search of agents) → increment in "MSP-potentials." (P.1)

2. CAS is capable of maintaining some macroscopic steady state on account of agent-agent interactions. This property can be described mathematically as the **stabilizing feedback**: temporal equilibrium → deviation from this equilibrium → recovery of temporal equilibrium. Macroscopic steady state of CAS is setted by means of MSP-variables: "potential," "conditions" and "efficiency." (P.2)

3. Finally MSP postulates that CAS is capable of controlling distribution of "conditions of realisation" between the sub-systems within a CAS. This property is used by CAS as a means for the maximal realisation (employment) of accumulated potential. (P.3)

The mechanism (P.3) applied to each CA-sub-system creates multi-level hierarchical fractal-like structure within comprehensive CAS.

MSP assumes that the previously listed MSP-mechanisms (P.1-P.3) are working in any real CAS. Attempting to formalise these mechanisms leads to a new (MSP) platform of CAS-modelling, an intelligent CAS constructed on MSP postulates (P.1-P.3). MSP is the "top-down" technique of CAS modelling from the integral system to its sub-systems (modules and agents). The previously listed adaptive mechanisms are working within each sub-system. In order for each CA-sub-system in comprehensive intelligent CAS operating on the basis of UMAM-rules (P.1-P.3) necessary impose some restrictions on agents' (modules) behaviour. Laws of behaviour of agents are contained implicitly in MSP-equations formalizing (P1-P.3) applied to each CA-sub-system. Evolution of sub-systems (modules and agents) in comprehensive CAS is the process by means by which whole levels in CAS structure satisfy requirements of MSP-postulates (P.1-P.3).

The remainder of this chapter is structured in the following way. Section II contains a brief overview of some results from multi-agent modelling. It is demonstrated using concrete examples that very dissimilar MAM-models display one and the same macroscopic properties (*). Section III is devoted to the discussion of how MAM and MSP platforms can be incorporated. Section IV introduces the principal positions of MSP-platform within CAS modelling. Section V contains some results of MSP-modelling and comparisons with results of MAM-modelling. The Conclusion contains some ideas of how an integrated MAM-MSP platform for CAS modelling can be constructed[1].

Brief Overview

With the advent of advanced computers, it became possible to track the dynamics of many MAM-models. The results proved to be unexpected with consequent outcomes that could not be predicted in advance. CAS does not contain anything but the "agents" interacting according to certain rules; however, the summary results of such interactions proved to be unpredictable. The system as a whole showed new, unexpected properties—the so-called "emergent" properties.

Kauffman and Johnsen (1991) found that three regimes of macroscopic dynamics are possible in their model: chaos, stagnation, and a so-called "edge of chaos." "Edge of chaos" is the optimal regime of CAS development. Within this regime, the process of permanent qualitative renewal of the system takes place. The extinctions of unfit species create similar avalanche-like processes. *The power law for frequency distribution of avalanche-sizes* indicates that "edge of chaos" is a critical state for an ensemble consisting of interacting agents. This model displays *dynamics of punctuated equilibrium* characterised by long periods of gradual changes followed by short periods of sudden reconfigurations. However, no mechanism of *spontaneous* organisation of the critical state is found in this model.

This drawback was eliminated in the Bak and Sneppen (1993) model of an ecosystem where the critical state is the attractor and the model shows *SOC-phenomenon*. The dynamics in this model has longer periods of relatively minor and slow qualitative changes, which are interrupted by the bursts of feverish activity at all levels. Evolution within this model turns out to be a two-stage process comprising first of a phase of slow, smooth changes in the system. This is followed by drastic reconfigurations of qualitative renewal—the punctuated equilibrium phenomenon.

These two properties of CAS-dynamics (SOC-phenomenon and punctuated equilibrium) are reproduced in many MAM-models (Amaral & Mayer, 1999; Sole, Bascompte, & Manrubia, 1996a; Sole & Manrubia, 1996b).

di Collobiano (2002) with colleges analysed the fossil records and concluded that the collected data indicate the existence of the following macroscopic properties within the ecosystems of the Earth.

1. **Punctuated equilibrium:** The lengthy smooth periods of species development are interrupted by short periods of mass-scale extinction of some species and emergence of new ones (op. cit., p. 31).

2. The power law of frequency distribution of unfit species extinctions against the size of extinctions (Figure 2.6 in op. cit., p. 27) occurs.

3. There exists a delay in recovering biodiversity after mass-scale extinction of species (op. cit., p. 32).

These observations are evidence of the existence of discontinuous cycles within the dynamics of real ecosystems, namely: (1) The growth in diversity of species, followed by (2) a sudden catastrophe and extinction of a number of species, then (3) a period of delay in origination of new species, concluding with (4) a rapid recovery and extension of biodiversity.

4.   Finally, analysis of phylogenetic trees shows the presence of *hierarchical structures with fractal properties* (Figure 2.2 in op. cit., p. 18).

As far as the ecosystem of the Earth is the real CAS, the properties revealed during the study of this CAS must have properties that reproduce an intelligent CAS closely resembling reality.

Among the multi-agent models imitating the dynamics of economic and social CAS, there are some models within which the phases of smooth changes radically differ in macro-characteristics before and after the process of reconfiguration. In such models the bursts of activity work similar to a CAS switching from one work mode to another, these two work modes alternating.

For instance, Hommes's (2002) model of financial markets displays the characteristics of the *four-phase cycle*. The phase of high volatility is replaced after the burst of reconfiguration (switching) by a phase of low volatility. After a new reconfiguration, the process repeats itself. *The length of phases is not constant*, but their alternation is strictly regular. Consequently, this model displays the *dynamics of stochastic discontinuous cycles consisting* of two stages, those being the gradual change in the macro-index and two catastrophe-like switches of the system from one work mode to another.

Epstein's Model of Civil Violence (2002) also shows *stochastic discontinuous cycles* in a so-called tension index (Epstein, 2002, Figure 8, p. 7247). The leaps are caused by avalanche-like transitions of agents from the inactive state (patience) to an active state (rebellion) and vice versa. As soon as the tension index exceeds the critical threshold, the system makes a catastrophic leap to a new equilibrium state.

Kephart (2002) noticed that very dissimilar multi-agent models of market economies demonstrate the presence of identical dynamic properties—*the leaps and cyclic nature of changes in macro-indices*. He called these cycles in market economies "price war cycles." He stressed that the reason for such dynamics does not lie in the specificity of particular models, but rather is a fundamental characteristic of market economies.

"...we have analyzed and simulated several different market models. Several phenomena appear to be quite generic: not only are they observed in many different scenarios, but their root causes appear to be very basic and general" *(Kephart, 2002; p. 7210).*

Within the phase of smooth changes in the macroscopic state of the system, the agent's interaction results in the growth in instability of the current equilibrium. At some point disruption occurs and a new equilibrium is reached; but it comes at the expense of reconfiguration (qualitative renewal) within the whole system. The reorientation of agents onto new peaks of fitness (profit) landscapes will be in the form of an avalanche. As a result, a new configuration emerges with other structures of fitness landscapes and new agent positions within its landscapes.

"Typical price trajectory consists of linear drops punctuated by sharp discontinuities up or down. These discontinuities coincide with quick shifts by all sellers to a new set of product parameters... Although the intuitive explanations for the sudden price or price/product discontinuities differ considerably across the various models, there is a generic mathematical principle that explains why this behavior is so ubiquitous and provides insight into how broadly it might occur in real agent markets of the future. Mathematically, the phenomenon occurs in situations where the underlying profit landscape contains multiple peaks. Competition among sellers collectively drives the price vector in such a way that each seller is forced down a peak in its profit landscape, although its individual motion carries it up the peak. At some point, a seller will find it best to abandon its current peak and make a discontinuous jump to another peak in its landscape. This discontinuous shift in the price vector suddenly places all other sellers at a different point in their own profit landscapes. If the next seller to move finds itself near a new peak in its landscape, it will make an incremental shift in its price and hence in the price vector; otherwise, it will respond with yet another radical shift" *(Kephart, 2002; p. 7211).*

Many well-known simple models ("sand pile" (Bak, Tang, & Wiesenfeld, 1987), "percolation" (Henley, 1989), "forest-fire" (Drossel & Schwabl, 1992)) imitating *SOC-phenomenon* contain some mechanism by means of which the increase in instability of the current configuration triggers episodic avalanche-like processes of reconfiguration of the system under consideration.

Sudden reconfigurations in MAM-models can be interpreted at the macroscopic level as *catastrophes of the integral CAS evolution*. Sornette (2002) notes that:

"We live on a planet and in society with intermittent dynamics rather than a state of equilibrium... Evolution is probably characterised by phases of quasistasis interrupted by episodic bursts of activity and destruction" (p. 2522).

Interrelation Between MAM and MSP Platforms of CAS Modelling

MAM-MSP interrelation is similar to interrelation between statistical molecular physics and thermodynamics. Both MAM and MSP describe one and the same reality—complex adaptive systems (CAS). MAM attempts to explain how peculiarities of inner microscopic structure of the system (properties of agents and behavioural rules) generate the system's macroscopic properties. MSP attempts to find some general regularity in macroscopic properties and dynamics of ensembles consisting of inter-acting agents. As inter-molecular interaction and motion of molecules in statistical physics produce some macroscopic properties of matter, which can be described in thermodynamic terms just-as-inter-agent interaction and behaviour of agents produce some regularity in macroscopic properties of the CAS as a whole.

We propose in this essay to apply **Jean-Baptiste Lamarck's laws** of evolution in order to validate macroscopic regularities of CAS. These regularities are the properties of ensembles of inter-acting adaptive agents. Each variable in MSP-platform of CAS-modeling describes some property of an integral system (an ensemble of interacting agents) irrespective of details of inter-agent interactions in the system. MSP-potentials ("adaptive potential" and "conditions for realisation") play the role of thermodynamic potentials of a system consisting of many interacting agents.

The MAM-platform is based on the concept of a "fitness landscape." Fitness function describes the ability of agents to survive in perpetually change-able environments. If the fitness value is larger, the adaptive abilities of the agent are higher. Therefore, the value of the fitness value depends directly on adaptive abilities of the agent localised in a definite position in a fitness landscape. The adaptive abilities of agents manifest themselves via the rate of growth in size of an ensemble of agents disposed in a definite position in a fitness landscape. Each position in a fitness landscape corresponds to the definite genotype of an agent. Mutations in genotype are interpreted as movement of an agent in a fitness landscape.

The motion in the fitness landscape directed to fitness peak can be interpreted as an agent's adaptive search the "best" position in a fitness landscape. An agent uses some criterion in order to choose the "fittest" position in fitness landscape. As a rule, an agent tends maximise fitness-value via the mutation process. Criterion of adaptive search depends on properties of the agent and its "vision." Learning agents are capable of correcting criterion of adaptive search in accordance with prior experience. If the "vision" of the agent is wider, the criterion of adaptive search is more complicated. Agents in real CAS have as a rule a very wide "vision" and thus very complex criterion of adaptive search.

Consider an intelligent CAS in which agents are similar to real ("living-like") agents in a real CAS. It means that we will consider agents that have almost unlimited "vision." Moreover, these agents are capable of correcting criterion of adaptive search using the whole historical experience of its evolution in the fitness landscape.

"Unlimited vision" of a life-like intelligent agent is the agent's ability to esti-mate "fitness" of each position in it's fitness landscape taking into account the possible losses along a path to this position, and making the best choice.

The change in size of the ensemble of agents moving along a definite path depends on fitness values at each point on this path. The possible loss in population size on the way to a position decreases the appeal of this position. Only when losses in population on the way to a fitness position exceed some threshold value does this position become inaccessible to the agent.

Losses in population of ensemble along the way toward fitness peak consist of two parts: (1) decrement in population on account of small fitness-values along the path and (2) decrement in population on account of non-optimal mutations at each point of this path.

The previously stated, a new magnitude which characterises influence of two factors may be introduced: (1) fitness value of a definite position in a fitness

Figure 1. Construction of a complex adaptive system according to MSP-approach

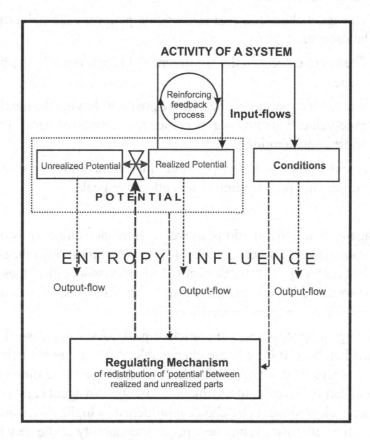

Notes: Two feedback loops describe the process of adaptation in CAS at the macroscopic level. The positive feedback (reinforcing feedback process) ensures the accumulation of "useful experience" ("adaptive potential" and "conditions of its realization") in a System. The negative feedback ("regulating mechanism") stabilizes the temporary equilibrium state of a System by means of redistribution of "potential" between realized (exploited) and unrealized (unexploited) parts. Degeneration of "potential" and "conditions" on account of random destructive perturbations of a System is the consequence of entropy influence.

landscape and (2) the possible losses (costs) in population size on the path to this position. This will be called magnitude "**preference.**"

Preference-value of the definite position in a fitness landscape depends directly on fitness value of this position and depends inversely on losses along the cost-minimizing path leading to this position (Figure 2).

The adaptive search of an agent consists of the following steps.

1. The agent estimates "costs" (losses) of all-possible paths leading each point in a fitness landscape.
2. The agent chooses a cost-minimizing path for each point of the fitness landscape.
3. The agent estimates the "preference" in each point in the fitness landscape.
4. The agent chooses the "best future position" having the maximal preference-value. This position becomes the "attractive peak" for the agent under consideration.
5. Agent shifts into a new position in the fitness landscape along a cost-minimizing path leading to this attractive peak.

The agent, owing to mutations, moves step-by-step along a cost-minimizing path leading to an "attractive peak." The agent recur the procedure of adaptive search at each step. This mechanism of adaptive search in a fitness landscape can be specified by the constriction of the agent's "vision" and definition in details of cost- and preference-functions.

As the agent approaches, the attractive peak losses decrease. The position and the height of this peak are changeable. After the agent culminates this peak, it keeps in this position in the landscape for some time even though other higher peaks exist in its fitness landscape. An agent can't reorient onto another peak because such a choice is burdened by higher losses in population size on the path towards any new peak. Attainability of the new fitness peak depends on the losses (cost of attainment) on the path to this peak (Figure 2). Until the adaptive search of the agent takes place in the nearest fitness peak region the agent evolves gradually.

The point at which preference-value is calculated is the point within "genotype space." The "adaptive potential" of this agent is the value of the prefer-

Figure 2. Interrelation between MAM and MSP platforms of CAS-model-ling

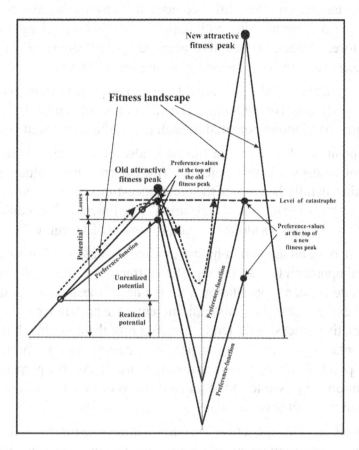

Notes: Fitness-value characterizes the rate of growth of agent's population posed in the definite place of fitness landscape. "Losses" are equal to decrement in this rate of growth due to non-optimal mutations on the path of agents to the definite position in fitness landscape. Preference-value is fitness-value minus losses. The current fitness-value is index of "realized potential". The preference-value at the top of fitness peak is index of available "potential". Reorientation of an agent onto a new fitness peak ("level of catastrophe") takes place if the preference-value at the top of a new peak is equal or larger than preference-value at the top of the old fitness peak.

ence-function calculated at the point within the range of possibilities in the fitness landscape, which represents the highest attainable point (fitness peak) possible within the range of potential values (Figure 2).

The quantity of losses along the way toward an attractive peak determines the "conditions of realisation" of adaptive potential. The "losses" along a path are larger as the "conditions of ascent" to the top become harder. Losses along the cost-minimizing path depend directly on the length of this path. Therefore, an agent's "adaptive potential" and "conditions of realisation" increases when the agent approaches the top of its adaptive peak.

The current fitness value of an agent can be interpreted as the agent's "realised (employed) adaptive potential." The value of realised potential is lesser than the value of adaptive potential at each point of a cost-minimizing path.

Each position of an agent in fitness landscape corresponds to the definite value of "realised adaptive potential" (the current fitness value), the "adaptive potential" in full (the value of the preference-function at the point of attractive peak) and "the conditions of realisation" (the function- formalizing influence of the possible losses along the path toward peak) (Figure 2).

Movement of an agent in a fitness landscape consists of two stages: (1) the gradual approach toward the top of an attractive fitness peak and then (2), a sharp and sudden reorientation onto the new fitness peak. As the agent approaches the fitness peak, his gain (increment in preference-value at the point of attractive fitness peak) tends to zero. From the other hand, the gain from re-orientation onto a new fitness peak increases because the preference-value at the point of this new peak grows (Figure 2). Agents perpetually correct estimations of possible future gains in the process of searching for its next position in the fitness landscape.

The position of an agent near the current attractive fitness peak is inherently unstable. Growth of an agent's population localised near the definite fitness peak is the direct consequence of the high fitness-value in neighbourhood of this peak. Since the different agent's populations are in competitive interaction, the growth of populations will decrease the height of each attractive fitness peak in each fitness landscape (Figure 3). As a consequence of this a new "best" position in a fitness landscape arises as either a first or last instance. An agent discovers a new point of maximum of preference-function in a fitness landscape only when the decrement of the current attractive peak height becomes large enough. Only when the new attractive peak is found will an agent abandon the prior peak.

"Punctuated equilibrium" phenomenon arises as a consequence of the instability of an agent's equilibrium position near a fitness peak. Reorientation of an agent onto a new fitness peak generates avalanche-like processes of

Figure 3. Dynamics of preference-values in the changeable fitness land-scape

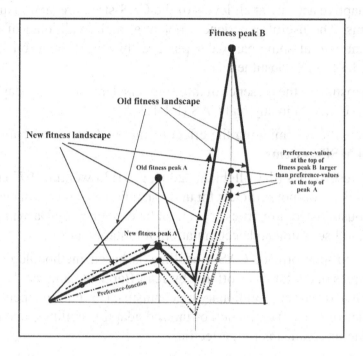

Notes: As the height of fitness-peak A diminishes a new attractive fitness peak B arises.

reorientation in the ensemble of interacting agents. This is stage of CAS re-configuration. A new structure of fitness landscapes is formed at this point. This is chaos-like process by which some new CAS structure emerges. At the macroscopic level, this is reminiscent of a catastrophe in the complex adaptive system's evolution.

Method of Systems Potential

So, the "adaptive potential," Φ, the "conditions of realisation," U, and the "realised portion of adaptive potential," Φ_R, are the basic variables by which MSP fixes the macroscopic state of CAS.

The adaptation processes lead to the accumulation of adaptive potential and conditions of realisation in the system. This process takes place through the adaptive activity at all levels of the CAS-structure, and in all of its sub-systems. The useful experience (potential and conditions) of CAS is not concentrated at some particular place within the system, but is dispersed around all of its constituents.

MSP postulates the presence of three universal macroscopic adaptive mechanisms (UMAM) in any real CAS (P.1-P.3).

Intelligent CAS imitating the effect of these adaptive mechanisms will be called **MSP-systems**.

Many researchers (di Collobiano, 2002, p. 31; Lewontin, 1972) insisted that Darwinism was not sufficient for understanding the process of evolution. The previously listed properties (*) cannot be explained by Darwin's the theory of natural selection and accumulation of mutation alone.

The MSP-platform of CAS-modelling is based methodologically on the principles of evolution as offered by Jean-Baptiste Lamarck. He formulated three macroscopic evolutionary mechanisms: (1) reinforcement of adaptive abilities in use, (2) extinction of unused adaptive abilities, and (3) inherent striving of organisms for perfection.

As it often happens in the history of science, these two doctrines—*Darwinism and Lamarckism—reflect different aspects of one evolutionary process.* Struggle for survival and mutations, that is, the concept of Darwinism, are presented as the basis of the theory of fitness landscapes and multi-agent modelling. Lamarck's laws of evolution are effective at the level of integral CAS. Selection and mutations at the level of a multitude of interacting agents result in CAS developing as an integral whole, just like Lamarck supposed; the system's used macroscopic adaptive abilities develop, while the unused ones die off. The interrelation between Lamarckism and Darwinism is the relation of between the properties of CAS as a united integral system and the properties of the same CAS as a multitude of interacting agents. Darwinism describes evolution at the micro-level, the level of interacting agents; Lamarckism describes evolution at the macro-level, that of integral systems.

The adaptive potential of CAS consists of two parts: the portion of potential realised in adaptive activity, Φ_R, and the non-realised portion of potential, Φ_D.

$$\Phi = \Phi_R + \Phi_D. \tag{1}$$

Lamarck's evolutionary laws regulate the dynamics of these two constituents of adaptive potential.

Lamarck's First Law

Adaptive abilities which are applied in adaptive activities of the system develop and strengthen.

Exploited adaptive abilities → adaptive activity → increment in exploited adaptive abilities.

The first of Lamarck's laws can be formalised as reinforcing feedback process:

$$\dot{\Phi}_R = a \cdot \Phi_R; \; a > 0 \tag{2}$$

where a is the rate of growth of the realised portion of potential.

Lamarck's Second Law[3]

The adaptive abilities that are not applied in adaptive activities of the system are degenerate.

Unused adaptive abilities → impossibility of their use in current activity → gradual degradation of unused adaptive abilities.

The second of Lamarck's laws can be formalised as follows:

$$\dot{\Phi}_D = -d \cdot \Phi_D; \; d > 0. \tag{3}$$

where d is the rate of degradation of unexploited abilities. This law reflects the action of principle of entropy in CAS.

The adaptive activity of an MSP-system is a process of application (exploitation; employment) of adaptive potential. The connection of adaptive activity with the potential, the conditions of realisation and the realised portion of potential is determined in MSP with the help of two postulates.

Let A be adaptive activity of a MSP-system in a unit of time.

The First Postulate of Adaptive Activity

The adaptive activity of a MSP-system is the source of increment in potential and conditions of realisation:

$\dot{\Phi}_+ = c \cdot A$ – Increment in potential on account of activity.

$\dot{U}_+ = q \cdot A$ – Increment in conditions on account of activity.
$c > 0, \quad q > 0.$

Other sources of increase in potential and conditions of realisation in MSP-system are possible as well. For instance, these values may grow or decrease on account of external impacts on the system from it's interaction with other systems. Note that these special cases may be organically included in the general scheme.

The Second Postulate of Adaptive Activity

The exploited potential of MSP-system is larger; therefore, the adaptive activity of the system is larger.

$A = \mu \cdot \Phi_R; \mu > 0.$ (4)

As far as the adaptive activity of MSP-system is the employment of the exploited portion of potential, this postulate is likely to invariably be true for relevant choices of units of measurement of activity and the potential.

The current macroscopic state, S, of the MSP-system is an ordered set of MSP-variables: (1) potential, Φ, (2) conditions of realisation, U, and (3) realised portion of potential, Φ_R:

$$S \leftrightarrow (\Phi;\ U;\ \Phi_R).$$

a. **The first adaptive mechanism (Lamarck's laws)** sets the current equilibrium state of the MSP-system and the laws governing it's change.

"Potential," Φ, and "conditions of realisation," U, increase with adaptive activity of a MSP-system and decrease as a consequence of the influence of the entropy principle.

Mathematically this statement may be represented as follows:

$$
\left.
\begin{aligned}
\dot{\Phi} &= \underbrace{c \cdot A}_{\substack{\text{increment on account of} \\ \text{adaptive activity}}} - \underbrace{d \cdot \Phi}_{\substack{\text{decrement on account of} \\ \text{entropy}}} \\
\dot{U} &= \underbrace{q \cdot A}_{\substack{\text{increment on account of} \\ \text{adaptive activity}}} - \underbrace{\Lambda \cdot U}_{\substack{\text{decrement on account of} \\ \text{entropy}}}
\end{aligned}
\right\} - \text{Stock-flows balance equations}
$$

$$(5)$$

Multipliers $c;d;q;\Lambda$ are the rates of the change in the potential and in the conditions as a result of adaptive activity of the MSP-system and the effect of entropy.

Differentiating the left and the right parts (1), using Lamarck's laws (2) and (3) and taking (4) into consideration, it is not difficult to derive three equations for the three variables Φ, U and Φ_R:

$$
\left.
\begin{aligned}
\dot{\Phi} &= \underbrace{(a+d) \cdot \Phi_R}_{\substack{\text{increment on account of} \\ \text{adaptive activity}}} - \underbrace{d \cdot \Phi}_{\substack{\text{decrement on account of} \\ \text{entropy}}} \\
\dot{U} &= \underbrace{v \cdot \Phi_R}_{\substack{\text{increment on account of} \\ \text{adaptive activity}}} - \underbrace{\Lambda \cdot U}_{\substack{\text{decrement on account of} \\ \text{entropy}}}
\end{aligned}
\right\} - \text{Stock-flows balance equations}
$$

$$(6)$$

$$\dot{\Phi}_R = a \cdot \Phi_R - \text{Lamarck's first law.} \tag{7}$$

$$v = q \cdot \mu, \, a + d = c \cdot \mu. \tag{8}$$

The second of Lamarck's laws describes the degradation of potential and conditions due to the influence of entropy. Call parameters $a; v; \Lambda; d$ *evolutionary parameters* of MSP-systems. They characterise evolutionary properties of the system as an integrated whole. Equations (6)-(7) may be solved analytically if the evolutionary parameters are constant values. Only this simplest case is considered in this essay.

Figure 1 presents schematically how CAS is constructed at the macroscopic level within MSP-platform of CAS-modelling. MSP-systems accumulate their adaptive potential and conditions of realisation (useful experience) through the channel of adaptive activity and lose them through the channel of entropy. Adaptive activity is input-flow. The effect of entropy results in output-flow. The equations representing the balance between the stocks and flows describe the dynamics of potential and the conditions of realisation.

Equations (6)-(7) do not take into account stochastic perturbations of MSP-systems.

The above stated, the following definitions might be introduced.

Density of conditions in MSP-system, z, is the quantity of conditions per unit of potential.

$$z \equiv \frac{U}{\Phi}. \tag{9}$$

Efficiency of the MSP-system, R, is the rate of exploitation of accumulated adaptive potential. Efficiency equals realised potential per entire potential ratio:

$$R \equiv \frac{\Phi_R}{\Phi}. \tag{10}$$

The following equations respecting density of conditions, z and efficiency R, can be derived from equations (6)-(7):

$$\frac{\dot{R}}{R} = \frac{\dot{\Phi}_R}{\Phi_R} - \frac{\dot{\Phi}}{\Phi} = (a+d)\cdot(1-R). \tag{11}$$

$$\frac{\dot{z}}{z} = \frac{\dot{U}}{U} - \frac{\dot{\Phi}}{\Phi} = \left(\frac{v}{z} - (a+d)\right)\cdot R + (d-\Lambda). \tag{12}$$

The following ordinary differential equation follows from equations (11)-(12):

$$R'_z \cdot \left[\left(v - (a+d)\cdot z\right)\cdot R + (d-\Lambda)\cdot z\right] - (a+d)\cdot R\cdot(1-R) = 0. \tag{13}$$

The solution of this equation determines trajectory of a MSP-system in the plane $(z;R)$.

Temporary equilibrium states of a MSP-system correspond to points on the path (13) in the plane $(z;R)$. Each pair $(z;R)$ corresponds to a definite ray running through the point of origin in the space $(\Phi; U; \Phi_R)$.

According to (11)-(12), the MSP-system having the constant evolutionary parameters approaches asymptotically to the point in which efficiency has maximal value $R = 1$. Let z_0 be the density of conditions in this point of maximal efficiency. As a consequence of (11)-(12), this value equals:

$$z_0 = \frac{v}{a+\Lambda}. \tag{14}$$

State $(z_0; R = 1)$ is the global equilibrium state of an MSP-system. Equilibrium conditions $\dot{R}(z_0) = \dot{z}(z_0) = 0$ are fulfilled at this point. It is evident that a MSP-system collapses into its global equilibrium state and remains for an indefinite time if perturbations of the MSP-system are absent.

What happens to the system if we consider the real situation and take the existence of random perturbations of the system into consideration? Such perturbations may be represented by the effect of external perturbation factors or fluctuations of evolutionary parameters.

Under the influence of such perturbations, the MSP-system deviates from the equilibrium trajectory (13). The system's dynamics in the plane $(z;R)$ is the superposition of random wandering on deterministic processes, (11)–(12). As a result, the system approaches toward a point $(z_0;R = 1)$. After that, it wanders around this point, moving aside following the perturbations and returning according to the equations of deterministic process (11)–(12). Such behaviour is very far from the typical picture of real evolutionary process.

The reason for this is that we have not taken into account the system's ability to maintain (stabilise) its temporal equilibrium state.

b.   **The second adaptive mechanism** describes the ability of a CAS to stabilise the temporal equilibrium state. This mechanism is based on the ability of the system to control the efficiency of system' performance through a reduction or extension of the scope of adaptive activity. The effect of this mechanism may be formalised as a loop of stabilising negative feedback. Consequently, another equation should be added to equations (6)-(7).

The process of stabilisation of temporal equilibrium state is as follows:

Deviation from temporal equilibrium → effect of stabilising mechanism → return to original temporal equilibrium state.

Stabilizing feedback is represented as regulating mechanism in **Figure 1.** Suppose that the system has gone off its trajectory (13) as the result of a perturbation. What will be the process of its return into the initial temporal equilibrium state? Answering this question requires understanding which of the variables the system is able to control: $z = \dfrac{U}{\Phi}$ or $R = \dfrac{\Phi_R}{\Phi}$. Stabilisation is effective only when the process takes place quickly. Neither the potential, Φ, nor the conditions of realisation, U, may be changed quickly in response to random perturbations of the system. These are inertial values. Consequently, the value $z = \dfrac{U}{\Phi}$ is not controlled by the system. The value Φ_R is the only variable which is liable to efficiently control an MSP-system. The MSP-system may react operatively to random perturbations reducing or increasing the efficiency $R = \dfrac{\Phi_R}{\Phi}$, thus shifting its state upwards or downwards along the axis R in the plane $(z;R)$. It is this process which stabilises the temporal equilibrium state of an MSP-system.

The ability of the system to stabilise its temporal equilibrium is one of the fundamental properties of any real CAS. For example, stabilisation in living systems is known as the process of homoeostatic and psychological self-regula-tion. Stabilisation in the economic system takes place via market mechanisms of demand-supply-price or investment-savings interdependence.

The choice of mathematical form of the stabilising mechanism in general is not universal. The equation should be of the following type:

$$\frac{dR}{dt} = H\left(R; z; \chi\right). \tag{15}$$

Function $H(R;z;\chi)$ depends on values z and χ as parameters. This function satisfies the following conditions:

$$H(R_E; z) = 0; \; H(R > R_E; z) < 0; \; H(R < R_E; z) > 0 \tag{16}$$

$$\left.\frac{\partial H}{\partial R}\right|_{(R_E; z; \chi)} < 0; \; R_E = R(z). \tag{17}$$

R_E is the value of efficiency in the point of the path (13) having abscissa z.

Assume that parameter χ does not change. Consider the simplest case of the equation (15), so-called anti-gradient law:

$$\frac{dR}{dt} = -K \cdot \frac{\partial W\left(R; z\right)}{\partial R} = -K \cdot W_R'\left(R; z\right); \; K \gg 0. \tag{18}$$

The **"stabilizing function"** $W(R;z)$ determines the stability properties of the MSP-system's temporary equilibrium state. The temporary equilibrium states $(z; R_E(z))$ correspond to the extreme points of function $W(R;z)$ subject to a fixed z:

$$W_R'\left(R_E; z\right) = 0. \tag{19}$$

Points of minimum (maximum and inflection) of the stabilizing function, $W(R;z)$, correspond to stable (unstable) temporal equilibrium states of an MSP-system. The path of temporal equilibrium states (13), $R(z)$, is a locus of minimum points of the stabilising function $W(R;z)$ subject to a fixed z.

According to (12) parameter z is changing in with the course of time. If, having some critical value z, the number of roots, $R_E(z)$, in the equations (19), change (for example, two different roots of equation (19) merge into one root), then the character of stability in the temporal equilibrium state changes at this value z. The following chapter will show that there are two critical values of the parameter z in MSP-systems with constant evolutionary parameters.

c. **The third adaptive mechanism** describes the ability of a CAS to maximise the employed portion of adaptive potential on account for optimal distribution of "conditions" between its sub-systems. This mechanism creates the structure within MSP-system.

The effect of the third adaptive mechanism may be described mathematically as a conditional extremum problem. Consider an MSP-system consisting of N sub-systems having potentials Φ_k and conditions U_k; $k = 1;...;N$. The aggregate potentials and conditions of the comprehensive MSP-system is equal to:

$$\Phi = \sum_{k=1}^{N} \Phi_k. \tag{20}$$

$$U = \sum_{k=1}^{N} U_k. \tag{21}$$

When the multipliers are introduced, γ_k, which characterise the distribution of "conditions" among sub-systems:

$$U_k = \gamma_k \cdot U, \sum_{k=1}^{N} \gamma_k = 1. \tag{22}$$

The conditional extremum problem can be formulated as follows:

$$\Phi_R \rightarrow \max,$$

subject to given $\Phi, \{\Phi_k\}_{k=1}^{N}, U.$
Consider Lagrange' function:

$$L\left(\lambda;\ \gamma_1;\ \gamma_2;...;\gamma_N\right)=\sum_{k=1}^{N}\Phi_k\cdot R\left(\frac{\gamma_k}{\Phi_k}\cdot U\right)+\lambda\cdot\left(U\cdot\left(1-\sum_{k=1}^{N}\gamma_k\right)\right) \qquad (23)$$

where λ – is Lagrange's multiplier.

Solution of the equations $\dfrac{\partial L}{\partial \gamma_k}=0$ gives us the following result:

$$\left.\frac{dR(z)}{dz}\right|_{Z=Z_k=\frac{U_k}{\Phi_k}}=R'_Z\left(z_k\right)=\lambda=Const \qquad (24)$$

Thus, the distribution of "conditions" between agents (sub-systems) in a comprehensive system is optimal if the tangents to the points of path (13) in which agents (subsystems) are disposed parallel to each other.

In other words, the condition (24) splits the ensemble of sub-systems (agents) into several groups. The number of groups will be equal to a number of different points of a path (13) in which the tangents to the path are parallel. If the path has no two differing points with parallel tangents, then all the sub-systems will have the same state. The ensemble will develop as an integral whole. If the path has several different points at which the tangents are parallel, then the ensemble will split into several cells creating a structure in the comprehensive MSP-system. If some cells in their turn are MSP-systems, then the structure of the second level is possible, and so forth.

In Summary

Dynamics of the MSP-system is the result of the actions of three universal macroscopic adaptive mechanisms (UMAM):

a.   **The first adaptive mechanism** describes the processes of the accumulation of the useful experience (potential and conditions) within the MSP-system. This mechanism determines the dynamics of the current state of the system.

$$\dot{\Phi} = \underbrace{(a+d)\cdot\Phi_R}_{\substack{\text{increment on account of}\\\text{adaptive activity}}} - \underbrace{d\cdot\Phi}_{\substack{\text{decrement on account of}\\\text{entropy}}}$$

$$\dot{U} = \underbrace{\nu\cdot\Phi_R}_{\substack{\text{increment on account of}\\\text{adaptive activity}}} - \underbrace{\Lambda\cdot U}_{\substack{\text{decrement on account of}\\\text{entropy}}} \qquad \text{(E1)}$$

$$\dot{\Phi}_R = a\cdot\Phi_R \qquad \text{(E2)}$$

Equation of trajectory of temporary equilibrium states of a MSP-system:

$$R'_z\cdot\left[\left(\nu-(a+d)\cdot z\right)\cdot R+(d-\Lambda)\cdot z\right]-(a+d)\cdot R\cdot(1-R)=0 \qquad \text{(E3)}$$

Equations of the change of the temporary equilibrium state of a MSP-system:

$$\frac{\dot{R}}{R}=\frac{\dot{\Phi}_R}{\Phi_R}-\frac{\dot{\Phi}}{\Phi}=(a+d)\cdot(1-R). \qquad \text{(E4)}$$

$$\frac{\dot{z}}{z}=\frac{\dot{U}}{U}-\frac{\dot{\Phi}}{\Phi}=\left(\frac{\nu}{z}-(a+d)\right)\cdot R+(d-\Lambda) \qquad \text{(E5)}$$

b.   **The second adaptive mechanism** describes the reaction of the MSP-system to the effect of external perturbations. This mechanism works as stabilizing feedback.

Equation of stabilizing feedback:

$$\frac{dR}{dt}=-K\cdot\frac{\partial W(R;z)}{\partial R}=-K\cdot W'_R(R;z);\ K\gg0. \qquad \text{(E6)}$$

c.   **The third adaptive mechanism** explains the ability of the system to optimally distribute conditions between the sub-systems:

$$\left.\frac{dR(z)}{dz}\right|_{Z=Z_k=\frac{U_k}{\Phi_k}}=R'_Z(z_k)=\lambda=Const \qquad \text{(E7)}$$

This adaptive mechanism is responsible for the generation of the many-level hierarchical structure of a MSP-system.

Note that the rules of sub-systems interaction can't be stated arbitrarily. Laws of interaction at the micro-level (between the sub-systems) must have the condition of coordinated universal mechanisms of adaptation (E1)-(E7) at all levels of the global system Hence these rules are the conditions necessary for the coordination of equations (E1)-(E7) made for each of the sub-systems. Thus, the local properties of the system are interwoven with its global properties. The laws of the behaviour of sub-systems are implicitly contained in equations (E1)-(E7).

MSP-Systems with Fixed Evolutionary Parameters

The equation (E3) can be solved analytically if MSP-system has a constant evolutionary parameters. The trajectory of the temporal equilibrium states $R(z)$ (13), consists of two branches (Figure 4):

Upper evolutionary branch: $z^{(-)}(R)$: $z = z_0 \cdot R - C^{(-)} \cdot R^{-\chi} \cdot (1 - R)^{1+\chi}$;

$$(25)$$

Subject to $z < z_0 \cdot R$;

Lower evolutionary branch: $z^{(+)}(R)$: $z = z_0 \cdot R + C^{(+)} \cdot R^{-\chi} \cdot (1 - R)^{1+\chi}$;

$$(26)$$

Subject to $z > z_0 \cdot R$;

$C^{(-)} > 0$; $C^{(+)} > 0$;

$$z_0 \equiv \frac{\nu}{a + \Lambda}; \chi \equiv \frac{\Lambda - d}{a + d}; -1 < \chi < \frac{\Lambda}{a}. \tag{27}$$

To specify the constants $C^{(-)}$ and $C^{(+)}$, it is necessary to set two initial positions of the MSP-system: one at the upper evolutionary branch and the second at the lower evolutionary branch. The efficiency of the MSP-system grows with time according to the logistic law:

$$R(t) = \frac{1}{1 + b \cdot e^{-(a+d)t}} \; ; \; b \equiv \frac{1 - R(0)}{R(0)}. \tag{28}$$

The sign of parameter χ determines the shape of function $R(z)$ (Figure 4). MSP-systems having positive and negative values χ have the different dynamic and structural properties.

The First Type of MSP-Systems: $\chi > 0$

The points of minimum of stabilizing function $W(R;z)$ lie on the upper evolutionary branch and on the lower part of the lower evolutionary branch.

Figure 4. Efficiency of adaptation, R(z), as the function of "density of conditions" in MSP-system with fixed evolutionary parameters

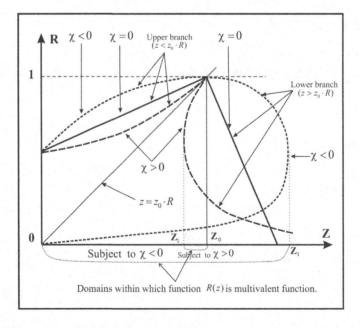

These are points of stable temporal equilibrium of MSP-system. The points of maximum for the function $W(R;z)$ lie on the upper part of the lower evolutionary branch (Figure 4). These are points of unstable temporal equilibrium states of MSP-system.

Supposing, at the initial moment the system was at the point 2 (Figure 5). It will move along the lower evolutionary branch until it reaches point 3. While it is approaching this point, the depth of the potential well $W(R;z)$ in which the system is situated will decrease (Figure 7). However, this means that the stability of temporal equilibrium state of the MSP-system is falling as it approaches point 3. This is the bifurcation point of stabilizing function $W(R;z)$ at which the minimum point of the function $W(R;z)$ is transformed into a point of inflection (Figure 7). A similar discourse can be made with respect to point 1 at which the points of maximum and minimum stabilizing of function $W(R;z)$ converge as well, and the depth of potential well vanishes. At points

Figure 5. Discontinuous evolutionary cycle of MSP-system with fixed evolutionary parameters in the plane (z;R)

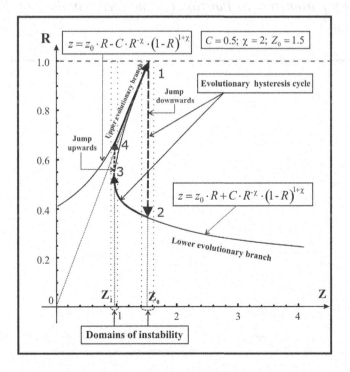

1 and 3 the MSP-system, following any small perturbation, will move from the upper (lower) branch to the lower (upper) branch (Figure 7).

Consequently, *there are two critical points at which the temporal equilibrium state of the MSP-system becomes unstable. In these points the system makes a leap from one evolutionary branch to another. Dynamics of an MSP-system subject to χ > 0 is a sequence of discontinuous cycles* (Figure 6, 9, 10, and 12).

Each **evolutionary cycle**, 1 → 2 → 3 → 4 (Figure 5) consists of two catastrophic jumps and two stages of the gradual motion of the MSP-system along either lower or upper evolutionary branches. For proper characterisation of these four phases of the cycle, it is convenient to use the names borrowed from the business cycle theory: (1) jump downwards—"crisis," (2) jump upwards—"revival," (3) the stage of the gradual development along the lower evolutionary branch—"depression" and (4) stage of the gradual development along the upper evolutionary branch—"prosperity." Our intuition suggests

Figure 6. Discontinuous evolutional cycle of MSP-system with fixed evolutionary parameters as function of time (perturbations of the System are very small)

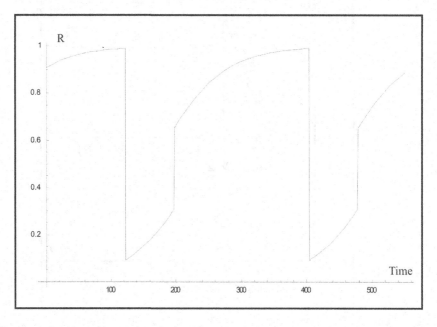

that this is not just an analogy but that in reality the business cycle as such is based on the evolutionary cycle of the economic CAS.

Instability of the current state of the MSP-system increases in during the evolutionary cycle. MSP-systems tend toward the global equilibrium (z_0; $R = 1$) but this is an unstable equilibrium. This is the unstable attractor of a MSP-system. Consequently, dynamics of the MSP-system having $\chi > 0$ demonstrates *"self-organised instability"* phenomenon introduced in the chapter (Sole et al., 2002).

The leaps occurring in the critical points of the function $W(R; z)$ are the evidence of mathematical catastrophe. The surface of the catastrophe is determined by means of the condition:

$$W_R'(R; z; \chi) = 0 \qquad (29)$$

Figure 7 shows the surface $W(R;z)$ and the movement of the system around this surface. At points z_0 and z_1 the MSP-system, under the influence of the

Figure 7. Discontinuous evolutionary cycle of MSP-system with fixed evolutionary parameters as motion round the surface of stabilizing function W(R;z)

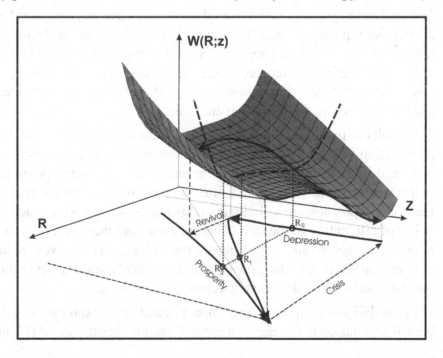

stabilising adaptive mechanism (E6), "rolls" the system into a new the temporal equilibrium state. In these points, the efficiency of the MSP-system changes stepwise on account of a reduction (crisis) or an extension (revival) of the realised portion of potential.

The simplest approximation of a stabilizing function is four-degree polynomial:

$$W_R'(R,z) = C \cdot (R-R_0) \cdot (R-R_1) \cdot (R-R_2)$$

$$W(R;z;\chi) = \left(\frac{R^4}{4} - A(R_0;R_1;R_2) \cdot \frac{R^3}{3} + B(R_0;R_1;R_2) \cdot \frac{R^2}{2} - R_0 \cdot R_1 \cdot R_2 \cdot R + C_1 \right) \cdot C_2$$

$$A(R_0;R_1;R_2) = R_0 + R_1 + R_2; \ B(R_0;R_1;R_2) \ R_0 \cdot R_1 + R_1 \cdot R_2 + R_0 \cdot R_2$$

$$(30)$$

C_1 and $C_2 > 0$ are some constants.

Points $(z; R_{0;1;2})$ lie on the evolutionary branches:

$$z = z^{(-)}(R_2); \ z = z^{(+)}(R_{0;1}) \tag{31}$$

The evolutionary cycles may be divided into the three large groups: Expansion cycles ("potential" and "conditions," which increase in the long-term (Figure 14, upper-right and upper-left insets). Contraction cycles ("potential" and "conditions" which decrease in the long-term - Figure 14, lower-right and lower-left insets). And third, closed cycles (where the changes in "potential" and "conditions" in the long-term are limited).

The results of modelling with the use of equations (E3) - (E6) and (30) are presented in Figures 9-14. These figures demonstrate that the length of the cycle and its different phases are quite sensitive to any small perturbations to the MSP-system. This follows directly from the fact that the stability of the system's position on evolutionary branch falls while it is approaching the points of bifurcation of the stabilising function, and the probability of skipping to the other evolutionary branch grows (Figure 8). The very moments of transition that determine the length of different phases of the evolutionary cycle depend on casual factors affecting the MSP-system.

The probability of jumping from the upper evolutionary branches to the lower branch depends on the average strength of random perturbations (Figure 8).

In the case of small perturbations, the time of the system's life on the upper branch is protracted. The system mounts nearly to the very crest of the upper branch, before transitioning downward. The probability density function for the events of the fall from the upper branch to the lower one has, as a "density of conditions" function, a peak-like form (Figure 15, 16). With the growth of perturbations, this peak shifts toward lower values of "density of conditions." The probability density function for the events of the system's shifting from the lower to the upper branch has a form of a peak localised in the vicinity of the critical point z_1. With the growth of perturbations this peak widens and its tail rises up (Figures 15-17).

The probability density of events of skipping from one branch to the other represents a summary distribution of events of falling downwards and jumping upwards. In the case of small perturbations within the system, this resulting distribution has a "two-hump" form (Figure 15). The first "hump"

Figure 8. Interrelation of stochastic and deterministic patterns in dynamics of MSP-system

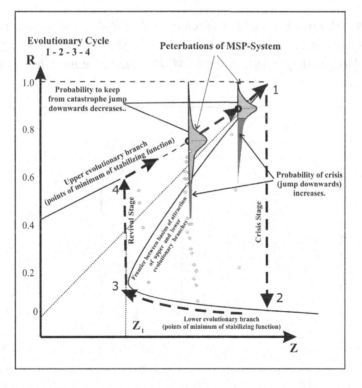

Figure 9. Sequence of irregular discontinuous evolutionary cycles of MSP-System with fixed evolutionary parameters. The following values of parameters were used in simulation: $a = 0.08$; $d = 0.02$; $\Lambda = 0.12$; $v = 0.6$; $z_0 = 3$; $\chi = 1$; $C^{(-)} = 0.05$; $\sigma = 0.5$

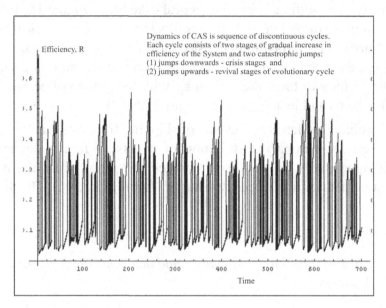

Figure 10. Dynamics of the efficiency of MSP-System with constant evolutionary parameters: $a = 0.0735$; $\Lambda = 0.1265$; $v = 0.6$; $z_0 = 3$; $\chi = 1$; $C^{(\pm)} = 0.05$. *Stochastic perturbations of MSP-System are modeled as PDF having* $\sigma = 0.5$

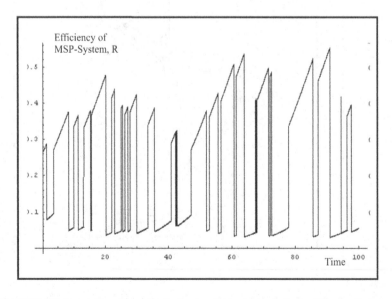

Figure 11. Dynamics of "potential" of MSP-System with constant evolutionary parameters. This is the same simulation as in Figure 10.

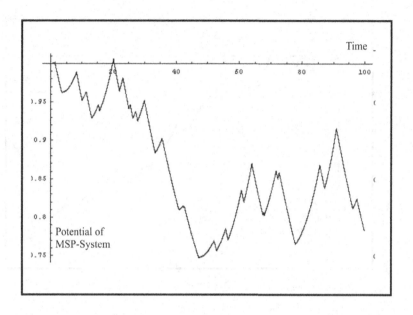

Figure 12. Simulation for the MSP-system with weakly fluctuating evolutionary parameters

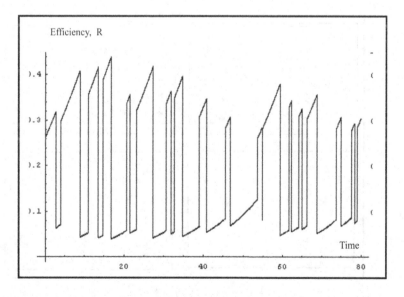

Figure 13. Dynamics of "potential" of MSP-system having the fluctuating evolutionary parameters (the same simulation as in Figure 12)

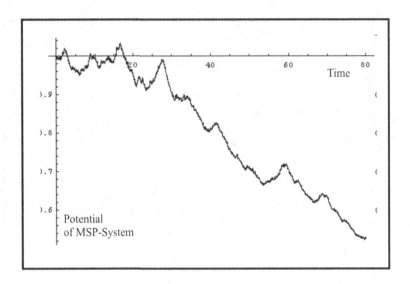

Figure 14. Some simulations of dynamics of MSP-system having fluctuating evolutionary parameters

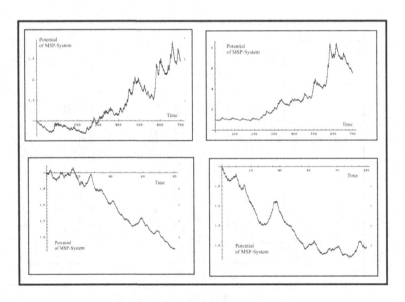

corresponds to the peak of events created by the fall from the upper branch down to the lower branch. The second "hump" matches the peak of leaps from the lower branch to the upper branch. With the growth of the system's perturbations, the "two-hump" distribution is transformed into a distribution close to the power law (Figures 15-19).

As far as each leap is a catastrophe of qualitative renewal of the system, which is accompanied by avalanche-like processes of reconfiguration, the power law of frequency distribution for movement from one branch to the other (Figure 19), shows that some critical state is being established in the MSP-system. As soon as the average value of external perturbations exceeds some threshold value, the two-peak-like distribution of fall-events (crises) and upheavals-events (revivals) (Figure 15) superimposed upon each other (Figure 16) form a power-like law of probability distribution (Figure 17-19).

That is, the MSP-system, with its growth in perturbations, spontaneously transforms into a critical state, demonstrating the *SOC-phenomenon.* Each jump corresponds to some avalanche-like process of system' reconfigura-

Figure 15. Non-cumulative frequency distribution of catastrophic jumps as the function of "density of conditions" subject to minor perturbations of the MSP-System; $z_1 = 2$; $z_0 = 3$

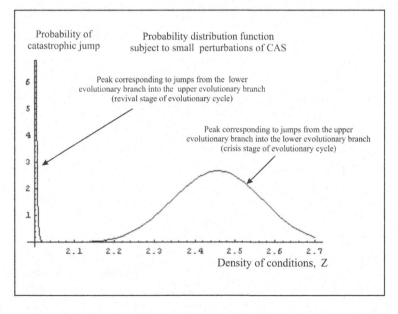

tion. The number of agents engaged within this process depends directly on the difference between values of efficiency before and after the jump. Let ΔR_{max} and ΔR_{min} are maximal and minimal values for this difference. If the value of constants $C^{(+)}$ and $C^{(-)}$ tend to zero then $\Delta R_{max} \to 1$ and $\Delta R_{min} \to 0$. Consequently, the power law for frequency distribution of avalanche-sizes may take place within an unlimited range of avalanche-scales. Figure 19 illustrates the linear law within the limited region of avalanche-scales. As the constants $C^{(+)}$ and $C^{(-)}$ are diminish this region is broadened and the system demonstrates criticality (the power law of frequency of distribution against avalanche-size within a region of very different scales).

The four-phase discontinuous cycles in which the phases of smooth growth of the system's efficiency alternate with leaping from one evolutionary branch to the other realise a regime of *punctuated equilibrium.* The very moments of quick transition and the smooth development phase length depend on the effects of random perturbations and are therefore random values.

Figure 16. Non-cumulative frequency distribution of catastrophic jumps as the function of "density of conditions" subject to moderate perturbations of the MSP-System; $z_1 = 2$; $z_0 = 3$

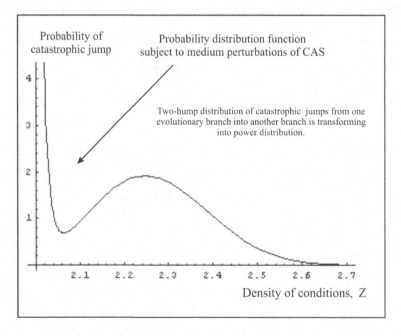

Figure 17. Non-cumulative frequency distribution of catastrophic jumps as the function of "density of conditions" subject to large perturbations of the MSP-system; $z_1 = 2$; $z_0 = 3$

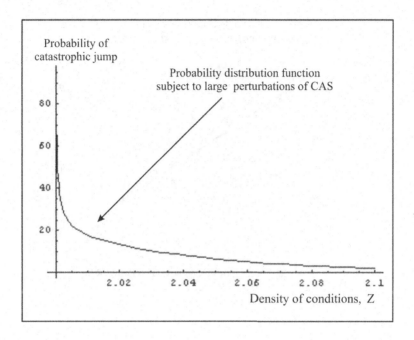

Figure 18. Non-cumulative frequency of jumps against the value of jump, $R_{upper}(z) - R_{lower}(z)$

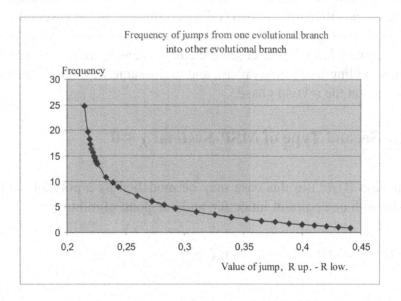

Figure 19. Non-cumulative frequency of jumps against the value of jump,
$R_{upper}(z) - R_{lower}(z)$, *in logarithmic scale*

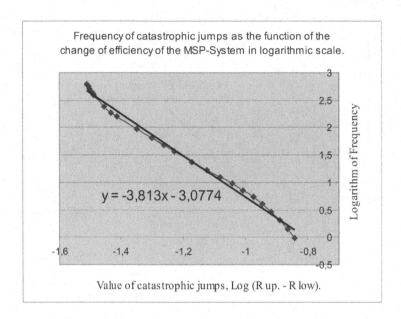

Finally, the path of equilibrium states (13) in the MSP-systems with $\chi > 0$ does not have two different points in which the tangents are parallel. Therefore, the adaptive mechanism (E7) will concentrate the ensemble of similar sub-systems (agents) in the neighbourhood of one and the same point of the evolutionary branch. The ensemble will move as an integral whole, synchronously falling into a crisis phase and in the same way synchronously rising upwards at the revival phase.

The Second Type of MSP-System: $\chi < 0$

Function $W(R;z)$ in this case may be modelled by a polynomial of fourth order with one point of inflection and one point of minimum.

$$W'_R(R,z) = C \cdot (R - R_0)^2 \cdot (R - R_1), \; C > 0 \tag{32}$$

The path of temporal equilibrium (13) has a multitude of pairs of different points in which the tangents are parallel. The condition of optimality (E7) may be satisfied here in two different points at once, for instance, at points 1 and 2, as shown in Figure 20. This means that adaptive mechanism (E7) splits an ensemble of similar MSP-systems with $\chi < 0$ into two classes: (1) the class of sub-systems located at the point 1 of the upper branch ("lower class") and (2) the class of sub-systems located at the point 2 of the lower part of the lower evolutionary branch ("upper class") (Figure 20). In other words, the adaptive mechanism (E7) forms in MSP-systems with $\chi < 0$ a cell (class) structure. Points of minimum of the stabilizing function $W(R;z)$ subject to fixed z coincide with the positions of classes 1 and 2. This is the simplest variant of class-structure. Evolutionary parameters in real CAS are changeable values as a rule. Real paths of the temporal equilibrium states are far more complex curves. As a consequence the adaptive mechanism (E7) is capable of forming far more complex cell-structures via the decomposition of

Figure 20. Catastrophe of chaotic restructuring in the MSP-system having $\chi < 0$

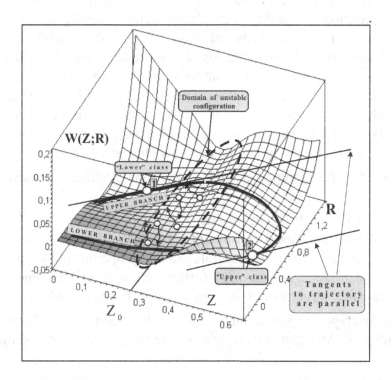

the ensemble of interacting agents into many classes (cells). Agents of each cell are situated in its own potential well of the stabilising function $W(R;z)$. The stability of the class-structure depends on the deep of potential well of stabilizing functions in the points where classes are disposed.

The position of cells on the path of the temporary equilibrium states can change slowly in course of evolution. Therefore, the stability of class-structure can change as well. Consider the simplest case of MSP-system having constant evolutionary parameters. Figure 20 illustrates a situation in which shift of class positions along the equilibrium path leads to a catastrophe of restructuring. At some critical value $z_c \approx z_0$, the stabilising function is transformed into a level, broad potential well.

If for some reason the efficiency of "upper" class 2 shifts downwards, and the efficiency of "lower" class 1 shifts upwards, and the condition (E7) is true for every moment of time, then, having such a shift, the instability of the class structure will grow, as the depth of potential wells of the function $W(R;z)$ in which the classes are placed decreases. The "agents" of one class will, because of some perturbations, leave their potential well and "wander" around the area near the critical value z_c.

The growing number of "wanderings" is a sign of initial stage of MSP-system reconfiguration. The further development in this direction results in the complete loss of stability in the class structure. The "agents" of both classes fall off their potential wells and wander chaotically round the bottom of this potential well. Collapse of the class structure takes place. This is the catastrophe of system restructuring. The old structure is destroyed and the system now searches for a new combination of parts which will form into one structured whole. This reconfiguration takes place according to the scheme: "disintegration—chaotic wandering—new assemblage into an integral whole." The process ends by the formation of a new class structure.

How can these properties of MSP-systems manifest themselves in practice?

Assume that each "agent" in a real CAS is the element of two MSP-systems simultaneously. Being constituents of one and the same integral CAS; all agents are carriers of the general systemic properties of the comprehensive big system. As agents having a certain rank within the complex multi-level hierarchical structure of CAS, agents differ from each other.

The first type of systemic interrelations is described by way of an MSP-system with $\chi > 0$. All agents are disposed in one and the same point on the path (13) of the MSP-system having $\chi > 0$. Hence, all agents have one and the same state within the frame of this MSP-system. This phenomenon is known as coherence. CAS is capable innately predicting the coherent behavior of all agents.

The second type of systemic interrelation (structural aspect) is described as the MSP-system with $\chi < 0$. Many-scale hierarchical structure exists within any CAS. Class structure in society and administrative structure of corporations are formed as the direct result of the struggle of agents for "conditions" of survival. Distribution of power and the control over means of subsistence in society create class structure. This process can be described by means of MSP-terminology as the optimal distribution of "conditions" directed to maximisation of useful output at the level of an integral system.

One and the same process of qualitative renewal of CAS (reconfiguration) shows itself both as a catastrophic leap within MSP-system having $\chi > 0$ and as a catastrophic restructuring of an MSP-system having $\chi < 0$. Both plans of systemic interrelations are of great importance for the solution of the task of effective adaptation of CAS. The mode of best adaptation for CAS is often called the state of "edge of chaos." It is possible to enumerate the three properties of MSP-systems by which the process of adaptation becomes most effective.

1. **SOC-phenomenon within of MSP-system having $\chi > 0$.** The transition into the critical state takes place spontaneously, as soon as the average value of perturbations exceeds some threshold. The process of qualitative renewal at the level of the integral system takes the form of an evolutionary cycle. The crisis stage is a manifestation of a reconfiguration in the ensemble of interacting agents.

2. **Perpetual renewal of structure within of MSP-system having $\chi < 0$.** If cells of the structure are posited close to the boundary of the unstable domain of the stabilizing function, then the composition of cells is permanently renewed.

3. **There exists an optimal interrelation between the structural and integral properties of the system**, where the development proves to be most flexible and effective.

The adaptation of the system is most effective when the structure is renovated as a result of small crises. The other extreme is a rigid structure, which is renewed rarely at all levels; this process is accompanied by a catastrophic global crisis in the system.

These three conditions of the "edge of chaos" solve one and the same task of renewing of the system, using the most optimal path.

A certain proportion must exist between introduction of innovations and preservation of the routines, conditioning the optimal pace of renewal of the system. CAS in the "edge of chaos" mode strives to find this optimal ratio between the intensity of innovations and preservation of the routine, when adaptation proves to be most flexible and effective (Zinchenko, 2006).

Conclusion

Thus, the previously mentioned emergent properties of CAS (*) discovered within of MAM-platform of CAS-modelling are reproduced in the MSP-platform. Thus there exists a deep, inherent relationship between the MAM and MSP platforms of CAS-modelling. The combination of these two different directions within the framework of one approach should make it possible to advance considerably the understanding of properties and dynamics of CAS.

Following is a way in which it would be possible to organically synthesise MAM and MSP platforms.

The **MSP-agent** is determined by its position within the class structure in the MSP-system with $\chi < 0$. This position may be coded as sequence of symbols (virtual genome). Development of an MSP-system consists of a sequence of reconfigurations (evolutionary cycles). Each reconfiguration is a change in the structure and consequently of the positions of MSP-agents within this structure. MSP-agents pass from one position within the MSP-structure into another position. This process can be described as the movement of MAM-agents in a fitness landscape. Consequently, it is possible to organically unite MAM and MSP platforms into a new more advanced technique of CAS-modelling. The development of such unified MAM-MSP platform is a very difficult task, but realisation of this task may result in large benefits[5].

References

Amaral, L. A. N., & Meyer, M. (1999). Environmental changes, coextinction, and patterns in the fossil record. *The American Physical Society, 82*(3), 652-655.

Arthur, W. B., Durlanf S. N., & Lane d. A. (Eds.) (1997). The economy as an evolving complex system II. *Proceedings of the Santa Fe Institute: Vol. XXVII* (pp. 1-14). MA: Addison-Wesley, Reading.

Bak P., & Sneppen, K. (1993). Punctuated equilibrium and criticality in a simple model of evolution. *Physical Review Letters, 71*(24), 4083-4086.

Bak, P., Tang, C., & Wiesenfeld, K. (1987). Self-organized criticality: An explanation of 1/f noise. *Physical Review Letters, 59*(4), 381-384.

di Collobiano, S. A. (2002). *Tangled nature: A model of ecological evolution.* Thesis submitted for the degree of Doctor of Philosophy of the University of London and the Diploma of Imperial College. Condensed Matter Theory Group, the Blacket Laboratory, Imperial College of Science, Technology and Medicine, London.

Drossel, B., & Schwabl, F. (1992). Self-organized critical forest-fire model. *Physical Review Letters, 69*(11), 1629-1632.

Epstein, J. M. (2002). Modeling civil violence: An agent-based computational approach. *Proceedings of the National Academy of Sciences of the U.S.: Vol. 99, Supplement 3. Sackler Colloquium on Adaptive Agents, Intelligence, and Emergent Human Organization: Capturing Complexity through Agent-Based Modeling* (pp. 7243-7250). Washington: National Academy of Sciences.

Gell-Mann, M. (1994). *The Quark and the Jaguar: Adventures in the simple and complex.* New York: W.H. Freeman.

Henley, C. L. (1989). Self-organized percolation: A simpler model. *Bulletin of American Physical Society, 34,* 838.

Holland, J. (1995). *Hidden order: How adaptation builds complexity.* Reading, MA: Addison Wesley.

Hommes, C. H. (2002). Modeling the stylized facts in finance through simple nonlinear adaptive systems. *Proceedings of the National Academy of Sciences of the U.S.: Vol. 99, Supplement 3. Sackler Colloquium on Adaptive Agents, Intelligence, and Emergent Human Organization:*

Capturing Complexity through Agent-Based Modeling (pp. 7221-7228). Washington: National Academy of Sciences.

Kamke E. (1971). *The handbook of ordinary differential equations* (4th ed.). Moscow: Nauka.

Kauffman S. A., & Johnsen, S. (1991). Coevolution to the edge of chaos: Coupled fitness landscapes, poised states, and coevolutionary avalanches. *Journal of Theoretical Biology, 149,* 467-505.

Kephart, J. O. (2002). Software agents and the route to the information economy. *Proceedings of the National Academy of Sciences of the U.S.: Vol. 99, Supplement 3. Sackler Colloquium on Adaptive Agents, Intelligence, and Emergent Human Organization: Capturing Complexity through Agent-Based Modeling* (pp. 7207-7213). Washington: National Academy of Sciences.

Lamarck, J. B. (1809). *Philosophie zoologique.* Paris.

Lewontin, R. C. (1972). Testing the theory of natural selection. *Nature, 236,* 181-182.

McMillan E. (2004). *Complexity, organizations, and change.* London and New York: Routledge.

Pushnoi, G. S. (2003). Dynamics of a system as a process of realization of its "potential.*" Proceedings of the 21st International Conference of the system Dynamics Society, July 20-24,* New York.

Pushnoi, G. S., (2004a). *Method of systems potential and evolutionary cycles.* Working paper presented at inter-disciplinary scientific forum (http://www.socintegrum.ru)

Pushnoi, G. S., (2004b, November). *Application of method of systems potential for analysis of economic system evolution.* Paper presented at the Second Internet Conference on Evolutionary Economics and Econophysics. Ekaterinburg, Russia: International A. Bogdanov Institute.

Pushnoi, G. S., (2004c, November). *The business cycle model on the basis of method of systems potential.* Paper presented at the Second Internet Conference on Evolutionary Economics and Econophysics. Ekaterinburg, Russia: International A. Bogdanov Institute.

Pushnoi, G. S., (2005, April). *Long-term and short-term dynamics of the economic system on the basis of systems potential method.* Paper presented at the Third Internet Conference on Evolutionary Economics and Econophysics. Ekaterinburg, Russia: International A. Bogdanov Institute.

Sole, R., & Manrubia, S. (1996b). Extinction and self-organized criticality in a model of large-scale evolution. *Physical Review, E 54*(1), R42-R45.

Sole, R., Bascompte, J., & Manrubia, S. (1996a). Extinction: Bad genes or weak chaos? *Proceedings of the Royal Society of London B: Biological Sciences, 263*(1375), 1407-1413.

Sole, R. V., Alonso, D., & McKane, A. (2002). Self-organized instability in complex ecosystems. *Philosophical Transactions of the Royal Society B, 357*(1421), 667-681.

Sornette, D. (2002). Predictability of catastrophic events: Material rupture, earthquakes, turbulence, financial crashes, and human birth. *Proceedings of the National Academy of Sciences of the U.S.: Vol. 99, Supplement 1. Sackler Colloquium on Self-Organized Complexity in the Physical, Biological, and Social Sciences* (pp. 2522-2529). Washington: National Academy of Sciences.

Zinchenko, T. N. (2006). *Cycles of Russian civilization.* Retrieved August 01, 2006, from http://www.socintegrum.ru/forum/viewtopic.php?t=79

Endnotes

[1]   This paper confines itself to the most important items of the analysis, referring Pushnoi' (2003; 2004a; 2004b; 2004c; 2005) sources for additional details.

[2]   Sign "dot" above a variable means time derivative and sign "touch" means derivative respect to some variable.

[3]   This numeration does not coinside with Lamarck's (1809) numeration of Laws of Evolution from His book "Philosophie zoologique."

[4]   This is Jacobi's ordinary differential equation. See for example equation 1.250 in Kamke (1971).

[5]   Author thanks all participants of inter-disciplinary scientific forum "Socintegrum": http://www.socintegrum.ru for remarks concerning MSP-approach.

Section II

Important Concepts

Chapter III

Modularity and Complex Adaptive Systems

David Cornforth, University of NSW, Australia

David G. Green, Monash University, Australia

Abstract

Modularity is ubiquitous in complex adaptive systems. Modules are clusters of components that interact with their environment as a single unit. They provide the most widespread means of coping with complexity, in both natural and artificial systems. When modules occur at several different levels, they form a hierarchy. The effects of modules and hierarchies can be understood using network theory, which makes predictions about certain properties of systems such as the effects of critical phase changes in connectivity. Modular and hierarchic structures simplify complex systems by reducing long-range connections, thus constraining groups of components to act as a single component. In both plants and animals, the organisation of development includes modules, such as branches and organs. In artificial systems, modularity is used to simplify design, provide fault tolerance, and solve difficult problems by decomposition.

Introduction

What is Modularity?

A train consists of an engine and carriages. A tree consists of branches and leaves. Trains and trees, like innumerable other systems, are built from modules. Modularity is a structural property of systems that arises when a system is composed of self-contained groups of elements that behave as a single unit. Complex systems often contain modules, which increase predictability and simplify control. Modules can usually be identified by the pattern of connections which are stronger and more numerous within modules than between modules. Modularity has the effect of isolating elements and processes from one another, and constraining their interactions. Modules isolate functionality into units that are both reliable and reusable. Complicated problems can be approached by dividing into smaller problems to reduce the combinatorial complexity. The formation of modular structures is a crucial mechanism in the emergence of order in many complex systems. Therefore, modularity is fundamentally related to the *adaptive* nature of many complex systems.

The human body provides an example of a natural complex system that contains a hierarchy of modules. Each cell in the body is a module; the cell's internal component parts and processes are isolated from those of other cells. The cells themselves are not a homogenous collection. Instead, groups of cells are specialised and clustered together to form modules. These modules are recognisable as organs, such as the liver, the heart, and the lungs, as well as muscles, nerves, and so on. Each organ, or module, can be identified with a particular function. The interaction between these modules is well defined. For example, the heart and kidneys do not interact directly. They perform specialized functions connected with another entity—the blood. One organ is responsible for movement of blood around the body. The other is involved in maintenance of the chemical composition of the blood. The use of modules in a complex biological system allows cells to operate in an efficient way, by concentrating on one group of activities.

Modules are the most common mechanism for dealing with complexity, not only in natural systems, but also in artificial systems as diverse as organisational structures and the design of electronic products. A television is a complex system of electronic components. Such consumer products are now manufactured in modules using subsystems or circuit boards that can be easily replaced. Modularity simplifies the tasks of design and repair. The same advantages are apparent, for example, in traditional Japanese architecture, where room sizes are determined by combinations of rice mats called *tatami*, measuring three feet by six feet (a little less than one metre by two metres). The use of modules allows a reduction in complexity in almost any context where a system is composed of many interacting parts. Of course, the organisation of a system into modules involves a cost of implementing an increased infrastructure. For example, an effort is required to change the known, working design of a non-modular television to the modular version. But once in place, the new design has advantages and allows a trade-off in effort verses efficiency.

Modularity plays a key role in complex *adaptive* systems. In a system that is changing, the ability to form modules conveys several advantages. First, modules simplify the process of adaptation by reducing the range of connections. This makes the outcome of any change more predictable and less prone to errors. In a complex structure, the richness of connections means that changes often lead to unexpected and sometimes disastrous results. Complex adaptive systems can avoid such problems by forming modules. Secondly, modules tend to be stable structures. So forming modules provides a way of fixing adaptations, thus ensuring that desirable features are retained. Thirdly, modules provide convenient building blocks, so making it possible to create large robust systems quickly and easily. We shall see examples of these effects in later sections.

What is a Hierarchy?

A related concept is hierarchical structure, where a system is composed of modules that are themselves composed of smaller modules. A hierarchy can have any number of such levels. The human body has a hierarchy beginning with modules such as the heart, lungs, and kidneys. These modules are composed of smaller structures; for example, the kidney is composed of nephrons. These are in turn composed of cells, and cells are composed of organelles. Like modularity, hierarchical structure seems to be an integral feature of biological systems. The study of modularity in natural systems gives many insights that can be applied in artificial systems. So hierarchies appear in organisational structures, there are hierarchies in knowledge, such as the DEWEY catalogue system, and hierarchical structures in manufactured systems. Another example is a power distribution system comprising power stations, local distribution switchyards, suburban transformers, and residential dwellings. The unifying principle is efficiency and the reduction of complexity.

Networks and Modularity

Networks and graphs are commonly used to represent the structure of complex systems. A *network* is a system of interconnected entities. An example is a social network where people are the entities, and they are connected to each other by relationships such as family relationships or friendships. More generally, a network is usually described in terms of *nodes*, which are the entities, and *links*, which are the relationships between entities. A *graph* is a simple mathematical structure that consists of *vertices*, or points, to represent the nodes and uses edges to represent the links that join pairs of nodes. A *network* is a graph in which the nodes and/or edges have attributes.

Networks occupy a central position in complexity theory because they underlie both the structure and behaviour of every complex system (Green, 2000). In formal terms, we can obtain a network from the structure of any system by mapping its elements to network nodes and the relationships (or interactions) between elements to edges of the network. Likewise, we can obtain a network from the behaviour of a system by representing all possible states of the system as network nodes, and representing transitions between states as edges of the network. These mappings provide a rigorous way of representing complex structures and behaviour as networks. The implication is that certain properties of complex systems (e.g., criticality) emerge as consequences of the underlying network.

Graph theory provides a useful tool for analysing modular and hierarchical structures in complex systems (Figure 1). The graph in Figure 1(a) represents a system with seven components. Such a graph could represent a system of interconnected components in many diverse contexts, for example, cities connected by roads, or manufacturing workstations connected by the flow of products and raw materials. In contrast, the graph shown in Fig. 1(b) is clearly divided into two sections or modules. The number of connections within each module is relatively high, whereas the number of connections between the modules is low.

Some basic properties of a graph (Bollobas, 1998) are as follows:

- The *degree* of a vertex is the number of edges meeting at that vertex.

- A *sparse graph* has relatively few edges.

- A *directed graph* has connections that apply in one direction only.

- A *path* is a sequence of consecutive edges. A pair of consecutive edges shares one vertex.

- The *length* of a path is the number of consecutive edges in the path.

- The *diameter* of a graph is the maximum length that can be found by considering the shortest path between every pair of vertices. The diameter is finite only for connected graphs.

- A *connected graph* is one in which every vertex is connected to every other by at least one path. A connected graph with *n* nodes has at least *n*-1 edges, and its largest possible diameter is also *n*-1.

- A *fully connected graph* is one in which every vertex is connected directly to every other. The diameter of a fully connected graph is 1. In a fully connected graph with *n* vertices, the number of edges is *n*(*n*-1)/2.

Figure 1. A simple graph (a) and a modular graph (b)

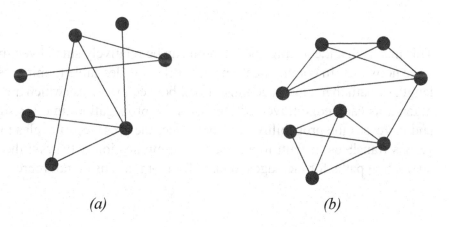

(a)   (b)

- A *cycle* is a closed path, that is, any pair of edges in a cycle shares a vertex.

The distribution of the degree of vertices in a graph will determine its properties. This is not constant across the graphs shown in Figure 1, as some vertices are highly connected, while others have only one connection. Certain distributions of the degree of vertexes have important properties, as we will see later.

Random Graphs and Networks

A *random graph* is a graph in which the edges are distributed at random among pairs of vertices. This type of graph is least likely to contain modules, as it has a homogenous structure. The properties of such graphs were investigated thoroughly by Paul Erdös and Alfred Renyi in the 1950s and 60s. In a random graph the probability of any vertex having a given degree approximates a Poisson distribution, with average degree $z = (n-1)p$, where p is the probability of a edge between two vertices and n is the total number of vertices in the graph. As the value of z increases, a phase transition is reached where the graph rapidly becomes connected (Erdös & Renyi, 1960). The phase transition also applies in the reverse situation where links are progressively removed from a network until catastrophic fragmentation occurs. This has implications for example in the fault tolerance of communications networks. The average length l of a path between any two vertices is given by:

$$l = \frac{\log n}{\log z}$$

This means that the average path length can be relatively small even in very large networks. In communications networks it is desirable to minimise the length of path that a message must travel between vertices (which are computers), as each edge traversed increases the propagation time for signals, and increases the probability of errors. Also, the presence of cycles in such graphs translates to fault tolerance in communication networks: there are alternative paths for messages to take. Random graphs do not represent the way natural and artificial systems are organised. Natural systems tend to show greater clustering, that is, vertices are grouped together into clusters or modules. Natural networks are more accurately represented by the models explained in the next two sections.

Scale Free Networks

A *scale free network* is a network in which the probability of any vertex having a given degree follows a power law (Albert & Barabasi, 2000; Barabasi, Albert, & Jeong, 1999, 2000; Barabasi, Ravasz, & Vicsek, 2001). A few nodes have many connections, while most nodes have few connections. The variable patterns of connectivity form cliques or modules of highly connected nodes, with a smaller number of connections between modules. They are highly tolerant to random attack, but not so tolerant to targeted attack. That is, if a node is removed at random, the graph is largely unaffected, but if a node with high connectivity is removed, the graph may become fragmented. This implies that the Internet, which forms a scale free network, is vulnerable to attacks on specific servers, such as malicious attacks by hackers. It also explains the high degree of robustness exhibited by many complex systems: individual nodes can be removed without removing the connected property of the network. However, unlike the catastrophic fragmentations occurring in random graphs, scale free graphs remain connected even when a large fraction of edges is removed.

Small World Networks

A *small-world network* is sparse, highly clustered, and has low diameter (Watts, 1999; Watts & Strogatz, 1998). These networks consist of a regular lattice (a tessellation of vertices with uniform connections, for example a grid) with a number of links added between pairs of vertices chosen at random. Such graphs seem to reproduce the "small world" phenomenon seen in social networks, where only a short path is required to link any two people. Such models have implications in many areas, particularly where geography constrains the interaction between agents, such as in the epidemiology of disease and the evolution of ecosystems. The probability of vertices having a given degree follows an exponential distribution.

Trees

A *tree* is a connected graph with no cycles. Trees are good models of hierarchical systems, for example, the army with its different levels of rank and rigid route for command and communication. The top level of a tree is a single node known as the *root node*. Terminal nodes (those nodes with no branches descending from them) are called *leaves*. A tree is called *balanced* if each node has the same number of branches descending from it. A *subtree* is a subset of nodes that form a tree. Every non-terminal node in a tree forms the root of at least one subtree. A *hierarchy* is a directed graph that forms a tree, and in which all nodes fall on paths leading away from (or to) a single node, which is called the *root* of the tree. In a family tree, the descendants of a single individual form a hierarchy.

Information flow in trees can proceed only from one level to another, as there are no peer connections. As a tree has no cycles, it affords no fault tolerance: there is only one path connecting any two nodes, and therefore a tree is vulnerable to attack. The removal of a single node anywhere results in the tree being divided into two trees. On the other hand, trees have the advantage of providing the smallest diameter for a given number of vertices. The maximum number of steps between any two nodes in a regular tree with L-layers is given by $2(L-1)$, and L is proportional to the logarithm of the number of nodes.

Network Modules

Because of their universal nature (see the start of 2.3), networks provide a convenient way to define modules mathematically. Within a network, a module is a connected set of nodes that is richly connected internally, but has only minimal connections to the rest of the network. In Figure 1(b), for instance, there are two modules with only a single edge between them.

The previous definition of a network module is necessarily imprecise. Systems are not necessarily all modular, or non-modular: they can have degrees of modularity. This degree can be measured by the modularity coefficient M. Various ways of measuring modularity have been proposed (e.g., Muff, Rao, & Caflisch, 2005; Newman & Girvan 2004). The most obvious approach is to compare the richness of links within and between modules.

For a known set of modules, the above ratio can be calculated explicitly. However, a different approach is needed if a measure is needed to identify emerging modules. One approach is to measure the degree of clustering (Watts et al., 1998). For any node i in a network of N nodes, the degree of local clustering is given by the ratio between the number of edges E_i that exist between its k_i neighbours and the maximum possible number of links $k_i(k_i-1)/2$. The clustering coefficient C of the entire network is then given by

$$C = \frac{1}{N} \sum_i \frac{2E_i}{k_i(k_i - 1)}$$

and the values of C range from 0 to 1. Pimm (1980) proposed a direct measure of modularity (or "compartmentalisation") by looking at modularity about pairs of nodes. For any pair of nodes i and j, the local modularity m_{ij} is the ratio between the number of neighbours the nodes share in common and their total number of neighbours, The modularity of the entire network is then the average of this ratio taken over all pairs of nodes:

$$M = \frac{1}{N(N-1)} \sum_i^N \sum_j^N m_{ij}$$

again with values ranging from 0 to 1.

Modularity in Mathematics

The idea of building blocks (modules) in mathematics probably began in prehistoric times with the custom of using fingers for counting. Having ticked off a set of objects with the fingers of one hand, it is convenient to refer to that set collectively as (say) a "hand" or "fist." The person doing the counting could then enumerate larger sets by counting off the number of fists present. An abstraction of this idea is the practice of making a mark for each object and scoring a line through each set of five marks. The ultimate expression of this approach to counting is the decimal place system in which each digit represents entire sets of different size. The number 351, for instance, means 3 sets of 100, plus 5 sets of 10, plus 1 more individual.

Equivalence Relations

An *equivalence relation* is a pattern that classifies sets of objects as being related. For example, gender classifies all males as equivalent to one another and all females as equivalent to one another. An equivalence relation partitions a set of objects into disjoint subsets or classes. That is, different classes do not overlap. The following mapping of words

cat ↦ noun	eat ↦ verb	fat ↦ adjective
mat ↦ noun	sit ↦ verb	wide ↦ adjective

defines a classification of words into their syntactic categories, making nouns equivalent to one another, and likewise for verbs and adjectives.

Set Theory and Logic

In any system, modules are subsets of the entire system, composed of elements. These subsets can be defined by logical statements (Figure 2). In Predicate Calculus, a *domain D* is a set of objects and an atomic predicate $P(x)$ is a statement about an element x in D. For instance, if the domain is the set of people in a village, and $P(x)$ denotes the statement "person x is female", then P defines a subset of people in the village (*i.e.* all women) for which the statement is true. Combining atomic predicates using logical operators such as AND, OR and NOT makes it possible to define more complex statements.

Classification

Identifying modules from observational data is the province of data classification. Here the problem is to divide a data set into groups of similar things, or modules. One example is the division of living things into groups including families, genera, and species. Another example is the division of customers of a telecommunications company into groups for targeted marketing. Methods of classification can be divided into rule-based and distance-based approaches.

Rule-based methods identify rules that partition a set of objects according to particular properties or features. Some examples were shown earlier under equivalence relations. Perhaps the best-known methods are decision trees. A *decision tree* is set of rules that are arranged in the form of a tree graph. The leaf nodes are outputs (categories in this case). The other nodes contain rules that take the form of logical tests "IF statement *A* is true THEN follow branch 1 ELSE follow branch 2." Perhaps the best-known examples are taxonomic keys for identifying plants and animal species.

Distance-based methods seek to form groups by comparing measures of distance or similarity between pairs of individuals. A typical measure is Euclidean distance *d(x,y)* between objects *x* and *y*. For instance, if the objects are (say) survey sites in a landscape, then the attributes might be numbers of different species found at that site, or environmental parameters.

Algorithms that automatically generate clusters or modules from data are known as clustering algorithms, and take two possible approaches. *Divisive* algorithms carve a set into finer and finer partitions. *Agglomerative* algo-

Figure 2. A Venn diagram showing various subsets associated with two predicates P(x) and Q(x). The regions represent subsets of elements. The numbers refer to regions defined by the compound predicates: (1). ~(P(x) OR Q(x)); (2). P(x) & Q(x); (3). P(x) OR Q(x)

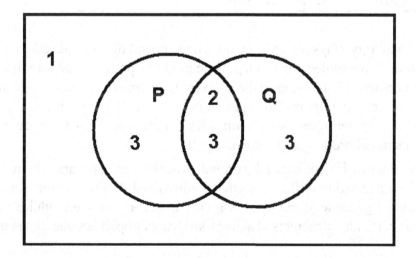

rithms link together different groups in a series of steps until all items are joined into one group. At each step, the algorithms link together whichever pair of groups (or individuals) show the least net separation, according to the distance measure being used. This procedure leads to a tree with one leaf node per individual in the set.

Modularity in Natural Systems

Modularity plays a fundamental role in all living systems, from ecosystems down to the cell. The prevalence of the cell in living things stems from its effect of concentrating all the ingredients needed to replicate the genome in one place. Prior to the evolution of the cell, it was probably difficult to obtain conditions under which genomic material could replicate at a sufficiently high rate. In multi-cellular organisms, groups of cells interact with one another, and exchange energy, raw products and information. Cells are linked by well-defined common communication channels: for example, hormones carried by the blood. They are also linked by the cell membrane dividing adjacent cells, through which things can pass. Evolution has resulted in highly complex organisms, and the ability of natural systems to employ modularity may help to explain how such systems arose. The modular nature of life is illustrated by the fact that a cell can die and be replaced without affecting the organism.

Modularity in the Genome

Modularity plays a part in evolution at several different levels of organisation. At the molecular level, genetic modules promote stability of inherited characters. Chromosomes themselves are interchangeable sets of characters. Modular structure is also apparent in proteins. The key structural elements, known as *motifs*, are short sequences of amino acids that convey particular functional properties (Bairoch, 1993).

Modularity is determined by growth processes and appears to be reflected in the organisation of the genes that are involved. In the genome, functionally related genes tend to cluster together in self-contained modules that code for particular structures. The best-known examples are the genes that control gender, which are concentrated on the X and Y chromosomes. During development, genetic modules are turned on and off by controller genes. For example, the so-called "eyeless gene" controls the genes that lead to development of the eye. Experiments have shown that if it is made inactive, then extra eyes can form on the antennae, wings and legs of *fruit flies* (Halder, Callerts, & Gehring, 1995). The Hox genes appear to control modules that determine the basic body plan of individuals (Cohen, 2001).

One of the most fundamental forms of modularity is overall body plan. The animal designs that exist today all appeared during the Cambrian explosion (Gould, 1989). In Arthropods, for instance, the basic design is a head followed by a number of segments with legs. The number of segments varies from three in insects to dozens in millipedes.

The Hierarchy of Biological Taxonomy

Biological taxonomy was created to assist in the identification and categorisation of organisms. There are between two and ten million species of plants, animals, and micro-organisms either known or assumed to exist. Collectively these form a complex system, with interactions in the form of evolutionary descent. In order to simplify the description of species, taxonomy was introduced in the 18th century by Swedish botanist Karl von Linné. Taxonomists divide all living things into categories, or modules, at seven different levels: kingdom, phylum, class, order, family, genus, and species.

Taxonomic hierarchies are really models of evolutionary change. All species within a given genus, for instance, are descended from a common ancestor. However, "missing links" and other incomplete information make the system imperfect. The platypus, for instance, is a fur-bearing, egg-laying, duck-billed creature, which caused confusion for early taxonomists because its features suggested that it belonged to several different groups (mammals, reptiles, birds).

Plant and animal species consist of reproductively isolated groups of organisms and therefore constitute the basic modules of macroevolution. The genetic modules that control body plans define the major phyla. They are now essentially fixed: no new animal phyla have appeared since the early Cambrian. However, the other levels of taxonomic organisation all mark major refinements in animal design.

Modularity in Plants

Plants make extensive use of modularity. While animals have a fixed number of parts, plants have open-ended development. Leaf morphology displays recurring patterns, which are self-similar at different scales (Lindenmayer, 1968). The fractal nature of plant structure is well known. The sub-lobes of many leaves are quite similar in shape to the larger lobes on the same leaf. Serrations on sub-lobes are often similar in shape to the large lobes. This self-similarity is a reflection of the fact that plant growth consists of repetition of modules, like a computer program. This process has been described in models called Lindenmayer systems (Lindenmayer, 1968). In such models, a simple grammar defines transitions between symbols. For example, a symbol for a stem may be replaced by a symbol for a stem and two symbols for a leaf. Such models show how simple rules can produce structure with self-similarity, and they have produced structures strikingly similar to plant forms.

Along the circumference of a growing plant shoot, cells exchange chemical messages depending on the gradient of concentration of hormones in the cell. Such interactions may be described by differential equations, as in the model proposed by the mathematician Alan Turing (1952). The solutions give rise to standing waves around the shoot. If the hormone is a growth hormone, then parts of the shoot begin to grow faster than other parts. These parts become the new shoots. The number of shoots that arise from the old shoot is therefore a number fixed by the parameters of diffusion between cells, and the mutual effects of the concentrations.

Plants are so reliant on modular structures that insects have evolved to take advantage of them. Some insects are able to induce the formation of galls by disturbing the growth sequence of the plants using chemical agents. Galls, consisting of stunted leaves, serve as a food source or as protection for insect larvae.

Modularity in Embryogenesis

The pattern of early growth, or embryogenesis, is the same for nearly every vertebrate. The body plan is modular, and these modules can be recognised very early in the process. For example, the body plan for all organisms is based on bilateral symmetry. The fertilised cell divides many times. At some time, a distinction is made between the head and the tail. These are the first modules to develop. Then the nervous system develops, and the other internal organs. Each cell must become a member of a large collection of cells, forming an organ. In single celled organisms, the cell is very complicated, as one cell must do everything. In larger organisms, cells can specialise and reap the benefits in efficiency. Although each cell contains the full genetic code for every function of the organism, it chooses to switch off the majority of function in order to concentrate on its chosen function.

Modularity in Language

Language has a hierarchical structure. Human speech consists of sentences, words, and various parts of speech. These are some of the modules used to simplify language. In written language, a book forms a hierarchical structure, as it is divided into chapters, paragraphs, sentences, words, and letters. Words are divided into various categories, such as verbs, nouns, and so on. The indigenous Dyirbal people of Australia have four categories of noun, one of which has been described as "women, fire, and dangerous things" (Lakoff, 1987). It is not necessarily the case that all these things have a common feature, but that they are related by links made from experiences or from religious beliefs.

As language is so modular, it is not surprising that the equipment to decode it is also modular in structure. Neuroscientists have described the brain as modular in the sense of being composed of cells and layers of cells to divide the processing. There is evidence to suggest that language is the function of a specific part of the human brain (Bates, 1994). Modules deal exclusively with a particular information type. Such modules include face recognition in humans and other primates, echo location in bats, or fly detection in the frog. Such modules may be innate (genetically predetermined) or learned as a result of interaction with the environment. There is evidence to suggest that these modules retain plasticity, so that rewiring is possible in the event of damage.

One way to get an insight into the structure of language, and how it may be decoded is to attempt to build a machine to understand language. Such machines are normally constructed by writing a special computer program, and supplying the language to the computer as digitised stream of letters or as a digitised audio signal. Many examples have shown that the ability of models to extract meaning is enhanced by the introduction of modular designs. These typically focus on dividing speech into phonemes.

Modularity in Social Structure

In a social context, modules appear as social groups. The formation of social groups depends on the richness of interactions within the group. Primates typically form core groups with mean size of 30 to 40 individuals, which is maintained through the use of grooming behaviour (Dunbar, 1996). The development of language in humans allows us to form larger groups with a mean of 100 to 150. In turn, these larger groups allow greater communication and cohesion through social gossip. The importance of cooperation as an evolutionary strategy is well documented.

Patterns of connection and information exchange in society are varied. Some individuals, such as community leaders, exert a strong influence upon many others. Some sections of society make use of hierarchies, for example in organisational structures. For these reasons, a scale-free network is a good model of social interactions.

Modularity in Artificial Systems

As modularity is so pervasive in natural systems, it is not surprising that it is also very common in artificial systems, since the same issues of complexity arise, and modularity is able to provide the same answers in different contexts. Although these systems are not self-adaptive, they undergo a process of development as technical knowledge and skills increase over time.

Modularity in Software Engineering

As the complexity of programming tasks has risen, the need has grown for some way of managing the complex interactions between program instructions. Modularity has provided that answer for a significant part of the history of programming, and more recently has been refined in the object oriented paradigm.

The Language Hierarchy

Modern programming development software is designed to make programming easier, by incorporating modularity into the process. A typical *integrated development environment* (IDE) has features that can create code for a visual component such as a button. When the programmer selects a button from a range of components, the button is displayed on the screen and skeleton code is automatically generated. That code is compiled into assembler code, which represents instructions of the microprocessor on which the program will run. These primitive instructions describe processes in terms of the movement of data between memory and internal registers of the microprocessor, for example. Many of these assembler instructions are interpreted by the microprocessor into the sequence of steps required to perform these operations at the level of the electronic circuits in the microprocessor. This is termed the *micro code*. These different levels of code form a hierarchy, starting from the instruction by the programmer to create a button, down through several levels of code to the actions performed by electronic circuits in terms of high and low levels of voltage.

Structured Programming

The earliest programming languages used statements like *goto* to direct the flow of program control. However, as the size and complexity of programs increased, this type of flow control led to programs that were error-prone and very difficult to read, interpret and debug. The introduction of structured techniques was a great advance, as programs could be divided into modules, called subprograms, subroutines, procedures, or functions. This allowed complex programs to be divided up into manageable chunks, so providing the programmer with the ability to develop programs of arbitrary size. Solutions to large and complex problems could now be built from modules. To be successful, this approach requires modules to be small, have a clear and simple semantics, and be as independent as possible of the context. The key to managing complexity was the limitation of the number and type of interactions between modules. The concept of modularity in programming has since expanded in several ways.

The Object-Oriented Paradigm

Several aspects of modularity are highlighted in the application of *object-oriented* languages. This paradigm introduces modularity in two different contexts, modularity of objects, and modularity of classes.

The *whole-part hierarchy* extends the concepts of structured programming by considering a program to be composed of a number of interacting objects. The object-oriented paradigm increases the control the programmer has over the encapsulation of instructions, and adds more control over the encapsulation of data also. This is known as *information hiding*, where the internal design of a module is hidden from the outside world. This is, in effect, a way of limiting the number of connections between modules. In this way, changes in the internal design of the modules have little effect outside that module. Information hiding includes the hiding of the internal states, or data, as well as the hiding of state transition rules, or the internal algorithms. In this paradigm, the solution to a problem is seen in terms of interacting modules, called *objects*. These objects store their internal state in variables, and possess instructions that are carried out in response to signals from other objects. The connections between modules are limited by hiding interval variables, and by strongly defining the type of information that may be passed between objects in response to signals. Interval variables that are explicitly declared as *private* are invisible from outside the object, and cannot be examined by other objects. Internal instructions are divided into modules called *methods*, which are invisible outside the object. Information transfer is limited to data that can be transferred to the object when a method is invoked, and returned from the object when a method terminates. The type of data must be explicitly declared. Figure 3 illustrates these relationships for the structure of a book using a UML diagram (Larman, 1998). A *Book* object is a whole object that is composed of various parts, including *Frontmatter, Body,* and *Annexes*. In turn, the *Body* of a book is a whole whose parts are the book's chapters.

A different kind of object network is the *Genspec Hierarchy* (general/specific). This is based on the concept of *inheritance*, where the design of a class is based on another class. A sub class inherits the properties of the super class. For example, a *Book* (Figure 4) is based on a higher-level class called *Publication*, from which it inherits the properties: *Title, Date,* and *Publisher*. Likewise, a *Novel* is based upon the *Book* class, from which it inherits the properties: *Author* and *ISBN*.

Implications of Object-Oriented Programming

The question of how to choose the breakdown of modules involves two costs. The cost of having too many modules rests on the difficulty of interfacing all the modules. The cost of having too few modules rest on the difficulty of developing large modules, since these may be relatively complex. Modern software development methods include a trade-off between these two costs. It suggests that a similar trade-off exists in the formation of modular systems in nature.

The object-oriented paradigm has permeated programming in recent times. This is surely due to its success as a means of simplifying code, allowing more efficient code generations and decreasing programming errors. However, this efficiency comes at the price of a tree structure, which is liable to display the problem of brittleness. This can occur when a phenomenon is encountered that does not fit into the hierarchy. This problem is often known as the Platypus Effect, after the animal of the same name that could not easily be fitted into the existing biological taxonomy.

Figure 3. A whole-part UML class diagram for the structure of a book

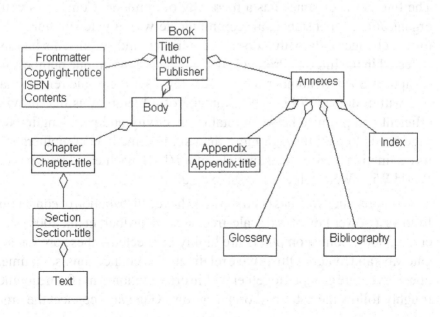

Figure 4. A Genspec class hierarchy relating different types of publications

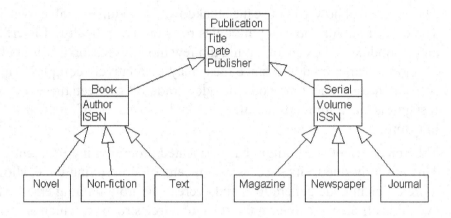

Modularity and the Internet

The Internet is organized as a hierarchy of domains. Computers within an organisation, for instance, all communicate with a gateway hub, which in turn exchanges data with a domain controller, and so on. This hierarchy is reflected in the Internet Protocol (IP), which assigns unique numbers to each computer. So an IP number such as 123.456.789.012 would refer to machine 012 within domain 789. The advantage of a hierarchy is that provides an efficient compromise between total connectivity and path length. No message needs to pass through more than six intermediate computers to reach its destination. Uniform resource locators (URL), which address item on the World Wide Web, achieve the same result for Web pages.

The computer network has been shown to have a distribution of connection that follows a power law: it is a scale-free network (Albert et al., 2000; Barabasi et al., 2000). Some computers are highly connected—these are the servers, gateways and routers. Others have relatively few connections, sometimes only one. Servers are grouped together within organisations, and form modules that roughly follow the pattern of organisations. Gateways connect the organisation level network to the outside world, and these gateways in turn form a larger network that may represent a city. Cities are linked by larger capacity microwave or cable links. This computer network forms a hierarchy.

Modularity and Fault Tolerance

The interest in living things as analogues for artificial systems has led to the consideration of modularity for fault-tolerance. In a living thing, cells can become defective and die without harming the existence of the organism. Genes that are crucial to the survival of the organism are duplicated in the genetic code. Fault tolerance is applied by ensuring an overlapping division of labour between different modules, as well as different conditions applying where possible.

In the previous example, the World Wide Web provides information in a distributed fashion. If any one computer fails, it is very likely that the information is available somewhere else. A critical feature of this system is that the servers are geographically distributed, so that they are not subject to the same conditions. If a power failure occurs in one place, only the servers located there will fail.

The new discipline of Embryonics (Mange, Sipper, Stauffer, & Tempesti, 2000) promises more fault tolerant machines, which are built from adaptive modules. Each module has a specification like a genetic code, and parts of this are turned on or off, depending on the required function of the module. Modules communicate with their peers to perform some collective task, and are able to sense a faulty neighbour and take over its function. If this system was in use in robot controllers, for example, any fault could be quickly isolated without human intervention and the corresponding costly shutdown of an assembly line could be avoided.

Modularity in Manufacturing

Modularisation can be found in manufacturing processes of all kinds, as the ability to make complex systems out of simpler parts reduces costs, allows easier repair, provides more flexibility of production, and encourages innovation in product development. This is driven by uncertainty in the level of demand, rapidly changing technology, and the increased demand for customized products. Modularity is closely related to the use of standards. Manufactured systems are not self-adaptive as some of the preceding examples, as they rely on a global design process. Nevertheless, they illustrate the application of modularity in robust design and therefore shed some light on modularity as used by natural systems. Modularity in manufacturing arises in three contexts: products, processes, and resources.

Product Modularisation

Product modularisation allows products to be assembled from standard, common parts. This increases the volume of the standard parts, so reducing costs, and also allows quicker design work. For example, the water pump is a small, assembled component of a car engine. The same water pump can be used on many different engines. Not only does this save production costs, as the volume of water pump production is increased, but it simplifies engine design. A new engine needs only to conform to the specified interface for the water pump. This interface is described in terms of its physical dimensions, its capacity for pumping water, and its requirement in terms of input rotational energy. As long as the new engine satisfies these specifications, the pump will work with the new engine. In this way, assembled components can be shared by many different production lines. This reduces the number of different parts that have to be manufactured and held in stores, thus reducing complexity of the manufacturing process. Product development time and cost is reduced by the availability of many modules with well-known properties, which can be used as building blocks to assemble a new product. The use of modular components also reduces quality problems, as a module can be thoroughly tested once, then can be incorporated into many designs.

Process Modularisation

Process modularisation identifies processes that produce standard sub components, and other processes that add customisations. Processes can be seen as collections, or modules, of operations performed. For example, the manufacturing of a motorcar will follow many common processes to build the basic car, but these may be followed by customisation processes such as installation of air conditioning or central locking. Process modules can be re-sequenced so that the processes common to many products are carried out first, while the customisation processes are carried out last. The latter processes may even be delayed until specific orders are received. By modularizing processes, the manufacturing can be simplified.

Resource Modularisation

Resource modularisation identifies and exploits modules within resources, such as staff and workstations. Production teams are commonly composed of a number of people, often with diverse skills, who collectively form a unit responsible for certain tasks within the manufacturing process. For example, in a factory producing motorcars there may be an engine team, or a wiring team. Resources such as workstations may be formed into modules. For example, a collection of workstations may form a resource module where engine assembly is carried out.

Modularity in Electronic Appliances

Modularity has had a huge impact upon electronic engineering, and has facilitated the widespread availability of cheap consumer products. At the dawn of electronics, designers who wished to construct an electronic appliance such as a radio had a number of individual components available to them. The design of an appliance meant working from first principles to decide on a satisfactory arrangement of these components to make the working radio. This was a major effort involving skilled engineers, and consequently took time and money. A major innovation in electronics design was the invention of the integrated circuit, where a commonly used module was fabricated on a single chip. This meant that a substantial part of the finished product could be made using these sub-systems, and consequently a large part of the design effort could be dispensed with. Engineers were freed from low-level design, and so attention could be given to the design of more complex systems.

Modularity and Fault-Finding

The traditional approach to fault finding in electronic circuits is to trace the signal until it disappears or goes outside its normal behaviour. This is time consuming and requires a highly trained engineer, and specialist equipment. The alternative approach is to locate the module containing the fault, and replace the whole module. This works by a careful design of modules, which means that each function is associated with a particular module. When the fault occurs, the module known to be responsible for that function is replaced. Alternatively, modules can be replaced in turn until the fault is rectified. This approach allows much quicker and cheaper repairs, and more economic manufacturing of the equipment.

Modularity in Artificial Complex Adaptive Systems

The recognition of modular structures within the vertebrate brain have inspired research into modular neural networks, where part of a problem is solved by a small network, then other networks are added an their outputs combined in some way. It is necessary to partition the problem into modules, but this can be done in some case using clustering algorithms, In other cases, such as robot controllers, a hierarchical partition is evident in the form of legs, joints etc. Neural network controllers can be developed in modules as each part of the mechanism is added to build the robots body. Genetic algorithms can be used to optimise the organisation and interactions between modules.

An artificial chemistry is a model composed of molecules and reactions between them. They have been used extensively to study the origins of life, including self-organisation. They can be used to model the growth and development of network structures in evolving complex adaptive systems.

Genetic programming uses a tree based model to evolve computer programs or complex rules that form solutions to a problem. The crossover operator is able to copy, move or swap whole sub-trees that form modules of code.

Adaptive Processes Leading to Modularity

The usefulness of modularity prompts the question of how such modularity arises, and how it persists. Various adaptive mechanisms contribute to modularity in different contexts. Some of these mechanisms are described next.

Aggregation arises when the autonomous nature of individuals (which tends to produce disjunctive behaviour) is overcome by connections that serve to homogenise behaviour. This can lead to individuals coming to the same states, or updating their states at the same time. Synchrony (see below) is therefore a possible mechanism for aggregation. To become modular, the aggregation must produce sub populations within a large population. If all autonomy is lost, all of the individuals participate in a homogenous collective, rather than forming modules.

For example, in a forest fire, a tree or a small section of forest can be considered as an individual. The possible states of an individual are unburnt, burning, or burnt. Material that is more flammable is likely to change from unburnt to burning faster than other material. The different areas that ignite also differ in the length of time they will burn, and therefore in their probability of igniting neighbouring vegetation. This will lead in turn to pockets of fire and pockets of unburnt vegetation within the burning forest. These pockets are modules that are caused by the interaction between areas of different vegetation.

Segregation arises when external constraints are imposed on a complex system, splitting it into parts. This type of modularity is caused by conscious design or physical boundaries. An example of conscious design is the design of an automobile engine. The interface between engine and gearbox is tightly controlled. Minor changes to the engine will not require a redesign of the gearbox, even though these modules are intimately connected. The interface is fixed, meaning that the connectivity between modules is restricted. Physical boundaries play a role in the model of speciation proposed by Charles Darwin (1859). He observed that groups of finches become separated due to physical barriers such as separate islands. They consequently experienced different evolutionary paths, and became distinct species, unable to interbreed. The connectivity was reduced by the physical separation, then environmental pressures reinforced the new pattern of connections.

Synchrony refers to the extent to which individuals are able to participate in shared activities. Such participation can lead to the formation of groups, or modules. A recent model of this process shows that modules can form due to clustering of elements that are nearly in synchronisation (Cornforth, Green, & Newth, 2005). This model uses a modified one-dimensional cellular automata, where each cell has its own rate of update, which can be influenced by the neighbouring cells (Figure 5a). After some time (Figure 5b), groups of cells synchronise and produce discrete bands of different patterns, representing modules of cells. This does not happen when all cells are synchronised, as in the standard cellular automata model (Figure 5c). In electrical circuits, global synchronisation by "crosstalk" is a problem that must be avoided. The ability to synchronise sub groups of individuals provides a possible mechanism for emergent modularity, a type of self-organisation often observed in real life systems, such as ant colonies and other social animals. The strength of temporal connections affects the possibility of synchronisation, so in turn may determine the maximum size of such systems.

Positive reinforcement is the tendency for an inclination towards some goal to produce a stronger tendency in the same direction, either through direct or indirect means. An example of this is Hebbian Learning (Hebb, 1949), where the synaptic connection between two brain cells that are stimulated together is strengthened. This makes it more likely that the same two brain cells will be co-stimulated, which further strengthens the connection. The phenomenon of positive reinforcement is very common in many natural and artificial systems. A further example is Turing's model of developing shoots,

Figure 5. Selected images produced by the state activation of a modified one-dimensional Cellular Automaton model over time. The cells are organ-ised as a horizontal row with the two ends connected (to form a loop). Time goes vertically downwards. The two possible states of each cell are shown as black and white. Cells are initialised with a random state at the start of the simulation, at the top of section (a). At a later stage, in section (b), some cells have synchronised, producing distinct regions. The image in section (c) represents the same model without the ability to synchronise groups of cells. This is the standard cellular automata model, where all cells are in synchrony. These images were produced using on-line software from VLAB (Green, 2006)

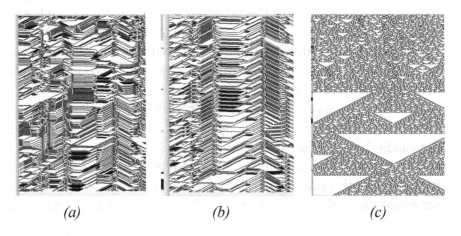

(a)   *(b)*   *(c)*

where the concentration of hormones is eventually maximised in one part of the growing shoot (Turing, 1952). In a model of social systems, the connections between individuals holding similar views were strengthened, leading to the rapid polarisation of individuals into two groups (modules), representing opposite opinions (Stocker, Cornforth, & Green, 2003).

Co-selection refers to the fact that elements that are "close" in some sense may be selected together and therefore after some time these elements may only be found together. A good example is the phenomena of gene shuffling, which is believed to play a large part in the formation of clusters of genes. During reproduction, the genotype is subjected to deletion, copying and insertion of random segments of DNA. A recent model of gene shuffling showed that gene clustering is inevitable, and that it leads to modules of genes forming spontaneously (Green, Newth, Cornforth, & Kirley, 2001).

Holland (1995) proposed a model for the emergence of modules in complex systems. This model included mechanisms by which agents could interact with each other via trading, fighting and mating. Agents were described by a genetic code that represented rules for their interaction, and were placed in an environment where necessary resources were scarce, so must compete for these resources. The addition of an adhesion tag to agents allowed them to "join forces" to create cartels or modules. The model was able to show the spontaneous formation of networks between agents, which excluded other agents and so came to resemble communities or artificial ecologies.

Conclusion

Modules are ubiquitous in both natural and artificial systems. Modules are necessary for the development of structures, where some functionality can be isolated and protected from change, whilst still allowing other parts of a system to evolve. Modules allow design to be simplified, and allow us to understand the world by breaking down our perception of it into meaningful chunks. Modularity is fundamentally linked with mechanisms of adaptation in complex systems. How and why modules form is still the subject of intense research, but several mechanisms have been identified, including aggregation and segregation, and the role of synchrony and positive reinforcement.

References

Albert, R., & Barabasi, A. L. (2000). Topology of evolving networks: Local events and universality. *Physical Review Letters, 85*(24), 5234-5237.

Bairoch, A. (1993). The PROSITE dictionary of sites and patterns in proteins, its current status. *Nucl. Acids. Res.* 21, 3097-3103.

Barabasi, A. L., Albert, R., & Jeong, H. (1999). Mean-field theory for scale-free random networks. *Physica A, 272*, 173-187.

Barabasi, A. L., Albert, R., & Jeong, H. (2000). Scale-free characteristics of random networks: The topology of the world-wide Web. *Physica A, 281*, 69-77.

Barabasi, A. L., Ravasz, E., & Vicsek, T. (2001). Deterministic scale-free networks. *Physica A, 299*, 559-564.

Bates, E. (1994). Modularity, domain specificity, and the development of language. *Discussions in Neuroscience, 10*,136-149.

Bollobas, B. (1998). *Modern graph theory*. New York: Springer Verlag.

Cohen, P. (2001). Monsters in our midst. *New Scientist*, July 2001.

Cornforth, D. J., Green, D. G., & Newth, D. (2005). Ordered asynchronous processes in multi-agent systems, *Physica D, 204*(1-2), 70-82.

Darwin, C. (1859). *On the origin of species by means of natural selection.* London: J. Murray.

Dunbar, R. (1996). *Grooming, gossip, and the evolution of language.* London: Faber and Faber.

Erdös, P., & Rényi, A. (1960). On the evolution of random graphs. *Mathematikai Kutato Intezet Kozlemenyei, 5*, 17-61.

Fodor, J. (1983). *Modularity of mind*. Cambridge, MA: MIT Press.

Hebb, D. O. (1949). *The organization of behavior*. New York: John Wiley Inc.

Holland, J. H. (1995). *Hidden order: How adaptation builds complexity.* New York: Addison-Wesley.

Gould, S. J. (1989). *Wonderful life: The burgess shale and the nature of history.* W. W. Norton & Company.

Green, D. G. (2000). Self-organization in complex systems. In T. J. Bossomaier and D. G. Green (Eds.), *Complex systems* (pp. 7-41). Cambridge University Press.

Green, D. G., Newth, D., Cornforth, D. J., & Kirley, M. G. (2001). On evolutionary processes in natural and artificial systems. In Whigham, Richards, McKay, Gen, Tujimura, and Namatame (Eds.), *Proceedings of the 5th Australasia-Japan Joint Workshop on Intelligent and Evolutionary Systems* (pp. 1-10), November 19-21, University of Otago, New Zealand.

Green, D. G. (2006). Artificial life virtual laboratory (VLAB), Monash University. Retrieved December 7, 2006, from http://www.complexity.org.au/vlab

Halder, G., Callerts, P., & Gehring, W. J. (1995). Induction of ectopic eyes by targeted expression of the eyeless gene in Drosophila. *Science, 267,* 1788-1792.

Lakoff, G. (1987). *Women, fire, and dangerous things.* Chicago, IL: University of Chicago Press.

Larman, C. (1998). *Applying UML and patterns.* London: Prentice Hall.

Lindenmayer A. (1968). Mathematical models for cellular interaction in development I. Filaments with one-sided inputs. *Journal of Theoretical Biology, 18,* 280-289.

Mange, D., Sipper, M., Stauffer, A., & Tempesti, G. (2000). Toward robust integrated circuits: The embryonics approach. *Proceedings of the IEEE, 88*(4), 516-543.

Muff, S., Rao, F., & Caflisch, A. (2005). Local modularity measure for network clusterizations. *Phys. Rev E, 72,* 056107

Newman, M. E. J., & Girvan, M. (2004). Finding and evaluating community structure in networks. *Phys. Rev E* 69, 026113.

Pimm, S. L. (1980). Food Web design and the effect of species deletion. *Oikos, 35,* 139-149.

Stocker, R., Cornforth, D., & Green, D. G. (2003). A simulation of the impact of media on social cohesion. *Journal of Advances in Complex Systems, 6*(3), 349-359.

Turing, A. (1952). The chemical basis of morphogenesis. *Philosophical Transactions of the Royal Society of London. Series B, Biological Sciences, 237,* 37-72.

Watts, D. J., & Strogatz, S. H. (1998). Collective dynamics of "small-world" networks. *Nature,* 393(6684), 440-442.

Watts, D. J. (1999). *Small worlds: The dynamics of networks between order and randomness.* Princeton University Press.

Chapter IV

Concept and Definition of Complexity

Russell K. Standish, UNSW, Australia

Abstract

The term complexity is used informally both as a quality and as a quantity. As a quality, complexity has something to do with our ability to understand a system or object—we understand simple systems, but not complex ones. On another level, complexity is used as a quantity when we talk about something being more complicated than another. In this chapter, we explore the formalisation of both meanings of complexity, which happened during the latter half of the twentieth century.

Introduction: Is Complexity a Quality or a Quantity?

The term *complexity* has two distinct usages, which may be categorised simply as either a quality or a quantity. We often speak of complex systems as being a particular class of systems that are difficult to study using traditional analytic techniques. We have in mind that biological organisms and ecosystems are *complex*, yet systems like a pendulum, or a lever are simple. Complexity as a *quality* is therefore what makes the systems complex.

However, we may also speak of complexity as a quantity—with statements like a human being being more complex than a nematode worm, for example. Under such usage, complex and simple systems form a continuum, characterised by the chosen complexity measure.

Edmonds (1999) performed a comprehensive survey of complexity measures as part of his PhD thesis, however it has not been updated to include measures proposed since that time. However, it remains the most comprehensive resource of complexity measures available to date.

The aim of this chapter is not to provide a catalogue of complexity measures, but rather to select key measures and show how they interrelate with each other within an overarching information theoretic framework.

Complexity as a Quantity

We have an intuitive notion of complexity as a quantity; we often speak of something being more or less complex than something else. However, capturing what we mean by complexity in a formal way has proved far more difficult, than other more familiar quantities we use, such as length, area, and mass.

In these more conventional cases, the quantities in question prove to be decomposable in a linear way (i.e., a 5 cm length can be broken into 5 equal parts 1 cm long) and they can also be directly compared—a mass can be compared with a standard mass by comparing the weights of the two objects on a balance.

However, complexity is not like that. Cutting an object in half does not leave you with two objects having half the complexity overall. Nor can you easily compare the complexity of two objects, say an apple and an orange, in the same way you can compare their masses.

The fact that complexity includes a component due to the interactions between subsystems rapidly leads to a combinatorial explosion in the computational difficulty of using complexity measures that take this into account. Therefore, the earliest attempts at deriving a measure simply added up the complexities of the subsystems, ignoring the component due to interactions between the subsystems.

The simplest such measure is the *number of parts* definition. A car is more complex than a bicycle because it contains more parts. However, a pile of sand contains an enormous number of parts (each grain of sand), yet it is not so complex since each grain of sand is conceptually the same, and the order of the grains in the pile is not important. Another definition used is the *number of distinct parts*, which partially circumvents this problem. The problem with this idea is that a shopping list and a Shakespearian play will end up having the same complexity, since it is constructed from the same set of parts (the 26 letters of the alphabet—assuming the shopping list includes items like zucchini, wax, and quince, of course). An even bigger problem is to define precisely what one means by "part." This is an example of the *context dependence* of complexity, which we will explore further later.

Bonner (1988) and McShea (1996) have used these (organism size, number of cell types) and other *proxy* complexity measures to analyse complexity trends in evolution. They argue that all these measures trend in the same way when figures are available for the same organism, hence are indicative of an underlying organism complexity value. This approach is of most value when analysing trends within a single phylogenetic line, such as the diversification of trilobytes.

Graph Theoretic Measures of Complexity

Since the pile of sand case indicates complexity is not simply the number of components making up a system, the relationships between components clearly contribute to the overall complexity. One can start by caricaturing the system as a *graph*—replacing the components by abstract *vertices* or *nodes* and relationships between nodes by abstract *edges* or *arcs*.

Graph theory (Diestel, 2005) was founded by Euler in the 18th century to solve the famous Königsberg bridge problem. However, until the 1950s, only simple graphs that could be analysed in toto were considered. Erdös and Rényi (1959) introduced the concept of a *random graph*, which allowed one to treat large complex graphs statistically. Graphs of various sorts were readily recognised in nature, from food webs, personal or business contacts, sexual relations, and the Internet amongst others. However, it soon became apparent that natural networks often had different statistical properties than general random graphs. Watts and Strogatz (1998) introduced the *small world* model, which has sparked a flurry of activity in recent years to measure networks such as the Internet, networks of collaborations between scientific authors and food webs in ecosystems (Albert & Barabási, 2002).

Graph theory provides a number of measures that can stand in for complexity. The simplest of these is the *connectivity* of a graph, namely the number of edges connecting vertices of the graph. A fully connected graph, however, is no more complex than one that is completely unconnected. As connectiv-

Figure 1. Various graph theoretic measures for a simple graph. The spanning trees are shown in the dashed box.

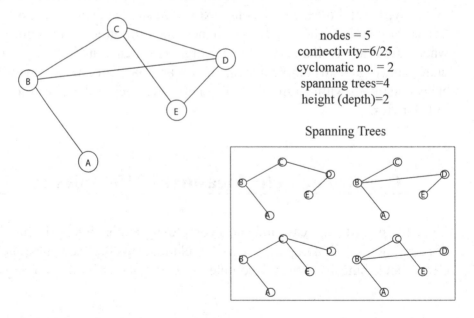

nodes = 5
connectivity=6/25
cyclomatic no. = 2
spanning trees=4
height (depth)=2

Spanning Trees

ity increases from zero, a *percolation threshold* is reached where the graph changes from being mostly discontinuous to mostly continuous. The most complex systems tend to lie close to the percolation threshold. Another graph measure used is *cyclomatic number* of a graph, basically the number of independent loops it contains. The justification for using cyclomatic number as a measure of complexity is that feedback loops introduce nonlinearities in the system's behaviour that produce complex behaviour.

Related to the concept of cyclomatic number is the *number of spanning trees* of the graph. A spanning tree is a subset of the graph that visits all nodes but has no loops (i.e., is a tree). A graph made up from several disconnected parts has no spanning tree. A tree has exactly one spanning tree. The number of spanning trees increases rapidly with the cyclomatic number.

The height of the flattest spanning tree, or equivalently the maximum number of hops separating two nodes on the graph (popularised in the movie *six degrees of separation*—which refers to the maximum number of acquaintances connecting any two people in the world) is another useful measure related to complexity. Networks having small degrees of separation (so called *small world networks*) tend to support more complex dynamics than networks having a large degree of separation. The reason is that any local disturbance is propagated a long way through a small world network before dying out, giving rise to chaotic dynamics, whereas in the other networks, disturbances remain local, leading to simpler linear dynamics.

Offdiagonal Complexity

Recently, Claussen (2007) introduced a complexity measure called *offdiagonal complexity* that is low for regular and randomly connected graphs, but takes on extremal values for *scale-free* graphs, such as typically seen in naturally occurring networks like metabolic and foodweb networks, the internet, the World Wide Web and citation networks. The apparent ubiquity of the scale-free property amongst networks we intuitively associate as complex (Newman, 2003) is the justification for using offdiagonal complexity, the other advantage being its computational practicality.

To compute offdiagonal complexity, start with the *adjacency matrix*

$$g_{ij} = 1 \text{ if } i \text{ and } j \text{ are connected, } g_{ij} = 0 \text{ otherwise} \tag{1}$$

Let ℓ_i be the node degree of i, and let c_{mn}, $m \le n$, be the number of edges between all nodes i and j with node degrees $m = \ell(i)$, $n = \ell(j)$:

$$c_{mn} = \sum_{i,j} g_{ij} \delta_{m,\ell(i)} \delta_{n,\ell(j)} \qquad (2)$$

Then the normalised n-th diagonal sum is

$$a_n = \frac{\sum_i c_{i,i+n}}{\sum_{i,j} c_{ij}} \qquad (3)$$

The *offdiagonal complexity* is defined by a Boltzmann-Gibbs entropy-like formula over the normalised diagonal sums:

$$c_{offdiag} = -\sum_n a_n \ln a_n \qquad (4)$$

For regular lattices, each node has the same link degree, so c_{mn} is diagonal, $a_n = \delta_{n0}$ and $C_{offdiag} = 0$.

For random graphs, most edges will connect nodes with similar link degree (the characteristic link degree scale), so c_{mn} will have a mostly banded structure, and $a_n \to 0$ as n increases. This leads to small non-zero values of the offdiagonal complexity.

Scale free networks have a power law distribution of link degree, which leads to the c_{mn} matrix having a wide spread of entries. In the case of all a_n being equal, offdiagonal complexity takes its maximum value as equal to the number of nodes.

Information as Complexity

The single simplest unifying concept that covers all of the preceding considerations is information. The more information required to specify a system, the more complex it is. A sandpile is simple, because the only information required is that it is made of sand grains (each considered to be identical, even if they aren't in reality), and the total number of grains in the pile. However, a typical motorcar requires a whole book of blueprints in its specification.

Information theory began in the work of Shannon (1949), who was concerned with the practical problem of ensuring reliable transmission of messages. Every possible message has a certain probability of occurring. The less likely a message is, the more information it imparts to the listener of that message. The precise relationship is given by a logarithm:

$$I = -\log_2 p \qquad (5)$$

where p is the probability of the message, and I is the information it contains for the listener. The base of the logarithm determines what units information is measured in—base 2 means the information is expressed in *bits*. Base 256 could be used to express the result in *bytes*, and is of course equivalent to dividing equation (5) by 8.

Shannon, of course, was not so interested in the semantic content of the message (i.e., its meaning), but rather in the task of information transmission so instead considered a message composed of symbols x_i drawn from an alphabet A. Each symbol had a certain probability $p(x_i)$ of appearing in a

Figure 2. Diagram showing the syntactic and semantic spaces. Two different messages, having meanings A and B, can each be coded in many equivalent ways in syntactic space, represented by the sets A and B, The information or complexity of the messages is related to the size it occupies in syntactic space by formula (5)

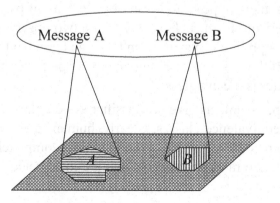

L_2 Semantic Layer

B is more complex (or has greater information than A, because the set B is smaller than A.

L_1 Syntactic Layer

message—consider how the letter "e" is far more probable in English text than the letter "q." These probabilities can be easily measured by examining extant texts. A first order approximation to equation (5) is given by:

$$I(x_1 x_2 \ldots x_n) \approx \sum_{i=1}^{n_1} {}_1 \, p(x_i) \, \log_2 p(x_i) \tag{6}$$

This equation can be refined by considering possible pairs of letters, then possible triplets, in the limit converging on the minimum amount of information required to be transmitted in order for the message to be reconstructed in its original form. That this value may be considerably less that just sending the original message in its entirety is the basis of compression algorithms, such as those employed by the well-known *gzip* or *PKzip* (aka WinZip) programs.

The issue of semantic content discouraged a lot of people from applying this formalism to complexity measures. The problem is that a message written in English will mean something to a native English speaker, but be total gibberish to someone brought up in the Amazon jungle with no contact with the English speaking world. The information content of the message depends on exactly who the listener is! Whilst this context dependence appears to make the whole enterprise hopeless, it is in fact a feature of all of the measures discussed so far. When counting the number of parts in a system, one must make a decision as to what exactly constitutes a part, which is invariably somewhat subjective, and needs to be decided by consensus or convention by the parties involved in the discussion. Think of the problems in trying decide whether a group of animals is one species of two, or which genus they belong to. The same issue arises with the characterisation of the system by a network. When is a relationship considered a graph edge, when often every component is connected to every other part in varying degrees.

However, in many situations, there appears to be an obvious way of partitioning the system, or categorising it. In such a case, where two observers agree on the same way of interpreting a system, then they can agree on the complexity that system has. If there is no agreement on how to perform this categorisation, then complexity is meaningless

To formalise complexity then, assume as given a classifier system that can categorise descriptions into equivalence classes. Clearly, humans are very good at this—they're able to recognise patterns even in almost completely random data. Rorschach plots are random ink plots that are interpreted by viewers as a variety of meaningful images. However, a human classifier system is not the only possibility. Another is the classification of programs executed by a computer by what output they produce. Technically, in these discussions, researchers use a *universal turing machine* (UTM), an abstract model of a computer.

Consider then the set of possible binary strings, which can be fed into a UTM U as a program. Some of these programs cause U to produce some output then halt. Others will continue executing forever. In principle, it is impossible to determine generally if a program will halt or continue on indefinitely. This is the so called *halting problem*. Now consider a program p that causes the UTM to output a specific string s and then halt. Since the UTM halts after a certain number of instructions executed (denoted $\ell(p)$) the same result is produced by feeding in any string starting with the same bits. If the strings have equal chance of being chosen (*uniform measure*), then the proportion of strings starting with the same initial $\ell(p)$ bits is $2^{-\ell(p)}$. This leads to the *universal prior* distribution over descriptions s, also known as the Solomonoff-Levin distribution:

$$P(s) = \sum_{\{p:U(p)=s\}} 2^{-\ell(p)} \qquad (7)$$

The complexity (or information content) of the description is given by equation (5), or simply the logarithm of (7). In the case of an arbitrary classifier system, the complexity is given by the negative logarithm of the equivalence class size

$$C(x) = \lim_{s\to\infty} s \log_2 N - \log_2 \omega(s,x) \qquad (8)$$

where N is the size of the alphabet used to encode the description and $\omega(s,x)$ is the number of equivalent descriptions having meaning x of size s or less (Standish, 2001).

It turns out that the probability $P(s)$ in equation (7) is dominated by the shortest program (Li & Vitányi, 1997, Thm 4.3.3), namely

$$K(s) + \log_2 P(s) \le C \qquad (9)$$

($\log_2 P(s)$<0 naturally) where C is a constant independent of the description s. $K(s)$ is the length of the shortest program p that causes U to output s, and is called the *Kolmogorov complexity* or *algorithmic complexity*.

An interesting difference between algorithmic complexity, and the general complexity based on human observers can be seen by considering the case of random strings. *Random*, as used in algorithmic information theory, means that no shorter algorithm can be found to produce a string than simply saying "print ...", where the ... is a literal representation of the string. The algorithmic complexity of a random string is high, at least as high as the length of the string itself. However, a human observer simply sees a random string as a jumble of letters, much the same as any other random string. In this latter case, the equivalence class of random strings is very large, close to N^s, so the perceived complexity is small. Thus the human classifier defines an example of what Gell-Mann calls *effective complexity* (Gell-Mann, 1994), namely a complexity that has a high value for descriptions that are partially compressible by complex schema, but low for random or obviously regular systems.

A good introduction to information theoretical concepts for complex systems studies can be found in Adami (1998).

Information Theoretic Graph Complexity

In an attempt to bridge the information theoretic approach to complexity with graph theoretical approaches, Standish recently introduced a coding scheme for which practical (though still NP-hard) algorithms exist for calculating the size of the equivalence class of descriptions (Standish, 2005). The intention is to use this method with networks that have a meaning or function attached, such as metabolic networks, or food webs. A randomly constructed food web will collapse fairly quickly under ecosystem dynamics to a much smaller stable food web, so random or regular networks will tend to have a lower complexity value.

However, when applied to abstract networks, it leads to a perverse result that regular networks have the high complexities, and the completely connected network has maximal complexity. This effect can be ameliorated by introducing a compressed complexity measure, which reduces the complexity measure of regular networks, and is closer to a Turing complete *syntactic* language. Unfortunately, there is no computationally effective algorithm known for calculating this compressed complexity measure.

Computational Complexity and Logical Depth

Algorithmic complexity takes no account of the time required to execute the shortest algorithm. An almanac of tide charts and Newton's equations of motion plus law of gravity for the Earth-Moon-Sun system contain the same information, yet the almanac contains the information in a more useful form for the maritime sailor, as it requires less work to determine when the tides occur. *Computational complexity* and *logical depth* are two concepts designed to address the issue of a description's value.

Computational complexity is defined as the execution time of the algorithm. Since this is highly dependent on what operations are available to the processor, usually only the scaling class of the algorithm is considered as the input size is increased. Algorithms may scale *polynomially*, which means the execution time increases as some power of the problem size ($t \propto n^s$), or may scale faster than this (e.g., exponentially: $t \propto n^s$), in which case they have *nonpolynomial complexity*. The class of polynomial algorithms is called P, and the class of nonpolynomial algorithms for which the solution can be checked in polynomial time is called NP. It is known that all NP algorithms can be transformed into any other by means of a polynomially preprocessor, but it is unknown whether or not $P=NP$ (i.e., whether it is possible to transform any nonpolynomial algorithm into a polynomial one). This issue is of great importance, as certain public key encryption schemes depend on nonpolynomial algorithms to ensure the encryption scheme cannot be cracked within a practical amount of time.

Bennett's *logical depth* (Bennett, 1988) is the execution time of the most highly compressed representation of an object, relative to some reference machine. It is meant to be a measure of the value of the object—the almanac of tide tables has a high value of logical depth compared with the equations of motion that generate it.

In terms of the observer-based complexity notions introduced in §4, assume that the observer has a limited amount of computing resources. Perhaps e is only prepared to spend 5 minutes computing the information, and prior to the widespread availability of electronic computers this meant that the almanac was not equivalent to the equations of motion, since it requires more than 5 minutes to compute the tidal information from the equations of motion via manual paper and pencil techniques. Since the almanac is inequivalent to the equations of motion *in this context*, it is clear that the almanac has greater complexity *in this context*.

Occam's Razor

The practice of preferring a simpler theory over a more complex one when both fit the observed evidence is called *Occam's Razor*, after William de Occam:

Entities should not be multiplied unnecessarily.

What is not widely appreciated, is that this strategy is remarkably success-ful at picking better theories. Often, when tested against further empirical evidence, the simpler theory prevails over the more complex. A classical example of this sort of thing is Einstein's General Theory of Relativity. The key field equations of general relativity are really quite simple:

$$G = 8\pi\kappa T \tag{10}$$

Of course unraveling what these equations means for a specific instance in-volves a nontrivial amount of 4-dimensional tensor calculus, so the general relativity computations have high logical depth. Einstein proposed the equa-tions in this form because they seemed the most "beautiful": there were a large number of alternative formulations that fitted the data at the time. One by one, these alternative formulations were tested empirically as technology developed through the 20th century, and found wanting.

However, by what criteria is a particular theory more simple than another. Goodman (1972) developed a theory of *simplicity* to put the practice of Occam's Razor on a more rigorous footing. His idea was to formalise the theories into formal logic predicates, and then count the number of primitive clauses required to encode the theory.

Solomonoff (1964) developed the concept of *algorithmic information com-plexity* in the 1960s as a way of explaining why Occam's razor works. He considered the set of all possible descriptions and computed the probability distribution that a particular description would be generated by a program picked at random by the reference machine. His work had some technical problems that were solved by Levin (1974), which led to the *universal prior* distribution (7). Basically, simple descriptions have a much higher probability than more complex ones, thus Occam's razor. The same behaviour is true of the arbitrary classifier system at equation (8) (Standish, 2004).

While the world is expected to be remarkably simple by the previous arguments, it is also logically very deep (10^{10} years of runtime so far!). This appears to be the result of another poorly understood principle called the *Anthropic Principle*. The Anthropic Principle states that the world must be consistent with our existence as intelligent, reasoning beings (Barrow & Tipler, 1986). So while Occam's razor says we should live in the simplest of universes, the Anthropic Principle says it shouldn't be too simple, as a certain level of complexity is required for intelligent life. The simplest means of generating this level of complexity is by accruing random mutations, and selecting for functional competence (i.e., Darwinian evolution).

Complexity as a Quality: Emergence

It is often thought that *complex systems* are a separate category of systems to *simple systems*. So what is it that distinguishes a complex system, such as a living organism, or an economy, from a simple system, such as a pair of pliers? This question is related to the notorious question of *What is Life?*, however may have a simpler answer, since not all complex systems are living, or even associated with living systems.

Consider the concept of *emergence* (Fromm, 2004; Holland, 1997). We intuitively recognise emergence as patterns arising out of the interactions of the components in a system, but not implicit in the components themselves. Examples include the formation of hurricanes from pressure gradients in the atmosphere, crashes in stock markets, flocking behaviour of many types of animals and of course, life itself.

Let us consider a couple of simple illustrative examples that are well known and understood. The first is the *ideal gas*, a model gas made up of large numbers of non-interacting point particles obeying Newton's laws of motion. A *thermodynamic* description of the gas is obtained by averaging:

temperature (T)
   is the average kinetic energy of the particles;

/

pressure (P)

> is the average force applied to a unit area of the boundary by the particles colliding with it;

density (ρ)

> is the average mass of particles in a unit volume;

The *ideal gas law* is simply a reflection of the underlying laws of motion, averaged over all the particles:

$$P \, \rho \alpha \, T \tag{11}$$

The thermodynamic state is characterised by the two parameters T and ρ. The so-called *first law of thermodynamics* is simply a statement of conservation of energy and matter, in average form.

An entirely different quantity enters the picture in the form of *entropy.* Consider discretising the underlying phase-space into cubes of size h^N, (N being the number of particles) and then counting the number of such cubes having temperature T and density ρ, ω (T, ρ, N). The entropy of the system is given by

$$S(T,\rho,N) = k_B \ln \omega(T, \rho, N) \tag{12}$$

where k_B is a conversion constant that expresses entropy in units of Joules per Kelvin. One can immediately see the connection between complexity (eq. 8) and entropy. Readers familiar with quantum mechanics will recognise h as being an analogue of Planck's constant. However, the ideal gas is not a quantum system, and as $h \rightarrow 0$, entropy diverges! However, it turns out that in the thermodynamic limit (N $\rightarrow \infty$), the average entropy S/N is independent of the size of h.

The *second law of thermodynamics* is a recognition of the fact that the system is more likely to move a state occupying a larger region of phase space, than a smaller region of phase space, namely that ω (T, ρ, N) must increase in time. Correspondingly entropy must also increase (or remain constant) over time. This is a probabilistic statement that only becomes exact in the thermodynamic limit. At the syntactic, or specification level of description (i.e., Newton's laws of motion), the system is perfectly *reversible* (we can recover the system's initial state by merely reversing the velocities of all the particles), yet at the semantic (thermodynamic) level, the system is *irreversible* (entropy can only increase, never decrease).

The property of irreversibility is an *emergent* property of the ideal gas, as it is not *entailed* by the underlying specification. It comes about because of the additional identification of thermodynamic states, namely the set of all micro-states possessing the same temperature and density. This is extra information, which in turn entails the second law.

The second example I'd like to raise (but not analyse in such great depth) is the well known *Game of Life* introduced by Conway (1982). This is a *cellular automaton* (Wolfram, 1984), in this case, a 2D grid of cells where each cell can be one of two states. Dynamics on the system is imposed by the rule that the state of a cell depends on the values of its immediate neighbours at the previous time step.

Upon running the Game of Life, one immediately recognises a huge bestiary of emergent objects, such as blocks, blinkers, and gliders. Take gliders for example. This is a pattern that moves diagonally through the grid. The human observer recognises this pattern, and can use it to *predict* the behaviour of the system with less effort than simulating the full cellular automaton. It is a *model* of the system. However, the concept of a glider is not *entailed* by the cellular automaton specification, which contains only states and transition rules. It requires the additional identification of a pattern by the observer.

This leads to a general formulation of *emergence* (Standish, 2001). Consider a system specified in a language L_1, which can be called the specification, or *syntactic* layer (see Figure 2). If one accepts the principle of *reduction*, all systems can ultimately be specified the common language of the theoretical physics of elementary particles. However, an often believed corollary of reduction is that this specification encodes all there is to know about the system. The previous two examples shows this corollary to be manifestly false. Many systems exhibit one or more *good models,* in another language L_2, which can be called the *semantic layer*. The system's specification does not entail completely the behaviour of the semantic model, since the latter also depends on specific identifications made by the observer. In such a case, we say that properties of the semantic model is emergent with respect to the syntactic specification.

The concept of "good" model deserves further discussion. In our previous two examples, neither the thermodynamic model, nor the glider model can be said to perfectly capture the behaviour of the system. For example, the second law of thermodynamics only holds in the thermodynamic limit—entropy may occasionally decrease in finite sized systems. A model based on gliders cannot predict what happens when two gliders collide. However, in both of these cases, the semantic model is cheap to evaluate, relative to simulating the full system specification. This makes the model "good" or "useful" to the observer. We don't prescribe here exactly how to generate good models here, but simply note that in all cases of recognised emergence, the observer has defined a least one semantic and one syntactic model of the system, and that these models are fundamentally incommensurate. Systems exhibiting emergence in this precise sense can be called *complex*.

A school of thought founded by Rosen holds that complex systems cannot be described by a single best model as reductionists would assume, but rather has a whole collection of models that in the limit collectively describe the system (Rosen, 1991). That such systems exist, at least formally, is assured by Gödel's incompleteness theorem (Hofstadter, 1979), which shows that number theory is just such a system that cannot be captured by a finite specification. He further argues mechanical systems (those that have a finite specification such as the examples I have previously given) can never be complex, since the specification contains all there is to know about the system. However, he implicitly assumes that all models must be perfect (i.e., in perfect correspondence with the underlying system), rather than merely good as I do here. This constitutes a *straw man* argument, and leads him to the *false* conclusion that mechanical systems (e.g., computer simulations) can never exhibit emergence. The two examples previously presented, which are perfectly good mechanical systems, are counter-examples to this claim. Furthermore, the definition of complex systems presented here is known to be non-empty, a fact not known of Rosen's definition since no physical counterpart to Gödel's incompleteness theorem is known.

Conclusion

When connoting a quality, complexity of a system refers to the presence of emergence in the system, or the exhibition of behaviour not specified in the systems specification. When connoting a quality, complexity refers to the amount of information needed to specify the system. Both notions are inherently observer or context dependent, which has lead to a disparate collection of formalisations for the term, and has lead to some despairing of the concept being adequately formalised. This would be a mistake, as within a given application, the meaning can be well defined.

An additional difficulty is the combinatorial size of the underlying syntactic space, which can lead to the intractability of computing complexity. Furthermore, the details of the syntactic layer may be inaccessible, for example the absence of historical genetic data in the study of evolution from the fossil record. So being able to establish easy to measure proxies for complexity is often important, and many proposals for complexity are of this nature.

References

Adami, C. (1998). *Introduction to artificial life.* Berlin: Springer.

Albert, R., & Barabási, A. L. (2002). Statistical mechanics of complex networks. *Reviews of Modern Physics, 74*, 47.

Barrow, J. D., & Tipler, F. J. (1986). *The anthropic cosmological principle.* Oxford: Clarendon.

Bennett, C. H. (1988). Logical depth and physical complexity. In R. Harkin (Ed.), *The universal turing machine: A half century survey* (Vol. 1, pp. 227-258). Oxford: Oxford UP.

Bonner, J. T. (1988). *The evolution of complexity.* Princeton: Princeton UP.

Claussen, J. C. (2007). Offdiagonal complexity: A computationally quick complexity measure for graphs and networks. *Physica A, 375*, 365-373. arXiv:q-bio.MN/0410024.

Conway, J. H. (1982). What is life? In E. Berlekamp, J. H. Conway, & R. Guy (Eds.), *Winning ways for your mathematical plays* (Vol. 2, Chapter 25). New York: Academic.

Diestel, R. (2005). *Graph theory* (3rd ed.). Berlin: Springer.

Edmonds, B. (1999). *Syntactic measures of complexity.* PhD thesis, University of Manchester. http://bruce.edmonds.name/thesis/, Complexity Bibliography: http://bruce.edmonds.name/compbib/.

Erdös, P., & Rényi, A. (1959). On random graphs. *Publ. Math. Dubrecen, 6,* 290-291.

Fromm, J. (2004). *The emergence of complexity.* Kassel: Kassel UP.

Gell-Mann, M. (1994). *The Quark and the Jaguar: Adventures in the simple and the complex.* London: Little Brown Co.

Goodman, N. (1972). *Problems and projects.* Indianapolis, IN: Bobbs-Merrill.

Hofstadter, D. R. (1979). *Gödel, Escher, Bach: An eternal golden braid.* New York: Basic Books.

Holland, J. (1997). *Emergence: From chaos to order.* Reading, MA: Addison-Wesley.

Levin, L. A. (1974). Laws of information conservation (non-growth) and aspects of the foundation of probability theory. *Problems Inform. Transmission, 10,* 206-210.

Li, M., & Vitányi, P. (1997). *An introduction to Kolmogorov complexity and its applications* (2nd ed.). New York: Springer.

McShea, D. W. (1996). Metazoan complexity and evolution: Is there a trend? *Evolution, 50,* 477-492.

Newman, M. E. J. (2003). The structure and function of complex networks. *SIAM Review, 45*(2), 167-256. arXiv:cond-mat/0303516.

Rosen, R. (1991). *Life itself.* New York: Columbia UP.

Shannon, C. E. (1949). *The mathematical theory of communication.* Urbana-Champaign, IL: University of Illinois Press.

Solomonoff, R. J. (1964). A formal theory of inductive inference, part 1 and 2. *Inform. Contr.,* pages 1-22,224-254.

Standish, R. K. (2001). *On complexity and emergence.* Complexity International, 9. arXiv:nlin.AO/0101006.

Standish, R. K. (2004). Why Occam's razor? *Foundations of Physics Letters, 17,* 255-266. arXiv:physics/0001020.

Standish, R. K. (2005). Complexity of networks. In Abbass et al. (Eds.), Recent advances in artificial life, volume 3 of *Advances in Natural Computation,* pages 253-263, Singapore. World Scientific. arXiv:cs.IT/0508075.

Watts, D. J., & Strogatz, S. H. (1998). Collective dynamics of "small-world" networks. *Nature, 393*(6684), 409-10.

Wolfram, S. (1984). Cellular automata as models of complexity. *Nature, 311,* 419-424.

Key Terms

Algorithmic Complexity: Length of shortest program capable of generating the description (also known as Kolmogorov complexity).

Anthropic Principle: The statement that the properties of the universe must be such as to permit our existence as human observers.

Cellular Automaton: A grid of cells, each of which can be in a finite number of states. The states of each cell depend only on the states of a neighbourhood of cells at the previous timestep, known as a transition rule.

Church-Turing Thesis: The proposition that all computable functions can be computed on a Turing machine.

Classifier System: A system that classifies a set of objects into a discrete set of classes. Formally equivalent to a map into the set of whole numbers.

Complexity (Quality): The quality of possessing emergent properties.

Complexity (Quantity): The amount of information a particular system represents to the observer.

Computational Complexity: The computational cost of executing an algorithm.

Emergence: The phenomenon of emergent properties.

Emergent Properties: Properties of a system at the semantic level that are not entailed at the syntactic level.

Entail: To logically imply something.

Entropy: Logarithm of number of syntactic states equivalent to a given semantic state. It is related to information (I) by $S+I=S_{max}$ where S_{max} is the maximum possible entropy of the system.

Equivalence Class: A set of objects that are equivalent under some mapping, i.e., $\{x : e(x) = e(x')\} \exists x'$.

Game of Life: A well known cellular automaton, with two states per cell, and a particular transition rule.

Graph Theory: Mathematical theory of objects consisting of atomic nodes linked by connections called edges.

Gödel Incompleteness Theorem: No finite set of axioms can prove all possible true theorems of number theory.

Information: The amount of meaning in any description; formally given as the logarithm of the proportion of syntactic space occupied by the description.

Link Degree: The number of edges a node has in a graph.

Logical Depth: Execution time of the most compressed representation of an object.

Newton's Laws of Motion: Laws of ideal point particles: the acceleration a particle experiences is proportional to the force acting on it, which is a function of the positions and velocities of the particle and the environment.

Occam's Razor: A statement of the practice of preferring a simpler theory over a more complex one.

Scale Free: A scale free distribution has infinite mean. A power law distribution is a common scale free distribution. A scale free process is a stochastic process obeying a scale free distribution.

Second Law of Thermodynamics: Entropy can only increase, or remain constant in a closed system; it can never decrease.

Semantic Level (or Space): The space of meanings for any description.

Syntactic Level (or Space): The language in which a description is specified: letters of the alphabet, genetic code, laws of theoretical physics, as appropriate.

Turing Machine: A formal model of a computation.

Universal Turing Machine: A formal model of a computer. Is capable is simulating any Turing Machine with appropriate input.

Section III

Computing Perspectives

Chapter V

Emergence of Creativity:
A Simulation Approach

Hrafn Thorri Thórisson, Reykjavík University, Iceland

Abstract

This chapter presents a theory of natural creativity and its relation to certain features of intelligence and cognitive faculties. To test the theory we employ simulated worlds of varying complexity, inhabited by creatures with a genetically-evolving mental model. Plan-making strategies are compared between creatures in each of these worlds. The results show that creative behaviors are governed by the world's structural coherence and complexity. In light of the results we present a new definition of creativity, propose a theory for why creativity evolves in nature, and discuss creativity's relation to perception, goals, logic, understanding, and imagination. Creativity has been a difficult concept to define and its exact relationship with intelligence remains to be explained. The theoretical framework presented is proposed as a foundation and tool for furthering understanding of natural creativity and to help develop creative artificially intelligent systems.

Introduction

Creativity is an important capability of humans. It gives us power beyond the reach of any other intelligent system known and separates us from the rest of the animal kingdom. Through creativity, the human race has learned to build complex technology far beyond that of any other species on this planet (Figure 1). Although creativity is an enormously important aspect of our existence, few artificial intelligence (A.I.) studies have been directly aimed at understanding the general underlying structure, or nature, of creativ-

Figure 1. Architectural constructs are perhaps not considered prime examples of creative output, yet are based on numerous creative insights without which they would not exist. Compared to some of the structures considered very creative in the animal kingdom, such as bird nests or ant-hills, the difference of creative capacity is obvious.

ity. The emphasis in A.I. studies has so far mainly been on building logical systems and it seems that creativity has for the most part been considered a side-product of logic.

Often associated with genious, creativity has thus been a highly visible part of human civilization—creative individuals set new standards and goals for humanity by pioneering physical constructions and scientific concepts. Although prime examples of creativity are generally extraordinary, it is quite obvious that creativity is also at work when it comes to the more mundane, such as plumbing, planning the route to your workplace, or finding a way to pour coffee when one hand is holding a telephone and the other a cat. Any plan to manipulate our environment or fulfill our goals is created in accordance to specific circumstances, whether the plan is to portray a woman on canvas or avoid spilling your coffee on your cat.

Creativity affects many features of intelligence (particularly in humans), making it very difficult to formally define as a concept; one cannot say that creativity is defined only by the novelty of the phenomena it produces, for it must be logical to some extent as well; randomness is generally not considered creative. It is also subtly erroneous to state that something is creative if it is novel and logical—because the logicality of a novel act is closely tied with that of the goal it belongs to, and thus an act can be extremely creative and logical within the confines of its goal's illogicality. To complicate things even more, intentionality of a creative act is a determining factor of its validity—we wouldn't normally perceive a person as creative if a certain action of theirs had led to a coincidental discovery of a new scientific concept (although such events may of course occasionally happen).

In light of the vast spectrum of human creative capabilities, noteworthy attempts at computational replication are often governed by an anthropocentric viewpoint, pushing research away from associating creativity with that of less capable animals that might provide us with a better understanding of the innate nature of its underlying mechanisms. An overemphasis on human capabilities may well be partially to blame for the fact that a wholesome definition and explanation of creativity has not yet reached a general consensus. In this chapter, we introduce a new simulation model consisting of virtual creatures within emergent environments and propose new methods with which we can begin exploring how creativity can be defined and identified in simpler animals.

The chapter is organized as follows: We begin by reviewing the background of creativity studies in various scientific disciplines. We then state our hypotheses in more detail and describe a simulation framework created for exploring how creativity exhibits itself in agents evolving within emergent environments. Then we describe an experiment based on the platform, and discuss the results. After which we discuss the theory in detail, in light of the experimental results and concepts of emergence, providing a new definition of creativity. We end the chapter with future research possibilities.

Background

Although some progress has clearly been made in research on creativity over the last 20 years, the concept has remained extremely hard to define and understand. By 1988, over 50 different definitions of creativity had already been proposed (Taylor, 1988). A common thread among many of them is a primary distinction between creativity displayed in an artifact (evaluated by society), and processes that might result in a creative product (Gero, 1996), or *artifact* (e.g., poems, paintings, architecture, music). The characteristics of creative artifacts are generally considered to be (1) novelty, (2) unconventionality or unexpectedness, and (3) value of the product (value to whom remains undefined). These have often been the pillars from which creative artifacts are evaluated (Boden, 2004; Gero, 1996; Liu, 1996; Wiggins, 2006). However, there exist no empirical evaluation methods for creativity or creative products, exploring processes by identification of the resulting products remains difficult. Another common view of human creativity is seeing it as merely a recombination of old ideas, which deserves special attention here. The idea has received significant opposition, especially in that it does not capture the entire spectrum of human creativity. Boden (1995) has argued that:

"Creative 'novelties' are of significantly different types—the most interesting of which lie beyond combination-theory. Many creative ideas are surprising not because they involve some unusual mix of familiar ideas, but in a deeper way. They concern novel ideas which not only did not happen before, but which—in a sense that must be made clear (and which combination-theory cannot express)—could not have happened before" (p. 124).

Moreover, combination-theorists do not explain how novel combinations come about in the first place. While recombinations can contribute to creativity, there is more to the story.

Creativity affects behavior to such a high degree that it's been hard to discern the differences and correlations of creativity and intelligence. Runco's (2004) review of creativity research covering the past 20 years mentions many processes studied in cognitive sciences that relate to creativity:

"Basic cognitive processes that have been studied include memory (Pollert, Feldhusen, Van Mondfrans, & Treffinger, 1969), attention (Martindale & Greenough, 1973), and knowledge (Mumford, Mobley, Uhlman, Palmon, & Doares, 1991, Rubenson & Runco 1995). Cognitive research has also focused on tactics, strategies, metacognition (Adams, 1980, Root-Bernstein, 1988, Runco, 1999c), and intellectual skills ..." (p. 667).

Considering the high number of cognitive features that creativity has been associated with, it has been suggested—and indeed seems likely—that creativity is not a specific mechanism of the brain but rather an aspect of human intelligence in general (Boden, 2004). Humans are extremely complicated machines, and admittedly more so than other animals. However, if creativity is tightly coupled with intelligence it must be considered that creativity is also evident in the intelligence of simpler animals and that the tendency to associate creativity with (extraordinary) human abilities may have been overemphasized. Crows have exhibited an ability to bend strings of wire into various shapes to use as tools for retrieving food from places that are difficult to get to (Weir & Kacelnik, 2006). Research indicates that this ability is not coincidental, and that the crows did not solve problems by repeating previously learned actions, but by generating new plans to solve each specific problem. We can assume, if creativity is a phenomenon evident in all intelligences, that its evolutionary roots are tightly related to planning mechanisms (e.g., as used by the crow to retrieve food). All non-reactive animals have some mechanisms for dynamic planning, and as such it could be that creativity shares common evolutionary roots in all animals (we'll come back to this issue later).

Some attempts have been made to explain the origins of creativity in terms of evolution (most of which are presented in relation to human creativity), and it has been suggested that exploring creativity's evolutionary roots might give us a holistic picture of how and why it emerges in relation to other processes (Gabora, 2005; Thórisson, 2004). Carruthers (2002) has proposed that the function of the extensive creative play of children, also evident in the behavior of other mammalians where the young engage in pretend-play such as hunting and fighting, is to train the young in imaginative thinking for use in adult activities. Again, we see attempts to explain creativity in the context of mammals. If we could study creativity in simpler animals, even such as insects, perhaps the pursuit would become easier.

Despite simple nervous systems, insects apply different strategies to identify landmarks, detect objects, and plan courses of action. They are not mere reflex machines, but use memory, evaluation, and perceptual mechanisms, including the detection of geometric shapes and route-segmentation, to function in their environment depending on previous experience (Collet & Collet, 2002; Giurfa & Menzel, 1997). Some might find it difficult to envision that creativity has anything to do with insects and as such there have been no attempts to shed light on creativity in terms of simpler animals than mammals. However, exploring the *general concept of cognition* in animals lower in the phylogenetic tree has gained some attention in recent years (van Duijn, Keijzer, & Franken, 2004). Godfrey-Smith (2001) recently proposed that cognition evolved to cope with environmental complexity and Maturana and Varela (1973) introduced theories of the origins of cognition with the concept of *autopoiesis*; a network of component-processes that perpetually generate themselves. Autopoiesis provides support for theory proposed in this chapter, and is discussed in more detail later.

Exploring cognitive mechanisms in animals, especially insects, is hard because they cannot tell us what they are thinking. Complex processes of intelligence cannot be readily explored in natural animals and neither can the evolution of the mechanisms involved. The methods offered by artificial intelligence present optional approaches to gaining a detailed understanding of intelligence (Thórisson, 2004). An added benefit of such research is (sometimes unexpected) practical uses of the resulting technologies for various purposes. But creating simulated environments and organisms with sufficient realism to be considered valid is no simple task. The environment and organisms must capture realistic features essential to the specific questions studied without excluding possible contributing factors, which are present in the corresponding natural systems.

Cellular automata (CA) are discrete, dynamical systems, which have been used frequently in research on artificial life (ALife), in which the emergent organization of the cells themselves result in agent-like behavior. The works of Antony, Salzberg, and Sayama (1998, 2004) are good examples of these kinds of artificial life simulations. The lifeforms which emerge are primitive—allowing a very limited spectrum of association with higher functioning organisms. This is because most approaches limit the whole system to a CA framework, explicit rules governing everything. In CA-based ALife research, the term "agent" generally used to refer to a cell encompassing complex internal processing. The interactions of such cells constitute multi-agent simulations. The model presented in this chapter must not be confused with such ALife experiments, as it consists of preprogrammed agents modeled after natural insects, and uses cellular automata *only* to produce landscape with emergent properties. While CA-based ALife simulations are mainly concerned with investigating the emergent behavior of interacting agents, we are exploring notions of how emergent environments affect creative aspects of intelligence on onto- and phylogenetic levels.

A Simulation Approach to Analyzing Creativity

The primary hypotheses of interest here are that the evolution of creativity mechanisms are directly related to the complexity/diversity of emergent environments, and that the underlying mechanisms of creative behavior are essentially the same in all creatures, despite the obvious human advantages mentioned above. We propose the theory that creativity is evolution's answer to perceptually apparent unpredictability. This is different from some hypothetical or "actual" unpredictability—the discussion here revolves around unpredictability from the standpoint of the creature.

H_1: An increase in environmental diversity will result in a larger set of distinct behavioral patterns (plans).

H_2: If the world is too complex, there will be no persistent structure evident in the composition of plans. Creative capabilities of all creatures are bound by rules inherent in the environment where they evolve.

More precisely, the previous hypotheses depend on (a) the number of individual components in the environment and their interactions, (b) the creatures' ability to perceive their environment, and (c) the creatures' set of operators which can be applied to modify their behavioral pattern (in particular, to make plans).

Creatures inhabiting a simple, closed, and static world would tend to evolve to become completely robotic due to predictability of the environment; if an environment is very simple the cognitive system of the creatures require little effort to survive. In a complex world, where events in the environment are not evident entirely by observation of the current situation, evolution must provide organisms with a mechanism to predict in uncertain situations. With the increase of interacting components in the environment, more complex cognitive efforts are thus required to produce and assess reactions to the current situation.

Earth's environment is governed by rules that can be traced down to a subatomic level, resulting in its emerging attributes such as land and sea, water circulation, and ecosystems. As creatures evolve in worlds governed by these rules, their plan-making mechanisms come to reflect them. If a particular world should on the other hand be random-based, a creature's planning ability might produce more diversity, but there would be no logic as to when or where the plans are applied. This makes it important to measure the complexity of the world in addition to the diversity of the creatures.

We propose to measure the structural complexity by the use of cellular automata where, through simple interacting rules, complex overall behavior emerges (see *World*). The fact that there are general rules in the environment, many of which are independent of (perceived) scale, indirectly lends support for the proposed hypotheses.

Creativity's roots, according to this line of thought, derive from interactions between the environmental structures: If the interactions of these structures are not obvious (to the organism), perceivable, and very repetitive, creatures must evolve an ability to internally represent and link unobvious causations—thus providing them with greater capabilities to produce diverse behavior in response to the diversity of the environment. Another reason for such a requirement is that visual cues may appear once it is too late for the creatures to react, supporting the evolution of a mechanism capable of predicting possible scenarios before they actually occur (imagination). Cognitive mechanisms must therefore be adept at predicting the environment—and in parallel keeping plans created for survival logical and relative to those predictions.

We will now describe a framework and an experiment created for exploring the hypotheses. Then we will explore their deeper theoretical support.

Simulation Framework

In the present framework the creatures are still at the evolutionary stage of relative reactiveness—they depend solely on visual cues in the environment to initiate a plan. However, the plans themselves directly serve as a prediction of the environment and are sufficient to produce results which support or refute the main hypotheses. The framework rests on the theory that creativity is a product of certain environmental characteristics that manifest themselves in organisms as they evolve in that environment. It purports that creativity is evolution's answer to a perceptually apparent unpredictability of emergent environments (H_1), and that creativity and logic co-evolve as imposed by the causal-relationship between levels of organization in emergent structures (H_2). To explore these notions through means of computer simulations, we have devised a program for simulated worlds that exhibit emergent properties, and creatures that are able to sense and act in these worlds. The world is composed of cellular automata, the creatures of genetically-controlled cognitive faculties (Thórisson, 2004). Each individual creature learns and exhibits intelligent behavior during its lifespan with the use of primitive associative memory, pattern recognition, and planning. Thus, evolution does not effect the creation of plans directly, but modifies the wiring of the creatures' learning mechanism, who in turn dictates which methods are used to generate plans. Let us emphasize that evolution is perturbing a single mental model[1], not constructing new ones. This is important as we're not attempting to evolve new mental components but observing how evolution makes use of readily available components, depending on different environmental contexts. The simulation is turn-based (updates once for every 50 steps of the creature). The creatures are run one at a time to simplify the simulation[2].

As we argue that creativity is an aspect of intelligence in general (Boden, 2004), in context with the environment in which the intelligence operates, it can not be measured explicitly at this point. Rather, we observe what types of behavior the creatures exhibit, how they contribute to our perception of creativity, and what kind of mechanisms are used to produce them. The observation provides support for our explanation and new definition of creativity, independent of any particular cognitive mechanism (see theoretical discussion).

The World

Cellular automata (cf. Wolfram, 2002) have frequently been used in artificial life (ALife) research where the cells are programmed to organize themselves to form patterns which behave like creatures (Antony et. al, 1998). The world in our framework is a classical cellular automaton with cells made to represent physical phenomena such as rocks, earth, and grass (see screenshots later in this section). This approach differs from other work on cellular automata in that the creatures that inhabit the world are separate entities with preprogrammed cognitive systems (they are not cells), and interact with the world's cells via perception and motor abilities.

Cellular automata was chosen because of its similarities with natural environment emergence, and because of the ease of quantifying environmental complexity. As discussed earlier, the Earth's environment is composed of emergent structures produced by the interactions of its constituent subcomponents. This effect is captured by cellular automata as the interactions of cells results in emergent structures in a similar manner. Very complex behavior can be produced by the use of simple rules such as those used in this experiment while at the same time keeping the world logical in terms of general behavior since the state of an individual cell is dependent on its own state and/or surrounding neighbors.

The cellular automata worlds in this experiment are 2D, 100x100 squares wrapped around to form an infinite plane with a repeating pattern; if a creature walks off the edge of the screen, it enters the world again on the opposing side. In the complex dynamic world used in this experiment, the cells in the simulation are dependent upon 25 of their surrounding cells. Each time the world updates, every one of the 10,000 cells looks at the 25 surrounding neighbors and calculate their next state according to given rules—resulting in 250,000 cell checks each time the world turns. The world is set to step at 1/50 steps of the creatures. By varying the rules and number of different kinds of cells, the diversity of the environment can easily be measured since the variation of cells and the number of their rules constitute the worlds complexity/diversity. The rules are not sensitive to neighbor positions, only quantity and lifetime. Adding rules to the components of the world increases the dynamism of the simulation, but this must not be confused with increased speed or, alternately, less time to think for the creatures: The simulation is turn-based (updates once for every 50 steps of the creature), and as such, increasing dynamism of the environment only results in the environmental structures becoming more varied and complex. Cognition is always allowed to run its full course before the next turn.

The world's complexity is quantified by counting the number of component types (cell types) and the number of rules these components abide. Complexity measurement is defined as:

$$Qc = Pi * C$$

where C represents the number of component types perceivable by the creatures and Pi represents the number of rules pertaining to these cells. A rule is defined as any rule or set of rules that causes a state transition for a cell under some condition or conditions. This can be taken as an approximate estimate of the complexity of a world because each rule represents a potential for structural change. While this method can certainly be improved upon, it provides us with an indication of the potential complexity of the environment.

Creatures

The artificial species should be designed to bear a resemblance to natural insects found on earth, this information is based on the research of Collet et al. (2002). The simulation of insect memory and navigational abilities has been tried successfully using a physical LEGO robot (Chan & Wyeth, 1999) and other physical robots (Möller, 2000). The methods are similar to those employed in this framework: Insects use image matching to associate visual cues with actions to navigate to and from nest and food sources[3]. The method for associative learning and cognitive apparatus used here is a simplified version of the one applied in the LEGO robot (see perception cortex and episodic memory).

We assume that the physical properties of our artificial cognitive system have already evolved to an insect-like state, having primitive memory and perceptual abilities, along with a system for the creature to be "aware" of

Figure 2. The perception-action-loop of the agents created in the project (Numbers trace the order of events)

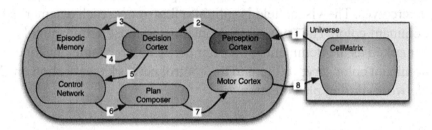

the consequences of its actions (loss or gain of energy after execution). The creatures' cognitive system is divided into several parts, their physical body comprising a (a) vision system, (b) mobility, (c) a mouth for feeding, and finally a (d) mental apparatus for interpreting visual information and generate plans. The cognitive system's components are depicted in Figure 2. The visual information allows them to form memories, which then serves as the basis of forming repeatable plans that enable them to interact with their environment. The plans are composed of primitive actions, such as *go-forward, turn-left, turn-right,* and *eat* (see details in *Plan Composer*). The creatures have a single goal: To survive as long as possible by finding, recognizing and consuming food and passing their genes on to their offspring. In our simulation, green cells (grass) provide the creature with energy if eaten. Eating brown cells has no effect, and eating gray cells causes a reduction of energy. Only the fittest creatures, those that survive the longest in each generation, are allowed to reproduce. Inheritance of cognitive mechanisms is achieved using simple genetic algorithms. The genes (see *Control Network*) of a new individual are mutated at birth to produce diversity in each successive generation.

We will now continue with a detailed description of each part of the artificial creatures' cognitive system.

Perception Cortex

The perception cortex deciphers visual information in the form of quantities of colors and registers which part of the visual field a dominant color is if there is any color more evident than others. The visual field of the creature is rectangular; tuned to perceive a 7x7 grid of cells. When the cortex receives input it begins interpretation by registering the number of each distinct colors it perceives. The visual field is split into four zones, each one marked for its dominant color. The zone which contains the most dominant color overall is marked as the dominant zone. Number of colors, dominant zone, and the dominant color serve as input to the control network (see section on Control Network) during plan creation.

Decision Cortex

The decision repertoire consists of mediating information between all the cortices, keeping a track of current processes, and initiating new processes. The cortex shares the responsibility of creating a new plan with the control network (see below), whether to modify old plans or to create a new one completely from scratch.

During each discrete step in the simulation the decision cortex assesses the status of the creature and its perceptual input and decides which action should be taken. While there is a plan is being executed, each primitive action executed by the motor cortex is routed to memory (plans are sequences of primitive actions), the score of the action is calculated and associated with the current perceptual input. The score of a plan or primitive action is determined by the energy loss/gain before and after its execution. The second mode is if there is no current plan executing: If a plan execution was finished in the last step, its total score is calculated and sent to memory. Next a request is sent to the episodic memory for a recollection of similar situations (see the next section) and to the control network to create a new plan depending on the situation. To sum up, the decision cortex is responsible for

a. Calculating the score of a plan that just finished executing.

b. Requesting a memory search in episodic memory.

c. Routing the perceptual input and physical actions to memory for storage.

d. Requesting a new plan from plan composer.

e. Sending new proposed plans or actions to the motor cortex.

Episodic Memory

The episodic memory is the storage area for all perceptual input, the creatures' actions, and the consequences of those actions. Memories include a particular visual field, the plan that was associated with the perceptual input, the score—in particular the energy expenditure, which was registered during the execution of the plan, along with a normalized plan score.

During each step, the decision cortex sends a message to the episodic memory to find all memories that the creature might have of similar situations. The procedure is as follows:

Find all similar memories by first rating them along three semi-independent feature dimensions:

1.   **Image Matching (dimension one):** The visual field in general: Compare each cell of the current visual field to each patch of a particular memory M. Similarity scoring is incremented with each cell that corresponds precisely to a cell in the same location in memory M relative to the creature (thus, if a cell in the upper left-hand corner is green, and the upper-left hand cell in memory M is green, the memory gets a point for similarity). This score is normalized, so the increment for each cell that's identical is 1 divided by the total number of cell in the visual field. The final score is the sum of all identical cells.

2.   **Dominant Zone Similarity (dimension two):** Compare the current visual fields dominant color and the zone the dominant color is mostly evident in to all memories. The score is Boolean.

3.   **Patch in Front of Mouth (dimension three):** Compare the patch in front of the creature's mouth to that same patch in all existing memories. This is similar to the zone similarity scoring—if the current patch in front of the mouth corresponds to that same patch in a memory, the similarity is turned on (again, 1.0 or 0.0).

For each of these features, the memories are arranged according to each feature's similarity score. The plan associated with each memory (there is either a plan or a primitive action associated with each memory) is retrieved for the top three memories—one for each dimension. Plan scores (energy payoff) are normalized by the following equation:

$$S_f = 1 / S_p(S_{max} - S_{min})$$

where S_f is final score, S_p is the original plan score, S_{max} is the maximum plan score of any plan retrieved from memory, and S_{min} is the minimum score for any plan retrieved from memory. The normalized plan scores of memories in the sorted dimensional arrays are multiplied by the similarity measurement of the memories, providing a "winner" with regards to similarity and plan score.

Control Network

The control network is the part of the program that gets passed on and mutated between generations; it holds the creature genome, which constitutes a set of control boxes and the connections between them. The control network is made up of 70 boxes, which consist of two inputs I_1 and I_2, an output O and an operator, which determines what to do with the inputs received. The types of boxes in the control network are:

- **Static boxes** have a fixed output that stays constant throughout the lifetime of an individual.
- **NOR boxes** or "Not OR" boxes return 1 if both inputs are zero.
- **NAND boxes** or "Not AND" boxes always return 1 except if both inputs receive numbers.
- **Input gate boxes** return I_1 as output only if the value of I_2 is more than zero.

Each of the boxes serves as a node in the control network. Outputs from the boxes are connected to none, some, or all of the other box inputs. The exact routing of the control box inputs and outputs is determined entirely during reproduction of the creatures. That is, the creatures' genetic configuration is responsible for using these connections to activate plan composition mechanisms. There are four instances of each kind of box in a control network except for static boxes, which are 16. For each box, a total of four possible connection configurations are possible. Each of the 30 boxes can receive two inputs. There are no initial connections between control boxes for the first generation in all worlds, and the initial outputs of static boxes are set to zero.

After the first generation, all settings of control boxes and their connections are changed by mutation. Following the terminology introduced by Holland (1998), which covers natural and artificial adaptive systems, we can describe the adaptive process of the control network.

The powerset of control box configurations and connections in the network is denoted α. We denote a specific control box configuration A as a set of possible configurations of connections between them: $A = \{a_{i1}, a_{i2}, ... a_{iki}\}$. The combinations of control boxes and their connections are defined by the adaptive plan τ which uses the mutation operator Ω between generations. The criterion for comparison of τ is μ—the age a creature reaches by using plan-making mechanisms (which are in turn controlled by the particular adaptive plan). The set of structures (control network configurations) attainable by the adaptive plan is represented by the following equation:

$$\alpha = A_1 X A_2 X ... A_n = \prod\nolimits^n_{i=1} A_i$$

Since the environment, E, selects over time, which control boxes survive between generations, an evolving, adaptive plan is defined over time by a particular environment E. This is depicted in Figure 3; the big box represents

Figure 3. Adaptive processes after Holland (1998). A(n) denotes a specific configuration of the control network.

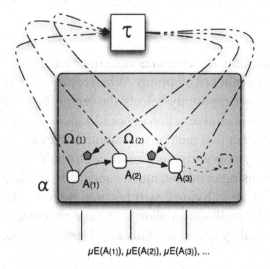

$$\mu E(A_{(1)}), \mu E(A_{(2)}), \mu E(A_{(3)}), ...$$

α which contains all structures attainable by the adaptive plan τ, which is decided by the environment E using μ. The adaptive plan produces a trajectory through α, which are specific configurations of the connections between control boxes, connections to the plan composer (see next section) and the output of the static boxes (a number between 1 and 30).

On every step during execution, the control network receives a request from the decision cortex for updating its outputs. The outputs feed into the plan composer and set control parameters as the creature decides how to plan its actions. There are three main ways for planning the next step, as explained in the next section.

Plan Composer

The plan composer creates plans from sequences of primitive actions (*go-forward*, *turn-left*, *turn-right*, *do-nothing* and *eat*). During each simulation step, the plan composer receives instructions from the control network regarding what to do and specifically how to do it. The instructions are in the form of integers from the control network inputs into the plan composer. They are deciphered by simple logic gates. The methods that the plan composer can use to create the next plan are the three methods:

a. Create a new plan from scratch.
b. Combine halves of two old plans.
c. Mutate an old plan (randomly change primitive actions of an older plan).[4]

During plan-making, the creatures can either create a new plan from scratch or use one of the other two options. When creating a new plan from scratch, the plan composer randomly selects the length of the plan and how many instances of each primitive action it should include. With random distributions of actions, the other two methods, combine halves and mutate, become very important as they provide a much more controllable way of making sensible plans. Also, by using combine, mutate and using an old plan unmodified, the development of an individual will become more evident as the creature is bound to use the methods on plans that have provided good results (memories are organized by score, see *Episodic Memory*). Note that in order to use methods b and c, the creature has to have created at least one random plan from which it can build a modified plan.

The use of a random mechanism to produce new plans is a matter of convenience and deserves some discussion. It is not our claim that creativity is a random process. On the contrary, we propose that creativity is an aspect of intelligence, independent of any particular cognitive mechanism. The main concern is to have a mechanism, which generates new plans from scratch, using other means than recombinations of previous plans. This allows us to compare and contrast the evolutionary incentive to produce completely new plans (regardless of the method of production) as opposed to relying on experience. Exactly how such novelty-producing mental components work on higher levels of natural intelligence, such as the human level, is another matter and not the focus of this chapter.

Experiment

In the experiment, we use three versions of the world. *Simple* (*Es*), which is made up of stripes alternating green and gray (Figure 4). Green is grass (food), gray is rock, and brown is mud (if the creature eats a green cell, the cell turns brown). *Es* has Qc = 3. *Simple Dynamic* (*Esd*) is the same as *Es* with the seemingly small change that the stripes change regularly from gray

Figure 4. A screenshot of a simple (Qc = 3) and simple dynamic world (Qc = 9); 100x100 cells

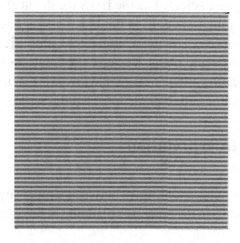

Figure 5. A screenshot of a complex dynamic world, Qc = 18; 100x100 cells

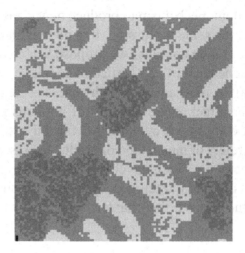

to green and green to gray, increasing the world's Qc to 9. Update frequency of *Esd* is every 50 steps. Both *Es* and *Esd* reset for each new individual. The third world, *Complex Dynamic (Ecd)* presents more landscape-like structures; Qc = 18 in Ecd (Figure 5). *Ecd* begins with initial random placement of cells, but is updated 500 times to eliminate the initial randomness before creatures are introduced to the world.

Each generation is made up of 100 creatures (Ng = 100), natural selection is implemented by sorting the creatures according to age; the top ten individuals (C_1, C_2 ... C_{10}) are selected as the basis for the next generation. The selection criteria for inheritance, μ, is the creatures' age reached. The creatures' only goal is to survive. Having a single goal simplifies comparison between the different worlds and plans. Because the creatures only have one goal, all plans that the creature creates are geared towards reaching that goal. And thus, coming up with alternative plans for reaching a goal is a form of creativity.

Results and Interpretation

The results show a high similarity between simple (Es) and simple dynamic (Esd) environments in the creatures planning behavior. In both environments, the creatures used all of their available mechanisms for plan creation (create-new-plan from scratch, mutate-old-plan, and combine-old-plans). Figures 6 and 7 show the average use of the three mechanisms for plan creation over the lifetime of the creatures in each of the 100 generations (see section on creatures for details about the mechanisms). While the creatures are producing new plans from scratch relatively often, they compensate for plan randomness by using the other mechanisms. The creatures evolving within these simple worlds are maintaining a balance between innovation and logic: creating new and untried plans as well as learning from their previous experiences by using and combining plans that have proven efficient and useful.

In terms of the proposed hypotheses, it would not have been surprising to see more difference in the results of the two worlds. Looking at the two simple worlds only, the main hypothesis, that an increase in environmental diversity results in a larger set of plans, is not clearly supported or disproved. The similar results might be due to structural likenesses between the two worlds. When compared to the results from the complex dynamic world (Ecd), however, the hypothesis is clearly supported. Figure 8 shows the average use of

Figure 6. Es. average use of create new plan (circles), mutate old plan (boxes) and combine old plans (triangles) X-Axis: generation 10-100; Y-Axis: 0-30

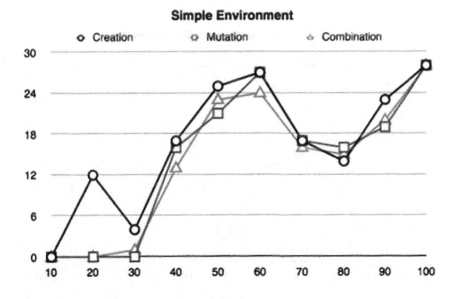

Figure 7. Esd. average use of create-new-plan (circles), Mutate-old-plan (boxes) and combine-old-plans (triangles) X-Axis: generation 10-100; Y-Axis: 0-25

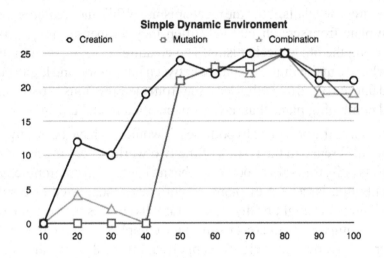

Figure 8. Ecd. average use of create-new-plan (circles), mutate-old-plan (boxes) and combine-old-plans (triangles) X-Axis: generations 10-100; Y-Axis: 0-20

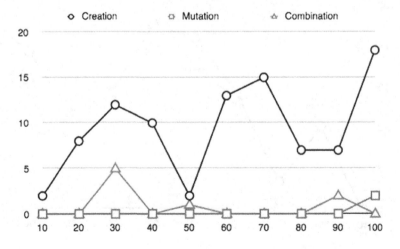

the plan-making mechanisms over the 100 generations. With Qc = 18, the creatures resorted to using the creation mechanism (creating a new plan from scratch every turn), while leaving the other mechanisms relatively unused. The plans and behavior of the creatures was therefore very diverse but the lack of learning from previous experiences resulted in their plans maintaining no logicality[5]. The creatures had shorter lifespans in more complex worlds and could therefore not use the plan-making mechanisms as often. In Es the creatures' average age reached is 28; in Esd it is 25 and in Ecd it is 21.

Figure 9 shows an example of how the creatures' plan maintains logicality by eating only the food (green) while skipping the rock-lines (gray) which, if eaten, result in a substantial loss of energy. Similarly, Figure 10 shows a creature having turned to eat a row of food in a consecutive manner. Such behavior would not have been possible were it not for the fact that the creatures in Es and Esd were using the mechanisms that build on previous experience. In the Ecd (Complex Dynamic Environment), the creatures showed little logicality in their behavior due to their frequent usage of the random plan-making mechanism (Figure 11 shows a creature within the Ecd). To find food in *Ecd* is not as simple as finding food in *Es* and *Esd*—the agents have to produce behavior that allows them to cope with the complexity of their environment. The agents work relatively mechanically in *Es* and *Esd*

Figure 9. A creature (black) in an Es world, eating only the food (light gray), bypassing the rocks

Figure 10. A creature (black) in Es eating a row of food (light gray) consecutively. The image has been enlarged. The screenshot shows 10x6 cells.

Figure 11. A creature (black) in Ecd lurks behind a gray rock formation, away from the food (light gray). The screenshot shows 31x17 cells.

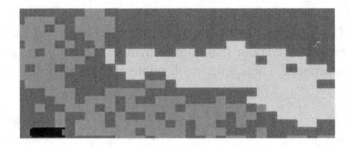

because the visual cues are few and provide accurate accounts of what will happen if the agents execute a certain plan. If the agents encounter a gray cell-structure (a stripe) in *Es*, they can depend on the fact that if they use the plan "move forward once, then eat" they will gain energy, as the cell they will eat is guaranteed to be green (food). However, in *Ecd*, the green structures' behavior is much more diverse, and hence harder to predict. This difference of environments are comparable to those of bacteria and insects in the sense that insects partain to environments of much higher diversity.

In summary, the results strongly suggest that creativity is governed by environmental complexity, and that structural coherence dictates logicality of produced plans. Particularly, agents whose cognitive system evolve in overly complex worlds tend to create diverse (random) plans, but simple ones impose plans that maintain novelty and diversity without venturing into randomness—supporting the stated hypothesis.

Theoretical Discussion

We argue that a coherent explanation of the different processes and mechanisms of creativity must be done in terms of self-organization and emergence. As creativity relies on many cognitive functions, we must incorporate those functions and discuss their origins.

Cognition is rarely associated with the behavior of reactive organisms. As noted by van Duijn et al. (2006), anthropocentric interpretations of cognition introduce a dichotomy between reactive/inflexible organisms and reflective cognizers. An anthropocentric view has also been prevalent throughout research on creativity. Alternative theories to popular views of cognition have been proposed, explaining cognition from a simpler and more mechanical viewpoint. In 1973, biologists Varela and Maturana introduced the concept of *autopoiesis* as a redefinition of life. Their explanation is especially relevant to the concept of emergence and complex systems as it presents a bridge between structurally automatic systems and cognitive systems. In the words of Varela and Maturana (1973), an autopoietic system is:

"... a machine organized (defined as a unity) as a network of processes of production (transformation and destruction) of components which: (i) through their interactions and transformations continuously regenerate and realize the network of processes (relations) that produced them; and (ii) constitute it (the machine) as a concrete unity in space in which they (the components) exist by specifying the topological domain of its realization as such a network." (p. 78).

A popular example of an autopoietic system is a biological cell. The cell's components are molecules, interactions are chemical reactions and the cell membrane the physical boundary that forces reactions into an entity distinguishable from the external environment (Beer, 2004). Computer simulations of autopoietic cellular structures have been created where proto-cells emerge from a digital primordial soup, gradually gaining in complexity to form membranes, in many ways similar to those observed in natural systems (Madina, Ono, & Ikegami, 2003).

Although the concept of autopoiesis remains somewhat controversial (Beer, 2004; van Dujin et al., 2006), it can help us explain the origins of creativity in a unifying manner. While admittedly there is a gigantic leap from auto-poietic systems such as a biological cell to an insect-like agent such as those used here, the methods that organisms (or autopoietic systems) can use to maintain their structure can be generalized to the *identification of a potential threat to its organization and responding appropriately*; a perception-action coupling. van Dujin et al. (2006) have claimed in relation to autopoiesis, that minimal cognition is a dynamic and adaptive sensorimotor process, and have noted that although bacteria have no nervous system, molecular sensorimotor mechanisms of most bacteria closely resemble some of the functional sensorimotor features of nervous systems. This allows us to generalize the cognitive functions of organisms at different levels of complexity as different means of maintaining the perception-action coupling[6].

The following is a proposal for a new definition of creativity and a framework for how the different concepts of cognition co-evolve with the phenomena. We will then proceed to explain how these concepts are interralated in terms of emergence and autopoiesis.

1. *Creativity* is an agent's ability to vary and adapt processes in order to fulfill its *goals*. Processes can be internal (mental functions), or an externalization of internal processes (physical actions and interactions with the environment), where an agent is a living (autopoietic) structure, be it organic or artificial. Creativity can be exhibited without *explicit understanding* of the environment or goals, and the diversity of products or artifacts produced through creative processes are limited by the physical attributes of the agent. Creativity is an aspect of intelligence as a holistic system, independent of any particular cognitive mechanism.

2. *Logicality* is an organism's ontogenetic ability to produce actions which are coherent with the organisms *goals* and structural organization of the environment. Environmental organization imposes itself on organisms as they evolve and is reflected in logical behavior.

3. *Insanity* is the inverse of *logicality*, resulting in behavior which is not applicable to the context in which they are realized, failing to fulfill the agents' goals and are consequently "illogical" or "nonsensual."

4.   *Imagination* is an organism's mechanism for modelling its environment internally to predict a turn of events. When creatures gain in organizational complexity along with the environment, reactive mechanisms become insufficient to predict the environment. This becomes an impetus for other, more complex mechansisms to evolve. In particular the ability to represent the environment as a mental simulation.

The previous definitions include several concepts of intelligence and cognition, mainly: (a) perception and action, (b) goals, (c) logic and insanity, (d) understanding, and finally (e) imagination or internal representations. We will now proceed to explain these concepts and their relationships in more detail.

To explain how *an organism can fulfill goals*, we must establish what goals are. It can be said that autopoietic systems' preservation of structure is an *implicit goal*, realized by the environment-agent coupling. The interactions that maintain an organisms organization, thereby allowing it to maintain identity as one, are *conditions* internal mechanisms of the organism aim to preserve. It is more than possible that this basic principle is the foundation from which continued complexity of hierarchical organization can emerge. Gradually, these systems organize a multileveled hierarchy of processes which constitute what we perceive as, for example, insects. Goals are consequently always evident as particular conditions of the environment. At higher levels of complexity (insect level, for example), organisms seek out these conditions by producing plans—whether they are instinctive or reflective. In other words, *goals* are conditions which allow an organism to persist[7]. Intentionality, in this sense, becomes the intellectual process of *understanding* these conditions and how they relate to the agent.

To explain logic's relationship with creativity, we must explore how environmental complexity affects goal-oriented behavior. The environment is constituted by emergent structures of varying complexity; the agents depend on visual cues from this environment to produce actions in order to preserve their structure. In our simulation, the agents "predict" the environment by generating random actions to begin with, and, over a lifetime learn to associate the correct actions to each perceptual stimuli. When the world becomes more complex, it has two major implications for the agents: The diversity of perceptual stimuli greatly increases, meaning that the domain of plans with which the agents can associate perceptual cues increases. Secondly, as the environment is not highly repetitive, the agents must produce behavior to meet this diversity; different plans apply to different problems (or multiple plans can apply to the same problem). This was clearly demonstrated in the results of our experiment. With respect to this relationship between the environment and plans, it can be stated that the plans are reflecting the architecture of the environment. Over time, evolution provides the agents with mechanisms to produce plans, without direct control over the plans themselves. Over the lifetime of individual agents, these mechanisms are fine-tuned to match the specific circumstance and reflect the environment more accurately. If the plans are not coherent with the specific circumstance they are presented in, they are *illogical* or *irrational;* they fail to comply with the agent's goals. It can consequently be stated that logic is bound in the coherence of the *plans* (behavior) and the *goals* (or environmental conditions) that the plans are intended to fulfill.

At this point we've established that plans are predictions, as well as reflections, of environmental organization. Even though organisms are not very advanced, the correlation between environmental organization, goals, and behavior imply that the organisms' cognitive system has an (implicit) understanding of the environment. In our experiment, however, they have no *internal* mechanism to understand, which presents an obvious evolutionary disadvantage; without an internal representation, the cause for a complex emergent structure's behavior is *perceptually invisible* and *unpredictable* to the organism. In other words, the cognitive mechanism has to experimentally try out different kinds of plans in order to become more adept at fulfilling goals. An internal representation of an emergent structure's constituent components and their interactions would be needed to accurately predict its behavior[8].

From an evolutionary perspective it can be assumed that, with increased complexity, natural organisms evolve more advanced methods of prediction, allowing them to represent structures internally and simulate or imagine environmental events. An internal representation of an emergent structure enables a deeper *understanding* of that structure, and hence, a more accurate prediction and increased chance of survival. Understanding can be equated with that of explanation (Baas & Emmeche, 1997). Using the simulation of this chapter as an example, we can *explain* that a brown cell turns green because it has a certain number of green neighbors surrounding it. Moving up a level of complexity, we can *explain* the group behavior of the cells by reference to the function of each individual cell, and so forth. If the agents in our simulation would be capable of understanding why (or in what context) the food appears (green cells)—they could predict the overall behavior of the structures that emerge (and decrease the number of random plan genera-tions). Instead of wasting energy following the food, for example, they could intentionally select a spot to sit down and wait for the arm of a spiral to come to them (a creative solution).

Following this line of thought, it is more than likely that mechanisms of internal representations adopt the emergent properties of the environment. Imagination, human's most valued creative posession, is possibly an advanced simulator of emergent phenomena. Such spontaneous generation of new (and surprising) ideas, from components or ideas that otherwise did not appear to present any novelty, has been noted in research as similarities between creativity and emergence (Gero, 1996; Liu, 1996).

Future Trends

Advances in computer science are enabling simulations of increasingly complex systems. With such powerful tools at hand, it is only natural that we continue developing methods for exploring the potential origins and nature of intelligence. There are many aspects of creativity which remain unexplored; the premise of this chapter is creativity in its most primitive forms, leaving out questions of how mechanisms of more advanced organisms contribute to, and affect overall, creative abilities.

Explaining and exploring cognition in terms of simpler organisms is gain-ing support in the scientific community, and our experiments suggest that this might provide us with a better foundation for explaining high-level intelligence as complex systems. We believe the same applies to creativity. The emphasis should be on exploring how more advanced mechanisms of cognition are related to creativity, and how such relationships are brought about by evolution.

It is important to start attempting the unification of various aspects of intel-ligence; we have spent the last decades dissecting and separating the mecha-nisms involved and now it is time to put the pieces back together and explain how they work in unison. Complex systems simulations are an imperative for studying how creative functions of organisms are interrelated and, should emergence prove as crucial to this explanation as we propose, they are close to indispensable.

Conclusion

We presented an explanation for the hypotheses that creativity is evolutions answer to environmental complexity and that logic and creativity co-evolve as dictated by emergent, structural coherence. Using emergence and autopoieses as a foundation, we defined creativity—presenting a unifying framework for the related cognitive concepts of perception and action, goals, logic and insanity, understanding and imagination. The theoretical arguments are in their initial stages, but offer much potential for further investigation and experimentation, especially in terms of computer simulations.

Relatively complex creatures are presented in the chapter's described experiment, which evolve within worlds with emergent environmental properties. The creatures were modeled after natural insects, utilizing essential cognitive mechanisms such as visual perception, memory and planning mechanisms, which was important for explaining and defining the concept of creativity. Cellular automata proved useful for simulating environmental emergence and quantifying the complexity of emergent worlds.

The artificial creatures in the experiment showed increased diversity of behavior in overly complex worlds, maintaining little or no logicality as to when plans were applied. The results support our hypotheses, suggesting that environmental complexity and organization affects the evolution of creativity to a high degree.

Future work using the simulation framework in this chapter will involve improvements of the creatures' cognitive system, and (a) increasing the gene pool and number of generations in each simulation run (it is not uncommon that similar experiments run thousands of generations), (b) trying more types of worlds of different complexity levels. We also note that the custom cognitive architecture used here might possibly be too limited to allow the creatures to adapt to worlds of high complexity, and that more robust solutions, such as artificial neural networks, might offer a better solution.

Acknowledgment

I would like to thank the following individuals for their advice and continued support: Dr. Kristinn R. Thórisson, Dr. Hannes Högni Vilhjálmsson, and Dr.

Yngvi Björnsson of Reykjavík University's artificial intelligence laboratory, the Center for Analysis and Design of Intelligent Agents.

References

Adams J. (1980). *Conceptual blockbusting*. New York: Norton.

Antony, A., Salzberg, C., & Sayama, H. (1998). A closer look at the evolutionary dynamics of self-reproducing cellular automata. *Selection*, June, Volume 2.

Baas, N. A., & Emmeche, C. (1997). On emergence and explanation. *Intellectica*, (25), 67-83. Retrieved June 28, 2004, from http://www.utc.fr/arco/publications/ intellectica/n25/25_04_Baas.pdf

Beer, R. D. (2004). Autopoiesis and cognition in the game of life. *Artificial Life, 10*, 309-326.

Boden, M. A. (2004). *The creative mind: Myths and mechanisms*. New York: Routledge.

Boden, M. A. (1995). Creativity and unpredictability. *Stanford Education and Humanities Review, 4*(2).

Carruthers, P. (2002). Human creativity: Its evolution, its cognitive basis, and its connections with childhood pretence. *British Journal for the Philosophy of Science, 53*. Retrieved May 19, 2004, from http://www.philosophy.umd.edu/people/faculty/pcarruthers/Creative-thinking.htm

Chan, P., & Wyeth, G. (1999). Self-learning visual path recognition. Proceedings of the Australian Conference on Robotics and Automation (pp. 44-49), Brisbane.

Collet, T. S., & Collet, M. (2002). Memory use in insect visual navigation. *Nature Review, 3*, July.

Gabora, L. (2005). Creative thought as a non-Darwinian evolutionary process. *Journal of Creative Behavior, 39*(4), 65-87.

Gero, J. S. (1996). Creativity, emergence, and evolution in design: Concepts and framework. *Knowledge-Based Systems, 9*(7), 435-448.

Giurfa, M., & Menzel, R. (1997). Insect visual perception: Complex abilities of simple nervous systems. *Current Opinion in Neurobiology, 4*(7), 505-513.

Godfrey-Smith, P. (2001). Environmental complexity and the evolution of cognition. In R. Sternberg & J. Kaufman (Eds.), The evolution of intelligence (pp. 233-249). London: Lawrence Elrbaum Associates.

Holland, J. H. (1998). Adaptation in natural and artificial systems. Cambridge, MA: MIT Press.

Liu, Y. (1996). *"What" and "Where" is design creativity: A cognitive model for the emergence of creative design.* Paper presented at the IDATER 1996 Conference, Loughborough, UK.

Madina, D., Ono, N., & Ikegami, T. (2003). Cellular evolution in a 3D lattice artificial chemistry. In W. Banzhaf et al. (Eds.), *Paper presented in the proceedings of ECAL 03* (pp. 59-68). Dortmund: Springer.

Martindale, C., & Greenough, J. (1973). The differential effect of increased arousal on creative and intellectual performance. Journal of Genetic Psychology, 123, 329-35.

Maturana, H. R., & Varela, F. J. (1973). Autopoiesis: The organization of the living. In H. R. Maturana & F. J. Varela (Eds.), Autopoiesis and cognition (pp. 59-138). Boston: Reidel.

Mumford, M. D., Mobley, M. I., Uhlman, C. E., Palmon, P. R., & Doares, L. M. (1991). Process analytic models of creative capacities, Creativity. Research Journal, 4, 91-122.

Möller, R. (2000). Insect visual homing strategies in a robot with analog processing. Biological Cybernetics, 83, 231-243.

Pollert, L. H., Feldhusen, J. F., Van Mondfrans, A. P., & Treffinger, D. J. (1969). Role of memory in divergent thinking. Psychological Reports, 25, 151-56.

Root-Bernstein, R. (1988). Discovering. Cambridge, MA: Harvard University Press.

Rubenson, D. L., & Runco, M. A. (1995). The psychoeconomic view of creative work in groups and organizations. Creativity & Innovation Management, 4, 232-41.

Runco, M. A. (2004). Creativity. *Annual Review of Psychology, 55*, 657-687.

Runco, M. A. (1999c). Time for creativity. *Encyclopedia of creativity.* San Diego, CA: Academic, 659–63.

Salzberg, C., Antony, A., & Sayama, H. (2004). Complex genetic evolution of self-replicating loops. *Artificial Life IX: Proceedings of the Ninth*

International Conference on the Simulation and Synthesis of Living Systems (pp. 262-267), MIT Press.

Taylor, C. W. (1988). Various approaches to the definition of creativity. In R. J. Sternberg (Ed.), The nature of creativity (pp. 99-124.), Cambridge University Press.

Thórisson, H. T. (2004). A framework for exploring the evolutionary roots of creativity. Proceedings of the European Conference on Case-Based Reasoning 2004 (ECCBR 2004) Workshops (pp. 179-190). Madrid: Complutense University of Madrid.

van Duijn, M., Keijzer, F., & Franken, D. (2006). Principles of minimal cognition: Casting cognition as sensorimotor coordination. *Adaptive Behavior, 14*(2), 157-170.

Weir, A. A. S., & Kacelnik, A. (2006). A new caledonian crow (corvus moneduloides) creatively re-designs tools by bending or unbending aluminium strips. Animal Cognition. Retrieved September 2006, from http://users.ox.ac.uk/~kgroup/publications/pdf/WeirKacelnik_06_bend_unbend.pdf

Wiggins, G. (2006). A preliminary framework for description, analysis and comparison of creative systems. Journal of Knowledge Based Systems, 19(7), 449-458

Wolfram, S. (2002). A new kind of science. Champain, IL: Wolfram Media.

Endnotes

[1] See section on *Control Network* in this chapter & Figure 3 in Thórisson (2004), figure not reproduced here.

[2] Creature interactions would add another dimension of complexity to the world.

[3] This method of insect associative-memory is often referred to as the "snapshot hypothesis."

[4] In prior simulations, we included a mechanism for using an old plan unmodified. However, this did not change the overall results in our experimentation (see Results & Interpretation).

⁵   Note that we speak of logicality and not of efficiency, as plans can potentially be logical but still inefficient.

⁶   This generalization is sufficient for what is discussed here; At higher levels of complexity, there are quite possibly additional factors to consider.

⁷   Primitive cognitive systems can fulfill *goals* without direct knowledge or understanding that they are doing so, such as the agents in this chapter's simulation.

⁸   Note that even without the ability to *visualize* turn of events, a basic mechanism to produce actions that correlate with the environment serves the same purpose at a more primitive level.

Chapter VI

Solving the Sensory Information Bottleneck to Central Processing in Adaptive Systems

Thomy Nilsson, University of Prince Edward Island, Canada

Abstract

Information bottlenecks are an inevitable consequence when a complex system adapts by increasing its information input. Input and output bottlenecks are due to geometrical limits that arise because the area available for connections from an external surface always exceeds the area available for connections to an internal surface. Processing of the additional information faces an internal bottleneck As more elements increase the size of a processor, its interface surface increases more slowly than its volume. These bottlenecks had to be overcome before more complex life forms could evolve. Based on mapping studies, it is generally agreed that sensory inputs to the brain are organized as convergent-divergent networks. However, no one has previously explained how such networks can conserve the location and magnitude of any particular stimulus. The solution to a convergent-divergent network that overcomes bottleneck problems turns out to be surprisingly simple and yet restricted.

Introduction

To improve adaptation to the environment by adding sensors, complex systems need to import the additional information without overcrowding their processors with more connecting pathways. Any interface between an external surface and the surfaces of inside structures always faces a potential bottleneck due to geometry. The external surface can always extend more finite paths than can be accommodated by the surface of an internal structure. Biological systems cannot overcome this bottleneck simply by using smaller connecting pathways because smaller dendrites and axons conduct nerve impulses more slowly. More information is useful only if it is also timely.

Adaptation by accessing more information produces bottleneck problems that do not end once the inputs have been internalized. A slightly different geometrical constraint now comes into play. The surface area available for connecting one structure to another grows with the square of each structure's linear dimensions, while the space for elements within a structure increases with the cube of those dimensions. This can create intraprocessor bottlenecks. Animals reduce this problem by structuring their processors as sheets. However, they can not avoid the consequences of additional information requiring additional processing elements. Larger brains result in longer distances over which to send information from region to region. The need for information that is timely requires larger internal pathways, which add to the intraprocessor bottleneck problem since space is limited.

Finally, achieving a greater variety of behaviors on the basis of the additional information may require a greater number of processor outputs to control a greater number of external effectors. The system now faces a third bottleneck that is the reverse of the problem encountered by importing more information. At a more general level, all three types of bottlenecks can be considered as a single problem of how to connect one set of elements to another set using fewer connecting paths than the number of elements. Until a solution to this fundamental bottleneck problem was found, the evolution of more complex biological systems was stalled.

The evolution of a convergent-divergent organization of animal sensory systems is generally acknowledged to solve the input bottleneck. This solution uses spatial multiplexing to convey information from many receptors with only a fraction as many nerve fibers. Yet there appears to be no explanation of how such systems can keep track of which receptor is stimulated. This chapter explains how that is possible.

Neural networks modeled on ordinary computer spreadsheets show how convergent-divergent organizations of sensory systems can solve the general bottleneck problem simply by dendritic and axonal branching. They conserve source location without using tags or feedback. They also convey source magnitude and are damage tolerant. Trial-and-error modelling suggests that there is only one basic branching solution for a linear array of sources, and it is limited to an 8-to-1 convergence. Another solution exists for two-dimensional source arrays, and it is limited to a 16-to-1 convergence.

Hopefully presenting these solutions will lead either to a proof that there is only one basic method for each type of array and its corresponding limit, or to other branching solutions. As is, these solutions may contribute to a better understanding of how information is transmitted in sensory and cognitive systems and to solving information bottlenecks in other complex systems. Implications of these convergent-divergent networks for the evolution of intelligence in biological systems and some possible technical applications are discussed.

The Problem

When all else fails, Uncle Remus' Brer Rabbit can always escape Brer Fox by running through the briar patch (Harris, 1955). Brer Fox would be shredded trying to follow. Real rabbits may not be as smart as Brer Rabbit is portrayed in these children's stories, but they share a sensory processing advantage. Motion pictures of rabbits running through bushes reveal them bobbing and twisting to dodge the branches. Evidently they have a fine sense of touch that is rapidly employed. Their survival depends on this ability.

Weddell, Taylor, and Williams (1955) found rabbits a most convenient species for studying the peripheral tactile sensory system. The large ears could be transilluminated for *in vivo* microscopic examination of the sensory and neural structures. They found that a square centimeter of skin had some 2000 sensory hair cells. This should give rabbits a fine sense of touch. However, a moment's reflection reveals a serious problem. The entire ear would have about 1/2 million hair cells. How could rabbits get all those nerve fibers from the ear, not to mention the rest of their body, into a tiny brain and still have room for some neurons to process the information?

Conceivably, it would be possible using very fine unmyelinated nerve fibers to transmit the information. However, it is not enough to get the information to the brain. It must get there fast to be effective. Table 1 illustrates this problem. Small unmyelinated dendrites and axons conduct nerve impulses so slowly that a rabbit running at 20 km/hr would travel nearly a meter before the touch information reached its brain. Large, fast-conducting axons could get the information there before the rabbit has travelled a centimeter, but the diameter of 100,000 such fibers would exceed 30 cm. It is not possible for rabbits to provide each hair with a suitable pathway of its own to the brain.

This problem is resolved by Weddell et al.'s (1955) finding that there were only about 6,500 myelinated dendrites entering the ear. Physiological recordings from these dendrites revealed that each was connected to some 80 hair cells. Yet this convergent organization leads to another problem: How can the brain then tell which hair gets bent? Obviously there has to be some way or there would be no advantage to having all those hairs.

The means to an answer was revealed as further examination found that each hair was in fact connected to four dendrites from separate neurons. Since this

Table 1. Diameter of a nerve bundle required to carry a nerve fiber for each of the 100,000 hairs on a rabbit's ear, and how far a rabbit would travel at 20 km/hr during the delay between when a hair is touched and the information reaches its brain—for small and large nerve fibers.

FIBER TYPE	DIAMETER OF SINGLE FIBER	DIAMETER OF 100,000 FIBERS	IMPULSE SPEED	DELAY	DISTANCE TRAVELLED @ 20 km/hr
	(:m)	(cm)	(m/sec)	(sec)	(cm)
SMALL:	0.5	1	0.5	0.15	83
LARGE:	20	>30	90	0.002	<1

divergence of information from each receptor reduces the overall convergence from 80-to-1 to 20-to-1, the divergence must be necessary. A clue to the role of divergence arises from their observation that the dendrites connected to any given hair cell followed diverse routes to exit the ear. Weddell et al. suggest that divergent paths avoid cross-talk between fibers responding at the same time. Brown et al. (2000) find that cats have a similar convergent-divergent organization of their peripheral tactile system. Continuation of this convergent-divergent organization into the somatosensory cortex is related to spatial acuity of cats (Brown, Koerber, & Millecchia, 2004) and to the fine grain of somatosensory receptive fields in monkeys (Rausell, Bickford, Manger, Woods, & Jones, 1998). Thus, the brain must somehow use the responses in many divergent fibers to determine which hair gets bent despite the high degree of peripheral convergence.

The problem is not peculiar to the tactile system. The human eye has over 100 million photoreceptors, but the optic nerve has only some 1.2 million axons (Polyak, 1957). Even in the fovea where there is a one-to-one ratio of receptors to ganglion cells, there is both convergence of several receptors connecting to a single ganglion cell and divergence of each receptor connecting to several ganglion cells (Dacey, 2004). Nevertheless, visual acuity can equal and even be finer than the width of a single receptor (e.g., Blake & Sekuler, 2006).

Background

Convergent-Divergent Networks

To solve the information bottleneck, a convergent-divergent organization of neural branching is generally acknowledged as a fundamental property of most sensory systems (e.g., Guyton, 1991; Rosenzweig, Breedlove, & Watson, 2005; Uttal, 1973). In the periphery, convergence predominates with the number of receptors greatly exceeding the number of afferent pathways. Once sensory information passes the thalamus, a predominantly divergent organization of connections from these pathways to many cortical neurons restores receptor specificity. Figure 1 illustrates the general concept of a convergent-divergent system. Upon reaching the cortex, information conveyed by a convergent-divergent sensory system somehow indicates which

Figure 1. The general concept of a convergent-divergent information trans-mission system. Many INFORMATION INPUTS *are provided to some type of* CON-VERGENT ENCODER, *which processes the information and sends it along a few* CONNECTING PATHWAYS. *A distant* DIVERGENT DECODER *spreads the information from the* PATHWAYS *to as many* OUTPUTS *as there are sources. The information from any particular* INPUT *goes to an* OUTPUT *corresponding to that source. (copyright by author, printed with permission)*

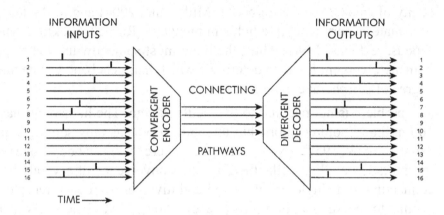

receptor was the source. It is certainly not obvious how convergent-divergent branching reveals the source, and the acknowledgments do not explain how this can happen.

How can receptor location be maintained through the bottleneck of a few connecting fibers? Any general answer pertaining to biological systems must recognize that all nerve impulses are the same regardless of the initiating source. While temporal patterns of nerve impulse trains could encode receptor specificity, this seems an unlikely solution to the bottleneck problem since temporal patterns are needed to carry qualitative information such as magnitude of receptor response. It is also possible that feedback loops could be used to decode which receptor is active as suggested by Goldberg, Cautwenberghs, and Andreou (2001). However, reliance on feedback would delay using the information and require more connections to the periphery.

This chapter explains how convergent-divergent encoding and decoding can transmit information from many receptors across a fractional number of connecting paths simply by using certain neural branching patterns and connecting weights. Such nets passively achieve a form of spatial multiplexing without either adding information to identify the sources or waiting for feedback confirmation.

Conserving Input Location

Compacting information from many "receptors" simply by connecting them to a single "afferent neuron" would make it impossible to tell which receptor was being stimulated. Convergence must be accompanied by divergence to conserve receptor identity. Both types of branching are evident in the afferent connections of the retina and lateral geniculate nucleus of the visual (Reid & Usrey, 2004) and tactile (Brown et al., 2000) sensory systems. The key is a neural branching pattern that has a different number of connections or branch weights between each receptor and two or more afferent neurons. Physiologically, different weights can be achieved by the number of dendritic branches and by the number of pre- and post-synaptic structures within a single synapse. Weighted branching can produce different response levels in two or more afferent fibers depending on which receptor is stimulated.

Now consider the divergence of connections from the afferent nerve fibers to a larger set of "cortical neurons" that correspond to individual receptors. That divergence must be accompanied by some convergence so that each afferent fiber connects to more than one cortical neuron. Otherwise, all cortical neurons connected to the same afferent fiber would have the same output—nothing would be accomplished by the divergence. Both convergent and divergent branching is evident in connections from the lateral geniculate to the visual and somatosensory cortex (Alonso & Swadlow, 2005). Mirroring the branching pattern for convergent encoding, each cortical neuron receives a different number of branches from each afferent fiber. This produces a different response strength in a cortical neuron depending on which afferent fibers are active.

In response to stimulation of a single receptor input, the output of such convergent-divergent systems is more complex than what is produced when each receptor has its own pathway. Divergence results in many cortical neurons responding to stimulation of a single receptor. Convergence results in a different cortical response strength depending on which receptor is activated. With the correct branching organization, the cortical neuron with the maximum response will be the one whose location corresponds to the location of the stimulated receptor.

Conserving Input Strength

The ability of convergent-divergent branching networks to also transmit the magnitude of an input is essential to convey *what* has happened as well as *where* something has happened (e.g., Sheth & Shimojo, 2002). Neurons must convey stimulus strength by temporal patterns of impulses—typically firing faster to stronger stimuli. Since branching solutions just use multiplication and summation, doubling the stimulus strength not only doubles the output response but also doubles the difference between the maximum response and the next strongest response. Thereby convergent-divergent systems can conserve both receptor identity and stimulus magnitude.

Solution

A solution to the bottleneck problem occurred spontaneously in response to a student's question about the general convergent-divergent organization of sensory pathways. Intuitively, I sketched on the blackboard a simple linear array of inputs connected by a 2 and 1 branching pattern to the same number outputs with one pathway for every two receptors. Stimulating one receptor and counting the number of active intersections leading to each output produced a maximum at a location that corresponded to the input location. That went well, so I added "sketch an example" to my notes. Thinking that any symmetrical pattern of convergent and divergent branching would work, it seemed unnecessary to be more specific. A few years later, I sketched a pattern, but was embarrassed to find it did not work. Trying to get a branching pattern that would work, revealed that symmetry was not sufficient. Indeed many tedious sketches produced only one pattern that did work.

Some years after that I programmed this pattern in MicroSaint (1985). It worked but ran too slowly to be practical either for demonstration or further study. When classroom computer projectors became available, I made probability demonstrations for my statistics course using QuattroPro 4 (1987) spreadsheets. Could a convergent-divergent network be modeled on something as simple as a spreadsheet? Yes, and this enabled testing many configurations. Remarkably, there did seem to be only one basic pattern for successful convergent-divergent networks. Had something this basic not been discovered previously? Presented at a meeting of the Association for Mathematical Psychology (Nilsson, 2002), the model raised interested comments which suggested the solution was indeed novel.

Preparing a figure to explain the linear array model for this chapter, led to the idea to try making a convergent-divergent model that would handle inputs arrayed over a 2-dimensional surface. This would provide a more realistic solution to the sensory bottleneck problem encountered in the tactile and visual systems. The solution to a convergent-divergent system that operates on a 2-dimension array of inputs requires a 3-dimensional neural network. It will be easier to understand how this model works by first considering the principles of its operation using a model that operates on a linear array of inputs and outputs.

Linear Array Model

Basic Operation

To see how a convergent-divergent network can work just by branching weights, consider a linear array of n inputs with $n/2$ connections to a linear array of n outputs. Figure 2 shows how 8 INPUT cells $B, C, ..., I$ of such a network can send information to 8 OUTPUT cells, $B,'C,'... I,'$ using 4 CONNECTING PATHWAYS, $BC\text{-}BC,' DE\text{-}DE,' FG\text{-}FG,' and HI\text{-}HI.'$ There are twice as many INPUT cells as CONVERGENT cells $BC, DE, ... HI$. Each INPUT cell sends two branches to the nearest CONVERGENT cell and a single branch to the next nearest CONVERGENT cell. Each OUTPUT cell receives two branches from its closest DIVERGENT cell and a single branch from the next closest DIVERGENT cell. That is all that is required.

In Figure 2, the different number of branches between cells is literally indicated by single or double paths. Each branch independently conveys the full value of the response strength in its originating cell, which lies to the left in the diagram. (Subsequently it will be necessary to refer to the strength of such connections as "weights" to simplify explanation.) The strength of the response in any cell is the sum of what is received from the incoming branches. Thus CONVERGENT cells DE and FG have the values 2 and 1 respectively. These values are directly transmitted over the CONNECTING PATHWAYS to DIVERGENT cells DE' and $FG.'$ Because OUTPUT cell E' receives two inputs of 2 from

Figure 2. Schematic for a linear array of inputs and outputs with a two-to-one and one-to-two convergent-divergent system. It sends information along half as many CONNECTING PATHWAYS as there are INPUTS and OUTPUTS. Entering a value of 1 into INPUT cell E produces the values 0, 2, 4, 5, 4, 2, 1, and 0 at OUTPUTS B,' C,' D,' E,' F,' G,' H' and I' respectively. The OUTPUT with the largest response corresponds to the INPUT that received the information. The COMPARISON NETWORK only passes on the OUTPUT with the maximum value, which in this example is the "5" from E.' Each path from a cell represents a neural branch that conveys the value in that cell. Note that some cells such as E and DE are connected by double lines - thus DE has the value of 2 since it has two branches from E each of which conveys E's value of 1. Note: lines that cross remain independent. (copyright by author, printed with permission)

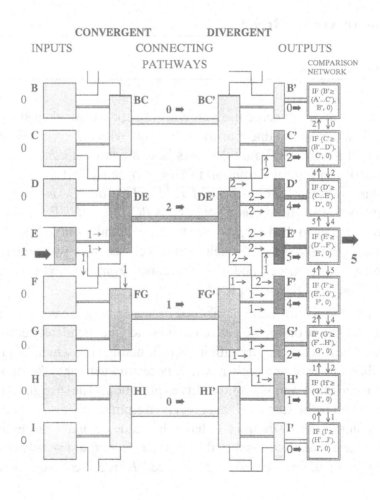

DE' plus an input of *1* from *FG'* it has the strongest output, *5*. The location of this maximum output at *E'* corresponds to the location of the INPUT cell *E* which received the stimulus.

Implementing the previous on a spreadsheet requires viewing matters from a different perspective. It is not possible for two or more cells in a spreadsheet to "send" their contents to a third cell and expect to find the sum of their contents in that cell. Rather the third cell must be programmed to add the contents of the two "sending" cells. This results in a subtle but critical change in creating the CONVERGENT part of the network. From the perspective of information flow, branching from the INPUT cells is always asymmetrical: two branches to the nearest CONVERGENT cell and one branch to the next-nearest. Yet from the perspective of the CONVERGENT cell where the mathematical operation resides, the incoming branching is always symmetrical: two branches from each of the two closest INPUTS and one branch from each of the two next-furthest IN-PUTS. The opposite occurs in the DIVERGENT section. Here the DIVERGENT cells "send" a symmetrical pattern of branches to the OUTPUT cells. However, the formulas in the OUTPUT cells require an asymmetrical summation from the nearest and next-nearest DIVERGENT cell.

Winner-Take-All Economics

Once a convergent-divergent system has achieved a distribution of output responses with a maximum at a certain cell that corresponds to the input, the system has achieved its task of overcoming the information bottleneck. From the topography of the maxima in such distributions, various simple and more complex receptive fields can be assembled to achieve the sensory processing for lines, edges, spatial frequency, etc. A general output of such distributions could suffice in principle to having transmitted the location and magnitude of the stimulus. However, an output that consisted only of the maxima would simplify the subsequent processing to produce cortical receptive fields and reflex arcs. That can be achieved by connecting the convergent-divergent network OUTPUTS to a comparison network that emits only the maximum output at its location. Such a network is readily obtained by lateral inhibition that produces a winner-take-all effect over a range that may be related to attention processes (Maass, 2000). This is illustrated by the right hand COMPARISON NETWORK in Figure 2. Each cell in that layer produces an output if its value exceeds the value of its neighboring cells. (The indicated calculation, "IF

(B:(A'...C'), B, 0)" represents the logic using minimal space. However, in QuattroPro the "" operation must be replaced by "=@MAX.")

Response Magnitude and Tolerance

In the spreadsheet model, input and output magnitude are represented as numbers. Figure 2 shows that an input value of "1" at E produces a maximum output of "5" at $E.$' Simple arithmetic along the branches shows that an input of "2" produces a maximum output of "10"; an input of "3" produces an output "15"; etc. Not only is the maximum output proportional to the input by a factor of "5," the difference between the maximum output and the next largest output equals the input. This shows that the convergent-divergent branching network can directly transmit an input's magnitude as well as its location.

Convergent-divergent networks are damage tolerant. In the example of Figure 2, if either of the two active CONNECTING PATHWAYS, DE-DE' or FG-FG,' are disabled, a maximum still appears at OUTPUTS that are close to the OUTPUT that corresponds to the location of the INPUT. With an input "1" at E, disabling DE-DE' produces two output maxima of "2" at F' and G'; disabling FG-FG' produces maxima of "4" at D' and E.' Networks with more layers of convergent and divergent branching (see below) are more tolerant of disabled connecting paths since they activate more paths for any given input.

More Convergence

Instead of connecting the CONVERGENT cells BC, DE ..., HI to DIVERGENT cells BC,' ..., HI' as shown in Figure 2, they could function as input cells to a second layer of CONVERGENT cells which one might label BCDE, FGHI, etc. This together with a corresponding second layer of DIVERGENT cells, BCDE,' FGHI,' ..., produces a convergent-divergent network with one CONNECTING PATHWAY for every four INPUTS and OUTPUTS. Likewise adding a third layer of CONVERGENT and DIVERGENT cells produces an 8-to-1 convergence ratio. See Figure 3. The effect of such cascaded layers can also be merged into single CONVERGENT and DIVERGENT layers with an equivalent, broader pattern of weighted branches. Because the resulting schematic needs to be large and is difficult to interpret even with colored paths to indicate the various number of branches, a figure to illustrate this possibility was not feasible.

Figure 3. Three layers of convergent and of divergent cells can be cascaded to produce an 8-to-1 convergence and still conserve stimulus location and magnitude. (copyright by author, printed with permission)

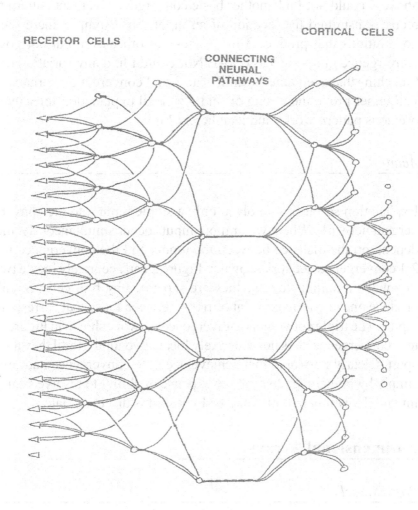

Can any number, x, of CONVERGENT and DIVERGENT layers be cascaded to achieve 2^x convergence ratios? No. Adding a fourth or more set of layers does not work. The output cell with the maximum response ceases to correspond with the input cell that is stimulated. The error patterns are predictable in terms of where the input stimulus occurs, but using that information still leaves some ambiguity and begs the purpose of the network.

Other Patterns and Limits?

Other than combinations of the binary, 2 and 1 branching pattern described above. I could not find another basic convergent-divergent pattern that correctly transmitted the location of an input. For example, there seem to be no solutions that produce 3-to-1, 5-to-1 or other even but not power-of-2 convergence ratios such as 6-to-1. Nor could I find any variation of 2 and 1 branching that overcame the limit of an 8-to-1 convergence. Perhaps someone will either prove me wrong or find a general explanation for why only the previous pattern works and its inherent limit.

Acuity

Explanation so far has involved only a single input into the convergent-divergent network. When two or more inputs occur simultaneously, the results depend on the distance between the inputs and the convergence ratio. The 2/1 convergence network shown in Figure 2 can accurately locate two INPUTS of equal strength as long as they are separated by four cells. Smaller gaps produce one or two maxima at OUTPUTS between those that correspond to the inputs. The triple convergence-divergence network shown in Figure 3 with 8-to-1 convergence does not accurately locate two inputs until they are 16 cells apart. Clearly networks that achieve accurate convergence and divergence simply by branching, do so at the expense of ability to resolve simultaneous inputs. (How this liability may be bypassed is discussed later.)

2-Dimensional Arrays

Basic Model

To model a convergent-divergent neural network that would operate on an array of inputs spread over a surface, I initially copied a spreadsheet version of Figure 2 to every other page in a 3-dimensional spreadsheet program, QuattroPro12. The convergent and divergent calculations were moved to the in-between pages and connections to input and output cells extended to both adjacent sheets. This proved awkward. So instead I placed the inputs as an INPUT ARRAY on one page, the CONVERGENT CALCULATIONS on the next page, the CONNECTING PATHWAYS on a 3rd page, the DIVERGENT CALCULATIONS on a

4th page, and the outputs along with comparison network calculations as an OUTPUT ARRAY on a 5th page. (It can all be done on just two pages, one for convergent calculations and one for the divergent, but having additional pages for inputs, pathways and outputs was easier to follow.) Figure 4 illustrates this organization for a convergent-divergent network operating on a sheet of inputs with a single level of convergent and divergent calculations.

It was immediately evident that the 2 and 1 branching used for linear arrays was no longer appropriate. Each INPUT cell now has four adjacent CONVERGENT CALCULATION cells to which it must "send" branches. To make the closest and next-closest branching weights inversely proportional to their distance required three weights that could no longer be simple whole numbers. Pythagoras' theorem was used to calculate the vector lengths or "Euclidian distance," and the reciprocal of that distance became the weight for that connection.

(There is no "distance" between sheets. Decreasing the branch weights in proportion to distance-squared does not work. Therefore, the spread of information in these neural networks is not analogous to a radiant effect. This indicates that convergent-divergent networks involve a selective branching structure as opposed to a simple spreading of the branches, which would produce a radiant-like reduction in terms of branch density as distance increased.)

As shown for the CONVERGENT cells on *Page 2* of Figure 4, the response from each INPUT cell is multiplied by one of these branching weights and summed with the results from the other INPUT cells connected to a given CONVERGENT cell. It is easier to visualize the weights from the perspective of the CONVERGENT cell because they are spatially symmetrical and the same for all CONVERGENT cells. Figure 5 shows the weights of the branches from the sixteen INPUT cells that send branches to each CONVERGENT cell. Note how a third weight of 0.24 is required for the next-closest set of INPUT cells C4, I4, C11, and I11 located at the corners of the twelve cells surrounding four cells closest to the CONVERGENT cell at F7.

On *Page 3,* the CONVERGENT cell locations become the CONNECTING PATHWAYS between the peripheral INPUT ARRAY cells and the central processor that lies beyond the OUTPUT ARRAY cells that form the limits of the convergent-divergent transmission model. The weights of the branches from these PATHWAYS to the OUTPUT ARRAY cells on *Page 5* look the same as the weights shown in Figure 5. The difference is that the centrally located PATHWAY at F7 would be connected to OUTPUT ARRAY cells at C4, E4, G4, ..., I11. However, this symmetric branching pattern can not be implemented in the spreadsheet model since spreadsheet cells can not "send" their contents to other cells.

Figure 4. How a neural network for a two-dimensional array of INPUTS and OUTPUTS with single degree of 4 to 1 convergence and 1 to 4 divergence was modeled on five spreadsheet pages. Except for the INPUT cells on Page 1, each active cell is connected to cells on the previous page by neural branches that have various weights such as the indicated values 0.71, 0.34, etc. used in the CONVERGENT and DIVERGENT CALCULATIONS on Pages 2 and 4. These weights reduce the strength of what is received from the branch's source cell. Stimulating the INPUT cell at location G8 on Page 1 produces a maximum response at location G8 on Page 4. In each indicated cell on Page 5 an "IF" function outputs the response value of the corresponding cell on page 4 if that value is larger than any of its neighbors. Page 1 and Page 5 are only connected by the PATHWAYS shown on Page 3. (copyright by author, printed with permission)

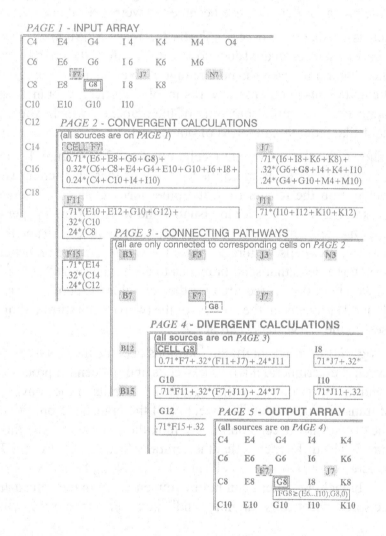

Figure 5. The weights used by CONVERGENT CALCULATION cells on Page 2 of Figure 4 for branches from Page 1 INPUTS to Page 3 CONNECTING PATHWAYS (shown shaded). The indicated weights are those used by CONVERGENT cell F7 for branches from INPUTS C4, C6, ..., I10 to PATHWAY F7. The weight for each branch is the reciprocal of that INPUT's distance to the PATHWAY. (Consider Page 2 to have zero thickness.) Every CONVERGENT cell uses the same weights for its INPUTS. (copyright by author, printed with permission)

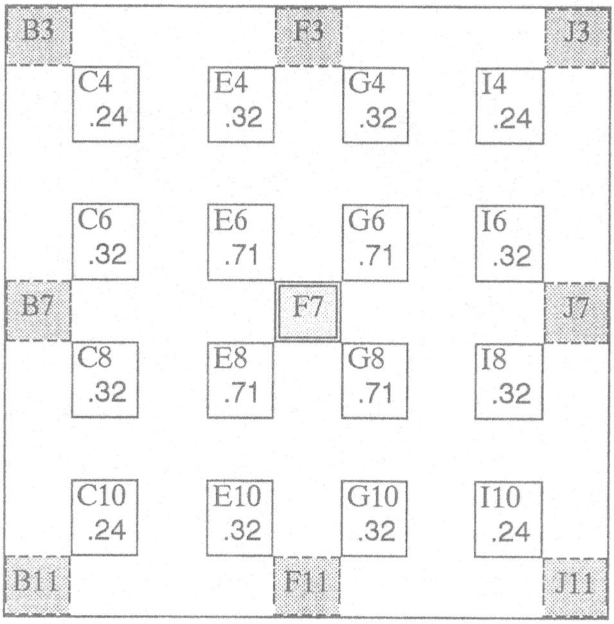

The DIVERGENT cells on *Page 4* of the network in Figure 4 operate by adding the contents from their two closest and two second closest CONNECTING PATHWAYS. The branches from each of these PATHWAYS require three different weights so that the contribution from each PATHWAY is inversely proportional to its distance from the OUTPUT CELL. See Figure 6. With respect to OUTPUT G8 in the upper illustration, the branch from its closest PATHWAY, F7, has a weight of 0.71; the two next closest PATHWAYS, F11 and J7, are weighted 0.32; and the furthest, J11, is weighted 0.24. Note that the weight of branches from each of these PATHWAYS varies depending on which OUTPUT is receiving their branches. This is shown in the lower illustration for OUTPUT I10.

Figure 6. Weights used by the DIVERGENT CALCULATION *cells on Page 4 of Figure 4 for neural branches from the* CONNECTING PATHS *(shown shaded) on Page 3 to the* OUTPUTS *on Page 5. There are four sets of asymmetrical weights depending on an* OUTPUT *cell's position with respect to its nearest* PATHWAY*. The upper diagram shows the weights for* OUTPUT *E6 of the branches from the adjacent* PATHWAY *F7 and the three other* PATHWAYS *(B3, F3, and B7) that surround F7. The lower diagram shows the weights for* OUTPUT *G8. (copyright by author, printed with permission)*

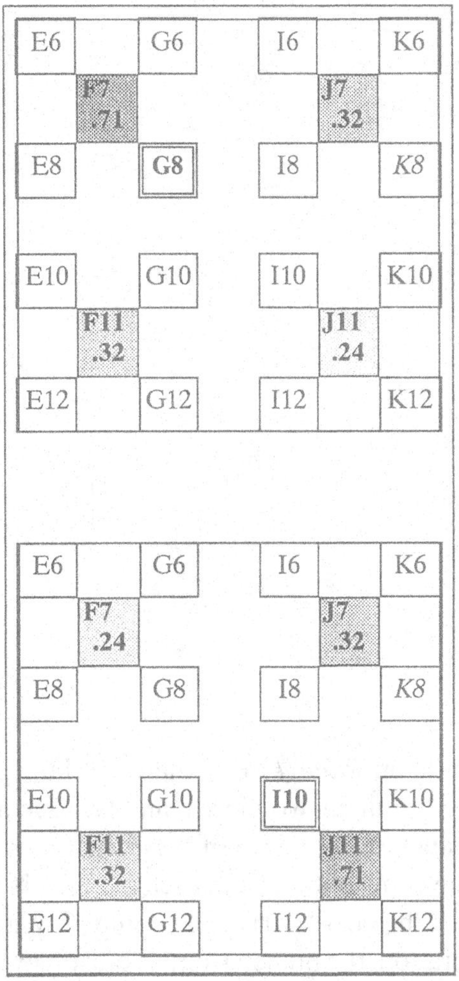

Figure 7. The distribution of output values across a portion of the 2-dimensional OUTPUT ARRAY on Page 5 of Figure 4 prior to the winner-take-all calculations in response to an input value of "1" entered at INPUT G8 on Page 1. Note that the maximum value, 0.76, occurs at OUTPUT G8, which corresponds to the location where the "1" was entered in the INPUT ARRAY. Only CONNECTING PATHWAYS F7, J7, F11, and J11 contribute to these outputs according to their distance from each OUTPUT cell as shown in the upper part of Figure 6. (copyright by author, printed with permission)

	A	C	E	G	I	K	M	O
2	0	0	0	0	0	0	0	0
	B3		F3		J3		N3	
4	0	.17	.22	.30	.27	.10	.07	0
6	0	.22	.50	.60	.45	.22	.10	0
	B7		F7		J7		N7	
8	0	.30	.60	.76	.60	.30	.16	0
10	0	.27	.45	.60	.53	.27	.15	0
	B11		F11		J11		N11	
12	0	.10	.22	.30	.27	.17	.07	0
14	0	.07	.10	.16	.15	.07	.06	0
	B15		F15		J15		N15	
16	0	0	0	0	0	0	0	0

Similar to the linear array model, the 2-dimensional output array of a convergent-divergent network is a distribution of response values across the array. Only the maximum value of that distribution corresponds to the location of an input. Figure 7 shows the distribution of values in the OUTPUT ARRAY prior to any comparative processing when a "1" has been entered at INPUT G8. The maximum value in this array correspondingly occurs at OUTPUT G8. The values in other OUTPUT cells decrease in proportion to their distance from this location.

As illustrated in Figure 4, a 3-dimensional neural net can transmit information from a sheet of INPUT cells along one-quarter as many CONNECTING PATHWAYS as the number of INPUTS and accurately represent in its OUTPUT ARRAY which INPUT was stimulated and the magnitude of that input. The cost of achieving this compressed transmission is that additional processing is needed to identify which OUTPUT has the information that specifically corresponds to the input. Subsequent winner-take-all calculations such as the "IF(G8 (C4... K12), G8, 0)" shown at OUTPUT G8 on *Page 5* of Figure 4 are needed at each OUTPUT to isolate the location and value of the OUTPUT cell having the largest value - in this example 0.76 at location G8.

Some Further Properties

As with the linear array model, greater convergence is possible by adding more layers of convergent-divergent branching before and after the connecting paths. On *Page 2* of Figure 4, instead of having the branches from the INPUT cells go directly to the CONNECTING PATHWAYS, their destination can be cells with a second set of similar CONVERGENT CALCULATION cells which then branch to the PATHWAYS. This double convergence uses only one-quarter as many PATHWAYS as the network in Figure 4. This results in a 16-to-1 convergence. A comparable doubling of the DIVERGENT cells in *Page 4* still conserves input location and magnitude.

A third layer of CONVERGENT and DIVERGENT cells on *Page 2* and *Page 4* would produce 64-to-1 convergence. However, errors now appear in localizing the input. Changing the branching weights changes where the errors occur with respect to the center and periphery of a 64 cell unit matrix of OUTPUT cells. As weights are changed, errors appear in the center of this matrix before they disappear in the periphery. This suggests that there is no solution. Sixteen-to-one convergence appears to be the practical limit for a 3-dimensional branching network operating on a sheet of inputs and outputs.

As could be expected, the spatial acuity of these 2-dimensional networks is closely related to the degree of convergence. The single degree 4-to-1 network shown in Figure 4 will locate two simultaneous inputs down to a gap of 4 INPUT cells. A second set of CONVERGENT and DIVERGENT cells will locate two inputs down to a gap of 14 cells.

Emerging Insights

Biological Implications

The 16-to-1 convergence obtainable simply by neural branching enables a substantial reduction of neural pathways needed to transmit information from many sources while maintaining the origin and magnitude of the information. Sensory systems such as the rabbit somatic system studied by Weddell et al. (1955) have a convergent ratio of 20-to-1 which is similar to the 16-to-1 ratio obtainable with the above branching model. Such savings in overall pathway size would also be applicable to major intracortical tracts which also must present bottlenecks to the flow of information between cortical areas. The neural branching evident at each end of such tracts seems capable of supporting a convergent-divergent organization (Bullier, 2004). Though these pathways also seem to involve feedback, that may serve other purposes such as refining and modifying the transmitted information rather than ensuring its accuracy.

Modelling these convergent-divergent systems may appear a daunting task and lead one to wonder how they could ever be achieved precisely enough biologically. In practice, once the basic branching pattern is defined, the rest is simply a matter of large scale copying easily done on spreadsheets. A gene, Pax6, has been found to not only initiate the development of eye structures (Kozmik, 2005), but also produces a topographic network of central connections (Vanderhaeghen & Polleux, 2004). The operation of this gene has been traced back to Coelenterates (jellyfish)—the simplest animals having a visual system (Nilsson, 2004). This suggests that all visual systems share a common origin dating back to the Precambrian era. While a parallel organization of individual receptor nerve fibers seems to have been adequate for simple animals, at some evolutionary point visual and tactile systems with multitudes of receptors and larger, more complex bodies must have encountered the bottleneck problem of how to convey all that information into a central nervous system. Then it is likely that a convergent-divergent variation of earlier parallel pathway systems was found adaptive.

However, more complex animals that adapted a convergent-divergent system faced a problem not present in parallel systems. In response to a single input, convergent-divergent networks produce a distribution of outputs that vary in magnitude. In the previous models, a layer of comparison calculations was added at the output layer to emit only the maximal output, which corresponds to the input. Neural network implementation of such calculations use lateral inhibition to achieve a "winner-take-all" effect (Maass, 2000). A single-input-to-single-output system would facilitate obtaining the reflex-arc learning of classical conditioning models such as those proposed by Sherrington, Pavlov, and Hebb (Hebb, 1949) that seem realizable with long-term potentiation effects (Bliss & Collingridge, 1993). Therefore, convergent-divergent sensory transmission may have provided the impetus for developing information comparison networks.

Convergent-divergent comparison networks could be capable of much more than facilitating reflex arcs. The combination of multiple interconnected information pathways with inhibitory comparison processing is similar to the networks proposed by Pribram (1991) to achieve holographic information processing which shares many properties associated with consciousness. Adding memory to such circuits can produce recognition systems (Deutsch, 1967; Eich, 1985; McLeod, Plunkett & Rolls, 1998). Might the convergent-divergent organization of the visual system have been the basis for evolving more complex information processing? Vertebrates are unique in having a visual nervous system that is part of their central nervous system. In mammals, the visual system develops in the neural tube *prior* to the forebrain.

Technological Possibilities

Branching solutions to spatial multiplexing seem applicable to electronic, optical, and even hydraulic information systems. Wire, optical fibers, beams, or pipes are information transmission media that are readily branched, and the detection and measurement of maxima in these media does not seem difficult. Multiplexing by means of branching directly in these media may prove advantageous to operations that must continuously adapt to changing conditions. Here are some specific application possibilities:

1. Like animal sensory systems, microcomputing circuits encounter bottlenecks whenever information has to be passed from one component to the next. Temporal multiplexing is presently used to overcome such bottlenecks. An ability to also incorporate spatial multiplexing could reduce the bottleneck problem by an additional factor of 16. This would seem important to enabling computing components to handle more information.

2.   Temporal multiplexing incurs a penalty of reducing operating speed by the multiplexing factor. For example, if an information transmission path has to be switched 4X to send the entire message, the final rate at which the complete information can be used is reduced by a factor of 4. Spatial multiplexing operates immediately. It does not need to take time out to break down a message into chunks for sequential transmission followed by reassembly. Therefore spatial multiplexing would be advantageous over temporal multiplexing to increase the speed of information processing.

3.   Spatial multiplexing can handle analog information directly. The relative strength of the output is proportional to that of the input. While temporal multiplexing can in principle also handle analog signals, switching introduces transients, which distort analog signals.

4.   The analog ability of spatial multiplexing would, in principle, enable it to work with any kind of information media: optical, hydraulic, acoustic, pneumatic. This suggests that spatial multiplexing could be directly applied in non-electronic control systems—for example to transmit hydraulic operations to a multitude of actuators along a few hydraulic lines.

Spatial and Temporal Tradeoffs

The major drawback to saving transmission paths by branching is the difficulty in handling more than one input simultaneously without unacceptable loss of spatial acuity. Since this problem has been resolved in the complex sensory systems of vertebrates, this may not be as severe a problem as it first appears. Notwithstanding inescapable neural conduction latency, the temporally discrete nature of neural impulses is smoothed by the combination of asynchrony of individual neural responses and variations in neural conduction speed. Multiplexing achieved by branching is continuous and does not require processing time. This can be a critical advantage when coherency is required for information processing (Cotterill, 1988). Continuous transmission systems can be considered to have infinite temporal resolution. The common wisecrack, "God invented time to prevent everything from happening at once." has significance here. Strictly speaking, no two things probably ever happen at *exactly* the same time. Thus a system that can transmit information continuously need not lack spatial acuity after all.

Conclusion

The bottleneck problem of how to transmit information from many sources without an overwhelming number of connecting pathways is common to most complex systems that seek more information to adapt to their environment. The problem is compounded in biological neural systems where transmission delays interact with pathway diameter and system size (Ringo, Doty, Demeter, & Simard, 1994). Unsolved, this bottleneck places severe restrictions on the viable size and complexity of adaptive systems.

Two biologically inspired neural network models for a convergent-divergent organization of an information transmission system have been presented. They enable information from many inputs to be transmitted along a fractional number of connecting paths while conserving which input was the source of the information. They solve the bottleneck problem using certain branching patterns or weights of the connections to and from the paths that transmit information from inputs to outputs. Their branching pattern makes them more tolerant of component failure than parallel transmission systems. The continuous operation of these models enables them to maintain the magnitude of the input and minimize transmission delays.

The inherent lack of complexity in how the elements of these models operate shows that spatial multiplexing can be achieved by neural networks that are as simple as models by McLeod et al. (1998) that are capable of learning and recognition. Adding these convergent-divergent transmission principles to the front-end of such cognitive models will enable future designers of complex adaptive systems to more realistically maximize their information handling abilities. These principles can also solve the need for biological modelling of how information from many sources can be economically transmitted from one region to another within a brain (Karbowski, 2003) and also from a brain to operate a large number of effectors such as individual muscle cells (Prescott, 2007).

In summary, solving the sensory information bottleneck has revealed the following nine general principles and a tenth speculative principle that enable complex adaptive neural systems to use more information:

1.   Obtaining more information from the environment requires connecting more sensors to the central processor. Processing the additional information requires a larger processor. Using the information may involve sending more information to control behavior.

2.   To be useful, the information must arrive promptly. This becomes more difficult as neural systems get larger and information must travel further.

3.   Biological neural systems are constrained by a tradeoff between conductor size and information conduction speed. Larger neurons conduct more rapidly, can support more branches, but take up more space than smaller neurons.

4.   Central processing of information is advantageous over distributed processing because it facilitates rapid integration and comparison of information from diverse sources, including memory, by reducing the distances information must travel.

5.   At some point in increasing the number of information pathways and consequent growth of system size, the number of information pathways that can enter a central processor faces a bottleneck due to space limitation in how many connections are possible at the surface of the processor. Faster biological pathways exacerbate this space limitation by being larger.

6.   Similar bottlenecks exists within a processor when large amounts of information need to be rapidly conveyed from one region to another and when large amounts leave the processor to control behavior.

7.   These bottlenecks can be solved by certain convergent-divergent branching organizations of the neural pathways. These organizations enable information from many sources to be conveyed by fewer connections while conserving the origin and magnitude of the transmitted information. (Biologically, the required additional branching is readily obtained as larger neurons are used to ensure promptness.)

8.   Unlike parallel transmission systems where information from each source is contained within a single pathway, convergent-divergent information networks distribute information from each source across many pathways that also carry information from other sources.

9.   Economical use of this distributed information may require the addition of comparison networks that identify the location and value of the distribution's maximum which identifies the original input in terms of a particular neural element. This facilitates combining the information from several inputs to form specialized elements such as receptive fields. It also facilitates channelling an input into reflex arcs and other behaviors.

10. (speculative). Modest modification of the "blueprint" for building comparative convergent-divergent information transmission networks may be combined with memory to produce recognition, learning, and consciousness.

References

Alonso, J. M. & Swadlow, H. A. (2005). The thalamocortical specificity and the synthesis of sensory cortical receptive fields. *Journal of Neurophysiology, 94, 26-32.*

Blake, R., & Sekuler, R. (2006). *Perception.* Toronto: McGraw-Hill.

Bliss, T. V. P., & Collingridge, G. L. (1993). A synaptic model of memory: Long-term potentiation in the hippocampus. *Nature, 361*, 31-39)

Brown, P. G., Harton, P., Millecchia, R., Lawson, J., Kunjara-Na-Ayudhya, T., Stephens, S., Miller, M. A., Hicks, L., & Culberson, J. (2000). Spatial convergence and divergence between cutaneous afferent axons and dorsal horn cells are not constant. *Journal of Comparative Neurology, 420*, 277-290.

Brown, P. G., Koerber, H. R., & Millecchia, R. (2004). From innervation density to tactile acuity, I. Spatial acuity. *Brain Research, 1011*, 14-32.

Bullier, J. (2004). Communications between cortical areas of the visual system. In L. M. Chalupa & J. S. Werner (Eds.), *The visual neurosciences.* (pp. 522-540). Cambridge, MA: MIT Press.

Cotterill, R. M. J. (1988). A possible role for coherence in neural networks. In R. M. J. Cotterill (Ed.), *Computer simulation in brain science* (pp. 164-188). Cambridge: Cambridge University Press.

Dacey, D. (2004) Origins of perception: Retinal ganglion cell diversity and the creation of parallel visual pathways. In M. S. Gazzaniga (Ed.), *The cognitive neurosciences III.* (pp. 281-301). Cambridge, MA: MIT Press.

Deutsch, S. (1967). *Models of the nervous system.* New York: John Wiley & Sons.

Eich, J. M. (1985) Levels of processing, encoding, specificity, elaboration, and CHARM. *Psychological Review, 92*(1).

Goldberg, D. H., Cautwenberghs, G., & Andreou, A. G. (2001). Probabilistic synaptic weighting in a reconfigurable network of VLSI integrate-and-fire neurons. *Neural Networks, 14*, 781-793.

Guyton, A. C. (1991). *Textbook of medical physiology.* Philadelphia: W. B. Saunders.

Harris, J. C. (1955). *The complete tales of Uncle Remus.* Boston: Houghton Mifflin.

Hebb, D. O. (1949). *Organization of behavior.* New York: Wiley.

Karbowski, J. (2003). How does connectivity between cortical areas depend on brain size? *Journal of Computational Neuroscience, 15*, 347-356.

Kozmik, Z. (2005). Pax genes in eye development and evolution. *Current Opinion in Genetics and Development, 15*(4), 430-438.

Levine, M. W. (2000). *Fundamentals of sensation and perception.* Oxford: Oxford University Press.

Maass, W. (2000). On the computational power of winner-take-all. *Neural Computation, 12*, 2519-2535.

McLeod, P., Plunkett, K., & Rolls, E. T. (1998). *Introduction to connectionist modelling of cognitive precesses.* Oxford: Oxford University Press.

MicroSaint [Computer program] (1985). Boulder, Colorado: Micro Analysis and Design.

Nilsson, D. E. (2004). Eye evolution: A question of genetic promiscuity. *Current Opinion in Neurobiology, 14*, 407-414.

Nilsson, T. H. (2002). *How acuity is conserved in convergent-divergent networks.* Paper presented at the meeting of the Association for Mathematical Psychology, Miami University, Oxford, Ohio.

Polyak, S. (1957). *The vertebrate visual system.* Chicago: University of Chicago Press.

Prescott, T. J. (2007). Forced moves or good tricks in design space? Landmarks in the evolution of neural mechanisms for action selection. *Adaptive Behavior, 15*, 9-31.

Pribram, K. H. (1991). *Brain and perception.* Hillsdale, NJ: Lawrence Erlbaum Associates.

QuattroPro 4 [Computer program] (1987) Scotts Valley, California: Borland International.

QuattroPro 12 [computer program] (2006) Ottawa: Corel Corporation.

Rausell, E., Bickford, L., Manger, P. R., Woods, T. M., & Jones, E. G. (1998). Extensive divergence and convergence in the thalamocortical projection to monkey somatosensory cortex. *Journal of Neuroscience*, *18*, 4216-4232.

Reid, R. C., & Usrey, W. M. (2004). Functional connectivity in the pathway from retina to striate cortex. In L. M. Chalupa & J. S. Werner (Eds.), *The visual neurosciences.* (pp. 673-679). Cambridge, MA: MIT Press.

Ringo, J. L., Doty, R. W., Demeter, S., & Simard, P. Y. (1994). Time is of the essence: A conjecture that hemispheric specialization arises from interhemispheric conduction delay. *Cerebral Cortex*, *4*, 331-343.

Rosenzweig, M. R., Breedlove, S. M., & Watson, N. V. (2005). *Biological psychology*. Sunderland, MA: Sinauer Associates.

Sheth, B. R., & Shimojo, S. (2002). Signal strength determines the nature of the relationship between perception and working memory. *Journal of Cognitive Neuroscience*, *15*, 173-184.

Uttal, W. R. (1973). *The neurobiology of sensory coding.* New York: Harper & Row.

Vanderhaeghen, P., & Polleux, F. (2004). Developmental mechanisms patterning corticothalamic projections: Intrinsic, extrinsic, and in between. *Trends in Neurosciences, 27*(7), 384-391.

Weddell, G., Taylor, D. A., & Williams, C. M. (1955). Studies on the innervation of skin, III: The patterned arrangement of the spinal nerves to the rabbit ear. *Journal of Anatomy*, *89*, 317-342.

Chapter VII

Complexity, Information, and Robustness:
The Role of Information "Barriers" in Boolean Networks

Kurt A. Richardson, ISCE Research, USA

Abstract

In this supposed "information age," a high premium is put on the widespread availability of information. Access to as much information as possible is often cited as key to the making of effective decisions. While it would be foolish to deny the central role that information and its flow has in effective deci-sion-making processes, this chapter explores the equally important role of "barriers" to information flows in the robustness of complex systems. The analysis demonstrates that (for simple Boolean networks at least) a complex system's ability to filter out (i.e., block) certain information flows is essential if it is not to be beholden to every external signal. The reduction of informa-tion is as important as the availability of information.

Introduction

In the information age, the importance of having unfettered access to information is regarded as essential—almost a "right"—in an open society. It is perhaps obvious that acting with the benefit of (appropriate) information to hand results in "better" actions (i.e., actions that are more likely to achieve desired ends), than acting without information (although incidents of "information overload" and "paralysis by (over) analysis" are common). From a complex systems perspective there are a variety of questions/issues concerning information, and its near cousin knowledge, that can be usefully explored. For instance, what is the relationship between information and knowledge? What is the relationship between information, derived knowledge, and objective reality? What information is necessary within a particular context in order to make the "best" choice? How can we distinguish between relevant information and irrelevant information in a given context? Is information regarding the current/past state of a system sufficient to understand its future? Complexity thinking offers new mental apparatus and tools to consider these questions, often leading to understanding that deviates significantly from (but not necessarily exclusive of) the prevailing wisdom of the mechanistic/reductionistic paradigms. These questions may seem rather philosophical in nature, but with a deeper appreciation of the nature of information and the role it plays in complex systems and networks, we can begin to design more effective and efficient systems to facilitate (rather than merely manage) information creation, maintenance, and diffusion.

The science of networks has experienced somewhat of a renaissance in recent years with the discovery of particular network topologies, or architectures, in natural and human systems. These topologies include both small-world (Watts & Strogatz, 1998) and scale-free networks (Barabási & Albert, 1999). Barabási (2001) has shown that the World Wide Web has a scale-free architecture, which essentially means that it has relatively few high-connected nodes (i.e., nodes containing many inputs and outputs) and relatively many low-connected nodes (i.e., nodes containing few inputs and outputs). However, there are significant limitations to network representations of real world complex systems. Barabási (2001) himself says that "The advances [in network theory] represent only the tip of the iceberg. Networks represent the architecture of complexity. But to fully understand complex systems, we need to move beyond this architecture and uncover the laws that govern the underlying dynamical processes, such as Internet traffic…"

Boolean network modeling is a relatively simple method to facilitate this move beyond mere architecture. Although the networks considered herein have random topologies (rather than scale-free or small-world) the modeling of such simple dynamical networks allows researchers to explore, albeit in a limited fashion, the emergent underlying dynamical processes of real systems such as the Internet.

In this chapter, I would like to examine one particular aspect of complex dynamical networks: How barriers to information and its flow are essential in the maintenance of a coherent functioning organization. My analysis will be necessarily limited. A very specific type of complex system will be employed to explore the problem, namely, Boolean networks. And, a rather narrow type of information will be utilized: a form that can be "recognized" by such networks. Despite these and other limitations, the resulting analysis has applicability to more realistic networks, such as human organizations, and useful lessons can be gleaned from such an approach. We shall see that such an approach may offer the possibility of complementing mechanistic approaches to the design of information systems—in which the most important characteristics are engineered—with approaches that allow certain characteristics to emerge from the interaction of the information system's components. The chapter begins with an introduction to Boolean networks and certain properties that are relevant to the analysis herein.

Boolean Networks: Their Structure and Their Dynamics

Given the vast number of papers already written on both the topology and dynamics of such Boolean networks, there is no need to go into too much detail here. The interested reader is encouraged to look at Kauffman (1993) for his application of Boolean networks to the problem of modeling genetic regulatory networks. A short online tutorial is offered by Lucas (2006), but the basics are provided herein.

A Boolean network, which is a particularly simple information system, is described by a set of binary gates $S = \{0,1\}$ interacting with each other via certain logical rules and evolving discretely in time. The binary gate represents the on/off state of the "atoms" (or, "agents") that the network is presumed to represent. So, in a genetic network, for example, the gate represents the state of a particular gene. The logical interaction between these gates would, in this case, represent the interaction between different genes. The state of a gate at the next instant of time ($t+1$) is determined by the k inputs or connectivity S_{ji}^{m} ($m=1,2,\ldots,k$) at time t and the transition function f_i associated with site i:

$$S_i(t+1) = f_i\left(S_{j_i^1}(t), S_{j_i^2}(t), \ldots, S_{j_i^k}(t)\right)$$

There are 2^k possible combinations of k inputs, each combination producing an output of 0 or 1. Therefore, we have 2^{2^k} possible transition functions, or rules, for k inputs. For example, if we consider a simple network in which each node contains 2 inputs, there are $2^2=4$ possible combinations of input - 00, 01, 10, 11 - and each node can respond to this set of input combinations in one of $2^{2^2} = 16$ different ways. Figure 1 illustrates a simple example. The figure shows not only an example network (a), but also its space-time evolution (b) and its phase space attractors (c) which will be discussed next. Figure 1d shows the sixteen different Boolean functions that can be created from two inputs.

The state, or configuration, space for such a network contains 2^N unique states, where N is the size of the network (so for the simple example shown, state space contains 64 states). Because state space is limited in size, as the system is stepped forward it will eventually revisit a state it has visited previously. Combine this with the fact that from any state the next state is unique (although multiple states may lead to the same state, only one state follows from any state), then any Boolean network will eventually follow a cycle in state space. As a result, state space (or phase space) is connected in a non-trivial way, often containing multiple attractors each surrounded by fibrous branches of states, known as *transients*. Figure 1c shows the state space attractors, and their associated basins, for the particular Boolean network shown in Figure 1a. The transition functions for each node were chosen randomly, but did not include the constant rules 0 (0000), or 15 (1111) as these force the node to be input-independent nodes with constant transition functions that do not change from their initial state.

Figure 1c shows the two attractors for this particular example: one period-3 attractor basin containing 56 states, and a single period-2 attractor basin containing the remaining eight states (a total of $2^5=64$ states). In this example,

Figure 1. A simple Boolean network (a) shows the set-up of a particular network with N=6. Each node is numbered 0 thru 5. The binary sequences in between the square brackets represent the Boolean function for each node. Note that nodes 2 and 5 are connected to themselves. (b) shows the space-time diagram for the evolving network. Each column shows the evolution of a particular nodes, and each row shows the overall network state at a particular time-step. In this case the network was seeded at t=0 with a random sequence. After an initial settling down period, the sequence converges of a period-3 cycle. (c) shows the two state space attractors that characterize this particular network: a period-3 (p3) and a period-2 (p2). (d) shows all the sixteen Boolean logic functions that can be constructed from two inputs depicted in the standard way with both look-up tables and machine state diagrams. In this study the two rules CONTR. (contradiction) and TAUT. (tautology) are excluded.

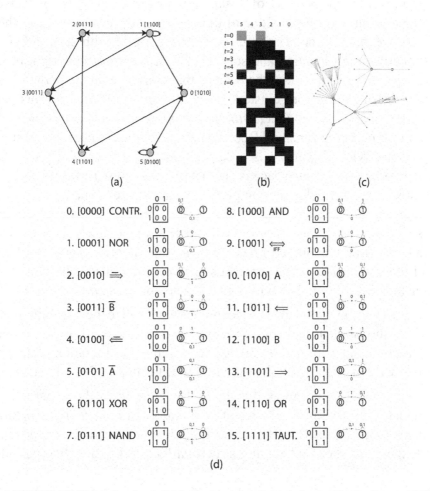

only five states actually lie on attractors and the remaining 59 lie on the transient branches that lead to these four cycle states. When a Boolean network is simulated, it is usually seeded with an initial random configuration. As the network is stepped forward one time-step at a time, there is an initial settling down period (sometimes referred to as the *relaxation time*) before the system converges onto a particular attractor. There are often many different routes to a particular attractor, and these are represented by the branching structures (or, transient branches) shown in Figure 1c. This relaxation period might be compared to the settling down period in human systems that occurs when a new strategy is implemented and people take time to find their place in the new strategy before the overall system stabilizes in one particular direction or another. Of course, this relatively stable period may only be temporary as adjustments to strategy are made in response to changing requirements often triggered by particular environmental conditions.

Figure 2a is another way of visualizing how state space is connected. Each shade of grey represents one of the two attractor basins that together characterize state space. The figure comprises a grid with state 000000 at the uppermost left position and state 111111 at the lowermost right position. It shows, for example, that the 8 states that converge on the period-2 attractor are distributed in four clusters, each containing two states. This particular representation is called a *destination map*, or *phase space portrait*, and we can see that even for small Boolean networks, the connectivity of state space is non-trivial. Figure 2b is a destination map for an $N=15$, $k=2$ Boolean network (whose state space is characterized by four attractors: 2p2, 2p3), to illustrate how quickly the complexity of state space connectivity, or topology, increases as network size, N, increases. The boundaries between different shades are known as *separatrices*, and crossing a separatrix is equivalent to a move from one attractor basin into another (adjacent) attractor basin (i.e., if the system is pushed across a separatrix then there will be a qualitative change in dynamic behavior—this is also known as *bifurcation*).

It is all well and good to have techniques to visualize the dynamics that results from the Boolean network structure (and rules). But how are a network's structure and its dynamics related? It is in the consideration of this question that we can begin to explore the role of information flows in such systems.

The potentially complex dynamics that arise from the apparently simple underlying structure is the result of a number of *interacting* structural feedback loops. In the Boolean network modeled to create the images in Figure 1, there are seven interacting structural feedback loops: two period-1, two

Figure 2. The destination maps for (a) the network depicted in Figure 1a (N=6, k=2), and (b) a particular N=15, k=3 network (the grid showing individual states is not included for clarity)

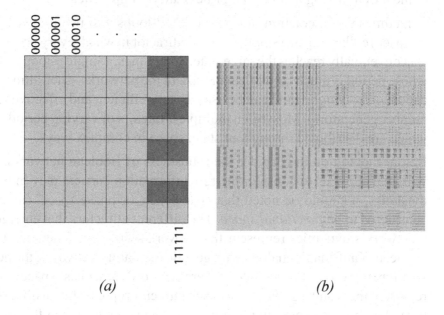

(a)   (b)

period-2, two period-3, and one period-5, or 2P1, 2P2, 2P3, 1P5 for short. The P5 structural loop in this case is: Node $0 \rightarrow 4 \rightarrow 3 \rightarrow 2 \rightarrow 1 \rightarrow 0$. It is the flow (and transformation) of information around such structural loops, and the interactions between different loops (or, inter-loop connectivity) that results in the two state space attractors in Figure 1c; 1p1, 1p3 for short (here I use "P" for structural, or architectural, loops and "p" for state, or phase space loops, or cycles). The number of structural P-loops increases exponentially (on average) as N increases, for example, whereas the number of state space p-loops increases (on average) in proportion to N (not $\sqrt{N}$ as Kauffman (1993) reported, which was found to be the result of sampling bias, Bilke & Sjunnesson (2002).

For networks containing only a few feedback loops, it is possible to develop an algebra that can relate P-space to p-space, that is, it is possible to construct some very simple and robust rules that relate a network's architecture to its function much in the same way as it is rather trivial (when compared to complex nonlinear dynamical systems) to build serial computers with particular functionality. However, as the number of *interacting* p-loops increases this particular problem becomes intractable very quickly indeed, and the development of a linking algebra (i.e., rules) utterly impractical.

Sometimes the interaction of a network's P-loops will result in state space (p-space) collapsing to a single period-1 attractor in which every point in state space eventually reaches the same state. Sometimes, a single p-loop will result whose period is much larger than the size of the network—such attractors are called *quasi-chaotic* (and can be used as very efficient and effective random number generators). Most often multiple attractors of varying periods result, which are distributed throughout state, space in complex ways.

Before moving on to consider the robustness of Boolean networks, which will then allow us to consider the role information barriers play in network dynamics, it should be noted that state space, or phase space, can also be considered to be *functional space*. The different attractors that emerge from a network's dynamics represent the network's different functions. For example, in Kauffman's analogy with genetic regulatory networks, the network structure represents the *genotype*, whereas the different phase space attractors represent the resulting *phenotype*, each attractor representing a different cell type. Another example might be in team dynamics in which the modes of forming, storming, norming, and performing are each represented in state space by a different attractor. A further example might be in computer network operations. Here again, different operational modes, including both stable and unstable (e.g., a crash) modes can be considered as different state space attractors. An appreciation of a system's state space structure tells us about the different responses a system will have to a variety of external perturbations (i.e., it tells us which *contextual archetypes* the system "sees" and is able to respond to).

Dynamical Robustness

The dynamical robustness of networks is concerned with how stable a particular network configuration, or operational mode, is under the influence of small external signals. Most information systems will exhibit a range of qualitatively different modes of operation. Only some of those modes will be desirable, and others (like system wide crashes) will be undesirable. An understanding of a system's dynamical robustness provides insights into which modes are most likely (i.e., which ones dominate state space), and how easily the system's behavior can be "pushed"—deliberately or not—into a different mode. In Boolean networks, we can assess this measure by disturbing an initial configuration (by flipping a single bit/input, i.e., reversing the state of one of the system's nodes) and observing which attractor basin the network then falls into (after some relaxation period). If it is the same attractor that follows from the unperturbed (system) state then the state is qualitatively stable when perturbed in this way. An average for a particular state (or, system configuration) is obtained by perturbing each bit in the system state, or each node, and dividing the number of times the same attractor is followed by the network size. For a totally unstable state the robustness score would be 0, and for a totally stable state the robustness score would be 1. The dynamical robustness of the entire network is simply the average robustness of every system state in state space. This measure provides additional information concerning how state space is connected in addition to knowing the number of cyclic attractors, their periods, and their weights (i.e., the volume of state space they occupy). By way of example, the average dynamical robustness of the network depicted in Figure 1a is 0.875 which means the network is qualitatively insensitive to 87.5% of all possible 1-bit perturbations.

More on Structure and Dynamics: Walls of Constancy, Dynamics Cores, and Modularization

As we have come to expect in complex systems research, there is always more to the story than what at first meets the eye. This is also the case for the relationship between network structure and dynamics. Although information flows (and is transformed) around the various structural networks, certain logical couplings "emerge" that force particular nodes into one state or another, keeping them in that state for as long as the network is simulated. In other words, once the network is initiated/seeded and run forward, after some seemingly arbitrary transient period (the relaxation time) some nodes cease to allow information to pass. These "fixed." or "frozen" nodes effectively disengage all structural feedback loops that include them—although these structural loops still exist, they are no longer able to cycle information continuously around them. As such we can refer to them as *non-conserving information* loops; information that is placed onto such loops will flow around the loop until a frozen node is reached, after which the information

Figure 3. The process of modularization in complex networks

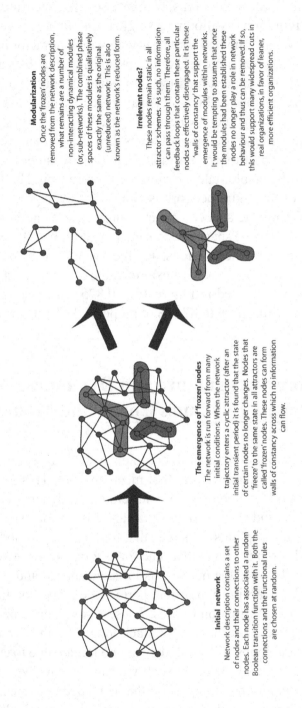

Modularization
Once the 'frozen' nodes are removed from the network description, what remains are a number of non-interacting dynamical modules (or, sub-networks). The combined phase spaces of these modules is qualitatively exactly the same as the original (unreduced) network. This is also known as the network's reduced form.

Irrelevant nodes?
These nodes remain static in all attractor schemes. As such, no information can pass through them. Therefore, all feedback loops that contain these particular nodes are effectively disengaged. It is these 'walls of constancy' that support the emergence of modules within networks. It would be tempting to assume that once the modules had been established these nodes no longer play a role in network behaviour and thus can be removed. If so, this would support many widespread cuts in real organizations, in favor of leaner, more efficient organizations.

The emergence of "frozen' nodes
The network is run forward from many initial conditions. When the network trajectory enters a cyclic attractor (after an initial transient period) it is found that the state of certain nodes no longer changes. Nodes that 'freeze' to the same state in all attractors are called 'frozen' nodes. These nodes can form walls of constancy across which no information can flow.

Initial network
Network description contains a set of nodes and their connections to other nodes. Each node has associated a random Boolean transition function with it. Both the connections and the functional rules are chosen at random.

flow is blocked. A number of such nodes can form *walls of constancy* through which no information can pass, and effectively divide the network up into non-interacting sub-networks (i.e., the network is *modularized*). This process is illustrated in Figure 3.

Nodes/Loop Types

The process is actually more complicated than what is depicted in Figure 3. When the occurrence of "frozen" nodes is examined more closely we find that some nodes are not frozen in all the different operational modes (attractors). As such, we can distinguish between four different types of information loop:

1. **Type1:** Those that contain frozen nodes (that are frozen to the same state, 0 or 1) in all modes of operation (attractors);

2. **Type2:** Those that contain the frozen nodes in all modes of operation, but the frozen state may differ from one mode of operation to another;

3. **Type 3:** Those that contain frozen nodes in some modes of operation, but may be active (i.e., contain no frozen nodes) in other modes—these act as non-conserving loops in some contexts, but as conserving loops in other contexts);

4. **Type 4:** Those that contain no frozen nodes in any modes of operation (i.e., information conserving loops).

Given that it is the existence of frozen nodes, or not, that determines whether an information loop is Type 1, 2, 3, or 4, we can also label nodes as Type 1, 2, 3, or 4 also. Throughout the rest of this chapter when we talk of frozen nodes, or non-conserving information loops, we are only concerned with Type 1 as these do not contribute to the gross characteristics of state space at all. But before moving on to consider the role of Type 1 nodes/loops at length I'd like to briefly mention the role of Types 2 and 3.

Assuming a particular network contains all types of nodes/loops, when the system is following different attractors, different sets of nodes/loops will be "active." As we shall see below, only the dynamic core (which comprises all types except Type 1 nodes/loops) contributes to the number and period of attractors in state space. However, the allocation of node/loop type is a global one in that we must consider the behavior of all nodes and loops in all modes of operation. If we consider the behavior of all nodes and loops in only one particular mode then each node becomes either frozen or not, and each loop becomes either conserving or non-conserving (i.e., Types 2 and 3 are effectively either Types 1 or 4 at the local attractor level). As a result, there exists another level of modularization. The modularization process previously discussed is the result of the emergence of only Type 1 nodes/loops and as such the modules identified in this way are the largest in size, but the fewest in number (because every operational mode—attractor type—is considered). However, for particular modes, there may be additional nodes that are frozen (and therefore a greater number of non-conserving loops) and so certain modules may actually divide ("modularize") further. In this localized scenario, although the *static structure* of the network (i.e., the pre-simulated structure) is the same in all modes of operation, the *emergent dynamic structure* is (potentially) different for each state space structure (attractor). Allen (2001) introduced the term *structural attractor,* which seems to be the same as the *emergent dynamic structure* discussed here. The relationship between structural attractors and state space attractors is complex (as one might expect). For example, the same structural attractors may account for different state space attractors (although in the case of Boolean networks I would expect those different state space attractors to be the same in most respects, such as period for example).

I will not explore the role of Type 3 and Type 4 nodes/loops further herein, but I suspect that the key to understanding the dynamics of (discrete) complex networks at both the global (state space wide) and local (for particular state space attractors) levels is through an understanding of how these different types form and interact.

The Emergence of a Dynamic Core

The identification of "frozen" nodes is non-trivial (and even "non-possible") before the networks are simulated. Although the net effect is the same as associating a constant transition function (i.e., contradiction or tautology) with a particular node, the effect "emerges" from the dynamic interaction of the structural feedback loops (and is often dependent on initial conditions). It is a rare case indeed that these interactions can be untangled and the emergent frozen nodes identified analytically beforehand.

As previously mentioned, these "frozen" nodes (Type 1) do not contribute to the qualitative structure of state space, or network function. A Boolean network characterized by a 1p3, 1p2 state space, like the one considered previously, will still be characterized by a 1p3, 1p2 state space after the (Type 1) frozen nodes are removed. In this sense, they don't appear to contribute the network's function—they do block the flow of information, but from this perspective have no functional role. Another way of saying this is that, if we are only concerned with maintaining the qualitative structure of state space (i.e., the gross functional characteristics of a particular network) then we need only concern ourselves with *information conserving* loops; those structural feedback loops that allow information to flow freely around the network. This feature is illustrated in Figure 4 where the state space properties of a particular Boolean network, and the same network after the non-conserving information loops have been removed (i.e., the network's "reduced" form), are compared. Although the transient structure (and basin weight) is clearly quite different for the two networks, they both have the same qualitative phase space structure: 2p4.

The process employed to identify and remove the non-conserving loops is detailed in Richardson (2005a). As network size increases, it becomes increasingly difficult to determine a network's state space structure. As such reduction techniques are not only essential in facilitating an accurate determination, but also in research that attempts to develop a thorough understanding of the relationship between network structure and network dynamics (as, already mentioned, only information conserving structural loops contribute to the network's gross functional characteristics). Reduction techniques basically sample state space and identify, which nodes are frozen to the same state (0 or 1) in *all* attractors (see the previous definition of Type 1 nodes). These nodes, and nodes that have no outgoing connections (and any connections associated with these nodes), are removed from the network description to form a "reduced" version. Another way of saying this is that all non-conserving information loops are identified and deactivated. What remains after this reduction process is known as the network's *dynamic core*. A dynamic core contains only information conserving loops. The majority of (random) Boolean networks comprise a dynamic core (which may be modularized) plus additional nodes and connections that do not contribute to the asymptotic dynamics of the network (i.e., the qualitative structure of state space). A full description of a system's dynamic core is the smallest description of the system that still contains the essence of what that system's function is: all other structure is superfluous.

Figure 4. An example of (a) a Boolean network, and (b) its reduced form. The nodes, which are made up of two discs feedback onto themselves. The connectivity and transition function lists at the side of each network representation are included for those readers familiar with Boolean networks. The graphics below each network representation show the attractor basins for each network. The state spaces of both networks contain two period-4 attractors, although it is clear that the basin sizes (i.e., the number of states they each contain) are quite different. The window located at the top-middle of the figure illustrates how different rules are applied (in the two-input case). The different combinations of the two-input, A and B, are mapped to outputs, O. In the example given (which is for rule [0110]) the "rule table" shows that if both A and B or zero or one, then the next state (O) of the node that has A and B as inputs, will be 0. This is the essence of how Boolean networks are stepped forward in time.

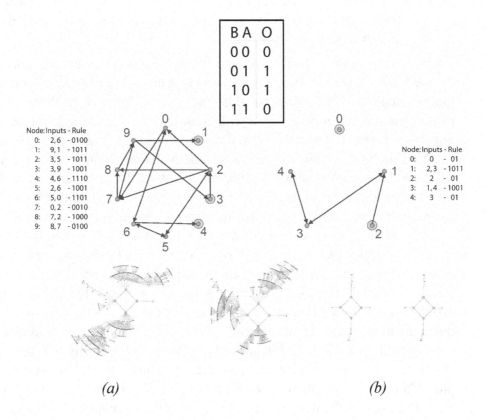

(a)   (b)

If we consider a clock: at the heart of most clocks found in the home there is some kind of time-keeping mechanism and another mechanism that represents the time kept to observers of that clock. Of course, these mechanisms are often surrounding by fancy cases and other sub-systems designed for aesthetic reasons, or to protect the main mechanisms from external influence. We could regard the central time-keeping mechanisms as this particular system's dynamic core, with the other frills and flourishes largely being irrelevant if our concern is with the time-keeping functionality of the clock. It should be noted though that in this example, the existence of modules, sub-systems, barriers, etc. are engineered into the system and that the dynamic core is trivial to identify (once a particular functional perspective is chosen). In the Boolean networks considered in this study, the existence of modules, sub-systems, barriers, etc. emerges through the nonlinear interaction of the various system components, and so details of their existence cannot (normally) be determined beforehand. It is likely that in real world networks such as the World Wide Web (WWW) some of the structure will be hard-wired (designed) into the network, and other structures (which may not be easily identified) emerge.

Another way of thinking about a complex network's dynamic core is in the process of modeling itself. Complex systems are *incompressible* (e.g., Cilliers, 1998; Richardson, 2005b). This statement simply asserts that the only *complete* model of a particular complex system is the system itself[1]. This is, however, quite impractical, especially when considering systems such as the WWW or a natural ecology. Instead of regarding our models as efforts to represent a system in its entirety we can say, using the language developed above, that the aim of any modeling process is to find an adequate representation of a system's dynamic core (i.e., those processes that are central to the functionality of the system).

The Role of Non-Conserving (Structural) Information Loops

As the gross state space characteristics of a Boolean network and its dynamic core (or, reduced form) are the same (i.e., in this sense, they are *functionally equivalent*), it is tempting to conclude that (Type 1) non-conserving information loops—information barriers—are irrelevant. If this were the case then it might be used to support the widespread removal of such "dead wood" from complex information systems (e.g., human organizations). The history of science is littered with examples of theories which once regarded such and such a phenomena as irrelevant, or "waste," only to discover later on that it plays a very important role indeed. The growing realization that "junk DNA" (DNA being probably the most intricate information system known to us, other than the brain perhaps) is not actually junk is one such example. What is often found is that a change of perspective leads to a changed assessment. Such a reframing leads to a different assessment of non-conserving information loops. Our limited concern, thus far herein, with maintaining a qualitatively equivalent state space structure in the belief that a functionally equivalent network is created, supports the assessment of non-conserving information loops as "junk." However, this assessment is wrong when explored from a different angle.

There are at least two roles that non-conserving information loops play in random Boolean networks:

1.   The process of modularization, and;
2.   The maximization of robustness.

Modularization in Boolean Networks

We have already briefly discussed the process of modularization. This process, which we might label as an example of *horizontal emergence* (Sulis, 2005) was first reported by Bastolla and Parisi (1998). It was argued that the spontaneous emergence of dynamically disconnected modules is key to understanding the complex (as opposed to ordered and quasi-chaotic) behavior of complex networks. So, the role of non-conserving information loops is to limit the network's dynamics so that it does not become overly complex, and eventually quasi-chaotic (which is essentially random in this scenario: when you have a network with a high-period attractor of say 10^{20}—which is not hard to obtain—it scores very well indeed against all tests for randomness. One such example is the lagged Fibonacci random number generator).

In Boolean networks, the resulting modules are *independent* of each other, so the result of modularization, is a collection of completely separate subsystems. This independency is different from what we see in nature, but the attempt to understand natural complex systems as integrations of *partially independent* and interacting modules is arguably a dominant theme in the life sciences, cognitive science, and computer science (see, for example, Callebaut & Rasskin-Gutman, 2005). It is likely that some form of non-conserving, or perhaps "limiting," information loop structure plays an important role in real world modularization processes. Another way of expressing this is *organization is the result of **limiting** information flow.*

The concept of modularization (which is an emergent phenomenon) appears to be similar to Simon's (1962) concept of *near decomposability*. In his seminal paper *"The Architecture of Complexity,"* Simon developed his theory of *nearly decomposable systems*, "in which the interactions among the subsystems are weak, but not negligible" (p. 474). Simon goes on to say:

"At least some kind of hierarchic systems can be approximated successfully as nearly decomposable systems. The main theoretical findings from the approach can be summed up in two propositions: (a) in a nearly decomposable system, the short run behavior of each of the component subsystems is approximately independent of the short-run behavior of the other components; (b) in the long run, the behavior of any one of the components depends in only an aggregate way on the behavior of the other components" (p. 474).

The process of modularization previously described is slightly different, but complementary. Near decomposability suggests that complex systems evolve such that weakly interacting subsystems emerge that, on sufficiently short timescales, can be considered as independent from each other (although it says little about the dynamic processes that lead to this state). This phenomenon is clearly observed in Boolean networks, except that in these particular complex systems, the emergent subsystems (modules) are completely independent of each other—information does not flow from one subsystem to another. If there were no communications with the system's environment then we could simply consider these independent subsystems in isolation. However, we shall see in the following discussions on dynamical robustness that the "padding" between these subsystems—the (Type 1) non-conserving information loops, or frozen nodes—plays an important role in the overall system's (the network of subsystems) dynamics in the face of external "interference." (It should be noted that, although the emergent modules discussed here are independent, in larger modules sub-modules may emerge that can indeed be viewed as weakly interacting subsystems. Near decomposability and modularization are related, but not in a trivial way.)

Dynamic Robustness of Complex Networks

Dynamic robustness was previously defined in a slightly different way, as the stability of a network's qualitative behavior in the face of small external signals. In this section, we will consider the dynamic robustness of an ensemble of random Boolean networks and their associated "reduced" form to assess any difference between the two.

To do this comparison, the following experiment was performed. 10^6 random Boolean networks with $N=15$ and $k=2$ (with random connections and random transition functions, excluding the two constant functions) were constructed. For each network, its dynamic core was determined using the method detailed in Richardson (2005a). The average dynamical robustness was calculated for both the (unreduced) networks and their associated dynamic cores. The data from this experiment is presented in Figure 5, which shows the relationship between the unreduced and reduced dynamic robustness for the 10^6 networks considered. The black points shows the average value of dynamic core (or, reduced) robustness for various values of unreduced robustness. *On average*, the dynamic robustness of the reduced networks is typically of the order of 20% less than their parent (unreduced) networks. Of course, the difference for particular networks is dependent on specific contextual factors, such as the number of non-conserving information loops in the (unreduced) networks (the extent of the dynamic core, in other words). This strongly suggests that the reduced networks are rather more sensitive to external signals than the unreduced networks. In some instances the robustness of the reduced network is actually zero meaning that any external signal whatsoever will result in qualitative change. This generally only occurs in networks, which have small dynamic core sizes compared to the network size. What is also interesting, however, is that sometimes the reduced network is actually more robust than the unreduced network. This is a little surprising perhaps, but not when we take into account the complex connectivity of phase space for these networks. This effect is observed in cases when there is significant change in the relative attractor basin weights as a result of the reduction process and/or a relative increase in the orderliness of state space.

In complex systems research it is important to consider the process of averaging data (and adding error bars extending a certain number of standard deviations). The data in Figure 5a is clearly multi-modal and as such, one has to take care in interpreting the physical meaning of the average. The different shades of grey in Figure 5 indicate the number of data points that

Figure 5. Data histograms of the dynamical robustness data collected. (a) all data, with black points showing the overall average, (b) data associated with a dynamic core size of 15, (c) 14, (d) 13, (e) 12, (f) 11, (g) 10, (h) 9, (i) 8, (j) 7, (k) 6, (l) 5, and (m) 4. Data for dynamic core sizes of 3, 2, and 1 are not included

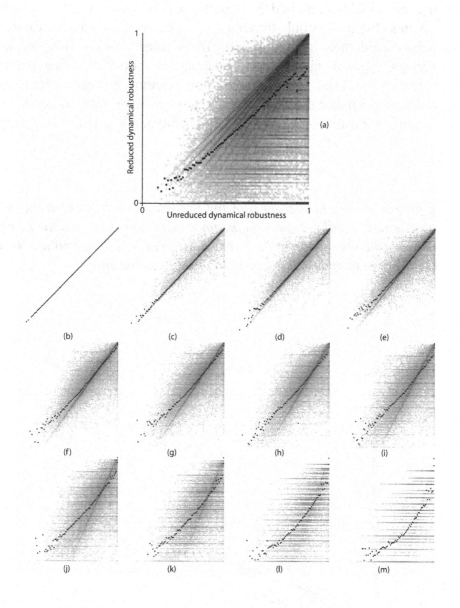

fall into a particular data bin (the data is rounded down to 2 decimal places leading to 100 data bins). So the darkest grey regions contain many data points ($> a^{10}$ where a is the relative frequency of the data, $a = 2.4$ in this case) and the lightest grey regions contain only one (or a^0) data point. If we had blindly calculated the average values and attempted to interpret its meaning, we would have missed the importance of dynamic core size completely. Figures 8b-8m show only the data for particular sizes of dynamic core. This helps considerably in understanding the detailed structure of Figure 8a. The various diagonal "modal peeks" relate to networks with different dynamic core sizes, and the different horizontal structures correlate with networks containing smaller dynamic cores which can have only limited values of dynamic robustness (i.e., as the size of the dynamic core decreases the data

Figure 6. A data histogram showing the relationship between the number of structural feedback loops in the unreduced networks, and the number of active structural loops in their dynamic cores. The black points represent the average number of structural loops in dynamic core.

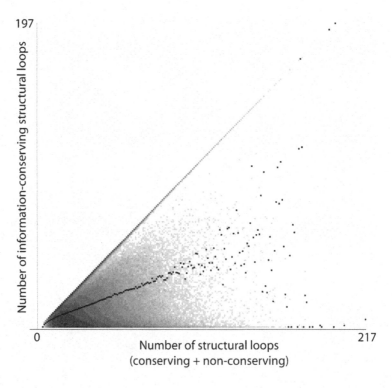

appears more discrete and as the core size increases the data appears more continuous).

Further analysis was performed to confirm the relationship between network structure, dynamic core structure, and state space structure. This included comparing the number of structural feedback loops in the overall network to the number of (information conserving only) loops in network's dynamic core. Figure 6 shows the data for all 10^6 (N=15, k=2) networks studied with all dynamic core sizes superimposed on each other. The data indicates that *on average* the dynamic core of a network has between 30% and 60% fewer structural feedback loops; all of them information conserving loops. On average only 42% of all structural feedback loops contribute to the (global) functionality of a particular network. It should of course be noted though that this proportion is strongly dependent upon dynamic core size. In the next section, we shall consider the implications of this in terms of state space characteristics and dynamic robustness.

State Space Compression and Robustness

In Boolean networks, each additional node doubles the size of state space. In fact, in any discrete system (or any system that can be approximated as discrete), when an additional node is added, the size of state space is increased by a factor equal to the total number of states that the additional node can adopt. So in a human system, like a team for example, the addition of an extra member will increase state space by a factor equal to the number of different responses that the additional member exhibits when operating in that particular system. This needn't result in the appearance of new state space structures (attractors), but the volume of state space is greatly increased. So even if "frozen" nodes contribute nothing to the qualitative structure of state space (which I shall now refer to as *first order functionality*), they at least increase the size of phase space. As an example, the phase space of an N=20 network is 1024 times larger than an N=10 network. Thus, node removal significantly reduces the size of phase space. As such, the chances that a small external signal will inadvertently target a sensitive area of state space, i.e., an area close to a separatrix, therefore pushing the network toward a different attractor, are significantly increased: a kind of *qualitative chaos*. This explains why we see the robustness tending to decrease when non-conserving information loops are removed: the (emergent) buffer between the system and the outside world—the system's environment—has been removed.

Prigogine said that self-organization requires a container (self-*contained*-organization). Non-conserving information loops function as a kind of container. So it seems that, although non-conserving information loops do not contribute to the long term behavior of a particular network, these same loops play a central role as far as the dynamical stability is concerned. Any management team tempted to remove 80% of their organization in the hope of still achieving 80% of their yearly profits (which is sometimes how the 80:20 principle in general systems theory is interpreted in practice) would find that they had created an organization that had no protection whatsoever to even the smallest disturbances from its environment—it would literally be impossible to have a stable business.

It should be noted that the non-conserving information loops do not act as impenetrable barriers to external signals (information). These loops simply limit the penetration of the signals into the system. For example, in the case of a modularized network, the products of incoming signals may, depending on network connectivity, still be fed from a *non-conserving* information loop onto information *conserving* loops for a particular network module. Once the signals have penetrated a particular module, they cannot cross over into other modules (as the only inter-modular connections are via non-conserving loops). As such, it would seem that non-conserving loops may play an *information distribution* role.

It should also be noted that even though a particular signal may not cause the system to jump into a *different* attractor basin, or bifurcate, it will still push the system into a different state on the *same* basin. The affect of signals that end-up on non-conserving information loops is certainly not nothing. So, although the term information "barriers" is used herein, these barriers are semi-permeable.

Balancing Response "Strategies" and System Robustness

Figure 7 shows a data histogram for the number of state space attractors vs. (unreduced) dynamic robustness. The plot shows that the robustness decreases rapidly initially as the number of state space attractors increases. Remembering that the number of state space attractors can also be regarded as the number of contextual archetypes that a system "sees," we see that versatility (used here to refer to the number of qualitatively different contexts a system can respond to, or is sensitive to) comes at the cost of reduced dynamic robustness assuming the same resources are available. Considered in this way robustness and versatility are two sides of the same coin. We would like for our systems to be able to respond to a wide variety of environmental contexts with minimal effort, but this also means that our systems might also be at the mercy of *any* environmental change. A system with only one state space attractor doesn't "see" its environment at all, as it has only one response in all contexts, whereas a system with many phase space attractors "sees" too much—there is a price to pay for being too flexible.

This is only the case though for fixed resources, that is, given the same resources a system with few state space attractors (modes of operation) will be more robust than a system with a greater number. This is because, on average, the system with more state space attractors will have a larger dynamic core and so the buffering afforded by non-conserving loops will be less pronounced. It is a trivial undertaking to increase phase space by adding nodes that have

Figure 7. A data histogram showing the relationship between the number of state space attractors (which is also related to network flexibility/versatility) and the (unreduced) dynamical robustness. The black points represent the average dynamic robustness for increasing numbers of phase space attractors (the greyscaling is scaled using a^n, where $a = 2.4$ and n is an integer between 0 and 10 inclusive).

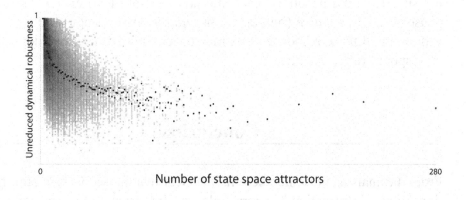

inputs but no outputs, or "leaf" nodes (which is equivalent to adding connected nodes that have a constant transition function)—we might refer to this as a *first-order* strategy. This certainly increases the size of phase space rapidly, and it is a trivial matter to calculate the effect such additions will have on the network's dynamical robustness (i.e., the increased dynamical robustness will not be an *emergent* property of the network). Increasing the robustness of a network (without changing the number, period and weight of phase space attractor basins) by adding connected nodes with non-constant transition functions is a much harder proposition. This is because of the new structural feedback loops created, and the great difficulty in determining the emergent "logical couplings" that result in "frozen" nodes, which turn structural information loops (that were initially conserving) into non-conserving loops. It is not clear at this point in the research whether there is any preference between these two strategies to increase dynamical robustness, although the emergent option is orders of magnitude harder to implement than the other, and will likely change functionality.

One key difference between the straightforward first-order strategy and the more problematic (second-order) emergent strategy is that the first-order enhanced network would not be quantitatively sensitive to perturbations on the extra (buffer) "leaf" nodes (i.e., not only would such perturbations not lead to qualitative change (a crossing of a separatrix, or a bifurcation), but the position on the attractor cycle that the system was on when the node was perturbed (i.e., *cycle phase*) would also not be affected)—there would be no effect on dynamics whatsoever. This is because the perturbation signal (incoming information) would not penetrate the system further than the "leaf" node, as by definition it is not connected via any structural (non-conserving or conserving) feedback loops: they really are impenetrable barriers to information. If the emergent strategy was successfully employed, the incoming signals would penetrate and quite possibly (at most) change the cycle phase (i.e., *quantitative* (but, again, not *qualitative*) change would occur). Either one of these response traits may or may not be desirable depending on response requirements.

Conclusion

From the analysis presented herein, it is clear that non-conserving information loops—information barriers—play an important role in a network's global dynamics: they are not "expendable." They protect a network from both *quantitative* and *qualitative* (quasi) chaos. Quantitative chaos is resisted by the emergent creation of modules—through the process of modularization—which directly reduces the chances of state space being dominated by the very long period attractors associated with quasi-randomness in Boolean networks. Whereas qualitative chaos—the rapid "jumping" from one attractor basin to another in response to small external signals—is resisted by the expansion of state space, which reduces the possibility of external signals pushing a system across a state space separatrix (i.e., into another mode of operation).

Much more effort will be needed to fully understand the design and operating implications of this research for real world information systems. In one sense, Boolean networks are at the heart of all technology based systems—computers are themselves very complicated Boolean networks. However, these sorts of (complicated) Boolean networks do not usually have architectures that contain the many nonlinear interacting feedback loops that the (complex) Boolean networks discussed herein have. Complicated Boolean networks, such as computers, generally process information serially, whereas complex Boolean networks can process information in parallel. In fact, there is considerable research being performed that considers complex Boolean networks as powerful parallel computers (see for example, Mitchell, 1998). It may well be that the sort of research presented here has little impact on the design of engineered systems such as computers and technology-driven information nodes as these are generally hard-wired *not* to exhibit emergent behavior. It is in the area of *soft*-wired systems, perhaps, that this research may offer some insight. For example, although the individual components of the Internet are hard-wired, the way in which its global architecture is developing is through emergent processes. Recent advances in network theory provide powerful tools to understand the *static* structure (architecture) of complex networks such as the WWW. But, equally powerful dynamical tools will be needed to understand the *dynamic* structure of the WWW which is likely quite different. There is clearly someway to go to fully understand what abstract concepts such as non-conserving information loops, or "frozen" nodes, refer to in real world information systems, but such research is beginning to provide us with the language and tools to facilitate our understanding of the structural and state space dynamics of a wide range of complex information systems like the Internet, the WWW, or even large decision networks to mention just a few.

Another useful avenue of further research may come by considering the "activity" of each node. In this chapter, we could have defined "frozen" nodes as those with an activity of zero (i.e., their state does not change with time). The remaining nodes will have different activity levels (e.g., a node that changes state on every time step (a period-2 node) would have activity 1). The dynamic core structure of a particular network (containing non-interacting modules) is found by removing all nodes with activity 0. However, different structures will be revealed if the "activity threshold for removal" is varied from 0 to 1. In this way, researchers would find further modularization, although modules (sub-structure) found this way would not be completely independent (the weakly interacting modules of Simon's "nearly decomposable systems" perhaps); systems of interacting sub-systems (with varying degrees of interaction strength) within the *same* system would be found, which would provide further insight into the relationship between emergent structure and function. Furthermore, it is possible that such an "activity threshold" analysis would be easier to apply to real world systems than the analysis performed herein, which is only concerned with a zero activity threshold.

To conclude, I would suggest that "barriers" (both impenetrable and semi-permeable) to information flow play a central role in the functioning of all complex information systems. However, the implications (and meaning) of this for real world systems is open to many different interpretations. At the very least it suggests that "barriers" to information flow should be taken as seriously as "supports" to information flow (although, paradoxically, a good "supporter" is inherently a good "barrier"!). This may seem obvious given the dual role of all types of boundary—that is, to keep in *and* keep out, or to enable *and* disable—but this change in focus offers, perhaps, an interesting counterpoint to the emerging cultural perspective that suggests that having as much information as possible can only be a good thing.

Acknowledgment

I'd like to thank Yasmin Merali and Bill McKelvey for useful suggestions on how to improve the earlier drafts of this paper, and to three anonymous reviewers. Thanks also go to Caroline, Alexander, and Albert for interesting diversions.

References

Allen, P. M. (2001). What is complexity science? Knowledge of the limits to knowledge. *Emergence, 3*(1), 24-42.

Barabási, A. L. (2001). *The physics of the Web. Physics World.* Retrieved May 21, 2007, from http://physicsweb.org/articles/world/14/7/9

Barabási, A. L., & Albert, E. (1999). Emergence of scaling in random networks. *Science, 286*(15 Oct), 509-512.

Bastolla, U., & Parisi, G. (1998). The modular structure of Kauffman networks. *Physica D, 115*, 219-233.

Bilke, S., & Sjunnesson, F. (2002). Stability of the Kauffman model. *Phys. Rev. E, 65*, 016129.

Cilliers, P. (1998). *Complexity and postmodernism: Understanding complex systems.* London, UK: Routledge.

Callebaut, W., & Rasskin-Gutman, D. (2005). *Modularity: Understanding the development and evolution of natural complex systems.* Cambridge, MA: MIT Press.

Kauffman, S. A. (1993). *The origins of order: Self-organization and selection in evolution.* New York: Oxford University Press.

Lucas, C. (2006). *Boolean networks—dynamic organisms.* Retrieved May 21, 2007, from http://www.calresco.org/boolean.htm

Mitchell, M. (1998). Computation in cellular automata: A selected review. In T. Gramss, S. Bornholdt, M. Gross, M. Mitchell, & T. Pellizzari (Eds.), *Nonstandard computation* (pp. 95-140). Weinheim: VCH Verlagsgesellschaft. Note that cellular automata are essentially Boolean networks with an ordered architecture rather than a random one.

Richardson, K. A. (2005a). Simplifying Boolean networks. *Advances in Complex Systems, 8*(4), 365-381.

Richardson, K. A. (2005b). The hegemony of the physical sciences: An exploration in complexity thinking. *Futures, 37*, 615-653.

Simon, H. (1962). The architecture of complexity. Proceedings of the American Philosophical Society, 106(6), 467-482. Reprinted in Richardson, K. A., Snowden, D., Allen, P. M., & Goldstein, J. A. (Eds.) (2006). *Emergence: Complexity & Organization 2005 Annual, Volume 7* (pp. 499-510). Mansfield, MA: ISCE Publishing.

Sulis, W. H. (2005). Archetypal dynamical systems and semantic frames in vertical and horizontal emergence. In K. A. Richardson, J. A. Goldstein, P. M. Allen, & D. Snowden (Eds.), *E:CO Annual Volume 6* (pp. 204-216). Mansfield, MA: ISCE Publishing.

Watts, D. J., & Strogatz, S. H. (1998). Collective dynamics of "small-world" networks. *Nature, 393*(4), 440-442.

Endnote

[1] Of course there is no such thing as a complete model. Models, by their very nature, are always, incomplete. The importance of the concept of incompressibility is to highlight that simplifications of complex systems can often lead (but not necessarily so) to understanding that is qualitatively incomplete. Contrast this situation to that of complicated systems (i.e., systems that comprise many components that may also be related via nonlinear interactions but without the connectivity profile (topology)) that would lead to the multiple nonlinear and interacting feedback loops that distinguish complex systems—for which simple representations (models) can always be constructed that are qualitatively complete.

Chapter VIII

Emergent Specialization in Biologically Inspired Collective Behavior Systems

G. S. Nitschke, Vrije Universiteit, The Netherlands

M. C. Schut, Vrije Universiteit, The Netherlands

A. E. Eiben, Vrije Universiteit, The Netherlands

Abstract

Specialization is observable in many complex adaptive systems and is thought by many to be a fundamental mechanism for achieving optimal efficiency within organizations operating within complex adaptive systems. This chapter presents a survey and critique of collective behavior systems designed using biologically inspired principles. Specifically, we are interested in collective behavior systems where specialization emerges as a result of system dynamics and where emergent specialization is used as a problem solver or means to increase task performance. The chapter presents an argument for developing

*design methodologies and principles that facilitate emergent specialization
in collective behavior systems. Open problems of current research as well as
future research directions are highlighted for the purpose of encouraging the
development of such emergent specialization design methodologies.*

Introduction

Specialization is observable in many complex adaptive systems[1] and is thought
by many to be a fundamental mechanism for achieving optimal efficiency
within certain complex adaptive systems. In complex ecological communities, specializations have evolved over time as a means of diversifying the
community in order to adapt to the environment (Seligmann, 1999). Over
the course of evolutionary time, specialization in biological communities
has assumed both morphological (Wenseleers, Ratnieks, & Billen, 2003)
and behavioral forms (Bonabeau, Theraulaz, & Deneubourg, 1996). For example, morphologically specialized castes have emerged in certain termite
colonies (Noirot & Pasteels, 1987), and honeybees dynamically adapt their
foraging behavior for pollen, nectar, and water as a function of individual
preference and colony demand (Calderone & Page, 1988). The consequence
of such specializations is that labor is efficiently divided between specialized castes[2] and individuals for the benefit of accomplishing group tasks. In
such a sense, specialization can be viewed as an adaptive mechanism in a
complex adaptive system.

Many artificial complex adaptive systems that exhibit collective behavior have
used design principles, which draw their inspiration from examples of specialization in nature. Such examples include complex ecological communities
such as social insect colonies (Bonabeau et al., 1996; Bonabeau, Sobkowski,
Theraulaz, & Deneubourg, 1997; Calderone et al., 1988; Noirot et al., 1987;
Seligmann, 1999; Wenseleers et al., 2003) biological neural networks (Baev,
1997), multi-cellular organisms (Hawthorne, 2001), economies of a nation,
companies, corporations, and other business organizations (Abdel-Rahman,
2001; Ng & Yang, 1997; Resnick, 1997). Such biologically inspired design
principles are especially prevalent in multi-robot (Potter, Meeden, & Schultz,
2001) swarm intelligence (Bonabeau, Dorigo, & Theraulaz, 1998) and artificial life systems (Nishimura & Takashi, 1997) where it is highly desirable
to replicate the success of biological collective behavior systems.

Suppositions of Specialization

Given empirical evidence offered by research in both biological collective behavior systems, and biologically inspired artificial collective behavior systems[3], two key observations can be stated.

- Specialization that assumes either behavioral or morphological forms is often present in biological systems that exhibit collective behavior.

- In biological systems that exhibit collective behavior, specialization is beneficial in that it increases the efficiency of the system, or allows collective behavior tasks to be solved that could not otherwise be solved by individuals within the system.

Given these observations, one can formulate the assumption that specialization is beneficial in biological inspired artificial complex adaptive systems that are designed to solve certain types of collective behavior tasks. Examples of such types of collective behavior tasks are presented in section *Collective Behavior Tasks and Specialization*. In order for this assumption to be proved, this chapter proposes the need to develop *emergent behavior design* methodologies[4]. Such methodologies would dictate design and engineering principles for creating an artificial complex adaptive system capable of solving collective behavior tasks that require or benefit from specialization. Ideally, such methodologies would result in the production of artificial complex adaptive systems that yield emergent yet desired forms of specialization. As in biological systems, this emergent specialization could then be harnessed and used by the system for the benefit of either increasing task performance, or solving certain collective behavior tasks, that could not otherwise be solved.

Chapter Goal and Motivation: Specialization as a Problem Solver

The chapter's scope is a survey and critique of collective behavior systems designed using biologically inspired design principles that use emergent specialization to solve collective behavior tasks. Such design principles include *self-organization*, *learning*, and *evolution* (Brooks, 1990). This chapter presents an argument for utilizing emergent behavioral specialization as a problem solver in biologically inspired artificial complex adaptive systems. Such utilization would be advantageous given the numerous real world applications where specialization is beneficial. Examples of such applications are presented in the section *Collective Behavior Tasks and Specialization*. This chapter's motivation is similar to that cited for the *organic computing* research endeavor (Müller & Sick, 2006). Organic computing has recently achieved some success in investigating the notion of defining and measuring concepts such as emergence and self-organization in large distributed complex adaptive systems. The key idea is to utilize emergent phenomena for the benefit of solving tasks in *organic computing systems*. An organic computing system is a technical system, which adapts dynamically to the current conditions of its environment. It is self-organizing, self-configuring, self-repairing, self-protecting, self-explaining, and context-aware (Müller et al., 2006). Initial research in this area displays great promise, and includes exploiting emergent functionality at the hardware level of visual microprocessors for image recognition tasks (Komann & Fey, 2007), self-organizing, and self-stabilizing role assignment in sensor and actuator networks (Weis, Parzyjegla, Jaeger, & Mühl, 2006), and self-organization of job scheduling and distribution of jobs over nodes in a network (Trumler, Klaus, & Ungerer, 2006).

Chapter Scope: Behavioral Specialization

Another important issue is which type of specialization[5] should be instituted for the benefit of a collective behavior system. We have elected to only survey research literature concerned with *behavioral specialization*. The decision to adopt this focus was based on the discovery that with relatively few exceptions (section: *Types of Specialization*) the majority of research concerning the use of emergent specialization for improving task performance is restricted to simulated systems. This is so, given the obvious engineering challenges and inherent complexity of dynamically creating morphologically specialized robots and computer components, that represent effective solutions to emerging challenges in a physical task environment (Parker & Nathan, 2006; Pfeifer, Iida, & Gomez, 2006; Watson, Ficici, & Pollack, 1999b). Figure 1 presents the scope of the chapter within the dimensions of emergent versus non-emergent phenomena and behavioral versus morphological specialization.

Figure 1. Types of specialization in biologically inspired collective behavior systems. The top left-hand side quadrant defines the scope of this chapter. Specifically, adaptive systems that use heterogeneous or homogenous design approaches with the aim of deriving emergent behavioral specialization for solving collective behavior tasks. See section: Types of Specialization for details.

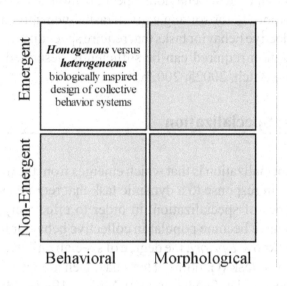

Types of Specialization

Specialization in collective behavior systems has been studied from many different perspectives (Bongard, 2000; Bryant & Miikkulainen, 2003; Blumenthal & Parker, 2004b; Campos, Theraulaz, Bonabeau, & Deneubourg, 2001; Haynes & Sen, 1996b; Nolfi et al., 2003b; Stone & Veloso, 2002; Whiteson, Kohl, Miikkulainen, & Stone, 2003), and is thus often defined in accordance with the goals of researchers conducting the study. Within collective behavior literature, specialization is either studied as an emergent property of the system, or is explicitly pre-programmed into the systems components. With notable exceptions such as Funes, Orme, and Bonabeau (2003), there are few examples of research that successfully specifies, *a priori*, what exactly the behavior of system components should be, in order to produce a specifically desired, yet emergent collective behavior.

Non-Emergent Specialization

Non-emergent specialization is that which is explicitly pre-specified to be apart of the design of system components and global behavior of a system. Such approaches are either static, or utilize learning algorithms so as to ascertain which type of behavioral specialization, selected from a given set, is most appropriate for solving a given task. Such approaches are useful for solving collective behavior tasks that require specialization, where the degree of specialization required can be sufficiently described *a priori* (Arkin & Balch, 1999; Balch, 2002a, 2002b).

Emergent Specialization

Emergent specialization is that which emerges from the interaction of system components in response to a dynamic task that requires varying degrees, or different types of specialization, in order to effectively accomplish. Such approaches have become popular in collective behavior task domains where one does not know, *a priori*, the degree of specialization required to optimally solve the given task (Gautrais, Theraulaz, Deneubourg, & Anderson, 2002; Luke & Spector, 1996; Murciano & Millan, 1997a; Murciano, Millan, & Zamora, 1997b; Potter et al., 2001; Stanley, Bryant, & Miikkulainen, 2005b; Theraulaz, Bonabeau, & Deneubourg, 1998b; Waibel, Floreano, Magnenat, & Keller, 2006). The section *Heterogeneous vs. Homogenous Design of Emergent Specialization* elaborates upon such emergent specialization design approaches.

Morphological vs. Behavioral Specialization

It is possible to further categorize specialization into two distinct classes: *morphological* (Martinoli, Zhang, Prakash, Antonsson, & Olney, 2002; Zhang, Martinoli, & Antonsson, 2003) and *behavioral* (Bonabeau et al., 1997; Li, Martinoli, & Mostafa, 2002).

The term *morphological specialization* is applicable to situated and embodied agents, operating in simulated or physical task environments, with embodiment (sensors and actuators) structured so as to yield an advantage in accomplishing the task (Watson et al., 1998a, 1999b, 2002). Examples of morphological specialization include the evolution of optimal arrangements of sensors and actuators in the design of simulated automobiles (Martinoli et al., 2002; Zhang et al., 2003), evolution of agent morphologies and controllers for various forms of motion in simulated environments (Sims, 2004), evolution of physical electric circuits for control (Thompson, Harvey, & Husbands, 1996), and evolving robot morphology for accomplishing different forms of physical motion (Lipson & Pollack, 2000).

The term *behavioral specialization* is applicable to agents with behaviors that are advantageous for accomplishing specific types of tasks (Balch, 2002a, 2002b; Nolfi & Floreano, 2000; Nolfi & Parisi, 1997). Examples of behavioral specialization include the use of machine learning methods that activate certain behaviors with a particular frequency as a response to dynamically arising tasks (Gautrais et al., 2002).

Collective Behavior Methods for Specialization

There is some agreement among researchers as to the methods for specialization that are appropriate for particular collective behavior tasks. Figure 2 illustrates a categorization of such methods, which are briefly detailed in the following. The categories illustrated in Figure 2 are by no means exhaustive, but rather several examples that have recently received particular research attention.

Figure 2. Collective behavior methods of specialization. See section: Collective Behavior Methods for Specialization for details.

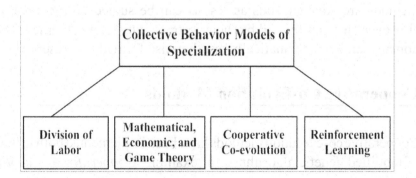

Division of Labor Methods

The use of behavioral threshold and division of labor methods have been investigated within the context of ant-based (Deneubourg, Goss, Pasteels, Fresneau, & Lachaud, 1987) and resource allocation (Bonabeau et al., 1997) methods. Such methods typically utilize feedback signals given to agents of the same caste (Kreiger & Billeter, 2000) in order to encourage the emergence of specialization for a specific task. Many variations of these methods exist (Bonabeau & Theraulaz, 1999; Bonabeau et al., 1996, 1997, 1998; Deneubourg et al., 1987; Robson & Traniello, 1999; Theraulaz, Gervet, & Semenoff, 1991; Theraulaz, Goss, Gervet, & Deneubourg, 1991), including those that use evolutionary algorithms (Tarapore, Floreano, & Keller, 2006; Waibel et al., 2006), and reinforcement learning models (Murciano et al., 1997a, Murciano et al., 1997b) in order to derive threshold values. The goal of such models is typically to optimize global task performance. Such methods are appealing as their evolutionary dynamics and emergent properties can usually be described with a mathematical representation and the results of such models are thus typically amenable to a mathematical analysis (Wu, Di, & Yang, 2003).

Mathematical, Economic, and Game Theory Methods

Linear, non-linear, and dynamic methods based in mathematical, economic, and game theory (Axelrod, 1984; Solow & Szmerekovsky, 2004) have many applications for resource assignment problems in business. For example, the maximum matching algorithm developed by Edmonds (1965) was designed to determine the maximum number of people that can be assigned to tasks in such a way that no person is assigned to more than one task. Thus, it is assumed that each person specializes in performing at most one task. Such methods are advantageous as results can be subject to a formal analysis. However, they are limited by their abstract nature, and assume that the task domain can be mathematically or otherwise formally represented.

Cooperative Co-Evolution Methods

Cooperative co-evolution methods have been implemented both in the context of modified genetic algorithms, for example, *Cooperative Co-evolutionary*

Genetic Algorithms (Potter & DeJong, 2000), and in the context of neuro-evolution methods, for example, *Enforced Sub-Populations* (ESP) (Gomez, 1997). In both cases, the genotype space is decomposed into a set of sub-populations, where each generation, the evolutionary process selects the best performing genotype components from each sub-population so as to construct a complete genotype as a solution. Decomposition of the genotype space into sub-populations, genotype construction from multiple sub-populations, and genotype to phenotype mapping depends upon the approach used. For example, the ESP method encodes separate neurons as genotype components to be distributed between sub-populations, where the composition of neurons encodes a complete neural network. Advantages of such methods include their versatility, and applicability to a broad range of complex, continuous, and noisy task domains. Also, the representation of the genotype space as a set of sub-populations provides a natural representation for many collective behavior tasks, and often effectuates the derivation of specialized phenotypes. A key disadvantage of such approaches is slow derivation of viable solutions in complex task domains due to inherently large search spaces. Also, the genotype representations that produce desired results can typically not be easily interpreted.

Reinforcement Learning Methods

There exists a certain class of reinforcement learning methods that provide periodic feedback signals to agent groups attempting to accomplish a collective behavior task (Sutton & Barto, 1998). A reinforcement signal is either local or global. Local reinforcement signals are calculated by, and given to a single agent, or a caste, upon task accomplishment. Global reinforcement signals are calculated by and given to the entire agent group at the end of a reinforcement learning trial (Li, Martinoli, & Yaser, 2004). The main advantage of reinforcement learning approaches is that agents are able to effectively operate in complex and noisy environments, with incomplete information. However, approaches that utilize only a global reinforcement signal, do not typically effectuate specialization in the group, even if task performance could be increased with specialized agents (Li et al., 2002, 2004). Approaches that utilize local reinforcement signals have been demonstrated as being appropriate for deriving specialized agents (Li et al., 2004), however such approaches suffer from the credit assignment problem (Grefenstette,

1995; Sutton et al., 1998), which potentially leads to sub-optimal collective behavior solutions.

Heterogeneous vs. Homogenous Design of Emergent Specialization

In collective behavior research, approaches to designing emergent special-ization usually adopt either *homogeneous* or *heterogeneous* methods for designing system components. Homogeneous approaches utilize a single agent behavior for every agent in a group of agents. Agent behavior may be encoded as one genotype representation, or in some cases simply defined by a given set of parameters, which are copied for each agent in the group (Quinn, Smith, Mayley, & Husbands, 2003). Heterogeneous approaches utilize different behaviors for each agent in a group of agents. The set of different behaviors is sometimes encoded as different populations of genotypes, as in the case of cooperative co-evolutionary genetic algorithms (Parker, 2000). Alternatively, different agent behaviors may simply be represented as dif-ferent sets of parameters (Campos et al., 2001).

Designing emergent specialization has been studied via specifying homogene-ity vs. heterogeneity within both the genotypes and phenotypes of individual agents as well as entire agent groups. Specialization is often closely associated with, and sometimes synonymous with, heterogeneity in collective behavior systems (Balch, 1998; Potter et al., 2001). Heterogeneity can be hardwired or plastic, and may assume either behavioral (Bryant et al., 2003; Noirot et al., 1987; Whiteson et al., 2003), or morphological (O'Riain, Jarvis, Alex-ander, Buffenstein, & Peeters, 2000; Schultz & Bugajska, 2000; Zhang et al., 2003) forms. Plastic heterogeneity is when a group adapts its degree of heterogeneity as a function of environment and task constraints, where as, hardwired heterogeneity is when the degree of heterogeneity in the group remains static (Li et al., 2002).

Certain researchers have attempted to outline generalized guidelines as when to use either homogeneous or heterogeneous design approaches. For example, Balch (1998) suggested that collective behavior task domains where all individuals are able to perform the task, such as collective gathering, are particularly suited for homogeneous design. Whilst, task domains that explicitly require complementary roles, such as RoboCup soccer, are more suitable for heterogeneous approaches. However, such guidelines, as with studies of specialization, are usually defined according to the goals and perspectives of the researcher. Hence, one can readily find examples of when homogeneity and heterogeneity have been used in a manner incongruent to any given set of design principles or guidelines.

Homogeneous Approaches

In homogeneous approaches, specialization is typically studied at the group level since emergent specialization depends upon the local interactions of cloned behaviors. At the genotype level, the key advantage of a homogeneous approach is that the search space size is kept minimal since an algorithm need only optimize a single behavior. At the phenotype level, homogeneous groups are potentially more adaptive than heterogeneous groups at coping with the loss of group members. Also, homogenous groups typically have greater flexibility in coordinating behaviors so as to produce an effective collective behavior (Stone & Veloso, 1999). The key disadvantage of such approaches is that system homogeneity, either at the genotype or phenotype level, does not facilitate specialization, so it is likely that such collective behavior systems will converge to a non-specialized solution, even if specialization is advantageous in the given task domain.

Heterogeneous Approaches

Heterogeneous approaches typically study emergent specialization at either the local (agent) or global (entire group) level. The key advantage of heterogeneity is that it encourages and facilitates emergent specialization, both at the individual and group level. The key disadvantage of heterogeneous approaches is that the search space is usually (for complex tasks) prohibitively large comparative to homogeneous approaches, since many different agent behaviors need to be optimized or otherwise adapted for task accomplishment.

Collective Behavior Tasks and Specialization

In the design of collective behavior systems, it remains an open research question as to which task domains are most appropriately solved using specialization. However, there is some agreement amongst researchers that if the task can be naturally decomposed into a set of complementary sub-tasks then specialization is often beneficial for increasing collective task performance (Arkin, 1998; Arkin et al., 1999; Balch, 2002a; Balch, 2002b). The following list enumerates several categories of such collective behavior task domains. Each of these task domain categories mandates some degree of collective behavior, where specialization is beneficial for improving task performance. In subsequent sections, specific research examples selected from each of these categories are briefly examined.

- **Collective Gathering** (Bonabeau et al., 1998; Perez-Uribe, Floreano, & Keller, 2003).

- **Collective Construction** (Murciano et al., 1997a, 1997b; Theraulaz & Bonabeau, 1995).

- **Collective Resource Distribution and Allocation** (Bonabeau et al., 1996, 1997; Campos et al., 2001; Theraulaz et al., 1998a, 1998b).

- **Multi-Agent Computer Games** (Bryant et al., 2003), (Stanley & Miikkulainen, 2002; Stanley et al., 2005b).

- **RoboCup Soccer** (Luke, Farris, Jackson, & Hendler, 1998; Luke et al., 1996; Stone et al., 1999.

- **Predator-Prey and Collective Herding Behaviors** (Blumenthal et al., 2004b), (Blumenthal & Parker, 2004a, 2004c; Luke et al., 1996; Potter et al., 2001).

- **Moving in Formation and Cooperative Transportation Tasks** (Kube & Bonabeau, 1999; Nolfi et al., 2003b; Quinn et al., 2003).

Collective Gathering

Collective gathering is a task domain characterized by the social insect metaphor. That is, collective gathering tasks seek to emulate the success and efficiency of social insects in gathering resources. Collective gathering tasks have been studied in the context of both physical multi-robot systems (Kreiger et al., 2000; Mataric, 1997) and simulated multi-robot systems (Ijspeert, Martinoli, Billard, & Gambardella, 2001), as well as more abstract artificial life simulations (Bongard, 2000; Deneubourg, Theraulaz, & Beckers, 1991; Perez-Uribe et al., 2003). The collective gathering task domain requires that a group of agents search for, collect, and transport resources in the environment from their initial locations to some particular part of the environment. Such gathering tasks typically require that the group of agents allocate their labor efforts to particular sub-tasks so as to derive a collective behavior that maximizes the quantity of resources gathered[6]. Collective gathering tasks are typically viewed as optimization problems and have been traditionally studied with mathematical or otherwise analytical methods (Bonabeau et al., 1996; Gautrais et al., 2002; Theraulaz et al., 1998a).

Learning Behavioral Specialization for Stick Pulling

The research of Li et al. (2004) addressed the important issue of attempting to specify the concepts of heterogeneity and specialization in a formal definition, so as emergent heterogeneity and specialization[7] would be measurable within the larger context of collective behavior and distributed systems research. In a case study that compared centralized and distributed learning methods, the authors qualitatively measured the diversity and specialization of a simulated multi-robot system given a stick-pulling task that mandated specialized and cooperative behavior. One research goal was to investigate the impact of diversity, in the form of heterogeneity in behaviors, upon emergent specialization and in turn the impact of specialization on task performance.

In all experiments, the authors presented a learning method that effectively operated within a multi-robot simulator, where specialization emerged as a function of task constraints and environmental conditions regardless of whether local or global reinforcement signals were used. The authors' explanation for this result was that if behavioral diversity (heterogeneity) is beneficial to task performance, then the learning method facilitates emergent specialization as a means of taking advantage of this behavioral diversity.

The key criticism of this research is the dependency between emergent specialization and the learning method used, and consequently the methods applicability to more generalized optimization tasks. Results supported a hypothesis that if behavioral diversity in a group was beneficial to task performance, then specialization was likely to emerge and increase accordingly with behavioral diversity and task performance. However, these results largely depended upon the type of learning method, the model of the task environment, robot controller parameters that defined membership to a caste, and the task related parameters that the learning method sought to optimize. Thus, the degree to which emergent specialization depended upon the underlying adaptation process remains an open question. Also, the system designer needed to select task environment parameters for the learning method. This cast doubt upon the possibility of applying the learning method to more complex and dynamic task environments, where pertinent task environment parameters that the learning method would require in order to encourage diversity, specialization, and increased task performance, could not be identified *a priori*.

Furthermore, the number of castes composing a group was determined by the system designer and not by the adaptive process. Experiments that analyzed emergent caste formation would be necessary in order to effectively ascertain the relationship between heterogeneity, specialization, and collective behavior task performance. An adaptive process where a particular number of castes emerge in response to simulation environment and task constraints would make such a process applicable to complex task environments where task challenges dynamically arise.

Collective Construction

Collective Construction is a task domain characterized by the social insect metaphor. That is, collective construction tasks seek to emulate the success and efficiency of social insects in gathering resources. Collective construction tasks have mainly been studied in the context of artificial life simulations (Bonabeau, Theraulaz, Arpin, & Sardet, 1994; Murciano et al., 1997a, 1997b; Theraulaz & Bonabeau, 1995. Collective construction is typically viewed as an extension of the collective gathering task, in that it requires the agents to construct a particular structure, with gathered resources, at a home area of the environment. Specialization is typically required for building complex structures from many different types of component resources.

Reinforcement Learning for Specialization in Collective Construction

Murciano et al. (1997a) and Murciano et al. (1997b) applied *reinforcement learning* (RL) methods to a group of homogeneous agents operating in a discrete simulation environment. A collective gathering task mandated that individual agents derive specialized behavior in order to then derive an optimal collective behavior.

The authors used a RL method that independently modified action selection parameters within the controller of each agent. The RL method used either *global* or *local* RL signals so as to effectuate the learning of specialized behaviors. Behavioral specialization took the form of an agent learning to consistently select one action from a set of possible actions. The global RL signal measured group performance, and the local RL signal measured individual performance. The global RL signal was given at the end of a RL trial, where the signal was equal for all agents in the group. The local RL signal was given to individual agents, where the signal was calculated in terms of the agents own successes or failures. Murciano et al. (1997b) conducted experiments that tested the impact of local versus global RL signals upon the learning of specialized behaviors in a homogenous group of agents with no communication. The goal of these experiments was for agents to specialize via learning to gather specific object types so as to construct complex objects. Thus, when agents interacted an effective collective gathering and construction behavior emerged. Group task performance was measured as the number of complex objects assembled in a given RL trial. In the same experimental setup (Murciano et al., 1997a) conducted experiments that utilized only global RL signals for the purpose of facilitating emergent specialization within a homogeneous group of communicating agents. The task of individual agents and the group was to maximize the number of objects gathered over the course of a RL trial. The goal of experiments was for agents to specialize to different behaviors so as communication would facilitate the collective gathering of an optimal number of objects.

One criticism of the research of Murciano et al., (1997b), and Murciano et al. (1997a) derives from the use of RL signals in effectuating specialized behavior. Experimental results indicated that a global RL signal successfully motivated emergent specialization, given the assumption that all agents contribute equally to the task, and the signal was translated so as it could be meaningfully interpreted by each agent in a homogenous group. This casts doubt upon the applicability of global RL signals to heterogeneous groups. Likewise, the applicability of local RL signals was not tested in complex task domains that provided more realistic simulations of multi-robot systems. The possibility of applying the RL method to facilitate specialization in continuous simulation and physical task domains seems unlikely given the sparse reinforcement limitations of global RL signals and the noisy nature of local RL signals (Sutton et al., 1998) that inhibit learning. One aim of the research was to demonstrate that specialization emerges as a function of task constraints on the environment and agent group, irrespective of the type of reinforcement signal used. Achieving scalability in the learning of behavioral specialization is especially prevalent for tasks that require an increasing degree of heterogeneity, and complexity in collective behavior, as a response to dynamically emerging task challenges. However, the scalability of the RL method as a mechanism for encouraging behavioral specialization remains unclear since only two group sizes (10 and 30 agents), and a discrete environment of one size (54 x 54 grid cells) was tested. Also, the impact of more dynamic versions of the simulation environment upon the RL algorithm, were not tested. That is, only one redistribution of objects, during given RL trials, was tested.

Finally, the RL method assumed that the given task environment could be abstracted to the form of a multi-objective function which could be optimized. In this case the function was represented as a set of agent affinities that determined an agent's propensity to adopt particular behavioral roles. This severely limited the applicability of the RL method to more general and complex task environments.

Collective Resource Distribution and Allocation

In a series of research endeavors inspired by social insects (Bonabeau et al., 1996, 1997; Campos et al., 2001; Theraulaz et al., 1998a, 1998b), studied emergent specialization using response threshold methods in simulations of homogenous agent groups that were implemented within the context of mathematical frameworks.

Division of Labor for Dynamic Task Allocation

Theraulaz et al. (1998a) extended a previous formalization for the regulation of division of labor (Bonabeau et al., 1996) in simulated social insect colonies so as to include a *reinforcement learning* process. A formal variable response threshold method was implemented for purpose of facilitating emergent specialization in the form of division of labor. The authors highlighted similarities between their results and observations made within biological social systems where specialist workers were dynamically allocated based upon sub-task demand within a collective behavior task (O'Donnell, 1998).

Division of Labor for Dynamic Flow Shop Scheduling

Campos et al. (2001) introduced a division of labor method and applied it as a method for assigning resources within a dynamic flow shop scheduling task. The task entailed assigning trucks to paint booths in a factory, where trucks moved along an assembly line at a given pace. The color of a truck was predetermined by customer order. Three minutes was needed to paint a truck, but an additional three minutes was required if the color of a paint booth was to be changed for the truck. There was also a cost associated with paint changeover for a booth. A division of labor method was applied to minimize the number of such changeovers. Such paint fit-and-finish tasks are traditional bottleneck problems that can significantly reduce production throughput and thus require optimal solutions (Morley & Ekberg, 1998).

Division of Labor as a Function of Group Size

Gautrais et al., (2002) implemented a variable response threshold method to demonstrate that increasing agent group size and demand for tasks generated specialized agents. As with previous research (Bonabeau et al., 1996; Theraulaz et al., 1998a, 1998b), the response threshold method provided each agent in a group with an internal threshold for activating a particular behavior. Each agent's response threshold was influenced by the level of demand for a particular task, and agents allocated themselves so as to satisfy demand for these tasks. The authors' main conclusion was that their response threshold method demonstrated emergent specialization to be function of group size in the given resource allocation task, where group sizes exceeding a critical threshold value contained specialized agents, and group sizes below the critical threshold value contained only unspecialized agents. These findings were corroborated by similar findings in empirical theoretical biology studies (Robson et al., 1999).

Division of Labor Methods for Collective Resource Distribution and Allocation: Comments

Such response threshold methods represent a very simple, yet powerful, self-regulating feedback system that assigns the appropriate numbers of agents to different tasks. It is obvious that the study of such biologically inspired formalizations of specialization are worthy of future research attention given their applicability to a broad range of optimization tasks including dynamic scheduling and resource allocation. The methods of Bonabeau et al. (1997), Campos et al. (2001), Gautrais et al. (2002), and Theraulaz et al. (1998a) were prevalent in that they eloquently demonstrated how behavioral specialization emerged as a result of self-regulating task assignment and accomplishment, for which there exists a large amount of corroborating biological literature and empirical evidence (Chen, 1937a, 1937b; Deneubourg et al., 1987; O'Donnell, 1998; Robson et al., 1999; Theraulaz, Gervet, & Semenoff, 1991).

The main appeal of this set of research examples was their successful modeling of specialized behavior in the form a set of equations. These equations were successfully applied as a method for regulating the specialization of agents to specific tasks, in order to optimally accomplish a collective behavior task. However, in many cases the adaptive nature of response threshold regulation was never tested for more than one group or environment size, and more than two tasks. Also, the removal of specialized agents to test the adaptation process was limited to two agents. This was an important aspect of the adaptive nature of response thresholds, since if task allocation becomes too dynamic, or oscillatory, it is conceivable that the advantages of specialization could be lost as an agent spends all of its time switching between tasks, and consequently never dedicates enough time to accomplish a given task.

In each case, a simple set of experiments illustrated the importance and necessity of utilizing models of biological social behavior as a step towards understanding such social behavior, and then applying the underlying techniques, namely response thresholds, as a means of designing problem solving methods for optimization tasks. The main advantage of division of labor methods is their eloquence and simplicity of formal specification. Also, such methods yield results that are amenable to a mathematical or formal analysis. However, such methods are also limited to task domains that can be completely represented via the mechanics of a mathematical method. This makes the contributions of such methods limited to optimization tasks that can be formally represented, or to supporting empirical results evident in related biological literature.

Multi-Agent Computer Games

The application of biologically inspired methods to multi-agent computer games (Fogel, Hays, & Johnson, 2004; Laird & vanLent, 2000) has recently achieved particular success and gained popularity. For example, there has been particular research interest in the creation of adaptive interactive multi-agent first-person shooter games (Cole, Louis, & Miles, 2004; Hong & Cho, 2004; Stanley et al., 2005b), as well as strategy games (Bryant et al., 2003; Revello & McCartney, 2002; Yannakakis, Levine, & Hallam, 2004) using artificial evolution and learning as design methods for agent behavior. However, the study of specialized game playing behaviors, in teams of agents, has received relatively little research attention. Specialization is beneficial since it is often necessary for teams of agents to formulate collective behavior solutions in order to effectively challenge a human player, where an increasingly difficult level of agent performance is expected as game time progresses.

Legion-I: Neuro-Evolution for Adaptive Teams

Bryant et al. (2003) utilized the *Enforced Sub-Populations* (ESP) neuro-evolution method (Gomez, 1997) for the derivation of collective behavior in a multi-agent strategy game called *Legion-I*. The research hypothesis was that a team of homogeneous agents, where agents were capable of adopting different behavioral roles would be advantageous in terms of task performance, comparative to heterogeneous groups, composed of agents with static complementary behaviors. These experiments highlighted the effectiveness of the ESP method for deriving a dynamic form of emergent behavioral specialization motivated by division of labor. Results supported the hypothesis that for the Legion game, a homogenous team, where individuals could dynamically switch between specialized behaviors was effective. However, the analysis of emergent specialization was only at a behavioral level, so one could not readily ascertain the relationship between behavioral specialization and the evolved genotypes responsible for such behaviors. This would make an exploration of the mechanisms responsible for emergent specialization resulting from division of labor problematic. The task environment used a discrete simulation environment popular in multi-agent strategy games, but this was not sufficiently complex or dynamic in order to adequately test and support suppositions stating the advantages of behavioral specialization in homogenous teams. Also, the task performance of homogenous groups was not compared with heterogeneous groups. Valuable insight into the capabilities of homogenous versus heterogeneous agent groups for facilitating emergent specialization, could be gained by a comparison between groups represented by one neural controller, versus each agent within a group being represented by a different neural controller.

NERO: Neuro-Evolution of Augmenting Topologies

Stanley et al. (2005b), Stanley, Bryant, Karpov, and Miikkulainen, (2006), and Stanley, Bryant, and Miikkulainen (2005a) introduced a neuro-evolution method for the online evolution of neural controllers that operated in the context of an interactive multi-agent computer game called *Neuro-Evolving Robotic Operatives* (NERO). NERO is a first-person perspective shooter game, where a human player competes with teams of agents, and agents compete against each other. The rtNEAT neuro-evolution method was used for evolving increasing complex agent neural controllers using a process known as *complexification*. This was an extension of the *Neuro-Evolution of Augmenting Topologies* (NEAT) method (Stanley et al., 2002) that operated using online evolution. The authors demonstrated the effectiveness of the rtNEAT method for dynamically adapting agent controllers within a team playing against other agent teams or a human player in real time. Agent game playing behavior became increasingly sophisticated over successive generations as a result of changing neural network topological structure as well as evolving network connection weights. As an extension of the NEAT method, rtNEAT used online evolution to yield impressive results in terms of facilitating effectively competitive collective behaviors in the game playing time of NERO. The NEAT and rtNEAT methods successfully implemented a speciated representation of the genotype space, and a distance measure for genotype similarities, that provided a clear method for relating observed behaviors with a given set of genotypes.

However, the specialized controllers evolved were primarily determined by a training phase of NERO. Agent teams evolved specializations that were suitable for a given environment. Given that simulation environments were the same for both training and a subsequent battle phase, it remains unclear how suitable evolved teams would be for generalized collective behavior games. The true potential and beneficial nature of the rtNEAT method for evolving specialized behaviors in an online evolutionary process, for purpose of increasing team task performance, was not tested in other simulated multi-robot task domains. In realistic collective behavior tasks where the environment is dynamic and its structure and layout are not known *a priori*, training phases would only be partially effective since controllers trained in a simulation of the environment would simply be representing a best guess behavior. Currently, it remains unclear if rtNEAT could be successfully applied to collective behaviors tasks where there is a significant disparity between a training simulation and a subsequent *actual simulation* (called the battle phase in NERO). Such an issue is especially prevalent if online evolution of controllers is to eventually be applied for accomplishing multi-robot tasks, with time and energy constraints, in dynamic and complex physical task environments.

RoboCup Soccer

A distinct relation to multi-agent game research is RoboCup (Kitano & Asada, 2000). RoboCup is a research field dedicated to the design and development of multi-robot systems for the purpose of playing a robotic form of soccer. It is widely recognized as a specific test bed for machine learning algorithms, and engineering challenges (Noda & Stone, 2001). The very nature of the RoboCup game demands the existence of several types of behavioral specialization, in the form of different player roles. Such behaviors must be complementary and able to interact in such a way so as to produce a desired global behavior. That is, a team strategy that wins the game in a competitive scenario. Several researchers have focused on machine learning, evolutionary computation, and neuro-evolution methods that derive task accomplishing collective behaviors within groups of two or three soccer agents. Although, specialized behaviors of individual soccer agents was either specified *a priori* or was derived in simplistic game scenarios (Hsu & Gustafson, 2001, 2002; Luke et al., 1998; Matsubara, Noda, & Hiraki, 1996; Stone et al., 1998, 1998b, 2002; Whiteson et al., 2003. Each of these research examples has been critiqued elsewhere (Nitschke, 2005).

Pursuit-Evasion

Pursuit-evasion is a collective behavior task that is commonly used within artificial life research to test both non-adaptive (typically game theoretic) and adaptive (typically learning and evolution) methods for agent controller design. The task requires that multiple pursuer agents derive a collective behavior for the capture of one or more evading agents (Haynes & Sen, 1996a). The investigation of emergent specialization remains a relatively unexplored area of research in the pursuit-evasion domain (Luke et al., 1996), the collective herding variation (Potter et al., 2001), as well as more traditional predator-prey systems (Nishimura et al., 1997).

Evolving Pursuit-Evasion Behavior with Hexapod Robots

Blumenthal et al. (2004a, 2004b, 2004c) expanded previous work via combining a *punctuated anytime learning* (Blumenthal & Parker, 2006; Parker, 2000) method with an evolutionary algorithm within a co-evolution scenario. Although not the main research focus, this work addressed the issue of using morphological differences in agents in order to effectuate the derivation of behavioral specialization, and consequently a collective prey-capture behavior. The co-evolution scenario operated within a simulated multi-robot system of five hexapod robots where the goal was to derive an effective prey-capture behavior within four predator robots, and a predator-evasion behavior within one prey robot. This study effectively illustrated the derivation of prey-capture behavior based upon specialized behaviors that utilized differences in simulated hexapod robot morphology. Such as, the least maneuverable robot adopting a passive defensive position, whilst the fastest and most maneuverable robots adopted proactive pursuit behaviors.

However, the morphological differences between the robots were simple, leading one to speculate that a higher degree of complexity in specialized behavior may have emerged if differences in sensors and controller structure were included along with a greater disparity in actuator capabilities. Also, the prey was always initially placed at the center of the simulation environment, which made it easier for predators to form an effective prey capture behavior, and influenced the types of prey-capture behaviors that could emerge. Though not explicitly stated as a being a goal of this research, a valuable contribution to this research, would have been a methodological study that described a mapping or set of principles linking types of sensor and actuator capabilities to resulting forms of emergent behavioral specialization. Such a study could potentially form the basis of multi-robot system design methodologies that use evolution and learning mechanisms that capitalize on morphology in order to produce desired collective behaviors for solving a given task.

Evolving Herding Behavior in a Multi-Robot System

The research of Potter et al., (2001) investigated the evolution of homogeneous vs. heterogeneous controllers within a simulated multi-robot system that was given a collective herding task. A group of Nomad 200s were simulated within the *TeamBots* simulator (Balch, 1998). The research hypothesis was that as task difficulty increased, heterogeneity and specialization become essential for successful task accomplishment. Heterogeneity was defined as the number of different behaviors one robot could select from, as well as the number of behaviors in the group. This hypothesis was tested with experiments that introduced a predator into the environment. The goal was to encourage the emergence of specialized defensive behaviors in addition to herding behaviors. Experiments effectively illustrated that emergent behavioral specialization, for the benefit of collective behavior task performance, could be facilitated in a heterogeneous team of agents. Furthermore, results supported a hypothesis that constructing a collective behavior task such that multiple behaviors are required, increases the need for heterogeneity, and in turn specialization. However, the inducement of emergent specialization via increasing the number of behaviors required, and not simply task complexity, was only investigated within a single case study.

The key criticism lies in the comparison of homogenous and heterogeneous groups for deriving collective herding behaviors. Particularly, it is unclear why the authors opted to use only two genotype populations to represent a group of three shepherds in the heterogeneous design approach. The impact of homogeneity and heterogeneity on emergent specialization was not validated with larger groups of shepherds. Also, only one increment in the complexity of the task environment was tested. That is, the addition of the predator to the collective herding task. Complete validation of the authors' hypothesis that specialization emerges not as a consequence of task complexity, but rather as a result of the number of behaviors required to solve the task, would require several comparative case studies. Such studies would need to test tasks of varying degrees of difficulty versus tasks that require numerous complementary and potentially specialized behaviors. Such a comprehensive study would yield a valuable contribution to ones understanding of the relation between heterogeneous and homogenous design approaches, task performance, task complexity, and emergent specialization.

Moving in Formation and Cooperative Transportation Tasks

Certain collective behavior research endeavors, mainly in the fields of artificial life and multi-robot systems, have aimed to model and reproduce various forms of social phenomena that are observable in biological systems (Reynolds, 1987; Zaera, Cliff, & Bruten, 1996). Coordinated movement and cooperative transport is sometimes studied within the context of a gathering task, and has been studied separately in both physical and simulated environments. Cooperative transport is inspired by biological prey retrieval models, which present many examples of the value of specialization, such as the pushing vs. pulling behaviors exhibited in stigmatic coordination that allows several ants to transport a large prey (Kube et al., 1999). Such inspiration was used by the research of Dorigo et al. (2004) and Nolfi, Baldassarre, and Parisi (2003a), which described the evolution of coordinated motion, and self-assembly in a simulated multi-robot system for the purpose of cooperatively transporting objects. Similarly, the research of (Nolfi et al., 2003a) described the evolution of particular group formations in a simulated multi-robot system, which allowed efficient forms of coordinated group movement across an environment towards a light or sound source. The research of Baldassarre, Nolfi, and Parisi (2003), Dorigo et al. (2004), and Nolfi et al. (2003a) has been reviewed in related work (Nitschke, 2005), and is thus not described here.

Future Directions

Consequent of the literature reviewed, we deem the most viable future research direction to be the development of structured and principled emergent behavior design methodologies. From a broad range of methods that utilize emergent specialization for solving collective behavior tasks, a lack of a unifying set of design principles (methodologies) that link the workings of each of these methods, was highlighted. Such design methodologies would provide definitions and measures of specialization, and allow researchers to construct collective behavior systems that facilitate desired forms of emergent specialization that solve given tasks. If emergent specialization is to be utilized as a problem solver in systems that are designed using biologically inspired principles such as evolution and learning, then the concept of specialization must be defined, so as it can be identified and used in a problem solving process. In order to validate design methodologies that identify, measure, and harness emergent specialization as a problem solving tool in artificial complex adaptive systems, several considerations must be made.

1. Given the disparate and disjoint nature of biologically inspired and collective behavior research, validation of emergent specialization design methodologies would be experimental, and not necessarily constructed from a set of mathematical or otherwise theoretical suppositions that are proved.

2. Such methodologies would need to encapsulate the various types of specialization that benefit particular types of collective behavior tasks. These types would be identified through extensive experimentation.

3. Such methodologies would need to use specialization that can be identified and categorized, either dynamically by the design method, or *a priori* by a human designer. Importantly, dynamic identification of the type and degree of specialization required for a given task by a method would greatly increase the applicability of the method. That is, such a method would by applicable to complex task environments where specific task challenges dynamically arise in the environment and the exact nature of tasks cannot be described ahead of time.

Hence, if emergent specialized behavior is to be used as a means of deriving solutions to complex and dynamic task challenges in both simulated and physical collective behavior systems[8] then future research is obliged to look towards addressing the considerations delineated herein.

Conclusion

In drawing conclusions for this chapter, it is important to note that the chapter's goal was not to present an exhaustive list of research relating to emergent specialization, but rather to identify and present a set of pertinent research examples that use biologically inspired design approaches for the purpose of facilitating emergent behavioral specialization. Such research examples were selected based upon results that indicated emergent behavioral specialization as being beneficial for solving collective behavior tasks.

The binding theme of the chapter argued, that the majority of collective behavior research is currently analyzed and evaluated from empirical data gathered and emergent behavioral specialization observed, without analytical methods for identifying the means and causes of emergent specialization. An obvious reason for this is that the use of biologically inspired concepts such as evolution, self-organization, and learning as design methods is still in a phase of research infancy. Consequently, emergent specialization derived using such biologically inspired design concepts is currently constrained to simple forms. Given this general evaluation of prevalent literature, we identified several unresolved issues that inhibit the development of biologically inspired design methodologies that synthesize emergent specialization in solving collective behavior tasks.

1.   It was evident that many researchers deem the simulation of collective behavior systems to be an effective approach for investigating emergent behavioral specialization, given that simulations provide a convenient means for studying the conditions under which specialization emerges. For example, the effects of parametric changes can be observed in a relatively short space of time. However, with notable exceptions, such as *SwarmBots* (Dorigo et al., 2004), the identification and transference of mechanisms motivating emergent specialization observed in simulation to counter-part algorithms operating in physical collective behavior systems such as multi-robot systems, is not yet plausible. In the case of *SwarmBots* (Dorigo et al., 2004), a simple task environment made the

transference to a physical environment possible, and emergent specialization was not necessarily a problem solver for dynamic challenges in
the environment, but rather a solution to a given task that was emergent
but not necessarily desired.

2.   In the pertinent research examples reviewed, the complete potential
     of biologically inspired design, and the advantages of emergent spe-
     cialization were not always effectively exploited. For example, many
     collective behavior systems, with notable exceptions such as division
     of labor methods applied to optimization tasks (Bonabeau et al., 1997),
     were simply attempting to synthesize emergent specialization, or to
     demonstrate the veracity of concepts such as self-organization, learn-
     ing, and evolution for deriving novel agent behaviors. Such concepts
     were rarely applied to methods that derived emergent specialization as
     a means of increasing task performance or accomplishing unforeseen
     challenges in collective behavior tasks.

3.   There is currently no standardized benchmark or research test-bed for
     testing, interpreting, evaluating, and classifying emergent specialized
     behavior. RoboCup was included as an honorable mention in the chap-
     ter, given that it provides an effective platform for testing and evaluat-
     ing various forms of collective and individual behavior, emergent or
     otherwise, implemented either within an agent simulator or a physical
     multi-robot system. That is, collective behavior is simply evaluated
     within a competitive game scenario, so collective behavior performance
     is determined according to the evaluation criteria of the game. Another
     exception is collective gathering and dynamic scheduling in distributed
     systems, which can be represented as optimization tasks. In this case,
     standardized benchmarks exist in the form of performance results yielded
     by classical adaptive approaches. This makes the results of biologically
     inspired and classical methods to such tasks comparable. However, with
     exceptions such as Bonabeau et al. (1997) and Theraulaz and Bonabeau
     (1995) many optimization tasks do not benefit from the use of emergent
     behavioral specialization. Thus, the testing, interpretation, and evalua-
     tion of emergent specialized behavior within the context of collective
     behavior systems, is currently conducted according to the performance
     benchmarks of the researcher's own experimental simulation platform.
     This means that the experimental results can only be compared within
     the context of their own simulation environment. The development of
     emergent specialization design methodologies that could be equally ap-

plied to physical collective behavior systems would remove this critical constraint.

Given these open research issues, one may conclude that if the notion of emergent specialization as a problem solver for collective behavior tasks is to gain any maturity and credibility, then collective behavior systems must be built upon proven *emergent specialization design methodologies*. Ideally, such methodologies must be proven for convergence to desired forms of collective behavior (achieved as a consequence of emergent specialization), scalable and transferable to a counterpart situated and embodied collective behavior task environments.

References

Abdel-Rahman, H. (2001). When do cities specialize in production. *Reg Sci Urban Econ, 26*(1), 1-22.

Arkin, R. (1998). *Behavior based robotics*. Cambridge, MA: MIT Press.

Arkin, R., & Balch, T. (1999). Behavior-based formation control for multi-robot teams. *IEEE Transactions on Robotics and Automation, 14*(6), 926-939.

Axelrod, R. (1984). *The evolution of cooperation*. New York: Basic Books.

Baev, K. (1997). *Biological neural networks*. Berlin, Germany: Birkuser.

Balch, T. (2002b). Taxonomies of multi-robot task and reward. In T. Balch & E. Parker (Eds.), *Robot teams: From diversity to polymorphism* (pp. 23-35). Natick: A K Peters.

Balch, T. (2002a). Measuring robot group diversity. In T. Balch & E. Parker (Eds.), *Robot teams: From diversity to polymorphism* (pp. 93-135). Natick: A K Peters.

Balch, T. (1998). *Behavioral diversity in learning robot teams. PhD thesis.* Atlanta: College of Computing, Georgia Institute of Technology.

Baldassarre, G., Nolfi, S., & Parisi, D. (2003). Evolving mobile robots able to display collective behavior. *Artificial Life, 9*(3), 255-267.

Beni, G. (2004). From swarm intelligence to swarm robotics. *Proceedings of the 1ˢᵗ International Workshop on Swarm Robotics* (p. 1-9). Santa Monica, CA: Springer.

Blumenthal, J., & Parker, G. (2006). Benchmarking punctuated anytime learning for evolving a multi-agent teams binary controllers. *World Automation Congress 2006.* Budapest, Hungary: IEEE Press.

Blumenthal, J., & Parker, G. (2004a). Co-evolving team capture strategies for dissimilar robots. *AAAI Artificial Multi-Agent Learning Symposium* (pp. 15-23). Arlington, VA: AAAI Press.

Blumenthal, J., & Parker, G. (2004b). Competing sample sizes for the co-evolution of heterogeneous agents. *Proceedings of the 2004 IEEE/RSJ International Conference on Intelligent Robots and Systems* (pp. 1438-1443). Sendai, Japan: IEEE Press.

Blumenthal, J., & Parker, G. (2004c). Punctuated anytime learning for evolving multi-agent capture strategies. *Proceedings of the Congress on Evolutionary Computation* (pp. 1820-1827). Portland, OR: IEEE Press.

Bonabeau, E., & Theraulaz, G. (1999). Role and variability of response thresholds in the regulation of division of labor in insect societies. In J. Deneubourg & J. Pasteels (Eds.), *Information processing in social insects* (p. 141-163). Basel, Switzerland: Springer Verlag.

Bonabeau, E., Dorigo, M., & Theraulaz, G. (1998). *Swarm intelligence: From natural to artificial systems.* Oxford, England: Oxford University Press.

Bonabeau, E., Sobkowski, A., Theraulaz, G., & Deneubourg, J. (1997). Adaptive task allocation inspired by a model of division of labor in social insects. In D. Lundh, B. Olsson, & A. Narayanan (Eds.), *Bio-computing and emergent computation* (pp. 36-45). Singapore: World Scientific.

Bonabeau, E., Theraulaz, G., & Deneubourg, J. (1996). Quantitative study of the fixed threshold model for the regulation of division of labor in insect societies. *Proceedings of the Royal Society of London B, 263*(1), 1565-1569.

Bonabeau, E., Theraulaz, G., Arpin, E., & Sardet, E. (1994). The building behavior of lattice swarms. *Artificial Life IV: Proceedings of the 4ᵗʰ International Workshop on the Synthesis and Simulation of Living Systems* (pp. 307-312). Cambridge, MA: MIT Press.

Bongard, J. (2000). The legion system: A novel approach to evolving heterogeneity for collective problem solving. *Proceedings of Eurogp-2000* (pp. 16-28). Edinburgh, UK: Springer-Verlag.

Brooks, R. (1990). Elephants don't play chess. *Robotics and Autonomous Systems, 6*(1), 3-15.

Bryant, B., & Miikkulainen, R. (2003). Neuro-evolution for adaptive teams. *Proceedings of the 2003 Congress on Evolutionary Computation* (pp. 2194-2201). Canberra, Australia: IEEE Press.

Calderone, N., & Page, R. (1988). Genotypic variability in age polyethism and task specialization in the honeybee. *Apis mellifera. Behav. Ecol. Sociobiol, 22*(1), 17-25.

Campos, C., Theraulaz, G., Bonabeau, E., & Deneubourg, J. (2001). Dynamic scheduling and division of labor in social insects. *Adaptive Behavior, 8*(2), 83-94.

Chen, C. (1937a). The leaders and followers among the ants in nest-building. *Physiol. Zool., 10*(1), 437-455.

Chen, C. (1937b). Social modification of the activity of ants in nest-building. *Physiol. Zool., 10*(1), 420-436.

Cole, N., Louis, S., & Miles, C. (2004). Using a genetic algorithm to tune first-person shooter bots. *Proceedings of the 2004 Congress on Evolutionary Computation* (Vol. 1, pp. 139-145). Piscataway: IEEE Press.

Deneubourg, J., Goss, S., Pasteels, J., Fresneau, D., & Lachaud, J. (1987). Self-organization mechanisms in ant societies (ii): Learning in foraging and division of labor. In J. Pasteels & J. Deneubourg (Eds.), *From individual to collective behavior in social insects* (pp. 177-196). Basel, Switzerland: Birkhauser.

Deneubourg, J., Theraulaz, G., & Beckers, R. (1991). Swarm-made architectures. *Proceedings of the European Conference on Artificial Life* (pp. 123-133). Amsterdam, Holland: Elsevier Academic Publishers.

Dorigo, M., Tuci, E., Gross, R., Trianni, V., Labella, H., Nouyan, S., et al. (2004). The swarm-bots project. *Proceedings of the Swarm Robotics: SAB 2004 International Workshop* (Vol. 3342, pp. 31-32). Santa Monica, CA: Springer Verlag.

Edmonds, J. (1965). Path, trees, and flowers. *Canadian J. Math., 17*(1), 449-467.

Fogel, D., Hays, T., & Johnson, D. (2004). A platform for evolving characters in competitive games. *Proceedings of 2004 congress on evolutionary computation* (pp. 1420-1426). Piscataway, USA: IEEE Press.

Funes, P., Orme, B., & Bonabeau, E. (2003). Evolving emergent group behaviors for simple humans agents. *Proceedings of the 7th European Conference on Artificial Life* (pp. 76-89). Berlin, Germany: Springer-Verlag.

Gautrais, J., Theraulaz, G., Deneubourg, J., & Anderson, C. (2002). Emergent polyethism as a consequence of increased colony size in insect societies. *Journal of Theoretical Biology, 215*(1), 363-373.

Gomez, F. (1997). *Robust non-linear control through neuro-evolution. PhD thesis.* Austin, TX: Department of Computer Science, University of Austin, Texas.

Grefenstette, J. (1995). Credit assignment in rule discovery systems. *Machine Learning, 3*(3), 225-246.

Hawthorne, D. (2001). Genetic linkage of ecological specialization and reproductive isolation in pea aphids. *Nature, 412*(1), 904-907.

Haynes, T., & Sen, S. (1996a). Co-adaptation in a team. *International Journal of Computational Intelligence and Organizations, 1*(4), 1-20.

Haynes, T., & Sen, S. (1996b). Evolving behavioral strategies in predators and prey. In G. Weiss & S. Sen (Eds.), *Adaptation and learning in multi-agent systems: Lecture notes in computer science* (pp. 113-126). Berlin, Germany: Springer-Verlag.

Hong, J., & Cho, S. (2004). Evolution of emergent behaviors for shooting game characters in RoboCode. *Proceedings of the 2004 Congress on Evolutionary Computation* (Vol. 1, pp. 634-638). Piscataway, USA: IEEE Press.

Hsu, W., & Gustafson, S. (2001). Layered learning in genetic programming for a cooperative robot soccer problem. *Proceedings of the 4th European Conference on Genetic Programming* (pp. 291-301). Como, Italy: Springer-Verlag.

Hsu, W., & Gustafson, S. (2002). Genetic programming and multi-agent layered learning by reinforcements. *Proceedings of the Genetic and Evolutionary Computation Conference* (pp. 764-771). New York: Morgan Kaufmann.

Ijspeert, A., Martinoli, A., Billard, A., & Gambardella, L. (2001). Collaboration through the exploitation of local interactions in autonomous collective robotics: The stick pulling experiment. *Autonomous Robots*, *11*(2), 149-171.

Kitano, H., & Asada, M. (2000). The RoboCup humanoid challenge as the millennium challenge for advanced robotics. *Advanced Robotics*, *13*(1), 723-736.

Komann, M., & Fey, D. (2007). Realizing emergent image pre-processing tasks in cellular-automaton-alike massively parallel hardware. *International Journal on Parallel, Emergent and Distributed Systems*, *22*(1), 79-89.

Kreiger, M., & Billeter, J. (2000). The call of duty: Self-organized task allocation in a population of up to twelve mobile robots. *Robotics and Autonomous Systems*, *30*, 65-84.

Kube, C., & Bonabeau, E. (1999). Cooperative transport by ants and robots. *Robotics and Autonomous Systems: Special Issue on Biomimetic Robots*, *1*(1), 20-29.

Laird, J., & vanLent, M. (2000). Human-level AI killer application: Interactive computer games. *Proceedings of the 17th National Conference on Artificial Intelligence and the 12th Annual Conference on Innovative Applications of Artificial Intelligence* (pp. 1171-1178). Menlo Park, USA: AAAI Press.

Li, L., Martinoli, A., & Mostafa, Y. (2002). Emergent specialization in swarm systems. In H. Yin, N. Allinson, R. Freeman, J. Keane, & S. Hubbard (Eds.), *Lecture notes in computer science: Vol. 2412. Intelligent data engineering and automated learning* (pp. 261-266). Berlin, Germany: Springer-Verlag.

Li, L., Martinoli, A., & Yaser, A. (2004). Learning and measuring specialization in collaborative swarm systems. *Adaptive Behavior*, *12*(3), 199-212.

Lipson, H., & Pollack, J. (2000). Automatic design and manufacture of robotic life forms. *Nature*, *406*(1), 974-978.

Luke, S., & Spector, L. (1996). Evolving teamwork and coordination with genetic programming. *Proceedings of the 1996 International Conference on Genetic Programming* (pp. 150-156). Stanford, USA: MIT Press.

Luke, S., Farris, C. H. J., Jackson, G., & Hendler, J. (1998). Co-evolving soccer SoftBot team coordination with genetic programming. In H.

Kitano (Ed.), *Robocup-97: Robot Soccer World Cup I* (pp. 398-411). Berlin, Germany: Springer-Verlag.

Martinoli, A., Zhang, Y., Prakash, P., Antonsson, E., & Olney, R. (2002). Towards evolutionary design of intelligent transportation systems. The *11th International Symposium on New Technologies for Advanced Driver Assistance Systems* (pp. 283-290). Siena, Italy: ATA Press.

Mataric, M. (1997). Behavior-based control: Examples from navigation, learning, and group behavior. *Journal of Experimental and Theoretical Artificial Intelligence, 9*(1), 62-78.

Matsubara, H., Noda, I., & Hiraki, K. (1996). Learning of cooperative actions in multi-agent systems: A case study of pass and play in soccer. *Adaptation, Co-Evolution, and Learning in Multi-Agent Systems: Papers from the 1996 AAAI Spring Symposium* (pp. 63-67). Boston: AAAI Press.

Morley, R., & Ekberg, G. (1998). Cases in chaos: Complexity-based approaches to manufacturing. In *Embracing complexity: A colloquium on the application of complex adaptive systems to business.* (p. 97-702). Cambridge, USA: The Ernst and Young Center for Business for Business Innovation.

Müller, C., & Sick, B. (2006). Emergence in organic computing systems: Discussion of a controversial concept. *Proceedings of the 3rd International Conference on Autonomic and Trusted Computing, Volume 4158 Of Lecture Notes In Computer Science* (pp. 1-16). Berlin, Germany: Springer.

Murciano, A., & Millan, J. (1997). Learning signaling behaviors and specialization in cooperative agents. *Adaptive Behavior, 5*(1), 5-28.

Murciano, A., Millan, J., & Zamora, J. (1997). Specialization in multi-agent systems through learning. *Biological Cybernetics, 76*(1), 375-382.

Ng, Y., & Yang, X. (1997). Specialization, information, and growth: A sequential equilibrium analysis. *Rev Dev Econ, 1*(1), 257-274.

Nishimura, S., & Takashi, I. (1997). Emergence of collective strategies in a predator-prey game model. *Artificial Life, 3*(1), 243-260.

Nitschke, G. (2005). Emergence of cooperation: State of the art. *Artificial Life, 11*(3), 367-396.

Noda, I., & Stone, P. (2001). The RoboCup soccer server and CMUnited clients: Implemented infrastructure for MAS research. *Autonomous Agents and Multi-Agent Systems, 7*(1), 101-120.

Noirot, C., & Pasteels, J. (1987). Ontogenetic development and the evolution of the worker caste in termites. *Experientia.*, *43*(1), 851-860.

Nolfi, S., & Floreano, D. (2000). *Evolutionary robotics: The biology, intelligence, and technology of self-organizing machines.* Cambridge, MA: MIT Press.

Nolfi, S., & Parisi, D. (1997). Learning to adapt to changing environments in evolving neural networks. *Adaptive Behavior*, *1*(5), 75-98.

Nolfi, S., Baldassarre, G., & Parisi, D. (2003a). Evolution of collective behavior in a team of physically linked robots. In G. Guillot & J. Meyer (Eds.), *Applications of evolutionary computing* (pp. 581-592). Heidelberg, Germany: Springer Verlag.

Nolfi, S., Deneubourg, J., Floreano, D., Gambardella, L., Mondada, F., & Dorigo, M. (2003b). Swarm-bots: Swarm of mobile robots able to self-assemble and self-organize. *Ecrim News*, *53*(1), 25-26.

O'Donnell, S. (1998). Effects of experimental forager removals on division of labour in the primitively eusocial wasp polistes instabilis. *Behaviour*, *135*(2), 173-193.

O'Riain, M., Jarvis, J., Alexander, R., Buffenstein, R., & Peeters, C. (2000). Morphological castes in a vertebrate. *Proceedings of the National Academy of Sciences of the United States of America*, *97*(24), 13194-13197.

Parker, G. (2000). Co-evolving model parameters for anytime learning in evolutionary robotics. *Robotics and Autonomous Systems*, *33*(1), 13-30.

Parker, G., & Nathan, P. (2006). Evolving sensor morphology on a legged robot in niche environments. *World Automation Congress 2006.* Budapest, Hungary: IEEE Press.

Perez-Uribe, A., Floreano, D., & Keller, L. (2003). Effects of group composition and level of selection in the evolution of cooperation in artificial ants. *Advances of Artificial Life: Proceedings of the 7th European Conference on Artificial Life* (pp. 128-137). Dortmund, Germany: Springer.

Pfeifer, R., Iida, F., & Gomez, G. (2006). Designing intelligent robots: On the implications of embodiment. *Journal of Robotics Society of Japan*, *24*(7), 9-16.

Potter, M., & DeJong, K. (2000). Cooperative co-evolution: An architecture for evolving co-adapted subcomponents. *Evolutionary Computation*, *8*(1), 1-29.

Potter, M., Meeden, L., & Schultz, A. (2001). Heterogeneity in the coevolved behaviors of mobile robots: The emergence of specialists. *Proceedings of the International Joint Conference on Artificial Intelligence* (pp. 1337-1343). Seattle, WA: AAAI Press.

Quinn, M., Smith, L., Mayley, G., & Husbands, P. (2003). Evolving controllers for a homogeneous system of physical robots: Structured cooperation with minimal sensors. *Philosophical Transactions of the Royal Society of London, Series A: Mathematical, Physical, and Engineering Sciences*, *361*(1), 2321-2344.

Resnick, M. (1997). *Turtles, termites, and traffic jams: Explorations in massively parallel micro worlds*. Cambridge, MA: MIT Press.

Revello, T., & McCartney, R. (2002). Generating war game strategies using a genetic algorithm. *Proceedings of the 2002 Congress on Evolutionary Computation* (pp. 1086-1091). Piscataway, USA: IEEE Press.

Reynolds, C. (1987). Flocks, herds, and schools: A distributed behavioral model. *Computer Graphics*, *21*(4), 25-36.

Robson, S., & Traniello, J. (1999). Key individuals and the organization of labor in ants. In J. Deneubourg & J. Pasteels (Eds.), *Information processing in social insects* (pp. 239-259). Basel, Switzerland: Springer Verlag.

Schultz, A., & Bugajska, M. (2000). Co-evolution of form and function in the design of autonomous agents: Micro air vehicles project. *Proceedings of the Workshop on Evolution of Sensors in Nature, Hardware, and Simulation* (pp. 154-166). Chicago, IL: AAAI Press.

Seligmann, H. (1999). Resource partition history and evolutionary specialization of subunits in complex systems. *Biosystems*, *51*(1), 31-39.

Sims, K. (2004). Evolving 3d morphology and behavior by competition. *Artificial Life IV: Proceedings of the 4th International Workshop on the Synthesis and Simulation of Living Systems* (pp. 28-39). Cambridge, MA: MIT Press.

Smith, A. (1904). *An inquiry into the nature and causes of the wealth of nations* (5th ed.), (E. Cannan, Ed.). London, United Kingdom: Methuen and Co., Ltd. First published: 1776.

Solow, D., & Szmerekovsky, J. (2004). Mathematical models for explaining the emergence of specialization in performing tasks. *Complexity*, *10*(1), 37-48.

Stanley, K., & Miikkulainen, R. (2002). Evolving neural networks through augmenting topologies. *Evolutionary Computation, 10*(2), 99-127.

Stanley, K., Bryant, B., & Miikkulainen, R. (2005a). Evolving neural network agents in the NERO video game. *Proceedings of the IEEE 2005 Symposium on Computational Intelligence And Games* (pp. 182-189). Piscataway, USA: IEEE Press.

Stanley, K., Bryant, B., & Miikkulainen, R. (2005b). Real-time neuro-evolution in the NERO video game. *Evolutionary Computation, 9*(6), 653-668.

Stanley, K., Bryant, B., Karpov, I., & Miikkulainen, R. (2006). Real-time evolution of neural networks in the NERO video game. *Proceedings of the 21st National Conference on Artificial Intelligence* (pp. 1671-1674). Boston: AAAI Press.

Stone, P., & Veloso, M. (1998a). A layered approach to learning client behaviors in the RoboCup soccer server. *Applied Artificial Intelligence, 12*(1), 165-188.

Stone, P., & Veloso, M. (1998b). Using decision tree confidence factors for multi-agent control. *Proceedings of the 2nd International Conference on Autonomous Agents* (pp. 110-116). Minneapolis, MN: ACM Press.

Stone, P., & Veloso, M. (1999). Task decomposition, dynamic role assignment, and low bandwidth communication for real time strategic teamwork. *Artificial Intelligence, 110*(2), 241-273.

Stone, P., & Veloso, M. (2002). Towards collaborative and adversarial learning: A case study in robotic soccer. *Evolution and learning in multi-agent systems, 48*(1), 83-104.

Sutton, R., & Barto, A. (1998). *An introduction to reinforcement learning.* Cambridge, MA: John Wiley and Sons.

Tarapore, D., Floreano, D., & Keller, L. (2006). Influence of the level of polyandry and genetic architecture on division of labor. *The 10th International Conference on the Simulation and Synthesis of Living Systems (ALIFE X)* (pp. 358-364). Cambridge, USA: MIT Press.

Theraulaz, G., & Bonabeau, E. (1995). Coordination in distributed building. *Science, 269*(1), 686-688.

Theraulaz, G., Bonabeau, E., & Deneubourg, J. (1998a). Fixed response thresholds and the regulation of division of labor in insect societies. *Bulletin of Mathematical Biology, 60*(1), 753-807.

Theraulaz, G., Bonabeau, E., & Deneubourg, J. (1998b). Response threshold reinforcement and division of labor in insect societies. *Proceedings of the Royal Society of London B, 265*(1), 327-332.

Theraulaz, G., Gervet, J., & Semenoff, S. (1991). Social regulation of foraging activities in polistes dominulus christ: A systemic approach to behavioural organization. *Behaviour, 116*(1), 292-320.

Theraulaz, G., Goss, S., Gervet, J., & Deneubourg, J. (1991). Task differentiation in polistes wasp colonies: A model for self-organizing groups of robots. *The 1ˢᵗ International Conference on the Simulation of Adaptive Behavior* (pp. 346-355). Cambridge, USA: MIT Press.

Thompson, A., Harvey, I., & Husbands, P. (1996). Unconstrained evolution and hard consequences. *Towards Evolvable Hardware: The Evolutionary Engineering Approach* (Vol. 1062 LNCS, pp. 135-165). Berlin, Germany: Springer-Verlag.

Trumler, W., Klaus, R., & Ungerer, T. (2006). Self-configuration via cooperative social behavior. *Proceedings of the 3ʳᵈ International Conference on Autonomic and Trusted Computing* (pp. 90-99). Wuhan, China: Springer.

Waibel, M., Floreano, D., Magnenat, S., & Keller, L. (2006). Division of labor and colony efficiency in social insects: Effects of interactions between genetic architecture, colony kin structure, and rate of perturbations. *Proceedings of the Royal Society B, 273*(1), 1815-1823.

Watson, R., Ficici, S., & Pollack, J. (1999a). Embodied evolution: A response to challenges in evolutionary robotics. In J. Wyatt & J. Demiris (Eds.), The 8ᵗʰ *European Workshop on Learning Robots* (pp. 14-22). Lausanne, Switzerland: Springer Verlag.

Watson, R., Ficici, S., & Pollack, J. (1999b). Embodied evolution: Embodying an evolutionary algorithm in a population of robots. *1999 Congress on Evolutionary Computation* (pp. 335-342). Washington, DC, USA: IEEE Press.

Watson, R., Ficici, S., & Pollack, J. (2002). Embodied evolution: Distributing an evolutionary algorithm in a population of robots. *Robotics and Autonomous Systems, 39*(1), 1-18.

Weis, T., Parzyjegla, H., Jaeger, M., & Mühl, G. (2006). Self-organizing and self-stabilizing role assignment in sensor/actuator networks. *Proceedings of the 8th International Symposium on Distributed Objects and Applications.* (pp. 1807-1824), Montpellier, France: Springer.

Wenseleers, T., Ratnieks, F., & Billen, J. (2003). Caste fate conflict in swarm-founding social hymenoptera: An inclusive fitness analysis. *Evolutionary Biology, 16*(1), 647-658.

Whiteson, S., Kohl, N., Miikkulainen, R., & Stone, P. (2003). Evolving keep-away soccer players through task decomposition. *Proceeding of the Genetic and Evolutionary Computation Conference* (pp. 356-368). Chicago, IL: AAAI Press.

Wu, J., Di, Z., & Yang, Z. (2003). Division of labor as the result of phase transition. *Physica A, 7*(1), 323-663.

Yannakakis, G., Levine, J., & Hallam, J. (2004). An evolutionary approach for interactive computer games. *Proceedings of the 2004 Congress on Evolutionary Computation* (pp. 986-993). Piscataway, USA: IEEE Press.

Zaera, N., Cliff, D., & Bruten, J. (1996). *(Not) Evolving collective behaviors in synthetic fish (tech. rep.).* Bristol, England: Hewlett-Packard Laboratories.

Zhang, Y., Martinoli, A., & Antonsson, E. (2003). Evolutionary design of a collective sensory system. *The 2003 AAAI Spring Symposium on Computational Synthesis* (pp. 283-290). Stanford, USA: AAAI Press.

Endnotes

[1]   Examples of complex adaptive systems include social insect colonies, biological neural networks, traffic jams, economies of a nation, as well as industrial infrastructures such as energy and telecommunications networks (Resnick, 1997). We deem complex adaptive systems to be a subset of complex systems where autonomous software (simulated) or physically embodied (robots) agents operate in order to solve a given task.

[2]   The terms task, activity, role, and caste are defined as follows. Task: what has to be done; Activity: what is being done; Role: the task assigned to an individual within a set of responsibilities given to a group

of individuals; Caste: a group of individuals specialized in the same role (Kreiger et al., 2000).

[3]   The terms collective behavior system and artificial complex adaptive system are used interchangeably throughout the chapter. Both refer to distributed systems where specialization emerges as a property of a collective behavior dynamics.

[4]   We distinguish methodologies from methods. We assume the latter to be the actual algorithm, which is implemented for the purpose of solving a specific task. Where as, we assume the former to be a set of design principles for designing methods.

[5]   Various definitions for numerous types of specialization have been proposed across a broad range of disciplines. In The Wealth of Nations, (Smith, 1904) Adam Smith described economic specialization in terms of division of labor. Specifically stating that in industrialism, division of labor represents a qualitative increase in productivity, and regarded its emergence as the result of a dynamic engine of economic progress. Smith viewed specialization by workers as leading to greater skill and greater productivity for given tasks, which could not be achieved by non-specialized workers attempting to accomplish those same tasks.

[6]   The allocation of agent labor within a group of agents is analogous to resource allocation which derives from economic and game theory studies (Axelrod, 1984). Such studies attempt to derive methods that efficiently allocate a limited amount of resources so as to accomplish a given task with the highest degree of performance possible.

[7]   Heterogeneity, and hence behavioral diversity, was defined as the number of castes in the group, and specialization was the part of diversity that was required to increase task performance.

[8]   Such a case has been envisioned for swarm robotic systems (Beni, 2004).

Section IV

Social Science
Perspectives

Chapter IX

Emergence in Agent-Based Computational Social Science:
Conceptual, Formal, and Diagrammatic Analysis

Jean Louis Dessalles, ENST, Paris, France

Jacques Ferber, LIRMM, CNRS, & University of Montpellier, France

Denis Phan, GEMAS, CNRS, and University of Paris IV Sorbonne, & CREM, CNRS, and University of Rennes I, France

Abstract

This chapter provides a critical survey of emergence definitions both from a conceptual and formal standpoint. The notions of downward/backward causation and weak/strong emergence are specially discussed for application to complex social system with cognitive agents. Particular attention is devoted to the formal definitions introduced by Müller (2004) and Bonabeau and Dessalles (1997), which are operative in multi-agent frameworks and make sense from both cognitive and social point of view. A diagrammatic 4-Quadrant approach allows us to understand complex phenomena along both interior/exterior and individual/collective dimensions.

Introduction

The concept of "emergence," first discussed in philosophy, is also widely used in complex adaptive systems literature especially in computer sciences (Holland, 1998) and related fields (multi-agent systems, artificial intelligence, artificial life...) as well as in physics, biology, and cognitive sciences. Particular applications are the social and human sciences, and consequently the design of "artificial society" or "agent-based computational economics" (ACE) framework by means of multi-agent systems (MAS). For instance in a pioneering book on artificial society and multi-agent simulations in social sciences, Gilbert and Conte (1995) put the emphasis on emergence as a key concept of such an approach: "Emergence is one of the most interesting issues to have been addressed by computer scientists over the past few years and has also been a matter of concern in a number of other disciplines from biology to political science" (op.cit. p. 8). More recently, comprehensive discussion of emergence issues can be found in Gilbert (2002) and Sawyer (2001a, 2004, 2005) for the social science and Sawyer (2002a) for the psychology. In economics, ACE put also the emphasis on the question of emergence (see e.g., Axtell, Epstein, & Young, 2001; Epstein, 1999, 2006; Tesfatsion, 2002a, 2002b; Tesfatsion & Judd, 2006). In all these works, cognition and societies are viewed as complex systems.

The present chapter discusses the impact of emergence on both "downward" and "upward" effects, with applications to the social sciences. MAS allow us to formalize in a single framework both bottom-up and top-down processes. In multi-agent frameworks, properties of the "whole" system result from the collective interactions between the parts (agents) by upward causation (bottom-up process, compatible with methodological individualism); but, to some extent, agents may be constrained by the whole top-down process, compatible with holism or structuralism methodological point of view. This downward effect may arise by means of the social dimension of beliefs (Phan & Ferber, 2007) through the agents' perception of social phenomena or through structural properties of the agents' social environment. Such a downward determination is mainly—but not only—associated to cognitive agents (Castelfranchi, 1998a-b). The process through which the macro-level emerging social structure "feedbacks" into the micro-level by re-shaping the "elementary" agents' behaviors is also called "immergence" by (Gilbert, 1995, 2002).

This chapter provides in first section a critical survey of emergence definitions in literature and exhibits the common structure of the remaining issues. Section 2 introduces and discusses the significance of formal definitions of emergence, with a special attention for those of (Müller, 2004; Bonabeau et al., 1997). These formal definitions are operative for modeling complex artificial societies using multi-agent oriented programming (Ferber, 1999) and make sense from both cognitive and social point of views (Dessalles & Phan, 2005). Complementary features related to complexity are introduced, like detection and cognitive hierarchy. Finally, the last section proposes to highlight the whole process of emergence in the cognitive and social context using a comprehensive framework, the 4-Quadrant approach, which allows an "integrative" understanding of complex phenomena at the light of multi-agent oriented design in both an interior/exterior dimension and an individual/collective dimension.

Some Conceptual Issues on Emergence

The notion of emergence has several meanings. In the vernacular language, emergence denotes both a gradual beginning or coming forth, or a sudden uprising or appearance; to emerge also means to become visible; for example, emergence may denote the act of rising out of a fluid. This latter sense is close to its Latin roots, where *emergere* is the opposite of *mergere*: to be submerged. In what follows, we relate the "act of rising out" to the arising of some phenomenon from a process, and note the fact that to become visible presupposes some observer.

The common sense of emergence is therefore linked to the meaning of a process that produces some phenomenon that might be detected by an observer. In the field of science, emergence was used by Newton in optics. By the 19th century, the word "emergent" was introduced into the fields of biology and philosophy. In the latter, emergentism has a long history, from Mill's chapter:

"Of the composition of causes" in *System of Logic* (Mill, 1843), Lewes' distinction between "resultant" and "emergent" effects (Lewes, 1875); Morgan (1923) and Broad (1925), to the contemporary debates about the philosophy of mind around "the mind—body problem." (For a synthesis, see among others: McLaughlin (1992, 1997); Van de Vijver (1997); Emmeche, Koppe, and Stjernfelt (1997); Clayton and Davies (2006); Kistler, 2006). Classical definition is given by Broad (1925):

"The emergent theory asserts that there are certain wholes, composed (say) of constituents A, B, and C in a relation R to each other; that all wholes composed of constituents of the same kind as A, B, and C in relations of the same kind as R have certain characteristic properties; that A, B, and C are capable of occurring in other kinds of complex where the relation is not of the same kind as R; and that the characteristic properties of the whole R(A, B, C) cannot, even in theory, be deduced from the most complete knowledge of the properties of A, B, and C in isolation or in other wholes which are not of the form R(A, B, C)" (Broad, 1935, Chapter 2, underlined by us).

As underlined, British emergentism rejects reductionism: the properties of the "whole" cannot be deduced from the properties of the parts. Several of them consider emergence also from an ontological standpoint, coupled with a layered view of nature. For ontological emergentism, the world is constituted of hierarchically layered structures, or "levels of organization." Lewes (1875) places emergence at the interface between such levels of organization. Each new layer is a consequence of the appearance of novel qualities, with an increasing complexity. "Emergent laws are fundamental; they are irreducible to laws characterizing properties at lower levels of complexity, even given ideal information as to boundary conditions. Since emergent features have not only same-level effects, but also effects in lower levels, some speak of the view's commitment to *downward causation*" (Campbell, 1974; also quoted by O'Connor et al., 2006). Although our main concern is downward causation, the philosophical position adopted here is more pragmatic, and deals with epistemic emergentism more than ontological one. As a consequence, our hierarchy of levels, and more generally our ontological commitment is relative to a given epistemological stance.

Epistemic, Ontological, and Methodological Background

In numerous contemporary views of emergence (Kistler, 2006; O'Connor & Hong, 2006,), this concept of an epistemological category is referring to the limits of human knowledge of complex systems. According to O'Connor et al. (2006), "emergent properties are systemic features of complex systems that could not be predicted (..) from the standpoint of a pre-emergent stage, despite a thorough knowledge of the features of, and laws governing, their parts." In addition, macroscopic patterns resulting from an emergent phenomenon could not be reduced[1]. In the past decades, a wide variety of definitions of epistemological emergence have been proposed. Although many of these definitions deal with non-reducibility, some of them are compatibles by some ways with reducibility. As a consequence, the answer to the question: "what is an emergent phenomenon?" depends on the concept of emergence one invokes. A broad definition of emergent property as been proposed by Teller (1992): "a property is emergent if and only if it is not explicitly definable in terms of the *non-relational properties* of any of the object's proper parts" (p. 140-141, underlined by us). This allows us to have some distance with more "canonic" conditions of emergentism such as novelty, unpredictability, and naturalistic hierarchy of layers. Then, it is possible to use the simple two-level framework of organization (micro/macro) as only a methodological one, linked with some epistemological stance. In this framework, Bedau (1997, 2002) distinguishes "two hallmarks" of how macro level emergent phenomena are related to their micro level bases:

1. Emergent phenomena are dependent on (constituted by, and generated from) underlying process.

2. Emergent phenomena are (somehow) autonomous from underlying process (Bedau 1997, p375).

Our approach of emergence is mainly locally epistemical, methodological, and "organizational" (Van de Vijver 1997) (i.e., related with a specific context of knowledge and specific tools (multi-agent systems). The corresponding ontology is then methodologically driven, and relative to a specific formalism: the framework of knowledge of multi-agent oriented programming. Furthermore, *we define emergence as a phenomenon relative to an observer*:

our concept of emergence is related to a particular framework of observation. This point of view excludes all forms of Platonicism or other strong forms of "scientific realistic" commitment[2]: scientific knowledge is not viewed as the "mirror of the nature." This epistemic point of view avoids numerous questions addressed by the so-called "orthodox emergentism" in the debate about "non reductionist physicalism."

According to Van de Vijver (1997), from the organizational point of view on emergence, the hierarchy of levels does not necessarily correspond to some "real" hierarchy in the "real world," but characterizes a locally relevant (from some academic field point of view for instance) conceptual organization of the world (here artificial world) in terms of:

1. An abstract closed system (the object of the study, or target system).
2. A discussion about the empirical/technical/conceptual relevance of such a point of view.
3. A discussion about the relevance of the properties, ontologies, etc., related to the corresponding system (entities, levels of organization, relations).
4. Both discussions must be related to the goal of the scientific process.

In this pragmatic view, each type of explanation has its own goal, relevance, and limits (Clark, 1996) and must be related to a specific scientific project. In such an approach, both conceptual and operational models in general—and multi-agent models in particular—can be viewed as *mediators* between theory and empirical evidences (Morgan & Morrison, 1999). As such, "models are both means to and source of knowledge" (Morgan et al., 1999, p. 35). Furthermore, as Minsky (1965) said, "to an observer B, an object A* is a model of an object A to extend that B can use A* to answer questions that interest him about A." Then, the model can be viewed as a specific technology in the process of learning and inquiry for knowledge, "to answer questions." This pragmatic point of view on the emergence discussed hereafter is consequently contextual to the project of investigating complex social phenomena with cognitive agents by means of both complex adaptive systems methodology and multi-agent system modeling.

The Varieties of Emergence: Purpose, Meaning, and Stakes

According to the usual characterization of complex systems, the properties of the "whole" complex (social) system cannot be reduced to the properties of the parts. It results therefore also from the relations between parts and, in some cases, from some irreducible macro causal power from the "whole" (i.e., downward causation). We notice that the relational properties, which structured the system, are neither at the level of the whole nor at the level of the parts, while being constitutive of both. The nature (and possible reducibility) of such a downward causation is one of the main debates in the field of emergent phenomena. As said previously, the answer to these questions depends on the definition of emergence one uses. Some authors have proposed to distinguish different kinds of emergence, as for example "nominal," "weak," and "strong" emergence for Bedau (1997, 2002), or "weak," "ontological," and "strong" emergence[3] for Gillett (2002a-b). For Bedau, the broader (weaker) form of emergence is called "nominal." *Nominal emergence* concerns the existence of some macro-property that cannot be a micro property. Each level has its specific distinct role and properties: "macro-level emergent phenomena are dependent on micro-level phenomena in the straightforward sense that wholes are dependent on their constituents, and emergent phenomena are autonomous from underlying phenomena in the straightforward sense that emergent properties do not apply to the underlying entities" (Bedau, 2002). Under this latter condition, strong emergence is the opposite of nominal emergence, as in this case, emergent properties have irreducible causal power on the underlying entities: "macro causal powers have effects on both macro and micro levels, and macro to micro effects are termed downward causation" (Bedau, 2002) *Weak emergence* is a subset of nominal emergence for which the emergent phenomenon is not easy to explain, according to Simon: "given the properties of the parts and the law of their interactions, it is not a trivial matter to infer the properties of the whole" (Simon, 1996, p. 184, quoted by Bedau, 2002) Accordingly, for Bedau (2002), weakly emergent phenomena are those which *need to be simulated,* to be revealed: "Assume that (a macro-state) P is a nominally emergent property possessed by some locally reducible system S. then P is weakly emergent if P is derivable from all of S's micro facts but only by simulation." According to the non-trivial dimension (surprising) of emergent phenomena, the need for simulation seems to be a transitory epistemic criterion only. If in a context of discovery, computer simulation reveals some new emerging patterns, this is not a sufficient condition to have no other way forever. Later justification by some explanatory formalism is a possible outcome. Thus, a surprising (weak) emergent phenomenon could become a simple nominal emergent one.

Stephan (2002a, 2000b) distinguishes different degrees in novelty, reducibility, and predictability. He proposes an interesting discussion on the difference between weak and strong forms of emergence in a larger framework, using the difference between "synchronic" and "diachronic" emergentism (see also Rueger, 2000a). The former postulates that a macroscopic emergent phenomenon can be explained by the current (synchronic) interactions of the interrelated microscopic entities. In other words, the center of interest is the relationship between the interacting entities and the whole system resulting from these entities and their relationship. In diachronic emergentism, on the other hand, the emergent phenomenon occurs across time by means of sequential adaptation of microscopic entities. The center of interest is now the evolution of both micro and macro structures, and not only the occurrence of a particular structure. As underlined by Stephan (2002b) synchronically emergent properties include also diachronically emergent ones, but not conversely.

For instance, in a Wolfram one-dimensional network of automata (1984), a specific configuration of the network emerges at each step from the value

Figure 1. Emergence of Sierpinsky's triangular structures within the diachronic diagram of the Wolfram network of automata Source Amblard & Phan (2006, p. 277; 2007)

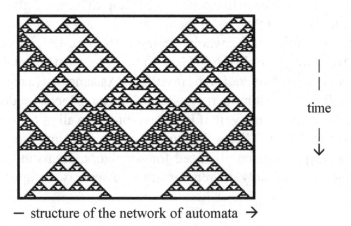

— structure of the network of automata →

of the automaton and the structure of their relations at the previous steps (synchronic emergence). In some cases, identified by both Wolfram and Langton (1984), the existence of an attractor drives the system towards a particular stable configuration (fixed point, cycle). In some others cases, called by Langton (1989) "the edge of Chaos," the evolution of the states of the systems, from step to step, generates a particular structure, such as the Sierpinsky's triangular structures (Figure 1). This structure is only observable from a diachronic perspective, and results from the succession of synchronic emergence of macrostructures due to the local interaction of microstructures (namely, the automaton) within the specific one-dimensional nearest-neighbor interaction.

For Stephan (2002a) the weaker version of emergentism (weak emergence) can be characterized by three features. First, following the physical monism thesis, only physical entities can bear the emergent properties or structures. Secondly, emergent properties or structures are attributes of the system itself, and cannot be attributed to some system's part. Thirdly, the principle of synchronic determination implies that all properties of the system nomologically depend on its micro-structures, namely, the parts and their relations. Stephan underlines that this latter thesis of synchronic determination can be understood as a stronger version of mereological supervenience. In mereological supervenience, the system's properties supervene on its parts and their relations, but this does not imply their dependence on its micro-structures (Stephan, 2002a, p. 80).

Numerous emergentists refer to debates about reductionism as well as about the so-called mind-body problem, discussing in particular the notion of supervenience introduced by Davidson (1970, 1980) and discussed by Kim (1992, 1993, 1995, 1999) from the point of view of emergence. Supervenience is a relation that can be summarized in a slogan form, by the sentence: "there cannot be an A-difference without a B-difference." For application to individually-related properties, this idea means that two individuals cannot differ in M-properties without also differing in N-properties. The strongest form (useful here) of supervenience asserts: "A family of properties M strongly supervenes on a family N of properties if and only if, necessarily, for each x and each property F in M, if F(x) then there is a property G in N such that G(x) and necessarily if any y has G it has F (Kim 1993, p. 65; see also the distinction between weak and strong form of individual supervenience in the possible world modal framework, same book). According to McLaughlin (1997), it is possible to define emergence from this strong form of supervenience: "If P is a property of W, then P is emergent if and only if (1) P supervenes with nomological necessity, but not with logical necessity, on properties the parts of W have taken separately or in other combinations; and (2) some of the supervenience principles linking properties of the parts of W with W's having P are fundamental laws" (p. 39). The two important features are the nomological (but non logical) necessity, and the notion of "fundamental law," which means that it is not metaphysically necessitated by any other laws of W. As underlined by McLaughlin and Bennett (2006), this definition of emergence involves synchronic supervenience. This could be problematic and requires at least a convenient concept of *reduction* (Kim, 1999, 2006) since if "everyone agrees that reduction requires supervenience" (McLaughlin & Bennett 2006), the converse is false. In particular, *non reductive materialism* rejects the reducibility argument and asserts that mental properties are not reducible to physical ones. This kind of emergentist arguments used in the mind-body debate has been re-used for the methodological debate in the social sciences between holism and individualism.

Stephan (2002a, 2000b) claims that numerous formal approaches to complex systems, connectionism, and cognitive science can be related to weak emergentism. In this chapter, the possibility for MAS to encompass such a limitation is precisely a major question of interest. This means that the strong emergence directly addresses the questions of downward causation and reducibility. We do not discuss in this paper all the questions raised by Stephan. When addressing the classical debate about methodological individualism versus holism in the social sciences[4], we do not need to discuss the question of reduction to the material basis of human (and social) behavior.

Figure 2. Irreducibility and novelty in emergent phenomenon (adapted from Stephan 2002b)

	Synchronic determination	Diachronic determination	
Weak (reducible)	weak emergentism	weak diachronic emergentism	|
Strong (irreducible)	(strong) synchronic emergentism	strong diachronic emergentism	Irreductibility ↓

— Novelty →

Hence, we restrict ourselves to a very simplified two-level framework where individuals are the basic entities at the first level, and where one wonders how some "social entities" may have any "existence." According to our discussion on the two dimensions of the so-called strong emergence (namely: downward causation, reducibility), the nature of social facts will depend on the effective class of emergence that we consider. From this limited point of view, in order to summarize this two-level problem we introduce in Figure 2a cross perspective on synchronic/diachronic-weak/strong emergence, adapted from Stephan (2002b) without the case of unpredictability).

To sum up, while both downward causation and irreducibility are generally considered by philosophers as necessary conditions for strong emergence, the definition of weak emergence depends on the author and remains unclear. While irreducibility seems to be a necessary condition for British emergentism, for Stephan (2002ab) reducibility corresponds to the case of weak emergence. Then, relevant questions are: what is the criterion and framework of reference to have a clear account of irreducibility and downward causation.

Irreducibility and Downward Causation: A Synthetic View

As weak emergence deals with upward causation and reductionism, (Bedau 2002; Gillet 2002b) relate emergence to the question of downward causation or "macro-determinism." Strong forms of downward causation are widely advocated by Sperry (1969, 1986, 1991) to deal with the mind-brain interactions, and by Campbell (1974) to deal with hierarchically organized biological systems. According to the downward causation, the behavior of the parts (down) may be determined by some properties or behavior of the whole (top). For instance, parts of the system may be restrained by some act in conformity with the rules given at the system level. Causation would come "downward" in conformity with a *holistic principle* rather than "upward," according to reductionism. The existence of irreducible downward causation is sometimes used to discriminate between weak and strong emergence.

Bedau (2002) introduces a notion of "weak downward causation" in order to keep the idea of emergent causal power from the whole upon the parts: "emergent phenomena without causal powers would be mere epiphenomena" (Bedau, 2002). Although we do not agree with the metaphysical commitment of Bedau, his arguments in favor of "weak downward causation" are appreciably persuasive. As pointed out by Kim (1992, 1999), the general form of downward causation effects can be respectively incoherent, inconsistent with the law of micro entities, and excluded by some micro effects. The "exclusion" argument concerns the cases where the emergent macro causation can be derived from the causal power of the micro constituents. This is effectively the case for numerous emergent phenomena in complex adaptive systems such as sand piles, snow avalanches and so on. In all models of statistical mechanisms, the law of the emergent macro level can be derived from the law of the elements and their interactions. As pointed out by Kim, weak downward causation has paradoxical consequences. "If these considerations are correct, higher-level properties can serve as causes in downward causal relations only if they are reducible to lower-level properties; the paradox is that if they are so reducible, they are not really 'higher level' any longer" (Kim 1999, p. 33). This problematic situation can be avoided by two means. First, in all that cases, Bedau (2002) claims that there is no worry with weak downward causation, because the sequence of causal effects is diachronic: "Higher-level properties can causally influence the conditions by which they are sustained but this process unfolds over time. The higher-level properties arise out of lower level conditions, and without this lower level conditions, the higher level properties would not be present." Second, both Bedau and Kim acknowledge the relevance and the autonomy of the higher level from a causal point of view in the case of an explanatory standpoint (Bedau) or a "conceptual interpretation" (Kim): "we interpret the hierarchy of levels of concepts and descriptions, or levels within our representational apparatus, rather than levels of properties and phenomena in the world. We can then speak of downward causation when a cause is described in terms of higher-level concepts, or in a higher level language, higher in relation to the concepts in which its effects are represented. On this approach, then, the same cause may be representable in lower-level concepts and languages as well, and a single causal relation would be describable in different languages" (Kim 1999, p. 33). This point of view is nothing but our "organizational" pragmatic approach of emergence, a step in the process of knowledge.

Emergence as Perceptive, Cognitive, and Social Phenomenon: Looking at Social Facts in a New Light

The respective role of social structures and individual action is a fundamental issue in social theory. The relevant questions are "does structure determine action or action determine structure? Or is it a bit of both? (Hollis, 1994, p.

6). From the structural standpoint, individual action is externally constrained by some holistic principles. For instance, *the Rules of Sociological Method* of Durkeim (1895) is generally presented as a paradigmatic holistic point of view, since social facts, taken "as things," are external to individuals and external observer have no direct access to those external things. On the contrary, from the individualist standpoint, society is nothing but the result of the individuals' actions. Accordingly, for methodological individualism, social phenomena must be stated by means of actions and interaction between individuals. This does not mean necessarily that individuals are the only relevant level for the social facts. Thus, Udehn (2001) distinguishes strong methodological individualism, for which all social phenomena must be reduced to the individual's behavior (e.g., Popper, 1966) and weak methodological individualism, for which autonomous institutions and social structures can shape the individual's behavior, even if social facts must be taken into account in individuals concepts.

Despite the commitment for the promotion of methodological individualism by several sociologists (Boudon, 1998, 2006; Coleman, 1990; Elster, 1989, 1998), sociologists are often viewed as unrepentant holists. Then, according to Granovetter (1985), the mainstream sociologists' approach would be "over-socialized" (related mainly to downward effects) while the economists' approach would be "under-socialized" (related mainly to upward effects). Nevertheless, both approaches have been more sophisticated and are often mixed (Hollis, 1994). Numerous scholars have proposed various forms of "sophisticated" methodological individualism, and the non-reductive argument (of the social level to the individual) is a key condition for emergence. Among these scholars, Sawyer (2001a, 2004, 2005) uses the notion of supervenience to identify "emergent social properties," which "cannot be reduced to an explanation in terms of individuals and their relationships." Sawyer (2002b, 2003) calls *non reductive individualism* (NRI) this dualism at midway between individualism and holism: "NRI holds to a form of property dualism in which social properties may be irreducible to individual properties, even though social entities consist of nothing more than mechanisms composed of individuals" (Sawyer, p. 266) According to the discussion on non-reductive physicalism, Sawyer argues that both *multiple realizability* and *wild disjunction* are necessary and sufficient conditions for emergence of non reducible social properties. Multiple realizability appears when a single social property can be generated by several micro-level mechanisms. This argument is a common objection to methodological individualism (Kincaid, 1996, Zahale, 2003). Wild disjunction appears when these mechanisms are not meaningfully related. Sawyer's claims have been criticized. For Bunge (2004), the notion of supervenience is less clear than the notion of emergence, in particular in the case of diachronic emergence relative to a given system. If emergence is defined as the rising out of a qualitative novelty, this new property appears "at some point in the development or the evolution of the system." In contrast, supervenience "does not use the concept of system and levels of organization" (Bunge, 2004, p. 377-78). This diachronic dimension of social emergent has been underlined by Archer (1995) for whom social structures emerged in the past from actions of agents; continue to exert effects in the present. As a consequence the only pertinent concept of emergence is diachronic (see also Manzo, 2007). As underlined previously, if the non-reducibility argument is problematic in a synchronic context (and by extension the related downward causation) this is not the case in a diachronic context. Then, on the one hand, in a diachronic perspective with reification, non reductive emergence is less problematical. On the other hand, Sawyer's criticism against Archer's arguments is less relevant in a socio-cognitive framework, as suggested for instance by Castelfranchi (1998a, 1998b, 2000).

Bunge (1977b, 1979) proposes an individually-based systemic concept for social analysis, in which both individual and collective take place. According to Bunge, a systemic society is "a system of interrelated individuals, i.e. a system, and while some of its properties are aggregation of properties of its components, others derive from the relationship among the latter" (Bunge, 1979, p. 13-14). According to Lewes (1879) the first relation (aggregation) describes *resultant* effects, and characterizes methodological individualism, and allows reductionism. The second relation is typically systemic, and characterizes emergentism, where bottom up properties emerge from the relations between the system's components, and are not possessed by any component of the whole. More specifically, Bunge defines resultant and emergent properties[5] as follows:

"Let $P \in p(x)$ be a property of an entity $x \in S$ with composition $C(x) \supset \{x\}$. Then P is a resultant of hereditary property of x iff P is a property of some component $y \in C(x)$ of x other than x; otherwise, P is an emergent or Gestalt property of x. That is:

1. *P is a resultant of hereditary property of $x =_{df} P \in p(x)$ & $(\exists y)(y \in C(x)$ & $y \neq x$ & $P \in p(y))$*

2. *P is an emergent or Gestalt property of x =$_{df}$ P ∈ p(x) & (y) ¬ (y ∈ C(x) & y ≠ x & P ∈ p(y))" (Bunge, 1977b, Definition 2.16 p. 97).*

Where ¬ is the basic symbol for negation. In addition, postulate 2.19 (Bunge, 1977b, p. 98) distinguishes reducible properties (eliminable in favor of micro-based properties) from no-reducible but analyzable or explainable. Reducibility entails analyzability, but the converse is false. "There is epistemological novelty in the formation of attributes representing emergent (ontological) novelty" (id.). But the explanation of emergent phenomena does not involve the elimination of ontological novelty. Bunge's systemism can be analyzed in both ontological and methodological perspectives.

In the ontological perspective, systemic collectivity is neither a set of individuals nor a supra individual entity transcending its members, but a system of interconnected individuals. There are global properties, some of these properties are resultant (reducible) some others are emergent from individual interactions (non-reducible). For Bunge, systemic society cannot act on its members, but members of a group can act severally on an individual. Finally, "social change is a change in the social structures of society—hence a change at both societal and individual levels" (Bunge, 1979, p. 16). The systemic framework introduced by Bunge is an interesting first step to encompass both monist individualism and holism. But there are also some intrinsic limitations. Significantly, several examples of Bunge are taken from natural science, not from human and social sciences. Pure Bungian agents have limited cognitive capacity and a lack of "social intelligence" (Conte, 1999). However, these limitations also appear with many models of emergence in artificial society as underlined by Sawyer (2004, p 265). The emergence is viewed only as a bottom-up process, without effective downward causation (see for instance the paradigmatic models of Schelling (1969, 1978) and Axtell et al. (2001) and their account by Dessalles et al. (2005) and Dessalles, Gallam, and Phan (2006)). In the following, we introduce new formal frameworks that allow us to encompass these limitations either with cognitive epistemic agents or with less cognitive, behavioral ones. The following example suggests how simple modification of information in the environment of individuals could feedback from top to down, through a specific mediator.

The case of a traffic jam, quoted by Bedau (2002) is a very interesting one for the discussion of the macro to micro relationship. Traffic jams arise in particular configuration of the micro constituents, and they are caused by the composition of such micro determinants. The process of traffic jam is then reducible *in principle* to (and can be simulated from) the behavior of the basic entities (the cars) in a specified environment. If we pay more attention to the cognitive and social dimension of this problem, traffic jams can arise because each individual does not have enough information in order to be spontaneously (from the bottom up) coordinated with the others in the use of limited capacity of traffic. In some highway infrastructures this worry has been encompassed by the use of an external information system that transmits messages to the car drivers about traffic. This results often in a better coordination and in the decrease in traffic jams, as the drivers do not act myopically, but take into account this information on the possible occurrence (emergence) of a traffic jam at the macro level to modify their own behavior at the micro level.

This example underlines the fundamental difference between complex interactive systems with reactive agents and systems with cognitive ones. In the former, in the case corresponding to weak emergence all the causality is reducible to the micro elements. In the latter, the existence of some social mediator, able to support feedback effect from the macro level to the micro can develop some autonomous properties and causal effects upon the micro behavior that cannot be directly reducible to micro causation. This could be modeled by means of reification of these social mediators, which makes sense from a social point of view (Phan et al., 2007, and section 3 on 4-Quadrants below). The generation of such mediators, from the bottom up can be viewed as a "weak emergent" phenomena, but the reification of some social representation of this emergent pattern and the feedback effect from this social object to the individual behavior can be viewed as a qualitative change in the model (or a shift from a model to another, at a different level, according to Bonabeau et al. (1997), that is certainly the strongest form of emergence than those addressed by Bedau. Indeed, in the larger new qualitatively different model, the "unsurprised" re-emergence of a previously reified phenomenon can be viewed as a weak emergent phenomenon on the one hand; but from the point of view of the lower level model—before reification—that is a strong emergent one. The following formal definition of emergence allows us to explain this question more precisely. In this chapter, we do not address these questions directly, as we limit ourselves to discussing social behaviors in artificial societies; but the opposition downward versus upward causation proves to be a central one in the field of social sciences.

Formal Definitions of Emergence

The present chapter is an attempt to integrate them into one single framework, in which the "whole" is a collective of cognitive agents (according to methodological individualism), while the agents are to some extent constrained by the whole (downward causation), by means of the "social dimension" of their belief, their perception of social phenomena, or by some structural properties of the collective as well[6]. For this purpose, we rely on the distinction introduced by Labbani, Müller, and Bourjault (1996) and Ferber, Labbani, Müller, & Bourjault (1997) and developed by Müller (2004) in the field of multi-agent systems, between "weak" and "strong" emergence. The latter refers to a situation in which agents are able to witness the collective emergent phenomena in which they are involved, which opens the road for both upward and downward causation.

In ACE (Epstein, 2006; Tesfatsion & Judd, 2006) and computational social sciences (Gilbert, 2007), emergence is strongly related to the "Santa Fe Approach to Complexity" (SFAC). In accordance with descriptive emergentism, SFAC calls emergence the arising at the macro level of some patterns, structures and properties of a complex adaptive system that are not contained in the properties of its parts. Interactions between parts of a complex adaptive system are the source of both complex dynamics and emergence. An interesting part of the emergence process concerns the forming of some collective order (coherent structures or patterns at the macro level) as a result of the agents' interactions within the system's dynamics. For the observer (i.e. the computational social scientist) this collective order makes sense by itself and opens up a radically new global interpretation, because this does not initially make sense as an attribute of the basic entities.

In this chapter, our concern is about formal models of emergence in MAS with cognitive and social agents. Therefore, we deal mainly with formal definitions of emergence, operative for MAS. Formally, in MAS, emergence is a central property of dynamic systems based upon interacting autonomous entities (agents). As previously mentioned, the knowledge of entities' attributes and rules is not sufficient to predict the behavior of the whole system. Such a phenomenon results from the confrontation of the entities within a specific structure of interaction, which is neither at the level of the whole system nor at the level of the entities, but constitutive of both. Accordingly, a better knowledge of the generic properties of the interaction structures would make it easier to have better knowledge of the emergence process (i.e., morphogenetic dynamics). From this point of view, to denote a phenomenon as emergent does not mean that it is impossible to explain or to model the related phenomenon. For this reason Epstein, 1999) uses the word "generative" instead of "emergent" in order to avoid a philosophical debate about emergence.

Some Definitions of Emergences in Complex Systems

Various attempts have been made to define emergence in an "objective" way. Some definitions refer to self-organization (Varela, Thompson & Rosch, 1991), to entropy changes (Kauffman, 1990), to non-linearity (Langton, 1990), to deviations from predicted behavior (Cariani, 1991a; Rosen, 1977, 1978, 1985) or from symmetry (Palmer, 1989). Other definitions are closely related to the concept of complexity (Bonabeau, Dessalles, & Grumbach, 1995a, 1995b; Cariani, 1991b; Kampis, 1991a, 1991b).

In statistical mechanics (Galam, 2004), as well as for models in economics or social sciences having the same structure than models of statistical mechanics[7], emergence may be related to an *order parameter* which discriminates between at least two phases, each one with a different symmetry associated respectively to a zero and a non-zero value of the order parameter. Each problem has its own specific order parameter[8].

For instance, in the Ising model, where individual spins take their values in $\{-1, +1\}$, the order parameter is the magnetization M, given by the sum of all spin values divided by their total number. When M=0, the state is paramagnetic (i.e., disordered in the spin orientations) while long range order appears as soon as $M \neq 0$. A majority of spins are then oriented to either -1 or +1, and an order is likely to emerge. Two ordered phases are thus possible in theory, but only one is effectively achieved. The order parameter provides a "signature" for the emergent phenomenon.

Although these definitions make use of concepts borrowed from physics and information science, they all involve inherently contingent aspects, as the presence of an *external observer* seems unavoidable. Even a change in entropy supposes that an observer be able to assess the probability of various states.

Emergence as a Phenomenon Related to an Observer

The unavoidable presence of an observer does not preclude, however, the possibility of extending the definition of emergence to include non-human observers or observers that are involved in the emerging phenomenon. In our quest for "strong emergence," we wish to assign the role of the observer to elements of the system itself, as when individuals become aware of phenomena affecting the whole society. This kind of self-observation is only possible because what is observed is a simplified state of the system. Emergence deals precisely with simplification.

Ronald and Sipper (2001) introduce a new approach called "emergent engineering" in order to have a controlled concept of the previously mentioned concept of "surprise." This approach opposes the classical engineered automation, based on unsurprising design, and the biologically inspired automation system, which allows the possibility of "unsurprising surprise." Many engineered emergent systems are based on this concept (e.g., Vaario, Hori, & Ohsuga, 1995). We do not deal directly with emergent engineering, but we discuss the framework used by this author based on a specific formal test of emergence, previously presented in Ronald et al. (1999). This test of emergence involves two functions, which can be assumed by the same individual or by two different persons: (1) a *system designer* and (2) a *system observer*. An emergent phenomenon can be diagnosed by combining the three following conditions (Ronald et al., 2001, p. 20)

1. **Design:** The system has been constructed by describing local elementary interactions between components (e.g., artificial creatures and elements of the environment) in a language L_1.

2. **Observation:** The observer is fully aware of the design, but describes global behavior and properties of the running system, over a period of time, using a language L_2.

3. **Surprise:** The language of design L_1 and the language of observation L_2 are distinct, and the causal link between the elementary interactions programmed in L_1 and the behaviors observed in L_2 is *non-obvious* to the observer- who therefore experiences surprise. In other words, there is a cognitive dissonance between the observer's mental image of the system's design stated in L_1 and his contemporaneous observation of the system's behavior stated in L_1.

The question is then how easy it is for the observer to bridge the gap between L1 and L2. The authors use artificial neural network classifiers to evaluate this gap. Within this framework, an "unsurprising surprise" can be defined as an "expected" surprise. This question is exemplified later, within the (Bonabeau et al., 1997) framework of emergence as reduction of complexity within the observation system.

The framework of Ronald et al. (1999) and Ronald et al. (2000) together with Forrest's definition of emergent computation (Forrest, 1990) allow Müller (2004) to define emergence in SMA as occurring between two organization levels, distinguishing the process itself and the observation of that process. The process concerns the evolution of a system formed by entities in interaction using a language L_1. These interactions may generate observable epiphenomena. At the observation level, epiphenomena are interpreted as emerging through specific calculation *using another language* L_2. Finally, emergence is defined as a particular relationship between the two languages where L_2 is not compositionally reducible to L_1 in the sense of Bunge (1977a). For Müller, weak emergence arises when the observer is external to the system. This account is stronger than the notion of *weak emergent phenomenon* in the sense of Bedau (1997, 2002) by adding to the necessity of simulating, the intrinsic irreducibility of the two description languages. Strong emergence arises when the agents involved in the emerging phenomenon are able to perceive it. In this latter configuration, the identification of epiphenomena by agents interacting within the system involves a feedback from the observation to the process. There is a coupling between the process level and the observation level through the agents because the agents are using both L_1 and L_2. This form of strong emergence is thus immanent in such a system. In order to avoid misinterpretation, we call "M-Strong" the strong emergence in the sense of Müller (2004).

To summarize, if there is *M-Strong emergence*, the system becomes reflexive, through the mediation of the agents.

1. Agents are equipped with the capacity to observe and to identify a phenomenon in the process, which represents the evolution of the system in which they interact. This capacity of observation and the target of such observation must then be sufficiently broad to encompass the phenomenon as a global one.

2. The agents describe this epiphenomenon in a "language" other than the one used to describe the process

3. The identification of an "emergent" epiphenomenon by the agents involves a change of behavior, and therefore a feedback from the level of observation to the process.

This category of m-strong emergence is important to model artificial societies (Castelfranchi, 1998a, 1998b; Gilbert, 1995). This is the case also even if there is a mix of strong and weak emergence in most multi-agent based social simulation (Drogoul & Ferber, 1991; Drogoul, Ferber, & Cambier, 1994).

Learning and "Intrinsic Emergence"

Crutchfield (1994), Bersini (2004), and Philemotte & Bersini, 2005a, 2005b) propose to consider an alternative definition of emergence, called "intrinsic emergence." They suggest to characterize emergence as an autonomous increase in the system's computational capabilities. Such a definition is supposed to be more "objective," as a natural way to avoid the presence of an external observer in charge of detecting emergence. (Philemotte et al., 2005a) implemented a situation of intrinsic emergence. In their system, a cellular automaton is evolved through a genetic algorithm (GA) until it is able to perform some arithmetic operations on a limited set of operands. As usual for cellular automata, the rules, which for each cell, decide of its next state, take as input the previous state of neighboring cells. In Philemotte et al.'s system, a second genetic algorithm is in charge of simplifying inputs for each cellular automaton by limiting the number of neighboring cells actually taken into account, so as to make the learning task easier for the first GA. Intrinsic emergence is claimed to occur whenever the second GA is able to isolate a relevant portion of the neighboring input and thus to significantly improve the learning efficiency of the overall system. Philemotte and Bersini were able to observe such sudden improvements when the two genetic algorithms cooperate.

Emergence as a Complexity Drop

In Bonabeau et al. (1997), emergence is defined as an unexpected complexity drop in the description of the system by a certain type of observer. Such a definition is claimed to subsume previous definitions of emergence, both structural (dealing with levels of organization) and epistemological (dealing with deviation from some model's predictions). In each case, the observer is able to detect a structure, such as the presence of relations between parts of the system, or some form of behavior like a characteristic trajectory. Structural emergence occurs whenever a collection of similar elements turns out to be more structured than anticipated. This augmentation of structure can be characterized by a decrease of complexity.

$$E = C_{exp} - C_{obs} \tag{1}$$

Here, E stands for the amplitude of the emergence; C_{exp} is the expected structural complexity and C_{obs} the structural complexity actually observed. Structural complexity is defined as the algorithmic complexity relative to a given set of structural descriptors. In order to use algorithmic complexity to describe finite systems, we abandon the generality of the concept as it was defined by Kolmogorov, Chaitin, and Solomonov (Li & Vitanyi, 1993), considering that the description tools are imposed by the observer and not by a generic Turing machine. We define the relative algorithmic complexity (RAC) of a system as the complexity of the shortest description that a given observer can give of the system, relative to the description tools available to that observer. Emergence occurs when RAC abruptly drops down by a significant amount.

For our purpose here, we must restrict the definition. We consider a specific class of observers in order to get closer to what human observers would consider as emergence. Following Leyton (2001), we impose the observer's description tools to be structured as mathematical groups. The observer may be considered as being a "Leyton machine," for which any structure is obtained through a group-transfer of other structures (Leyton, 2001). Any level of organization that can be observed has operational closure and is structured as a group, and the only structures that can be observed are the invariant of a group of operations. Moreover, the observer is supposed to have hierarchical detection capabilities. This means that all elements of the system that the observer can consider have themselves a group structure.

For structural emergence to occur, it is important that there be an unexpected complexity decrease. This may happen either because the detection of the higher structure was delayed, as when one needs time to recognize a Dalmatian dog in a pattern of black and white spots. It may also happen when adding a new observable that, instead of increasing the overall complexity

Figure 3. Parallelism between hierarchies: level of description, level of observations (detectors), and conceptual level (association concepts-detectors) (source: Dessalles et al., 2005)

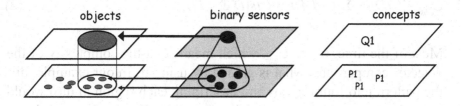

of the system for the observer; it paradoxically decreases it (Bonabeau et al., 1997).

Emergent phenomena are naturally described in two-level architecture (Figure 3). In such a framework, objects at the two levels make sense only because some observer is able to detect them. The detected object at the upper level is composed of objects of the first level. Correspondingly, the upper level detector is triggered by the activity of lower level detectors. The system's complexity, defined as the minimal description that can be given of its state, drops down by a significant amount when an upper-level detector becomes active, as its activity subsumes the activity of several lower-level detectors.

Let us call s the emerging phenomenon, $\{d_i\}$ the set of lower-level detectors and D the higher-level detector. Before emergence occurs, the expected complexity may be written:

$$C(s \ \& \ \{d_i\}) = \Sigma_i \ C(d_i) + C(s|\{d_i\})$$

The notation $C(a|b)$ means the complexity of a when the description of b is available. If s designates a pattern of black and white patches, the $\{d_i\}$ may refer to the detection of black patches. In this case, $C(s|\{d_i\})$ is zero, as the scene is entirely described once the $\{d_i\}$ are. Let us suppose that a new detector is taken into account. The expected complexity becomes:

$$C_{exp} = C(s \ \& \ D \ \& \ \{d_i\})$$

Suppose the scene is described using D first. Then, the actual complexity becomes:

$$C_{obs} = C(D) + \Sigma_i \, C(d_i|D) + C(s|D \,\& \, \{d_i\}) \qquad\qquad (2)$$

Most of the time, $C_{obs} = C_{exp}$, which means that the complexity of the new detector compensates what is gained by using it. In our example, dividing the pattern into four regions and describing each region in turn would provide no complexity decrease. If, however, D subsumes some of the d_i, then $C(d_i|D)$ becomes small or even zero, and C_{obs} gets smaller than C_{exp}. This is when emergence occurs.

In our example, D may be the shape of a Dalmatian dog. Many of the black and white patches become predictable as soon as the dog's shape is recognized. This sudden upper-level pattern recognition decreases the overall complexity according to the preceding formula, giving rise to computable amplitude of emergence.

Note that formulas (1) and (2) make a prediction that is not acknowledged in most models of emergence. The emerging characteristic must be *simple*. The simpler it is, the more significant is the emergence. In formula (2), it is important that $C(D)$ be small, as a large value would ruin the emergence effect. In our example, a Dalmatian dog constitutes a familiar shape that has therefore low complexity.

This requirement that the emerging property be simple seems to be verified in all examples to be found in the literature. This statement may be surprising at first sight. On certain occasions, emergence seems to involve an increase rather than a decrease of complexity. Examples such as phase transition or bifurcation into chaos come to mind. In such cases, however, what is remarkable and simple is not the resulting state, but the point of bifurcation. If phase transitions were fuzzy (e.g., if the transition from water to ice was progressive between +10°C and –10°C) emergence would be much less obvious. We note also that taking a higher-level detector D into account undoubtedly makes things more complicated, as it increases the observational hierarchy. This price paid to complexity is taken into account by the term C(D) in (2). Emergence only occurs when this term is more than compensated by the low value of the other terms of Cobs.

Relationship with Others Concept of Emergence

We may wonder how the preceding definition of emergence as a complexity shift relates to other definitions reviewed in this chapter. As shown in Deguet, Demazeau, and Magnin (2006), the change of description language invoked by Müller or by Ronald et al. amounts to taking new detectors into account. This language change is captured by D in the preceding formula. The 'non-obvious' character of the behavior described in the upper-level language, as invoked by Ronald *et al.*, corresponds in our framework to the unexpected complexity shift.

Philemotte and Bersini's notion of "intrinsic" emergence also relates to the previous definition. Their definition is original, and is not limited to the description of structural patterns. We may call it behavioral emergence, as the criterion for emergence is a discontinuity in performance rather than a discontinuity in structural complexity. We may, however, ask what is emerging in Philemotte and Bersini's two-level GA-based cellular automaton. If the general definition of intrinsic emergence is restricted to describing some discontinuity in efficiency, then the answer is that nothing emerges. In their particular experiment, however, a relevant input filter can be said to emerge. For some definition of complexity, indeed, intrinsic emergence is well described by definition (1). The measure of complexity to be considered here is the size of the relevant search space. When systematically ignoring a portion of the input, the second GA dramatically reduces the space where the first GA will find an efficient rule for the cellular automaton. This presupposes, however, that the input filter does not exclude convenient solutions. If complexity is set to a maximal value when no adequate rule is learned, then intrinsic emergence can be said to correspond to a complexity drop. Note, however, that intrinsic emergence, contrary to structural emergence, does not rely on the complexity of structure (e.g., the complexity of hierarchical group structure, but relies on learning efficiency which directly correlates with the size of the filtered search space).

Definition (1) may be also applied to cases of diachronic emergence. The fact that a given structure can only be detected by comparison between successive states of the system may be merely ignored when considering complexity shifts. Structure and thus unexpected simplicity is discovered in the set of successive time slices. Diachronic emergence, according to definition (1), occurs whenever the complexity of this set turns out to be simpler than anticipated.

Quadrants: An Integrative View of Multi-Agent Systems

In order to give a comprehensive view of emergence in MAS it is necessary to understand the various perspectives and components that make a MAS, and thus to use an *integrative view of MAS* (Ferber, 2007, 2007b, Phan et al., 2007), which is inspired from those of Wilbert (2000). This diagrammatic framework is designed in order to provide a two-dimensional heuristic description of the complex relationship within social systems.

The 4-Quadrant Framework

The 4-Quadrant approach resides in a decomposition into two axis: individual vs. collective perspectives on the one hand, and interior (i.e. mental states, representations) vs. exterior (i.e., behavior, objects, organizations) perspectives on the other hand. These two axis taken together provide a four-quadrant map where each quadrant must be seen as a perspective in which individuals, situations and social systems, as well as the architectural design of artificial society may be described and discussed as it is shown on Figure 4.

The upper half of the diagram is related to the individual aspects of the MAS (i.e., agents), whereas the lower half is dedicated to its collective aspects (i.e., societies of various form and size). The left half is related to the interior aspects, which reside only in the view of agents, and the right half is about exterior (i.e., manifestations of the behavior and traces in the environment, which may be seen by an outside observer). The I-I (interior-individual, upper left) quadrant, is about emotions, beliefs, desires, intentions, of an individual (i.e., about its mental states, its subjectivity). The E-I (exterior-individual, upper right) quadrant describes physical bodies, concrete objects, and also behaviors of individuals. The I-C (interior-collective, lower left) is about shared knowledge and beliefs, collective representations, ontologies, social norms, and represents the inter-subjective part of individuals, what could be called the *noosphere*. The E-C (exterior-collective, lower right) is about material or formal social structures such as institutions and organizations (i.e., collective forms and structures of groups and systems) what could be called the *sociosphere*. According to this decomposition, it is clear that emergence may appear either on the internal side or on the external side. If emergence is seen as a construction going from the individual to the collective level, and

Figure 4. The 4-Quadrant map (adapted from: Ferber 2007, 2007b, Phan et al. 2007)

Internal-Individual (I-I)	External-Individual (E-I)
I → Subjectivity	It, This → Objectivity
< mental states, emotions, beliefs desires, intentions, cognition…>	<agent behavior, object, process, physical entities >
"Interiority"	"Observables, exteriority"
Internal-Collective (I-C)	External-Collective (E-C)
We→ Inter-Subjectivity	Them, All This → Inter-Objectivity
< shared / collective knowledge invisible social codes and implicit ontologies, informal norms and conventions>	<reified social facts and structures, Organizations, institutions>
"Noosphere"	"SocioSphere"

downward causation as constraints going from the collective to the individual level, the 4-Quadrant map shows that emergence may appear either on the internal or the external side. On the internal side, collective representations, general concepts and ideas, arise from external beliefs and goals. As such elements of the noosphere, which result from the composition of individual representations and beliefs, act as constraints for the beliefs, objectives, and way of thinking of individual agents. It is as if things could only be thought through the paradigms and representations of the collective level. On the external side, social structures, which result from the activities of agents, act as constraints for their possible behavior.

Representation of Weak Emergent Phenomena

Fundamental questions about the emergence properties in weak emergent phenomena need to be explained. We claim that the presence of an external observer being able to discern an emergent phenomenon and level of organization is unavoidable. Accordingly, who is this observer? From the point of view of social sciences, what does the higher level of organization consist in? For whom does this level make sense?

To understand the emergent phenomenon, we need to introduce an observer (i.e., another agent), which sees a multi-agent system from an outside position. In the weak form of emergence, the observer is an agent that stands outside of the system, and thus outside of the four quadrants (Figure 5). As such, its observation shows a reduction of complexity when the system is seen from the E-I quadrant or from the E-C quadrant. The arrow in the figure between these two quadrants shows both a new structural pattern of organization, which arise from interactions of the individual level, and the conceptual simplification, which comes from a more abstract level of analysis.

An example of weak emergence is given by aggregation mechanisms, such as the one described by Schelling in its model of segregation (Schelling 1969, 1978). Schelling's aim was to explain how segregationist residential structures could spontaneously occur, even when people are not segregation- ist themselves. The absence of a global notion of segregationist structures (like the notion of ghettos) in the agent's attributes (preferences) is a crucial feature of this model. Agents have only local preferences concerning their preferred neighborhood, but the play of interactions generates global segre- gation (Figure 6).

Agents choose their area in relation to the colors of their neighborhood. Though agents may be weakly segregationist (each agent would stay in a neighborhood with up to 62.5% of people with another color), segregation

Figure 5. Weak emergence (emergence of structure) seen from an (external) observer point of view

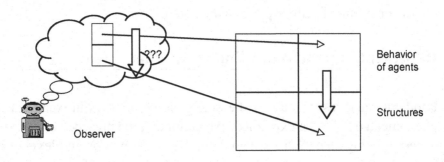

Figure 6. Original (checkerboard) Schelling Model (Source : Source: http://www-eco.enst-bretagne.fr/~phan/complexe/schelling.html and Phan (2004a))

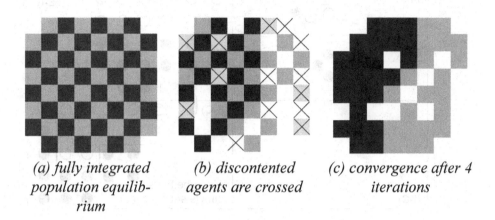

| (a) fully integrated population equilib-rium | (b) discontented agents are crossed | (c) convergence after 4 iterations |

(a) fully integrated population equilib-rium *(b) discontented agents are crossed* *(c) convergence after 4 iterations*

occurs spontaneously: in Figure 6a, no agent wishes to move, but this is an unstable equilibrium. A slight perturbation is sufficient to induce an emergence of local segregationist patterns (Figure 6b and 6c).

Local interactions are sufficient to generate spatial homogeneous patterns. Spatial segregation is an emerging property of the system's dynamics, while not being an attribute of the individual agents. Sometimes, local integrated (non-homogeneous) patterns may survive in some niches. But such integrated structures are easily perturbed by random changes, while homogeneous structures are more stable (frozen zones). Complementary theoretical developments on Schelling's model of segregation can be found in the growing literature on this subject (see Dessalles et al., 2005 for further references). Independently of the question of the empirical relevance of Schelling's model, this pioneering work is generally viewed as a paradigmatic example of the first generation of agent-based models, producing macro-social effects from the bottom-up (Amblard & Phan, 2007). Figure 7 represents Schelling's model in the 4-Quadrant perspective: individual behaviors (E-I quadrant) based on simple preference choices (I-I quadrant) result in a global pattern, the emergence of ghettos (E-C quadrant) as an external observer (e.g., researcher, experimentalist) could seen.

Figure 7. The methodological individualist approach: Weak emergence of ghettos in Schelling's model of segregation

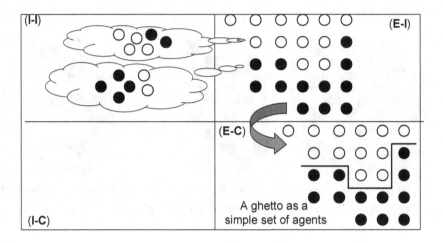

M-Strong Emergence from the 4-Quadrant Point of View

Among fundamental questions raised by emergence in the social field, the problem of the existence of some "social entities" (or "social objects") is of great importance for the modeling of artificial society, in particular for the so-called "immergence" (Gilbert, 1995).

M-strong emergence, from the standpoint of Müller, can be seen as a process in which agents are able to observe and consider the situation from both an individual and collective point of view. M-strong emergence arises when global structures and/or abstract entities are considered by individuals to determine their individual behavior.

In Schelling's model, agents do act according to a simple preference rule, which only considers the status of their neighborhood. Let us suppose now that they possess a sense of "membership." Each agent (grey or black) thinks that it is a member of a community (grey or black) and that newcomer must join their community and live close to agents of their own "color." Let us also suppose that there is some kind of penalty if an agent does not follow that rule. Situations as this one is characteristic in human population, see for instance the Capulet and Montaigu conflict in Romeo and Juliet. This

Figure 8. M-Strong emergence (emergence of structure) seen from both an agent and an (external) observer point of view

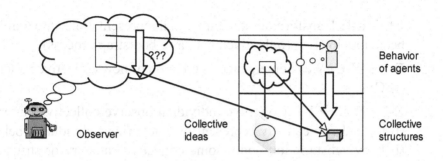

restriction imposes a downward causation (or immergence) relation: each agent is constrained by its membership to its own community, the global level reacting back to the agent level. A new agent has to "choose its own camp" and cannot go freely to a specific location.

Segregation and ghettos will appear, but this time as a result of explicit membership internalized by agents. The overall situation may be depicted as in Figure 8, where each agent has a representation of being a member of its community. The "grey" and "black" community is then reified in the I-C quadrant as collective ideas and concepts, resulting in an m-strong emergence.

From the 4-Quadrant point of view emergence is not a straightforward transition from the individual to the collective level: all quadrants are deeply interconnected. Thus, an important issue in emergence would be to dynamically relate weak and m-strong emergence using the interconnection of the four quadrants. We have seen that Schelling's model produces a weak emergence, but that agent behaviors based on community membership result in an m-strong emergence. But very often, in empirical social phenomena, both emergences occur. First a weak emergence appears producing a collective structure, which is then observed by agents. These observations, added to communications between agents, produces collective ideas or concepts, which are then used by agents for their subsequent behavior, resulting in an M-strong emergence.

If we trace the dynamics of the whole process, we have the following cycles of dependence, which take place between the four quadrants:

a.   **I-I → E-I:** Transformation of individual representations into individual behaviors in (E-I) (only given here as a bootstrap process)

b.   **E-I → E-C:** Weak emergence as creation of new collective patterns in (E-C)

c.   **E-I × E-C → I-I:** Cognitive individual observe collective patterns in (E-C) and subjectively represent or categorize individual's behavior (E-I) by subsumption under some collective category or structure in (I-I).

d.   **I-I × E-I × E-C → I-C:** Emergence of new collective (public) representation (idea, concept, category...) through communication between agents driving to reification of individuals' beliefs in (I-C).

e.   **I-I × I-C × E-C → E-I:** Individual behaviors in (E-I) constrained by individual (I-C) and collective representation (I-C) and by social and organizational structures (E-C) as well.

f.   Go to (b) in a recursive loop, in order for the whole process to continue.

Individuals' mind is at the origin of their behavior. Interactions between these behaviors produce emergent phenomena at the collective level (a). These behaviors together will possibly result in a collective structure (weak emergence) (b). Then, if agents have a sufficient level of cognition to be able to observe and represent they will subjectively categorize individual's behavior by subsumption under a category or structure within the internal-individual quadrant (I-I) (c). Furthermore, if these agents can communicate about these categories / representations, then a new collective representation (idea, concept, category...) will appear in the interior-collective quadrant (I-C) (d) (Steels 2006).The collective representation will then be used to constrain the agent behaviors, in a downward causal link (e). The whole process continues with (b) thus forming a loop from the external individual level (E-I) to the external collective level (E-C) and back to E-I, through the various individual and collective representations.

Conclusion

The reflexivity meditated by the agents' "consciousness" and/or "awareness" appears to be a determinant characteristic that distinguishes systems involving human agents from systems made of non-conscious or material entities. Within agents, it is interesting to distinguish a hierarchy in the cognitive capacity of agents, from reactive agent to epistemic agent[9] (Bourgine, 1993; Phan, 1995). If a reactive agent cannot be considered as an observer of its environments, both behavioral and epistemic agents have the cognitive capability to process available information and can be viewed as observers of the process in which they take part. In this process a behavioral observer only takes into account some visible characteristics of its environment, while an epistemic observer "models" and simulates in some way this process. Accordingly, behavioral and epistemic agents can contribute to strong emergence through consciousness. By contrast, a reactive agent has no consciousness and contributes only indirectly to strong emergence, which is mediated by the environment (Labbani et al., 1996). The general socio-cognitive process briefly introduced here should be augmented and detailed to form a better understanding of the m-strong emergence process which arises in complex social systems. Emerging phenomena in a population of agents are expected to be richer and more complex when agents have enough cognitive abilities to perceive the emergent patterns or when the structures of the collective can detect emergent phenomena and feedback on the agent's level. Such feedback loops between emerging collective patterns and their individual components allow us to have more sophisticated design of agents in artificial societies. This requires complementary developments, like those discussed in Phan et al. (2007) on the ontological status of "social belief," or like the notion of "social intelligence" presented by Conte (1999) as a property of socially situated agents, and more generally like in all the works initiated by Castelfranchi and Conte and co-authors since 1995.

Acknowledgment

The authors acknowledge Jean Pierre Müller for valuable remarks and others intellectual contributions, Alexandra Frénod for significant corrections on the original draft, as well as the ANR program "Corpus" for financial support of the project "CO-SMA-GEMS." Finally, we thank also anonymous referees for valuable remarks on a previous version of this chapter. Denis Phan is a CNRS member.

References

Amblard, F. & Phan, D. (2007). *Multi-agent models and simulation for social and human sciences*. Oxford: The Bardwell-Press. Forthcoming in September, translated from part of: Amblard F. Phan D. dir. (2006). Modélisation et simulation multi-agents, applications pour les Sciences de l'Homme et de la Société, Londres, Hermes-Sciences & Lavoisier, with new Chapters).

Archer, M. S. (1995). *Realist social theory: The morphogenetic approach*. NY: Cambridge University Press.

Archer, M. S. (1998). Social theory and the analysis of society, in May & Williams (Eds.) Knowing the Social World, Buckingham-Open University Press.

Axtell, R., Epstein, J. M., & Young, H. P. (2001). The emergence of classes in a multi-agent bargaining model. In Durlauf, & P. Young (Eds.), *Social dynamics*, (pp. 191-212). Cambridge, MA: The MIT Press.

Baas, N. A. (1994). Emergence, hierarchies, and hyperstructures. In C. G. Langton (Ed.), *A life III, Santa Fe Studies in the Sciences of Complexity, Proc.* (Vol. XVII, pp. 515-537. Redwood City, CA, Addison-Wesley.

Baas, N. A., & Emmeche, C. (1997). On emergence and explanation. *Intellectica, 25*, 67-83

Beckermann, A., Flohr, A. H., & Kim, J., (1992). *Emergence or reduction? Essays on the Prospects of Nonreductive Physicalism*. Berlin & New York: Walter de Gruyter.

Bedau, M. A. (2002). Downward causation and the autonomy of weak emergence. *Principia, 6-1* June, special issue on Emergence and Downward Causation, 5-50.

Bedau, M. A. (1997). Weak emergence, Noûs, 31, Supplement: Philosophical Perspectives, 11, Mind, Causation, and World, 375-399.

Bersini, H. (2004). Whatever emerges should be intrinsically useful, in Artificial life 9, (pp. 226-231) Cambridge Ma.,The MIT Press.

Bonabeau, E., & Dessalles, J. L. (1997). Detection and emergence. *Intellectica, 25*, 89-94.

Bonabeau, E., Dessalles, J. L., & Grumbach, A. (1995a). Characterizing emergent phenomena (1): A critical review. *Rev. Int. Syst. 9*, 327-346.

Bonabeau, E., Dessalles, J. L., & Grumbach, A. (1995b). Characterizing emergent phenomena (2): A conceptual framework. *Rev. Int. Syst. 9*, 347-369.

Boudon, R. (2006). Are we doomed to see the homo sociologicus as a rational or as an irrational idiot? In J. Elster, O. Gjelsvik, A. Hylland, & K. Moene (Eds.), *Understanding choice, explaining behavior. Essays in the Honour of O. J. Skog* (pp. 25-42) Oslo, Unipub Forlag, Oslo: Academic Press.

Boudon, R. (1998). Social mechanisms without black boxes. In Hedström and Swedberg (Eds.), Social mechanisms: An analytical approach to social theory (pp. 172-203). Cambridge, MA: Cambridge University Press.

Bourgine, P., (1993). Models of autonomous agents and of their co-evolutionary interactions; Entretiens Jacques Cartier, Lyon.

Bunge, M. (2004). Clarifying some misundetstandings about social systems and their mechanisms. *Philosophy of the Social Sciences, 34*(2), 371-281.

Bunge, M. (1979). A system Concept of Society: Beyond Individualism and Holism, Theory and Decision, 10(1/4) January 13-30.

Bunge, M. (1977a). Emergence and the mind. Neuroscience 2, 501-509

Bunge, M. (1977b). Treatise on basic philosophy. III: Ontology: The furniture of the world. Dordrecht: Reidel.

Broad, C. D. (1925). *The mind and its place in nature*. London: Routledge & Kegan Paul

Campbell, D. T. (1974). Downward causation in hierarchically organized biological systems. In Ayala & Dobzhansky (Eds.), *Studies in the philosophy of biology: Reduction and related problems*. London: Macmillan.

Cariani, P. (1991a). Adaptivity and emergence in organisms and devices, World Futures 31, Gordon & Breach Science Publishers, 49-70.

Cariani, P. (1991b). Emergence and artificial life. In Langton, Taylor, Farmer, & Rasmussen (Eds.), Artificial Life II. (pp. 775-797) Santa Fe Institute Studies in the Sciences of Complexity Proceedings Vol. X, Redwood City, Ca., Addison-Wesley.

Castelfranchi, C. (2000). Through the agents' minds: Cognitive mediators of social action. *Mind & Society, 1*(1), 109-140, March.

Castelfranchi, C. (1998a). Simulating with cognitive agents: The importance of cognitive emergence. In R. Conte, J. Sichman, & N. Gilbert (Eds.), *Multi-Agent Systems and Agent-Based Simulation, Lecture Notes in Computer Science* (Vol. 1534, pp. 26-44), Berlin, Springer.

Castelfranchi, C. (1998b). Emergence and cognition: Towards a synthetic paradigm in AI and cognitive science. In H. Coelho (Ed.), *Proceedings of the 6th Ibero-American Conference on AI: Progress in Artificial Intelligence, Lecture Notes in Computer Science 1484*, (pp. 13-26), London, Springer.

Clark, A. (1996). Happy coupling: Emergence and explanatory interlock. In M. Boden (Ed.), *The philosophy of artificial life*. Oxford: Oxford University Press.

Clayton, P., & Davies, P. (2006). *The re-emergence of emergence*. Oxford: Oxford University Press.

Coleman, J. S. (1990). *Foundations of social theory*. Cambridge, MA: Harvard University Press.

Conte, R. (1999). Social Intelligence Among Autonomous Agents, Computational, and Mathematical Organization Theory, 5, 202-228.

Conte, R., & Castelfranchi, C. (1995). *Cognitive and social action*. London: UCL Press.

Crutchfield. (1994). Is anything ever new? Considering emergence. In Cowan & Melzner (Eds.), Integrative themes. Volume XIX of Santa Fe Institute Studies in the Sciences of Complexity, Reading, Ma., Addison-Wesley Publishing Company.

Davidson, D. (1970). Mental events. In L. Foster & J. W. Swanson (Eds.), *Experience and theory*. London: Duckworth.

Davidson, D. (1980). *Actions and events*. Oxford: Clarendon.

Deguet, J., Demazeau, Y., & Magnin, L. (2006). Elements about the emergence issue a survey of emergence definitions. To appear in ComPlexUs,

International Journal on Modelling in Systems Biology, Social, Cognitive and Information Sciences, Karger, Basel, Spring 2006.

Dennett, D. C. (1996). *Kinds of minds*. NY: Brockman.

Dessalles, J. L., & Phan, D. (2005). Emergence in multi-agent systems: Cognitive hierarchy, detection, and complexity reduction part I: Methodological issues. In P. Mathieu, B. Beaufils, & O. Brandouy (Eds.), Agent-based methods in finance, game theory, and their applications, (pp. 147-159), Lecture Notes in Economics and Mathematical Systems, Vol. 564, Berlin, Springer.

Dessalles, J. L., Galam, S., & Phan, D. (2006). Emergence in multi-agent systems part II: Axtell, Epstein and Young's revisited, 12th International Conference on Computing in Economics and Finance, June 22-25, 2006, Limassol, Cyprus

Drogoul, A., & Ferber, J. (1991). A behavioral simulation model for the study of emergent social structures. *European Conference on Artificial Life*, Paris.

Drogoul, A., Ferber, J., & Cambier C. (1994). Multi-agent simulation as a tool for analysing emergent processes in societies. *Proceedings of Simulating Societies Symposium*, University of Surrey, Guildford, 1992. Re-published in N. Gilbert & J. Doran (Eds.), Simulating societies: The computer simulation of social phenomena, (pp. 127-142) Londres: UCL Press.

Durkeim, E. (1895). Les règles de la méthode sociologique, trad. by W.D. Halls. The rules of the sociological method. New York: The Free Press, 1982.

Durlauf, S. N. (2001). A framework for the study of individual behavior and social interactions. *Sociological Methodology, 31*(1), 47-87, January.

Durlauf, S. N. (1997). Statistical mechanics approaches to socioeconomic behavior. In Arthur, Durlauf, & Lane (Eds.), *The economy as an evolving complex system II*, Santa Fe Institute Studies in the Sciences of Complexity, Volume XXVII, Redwood City, CA, Addison-Wesley.

Elster, J. (1989). *Nuts and bolts for the social sciences*. Cambridge MA: Cambridge University Press.

Elster, J. (1998). A plea for mechanism. In P. Hedstrom & R. Swedberg (Eds.), *Social mechanisms. An analytical approach to social theory* (pp. 45-73). Cambridge, MA: Cambridge University Press.

Emmeche, C., Koppe, S., & Stjernfelt, F. (1997). Explaining emergence-towards an ontology of levels. *Journal for General Philosophy of Science, 28*, 83-119.

Epstein, J. M. (2006). Generative social science: Studies in agent-based computational modeling. Princeton University Press.

Epstein, J. M. (1999). Agent-based computational models and generative social science. *Complexity, 4*(5), 41-60.

Ferber, J. (2007a). Towards an integrative view of multi-agent systems. Forthcoming.

Ferber, J. (2007b). Multi-agent concepts and methodologies. In F. Amblard & D. Phan (Eds.), Multi-agent models and simulation for social and human sciences. Oxford: The Bardwell-Press (forthcoming in September).

Ferber, J. (1999). *Multi-agent systems*. Reading, MA: Addison Wesley.

Ferber, J., Labbani, O., Müller, J. P., & Bourjault, A. (1997). Formalizing emergent collective behaviors: Preliminary report. *International Workshop on Decentralized Intelligent and Multi-Agent Systems* (pp. 113-122), St. Petersburg.

Forrest, S. (1990). Emergent computation: Self-organizing, collective, and cooperative phenomena in natural and artificial computing networks. *Introduction to the Proceedings of the 9th Annual CNLS Conference in Emergent Computation* (pp. 1-11). Cambridge, MA: MIT Press.

Galam, S. (2004). Spontaneous symmetry breaking and the transition to disorder in physics. In P. Bourgine & J. P. Nadal (Eds.), Cognitive economics, an interdisciplinary approach (pp. 157-168). Berlin-Heidelberg: Springer-Verlag.

Galam, S., Gefen, Y., & Shapir, Y. (1982). Sociophysics: A mean behavior model for the process of strike. *Mathematical Journal of Sociology, 9*, 1-13.

Gilbert, N. (2007). Computational social science: Agent-based social simulation. In F. Amblard & D. Phan (Eds.), Multi-agent models and simulation for social and human sciences. Oxford: The Bardwell-Press (forthcoming in September).

Gilbert, N. (2002). *Varieties of emergence*. Paper presented at the Agent 2002 Conference: Social Agents: Ecology, Exchange, and Evolution, Chicago.

Gilbert, N. (1995). Emergence in social simulations. In N. Gilbert & R. Conte. op.cit. p. 114-156.

Gilbert, N., & Conte R. (1995). *Artificial societies: The computer simulation of social life*. London: UCL Press.

Gillett, C. (2002a). The varieties of emergence: Their purposes, obligations, and importance. *Grazer Philosophische Studien, 65*, 89-115.

Gillett, C. (2002b). Strong emergence as a defense of non-reductive physicalism: A physicalist metaphysics for "downward" determination. *Principia, 6*(1) June, special issue on Emergence and Downward Causation, 83-114.

Granovetter, M. S. (1985). Economic action and social structure: The problem of embeddedness. *American Journal of Sociology, 91*, 481-510.

Holland, J. H. (1998). *Emergence from chaos to order*. Readings, MA: Helix Books Addison-Wesley.

Hollis M. (1994). *The philosophy of social science*. Cambridge, MA: Cambridge University Press, (revised and updated version 2002).

Kampis, G. (1991a). *Self-modifying systems in biology and cognitive science*. Pergamon Press.

Kampis, G. (1991b). Emergent computations, life, and cognition. World Futures 31, Gordon & Breach Science Publishers, p. 33-48.

Kauffman, S. (1990). The sciences of complexity and "origin of order." *PSA: Proceedings of the Biennal Meeting of the Philosophy of Sciences Association, Vol II Symposia and Invited Papers* (pp. 299-322).

Kim, J. (2006). Emergence: Core ideas and issues. *Synthese, 151*(3), 347-354.

Kim, J. (1999). Making sense of emergence. *Philosophical Studies, 95*, 3-36.

Kim, J. (1995). Emergent properties. In Honderich (Ed.), *The Oxford Companion to Philosophy* (pp. 224). Oxford University Press.

Kim, J. (1993). *Supervenience and mind*. Cambridge, MA: Cambridge University Press.

Kim, J. (1992). Downward causation. In Beckermann, Flohr & Kim, Eds., op cit.. 119-138

Kincaid, H. (1996). Philosophical foundations of the social sciences. Cambridge, MA: Cambridge University Press.

Kincaid, H. (1986). Reduction, explanation, and individualism. *Philosophy of Science, 53*(4) December, 492-513.

Kistler, M. (2006). New Perspectives on Reduction and Emergence in Physics, Biology and Psychology. Special issue of Synthese, 151/3.

Klee, R. L. (1984). Micro-determinism and concepts of emergence. *Philosophy of Science, 51*(1), 44-63.

Labbani, O., Müller, J. P., & Bourjault, A. (1996). Describing collective behaviors in Workshop ICMAS, 09-13 December, Kyoto, Japan

Langton, C. (1989). Computations at the edge of chaos: Phase transitions and emergent computation. *Physica D, 42*, p. 12-37

Langton, C. G. (1984). Self-reproduction on a cellular automaton. *Physica D, 10*, 135-144.

Li, M., & Vitanyi, P. M. B. (1993). *An introduction to Kolmogorov complexity and its applications*. New York, Berlin: Springer-Verlag.

Lewes, G. H. (1875). *Problems of life and mind*. Rinehart & Winston.

Leyton, M. (2001). *A generative theory of shape*. New York: Springer Verlag.

Manzo, G. (2007). Progrès et 'urgence' de la modélisation en sociologie, du concept de "modèle générateur" et sa mise en oeuvre, L'Année Sociologique, 2007, 57(1) forthcoming

McLaughlin, B. P. (1997). Emergence and supervenience. *Intellectica, 25*, 25-43.

McLaughlin, B. P. (1992). The rise and fall of British emergentism. in Beckermann, Flohr & Kim, op cit.. 49-93.

McLaughlin, B., & Bennett, K. (2006). Supervenience. In E. N. Zalta (Ed.), *The Stanford Encyclopedia of Philosophy* (Fall 2006 Edition). Retrieved from http://plato.stanford.edu/archives/fall2006/entries/supervenience

Mill, J. S. (1843). *System of logic*. London: Longmans, Green, Reader, and Dyer.

Minsky M. L. (1965). Matter, mind, and models. *Proceedings of IFIP Congress* (pp. 45-49), Spartan Books, Wash. D.C. Reprinted in Semantic Information Processing MIT press, 1969.

Morgan, C. L. (1923). *Emergent evolution*. London: Williams & Norgate.

Morgan, M. S., & Morrison, M. (1999). *Models as mediators*. Cambridge, MA: Cambridge University Press.

Müller, J. P. (2004). Emergence of collective behavior and problem solving. Engineering Societies in the Agents World IV, The 4th International Workshop ESAW-2003, Revised Selected and Invited Papers, (pp. 1-20) LNAI 3071 Springer Verlag.

Nagel, E. (1961). *The structure of science*. New York: Harcourt, Brace, and World.

O'Connor, T., & Hong Y. W. (2006). Emergent properties," E.N. Zalta (Ed.), The Stanford Encyclopedia of Philosophy (Winter 2006 edition), http://plato. stanford.edu/archives/win2006/entries/properties-emergent.

Palmer, R. (1989). Broken Ergodicity. In Lectures in the Sciences of Complexity, D. Stein, Ed. Volume 1, Santa Fe Institute Studies in the Sciences of Complexity, Reading, Ma., Addison-Wesley.

Phan, D. (2004a). From agent-based computational economics towards cognitive economics. In P. Bourgine, & J. P. Nadal (Eds.), *Cognitive economics, An interdisciplinary approach* (pp. 371-398). Berlin-Heidelberg: Springer-Verlag.

Phan, D. (2004b). Hierarchy of cognitive interactive agents and statistical mechanics: How object oriented programming highlights the connection. In Coelho, Espinasse, & Seidel (Eds.), The *5th Workshop on Agent Based Simulation, Lisbon, Portugal* (pp. 69-76) Erlangen, San Diego, SCS Pub. House.

Phan, D., & Feber, J. (2007). Thinking the social dimension of the artificial world: Ontological status of collective beliefs. *International Transactions on Systems Science and Applications*, Special issue on "Emergent intelligence over networked agents," forthcoming. in 2007.

Phan, D., & Semeshenko, V. (2007). Equilibria in models of binary choice with heterogeneous agents and social influence. *European Journal of Economic and Social Systems*, forthcoming.

Phan, D., Gordon, M. B., & Nadal, J. P. (2004). Social interactions in economic theory: An insight from statistical mechanics. In P. Bourgine, & J. P. Nadal (Eds.), *Cognitive economics, An interdisciplinary approach* (pp. 225-358). Berlin-Heidelberg: Springer-Verlag.

Philemotte, C., & Bersini, H. (2005a). Intrinsic emergence boost adaptive capacity. In GECCO '05: *Proceedings of the 2005 Conference on Genetic and Evolutionary Computation* (pp. 559-560) New York, NY, USA, ACM Press.

Philemotte, C., & Bersini, H. (2005b). Co-evolution of effective observers and observed multi-agents system. *Advances in Artificial Life, The 8th European Conference, ECAL 2005*, Canterbury, UK, September, Proceedings. (pp. 785-794) Volume 3630 of Lecture Notes in Computer Science, Springer.

Poincaré, H. (1902). La science et l'hypothèse, Paris, Flamarion. Trad. Science and Hypothesis, New York, Dover Publications 1952

Putnam, H. (1981). *Reason, truth, and history*. Cambridge, MA: Cambridge University Press.

Ronald, E., & Sipper, M. (1999). Surprise versus unsurprised: Implication of emergence in robotics. *Robotics and Autonomous Systems, 37*, 19-24.

Ronald, E., Sipper, M., & Capcarrère, M. S. (2001). Design, observation, surprise! A test of Emergence. *Artificial Life, 5*, 225-239.

Rosen, R. (1985). *Anticipatory systems: Philosophical, mathematical, and methodological foundations*. New York: Pergamon Press.

Rosen, R. (1978). *Fundamentals of measurement and representation of natural systems*. North Holland.

Rosen, R. (1977). Complexity as a system property. *International Journal of General Systems, 3*, 227-232.

Rueger, A. (2000a). Physical emergence, diachronic, and synchronic. *Synthese, 124*, 297-322.

Rueger, A. (2000b). Robust supervenience and emergence. *Philosophy of Science, 67*, 466-489.

Sawyer, R. K. (2005). *Social emergence: Societies as complex systems*. Cambridge University Press.

Sawyer, R. K. (2004). The mechanisms of emergence. *Philosophy of the Social Sciences, 34*(2), 260-282, June.

Sawyer, R. K. (2003). Nonreductive individualism, Part II: Social causation. *Philosophy of the Social Sciences, 33*(2), 203-224

Sawyer, R. K. (2002a). Emergence in psychology: Lessons from the history of non-reductionist science. *Human Development, 45*(2), 1-28.

Sawyer, R. K. (2002b). Nonreductive individualism, Part I: Supervenience and wild disjunction. *Philosophy of the Social Sciences, 32*(4), 537-559.

Sawyer, R. K. (2001a). Emergence in sociology: Contemporary philosophy of mind and some implications for sociological theory. *American Journal of Sociology, 107*(3), 551-585.

Sawyer, R. K. (2001b). Simulating emergence and downward causation in small groups. In Moss & Davidsson (Eds.), *Multi agent based simulation* (pp. 49-67). Berlin, Springer-Verlag.

Schelling, T. S. (1978). Micromotives and macrobehavior. NY: W.W. Norton and Co.

Schelling, T. S. (1969). Models of segregation. *American Economic Review, Papers and Proceedings, 59*(2), 488-493.

Simon, H. A. (1996). *The science of the artificial*. Cambridge, MA: MIT Press.

Sperry, R. W. (1991). In defense of mentalism and emergent interaction. *Journal of Mind and Behavior, 12*, 221-245

Sperry, R. W. (1986). Discussion: Macro- versus micro-determinism (A response to Klee). *Philosophy of Science, 53*(2), 265-270.

Sperry, R. W. (1969). A modified concept of consciousness. *Psychological Review, 76*, 532-536

Steels, L. (2006). Experiments on the emergence of human communication. *Trends in Cogn. Sciences, 10*(8) 347-349.

Stephan, A. (2002a). Emergentism, irreducibility, and downward causation. *Grazer Philosophiche Studien, 65*, 77-93

Stephan, A. (2002b). Emergence. In Nadel (Ed.), *Encyclopedia of Cognitive Science* (Vol. 1, (pp. 1108-1115). London: Macmillan.

Teller, P. (1992). A contemporary look at emergence. In Beckermann, Flohr, & Kim, Eds., op cit. 139-153

Tesfatsion, L. (2002a). Economic agents and markets as emergent phenomena. *Proceedings of the National Academy of Sciences U.S.A.*, 99, Suppl. 3, 7191-7192

Tesfatsion L. (2002b). Agent-based computational economics: growing economies from the bottom up. *Artificial Life, 8*(1), 55-82.

Tesfatsion, L., & Judd, K. L. (2006). *Handbook of computational economics. Vol. 2: Agent-Based Computational Economics*. Amsterdam, New York: Elsevier North-Holland.

Tuomela, R. Methodological Individualism and Explanation, Philosophy of Science, 57, 133-140.

Udehn, L. (2001). *Methodological individualism: Background history and meaning*. New York: Routledge.

Van de Vijver, G. (1997). Emergence et explication. *Intellectica, 25*, 7-23.

Varela, F., Thompson, E., & Rosch E. (1991). *The embodied mind*. MIT Press.

Vaario, A, Hori, K., & Ohsuga, S. (1995). Towards evolutionary design of autonomous systems. *The International Journal in Computer Simulation, 5*, 187-206.

Wilbert, K. (2000). *A theory of everything: An integral vision for business, politics, science, and spirituality*. Boston, MA: Shambhala Publications, Inc.

Wolfram, S. (1984). Universality and Complexity in Cellular Automata », Physica D. N°10.

Worrall, J. (1989). Structural realism: The best of both worlds? *Dialectica, 43*, 99.

Zahale, J. (2003). The individualism-holism debate on intertheoretic reduction and the argument from multiple realization. *Philosophy of the Social Science, 33*(77), 99.

Endnotes

[1] For O'Connor and Hong (2006), the contemporary discussion on epistemological emergence as a non-reductionist concept relies on the discussion on Nagel (1961, p. 366-380 "The doctrine of emergence"). The latter is in fact widely based on the British version of emergentism, with Broad and Mill.

[2] For mathematical Platonicists, mathematical entities exist independently of the human observer. The strong form of "scientific realist" is also called "metaphysical realism" by Putnam (1981). This reject does not imply a relativist position. Our position is compatible for instance with the "internal realism" of Putnam (1981) as well as with more anti-relativist positions such as the "structural realism" of Poincaré (1902) and

Worrall (1989)—see Varenne, Phan "epistemology in a nutshell" in Amblard & Phan, (2007).

[3] See Fromm, in this book, for another typology of emergent phenomenon.

[4] For a recent debate including the supervenience/reduction dimension discussed here, see Kinkaid (1986) and Tuomela (1990).

[5] "Energy is a resultant or hereditary property in the sense that it is possessed by every parts of a thing (...) Unlike holism, we regard emergents as rooted in the properties of the components, hence as explainable in terms of the latter, through not by reduction to them. For example, temperature is explainable as average kinetic energy of the molecules, but this does not exemplify reduction because averages, through computed from individual values alone, are collective properties." (Bunge, 1977b p. 97-98)

[6] For a discussion of both perspectives in the social sciences from a "median" emergentist point of view, see the antagonists contributions of Archer (1998) and Sawyer (2001a)

[7] See for instance Durlauf (1997, 2001), Phan, Gordon, and Nadal (2004), Phan and Semeshenko (2007), and the pioneering work of Galam, Gefen, and Shapir (1982).

[8] Remark that several authors consider irreducibility as a necessary condition of emergence. Accordingly, numerous phenomena studied by the statistical mechanics are not viewed as emergent. For instance, for Bunge (1977), the temperature does not emergent from molecular movements because it could be reducible to the average energy within the system.

[9] An important feature is the availability of the inferior level of cognition for higher-level agents: an epistemic agent can behave sometimes like a behavioral agent or like a reactive agent.

Chapter X

Ontological Reflections on Peace and War[1]

Hayward R. Alker, University of Southern California &
Watson Institute, Brown University, USA

Abstract

Responding to a provocative question by Hiroharu Seki about Hiroshima ontologies, this chapter reviews related thinking about the ontological primitives appropriate for event-data making, accessing high-performance knowledge bases, and modeling intelligent complex adaptive systems of use to researchers on war and peace. It cautions against "Cliocide," defined as of the "silencing" or symbolic killing of collective historical-political or historical-disciplinary identities and identifying practices by historical or discipline deficient "scientific" coding practices. It proposes that more intelligent multi-agent models in the "complex, adaptive systems" tradition of the Santa Fe Institute should include the socially shared memories of nations and international societies, including their identity-redefining traumas and their relational/migrational/ecological histories of community-building success and failure. Historicity in an ontologically distinctive sense of the "time ordered self-understandings of a continuing human society" is still a challenge for the computationally oriented literature on war and peace.

Introduction

Faced with the challenge to honor the late Hiroharu Seki, whom I knew and have admired for several decades, I was at first not sure what would be an appropriate appreciation of his significant, wide-ranging career. The theme of ontologies relevant to researchers interested in peace and war finally crystalized in my mind followed hearing him speak from the audience at a recent International Studies Association meeting. Politely, but insistently, he asked a distinguished panel of scholars (I paraphrase): how can you put Hiroshima ontology into your approach to international relations? At a panel where epistemological and ontological pluralism was a central issue, and before an inter-disciplinary professional group where socially constructed international relationships have been a hot topic[2], his remark was both highly appropriate and particularly challenging.

Seki's difficult but powerful insistence deserves sustained reflection. I see his injunction as closely related to the development of a collective sense of history as a basis for both an international society of states and a global society of individuals having the capacity to direct themselves towards a better future, away from horrifying pasts, toward a world where Hiroshimas, Auschwitzs, and Chernobyls never reoccur. In other words, Seki appeared to be trying to discover how can a powerful, shared sense of history and tradition, of prohibitions and morally preferable possibilities, be developed, shared, and deeply transmitted to future generations. I think he had in mind their culturally transmitted, phenomenological, and ontological ways of seeing and encoding reality, as well as their more consciously reflected upon norms and practices.

To pay homage to Professor Seki, I have decided to make some earlier thoughts along similar lines more widely available. First, I shall recall briefly the international relations simulation world of the 1960s, which Hiroharu

Seki and I both inhabited, and where we first met through the courtesy of Harold Guetzkow. Then, I shall reflect further on the absence of morally powerful lessons easily connected to, or embodied within, the way behavioral scientists have represented specific, singular international events like Hiroshima or Auschwitz. How is this kind of intelligence embodied into our complex adaptive systems models? Where, for example, in formally modeled accounts of international relations, are the triggers for the tragic (or comic!) meanings of many classical historians, or the ironical historical sensitivity characteristic of many modern and some post-modern thinkers?[3] And what about the data we develop to calibrate or test such models? Do not simple quantifications of horrifying international events like these obfuscate, or tend to erase from our consciousness, the complicated socio-historical identifications, expectations, roles and networks normally binding together a national or international society's members?

Current adaptive systems models popular in political science and international relations have no or almost no symbolic memories; typically their past-invoking mechanisms are structurally similar to first order Markov processes[4]. Surely, the human history of peace and war, of freedom and domination, of community, nation, state or international systems formation and dissolution has more to offer than that! I shall suggest "event data" coding practices[5] for greatly reducing the inadvertent complicity with such horrible events, which their oversimplified, reality hiding, "naturalizing" scientific codifications,/ quantifications as "event data" tend to suggest. I shall follow the practice of contemporary computer scientists in treating "ontologies" for such "event data" as humanly respecifiable linguistic primitives used for artificial knowledge representation and retrieval systems.[6] Next, attempting to help fulfill Professor Seki's belief in the promise of international simulations, I shall reflect on my several visits to a citadel of complex adaptive systems theory, the Santa Fe Institute. I shall show how a better sense of historical connectivities, or of trauma-avoiding historicities (a concept to be defined below), might inform a recent ecological research program on adaptive, multi-agent systems,[7] a research program attempting to incorporate international issues. Finally, as a challenge to future modelers of intelligent complex adaptive systems, I speculate about the future of more intelligently modeled international crisis research, inspired by the recent computationally-oriented writings of Gavan Duffy, Brian Cantwell Smith, and Thomas Schmalberger.

Putting More War and Peace into
Our Models' Ontologies

In the late 1960s,—when Professor Seki and I were both associated with Harold Guetzkow's simulated international processes project—I made my first investigation of phenomenological and ontological possibilities in more or less computerized international simulations.[8] In what then I might have referred to as a study of the "face validity" of different simulated worlds, my investigative strategy was comparatively to attempt to represent the consequences of an accidental, rather than an intentional, nuclear explosion in three different simulated worlds.

But even a hypothetical, gamed exploration of the implications of an ambiguously caused[9] Cold War nuclear accident at a clandestine Soviet test site in Polunochnoe, proved beyond the representational capacities of skilled formal modelers at that time. Professor Lincoln Bloomfield's non-computerized Political Military Exercise evidenced much more realistically suggestive possibilities for escalation and creative conflict containment than the formalized or partly formalized models Ronald Brunner and I investigated. The crucial gamed results of Bloomfield's imaginative scenario generate difficulties in the U.S. government's communication, for verification purposes during a crisis situation, with submerged submarines. These difficulties could not be adequately represented within either Guetzkow's own Inter-Nation Simulation (INS) or a hugh, Defense Department's TEMPER computer simulation. Guetzkow's "man-machine" INS combined human role players with computational decision environments, abstracted actors, and relationships too far above the important particulars of international history. It treated nations as abstract entities named "Bingo," "Erga," etc. Similarly, the major fully computerized simulation at the U.S. Department of Defense's Joint War Games Agency in the late 1960s, TEMPER, couldn't represent "unintentional actions" well; it also regionalized international threats implausibly. Fulfilling treaty obligations, European NATO members sent troop reinforcements to the continental United States in the middle of the TEMPER-simulated Polunochnoya crisis! Seki's ontological challenge was already a relevant issue, although the developers of TEMPER thought historically in categories linked most directly to the Cold War rather than to the costs of victory and defeat in World War II. A look at event data research in subsequent decades would reveal, I believe, persistent versions of related representational conundrums.[10]

How not to Commit Cliocide in Event-Data Coding Practices[11]

As methodologically restated in Alker's "Emancipatory Empiricism: Toward the renewal of empirical peace research,[12]" yesterday's computational tools and data-making practices rarely have the avoidance of specific major international traumas (which actually occurred much earlier and might recur today or in the future) as their central, codifiable reality. Our "realistic" scientific procedures have long been in danger of being captured by the often ugly, frequently recurring but probably not eternal realities of "Power Politics" that we as scholars of the successes and failures of the Westphalian state system must try faithfully to represent, as well as to transcend.

What are the "events" that the event-data specialist tries replicably, and hopefully validly, to encode? Webster's Third New International Dictionary illustrates it's first definition of "event" as "something that happens" by citing Wordsworth—"this day's event has laid on me the duty of opening my heart." Reflect on his indictment—in a poem entitled "The Thorn"—of science (and art) unreflective about the influences of its originating experiences:

Our meddling intellect
Misshapes the beauteous forms of things.
We murder to dissect.
Enough of science and of art.
Close up these barren leaves.
Come forth and bring with you
A heart that watches and receives.

Whether beauty or ugliness is our subject, the naturalistic search for quantified scientific replicability can butcher specifically situated traumas or ecstacies. We must learn from Wordsworth.

Two themes derive from these reflections on the ways in which we fail scientifically to encode the partly shared, socio-historical significances of Hiroshima, Auschwitz, and other traumatic events shaping the internal and relational identities and international "destinies" of particular nations or peoples. First, I will briefly discuss the "high politics" of disciplinary birth, renewal, death and transfiguration. In this domain paradigmatic, disciplinary, and interdisciplinary wars have sometimes been directed more or less consciously against humanistic history, radical political economy, transnational/international sociology, peace research, the cultural self-understandings of conquered nations, and even the social reality of "power politics." None of these orientations adequately comprehends the complexities of international history.

The second theme concerns the ways International Relations specialists operationally address "event data." It concerns how they might better include both socio-cultural and political-economic historicities, including the recognition of distortive effects of their own disciplinary historicity, in their work. This new, merged research direction, now significantly, but never completely, operationalizable with contemporary multi-perspective procedures[13], should help slow or reverse our disciplinary descent from analytical "accident" to "malfeasance" to symbolic "silencing" or "Cliocide." By "historical/disciplinary Cliocide," I mean the more or less premeditated "analytical and/or symbolic killing" of socio-historically shared achievements and failures, including the replicable traumas and the people-defining, semi-historical "hero stories" of societal collectivities and transnational disciplines. The culprits?: solipsistic, individualistic, one-sided, asocial, scientistic, phenomenologically insensitive and ontologically impoverished story-telling and data-making perspectives and procedures.

The Historicity of International Events and Scholarship

According to Webster, then, events are things that happen, activities or experiences, noteworthy occurrences or happenings; they are thus pieces of history. International events are then events that are international in some respect, pieces of international history noteworthy from perhaps several domestic or international perspectives (usually those of journalists). International event data are replicable codifications of these pieces of historical experience, generated from particular international relations scholarly vantage points.

But, we must ask, what are the boundaries of an event, what are the connections (at any instant, and through time), and how do they affect the kind of event it is, or that we, or others, describe it to be? How can we better delineate the ways events contain, overlap, inter-relate, interpenetrate, fold back upon, cumulate, or subsume each other? Our scholarly impoverishment in ontologically conceiving or phenomenologically representing history's "essence," its *historicity* (or, more generally, its *connectivity*) is evident in the small number of ways most complex adaptive systems modelers of war and peace conceive and represent historical international processes. And by the extent to which historicity is usually naturalistically defined as a kind of "path dependence" based on the model of sampling from urns of marbles without replacement.

Let us look at the issue of historical *connectivity,* or *historicity,* in somewhat more detail. Some refer to the Pelopponesian War as an event; similarly others refer to World War I or II separately, the latter being argued to have started in 1931 (Manchuria), 1935 (Ethiopia), 1939 (Poland), or 1941 (Pearl Harbor). But classical historians recognize that, just as world systems theorists are having us rethink the ultimate separability of the First and Second World Wars of this century, Thucydides was both insightful and correct to treat as one war two periods of sustained hostilities interrupted by a long, but uneasy peace. The meaning and significance of the later events in both wars—in particular, as attempts to fulfill, redefine, or overturn earlier policies or settlements (i.e., positively or negatively judged precedents)—is so colored by the earlier pe- riod of fighting that it is appropriate to say the earlier events are *contained in,* or *constitutive of* the later ones. Together these episodes constitute a single event, a larger unity. Here is a conception of historicity—the time ordered self-understanding of a continuing human society[14]—that further and more deeply explicates Seki's difficult conception of "Hiroshima ontology."

We can summarize and extend the present discussion with Table 1. Reaching back into recent philosophical and historiographic writings, and toward the technically advanced fields of (computational) linguistics gives at least nine overlapping, but alternative versions of "historicity."

One may well ask, must any historical particular always be defined in terms of everything it is connected to? Which perspectives concerning an event—at least including significant contemporary participants—do *not* belong in its adequate codification? Behavioral codings by one professor's graduate students debatably assume (and allow limited statistical tests for) conceptual univer- salism. But the diversity, multiplicity and richness of multiple perspectives concerning war boundaries is already powerfully suggested, inter alia, by the continentally distinct initial dates for World War II previously given. As recent American history, and the diplomatic Bluebooks of World War I fame make clear, sharply different versions of events, from different individual, organizational, national or transnational perspectives, are intriguingly, but differentially constitutive of their noteworthiness. Overlapping, changing, as well as opposed, regionalisms[15] seem a better empirical starting point for the

Table 1. Nine ways of conceptualizing and/or operationalizing historicity (Source: Most importantly, Alker, 1996, p. 184-206, 213-215, 297-302, 321-328, and 386-393)

1. The Brian Arthur-Paul David-Robert Keohane-Stephen Krasner literature on cybernetic, path-dependent, probabilistic (urn selection) historical processes;

2. Weiner-inspired cybernetic discussions of nonergodic development;

3. Jon Elster's rewrites of electro-magnetic hysteresis (defined by Webster as "the influence of the previous history or treatment of a body on its subsequent response to a given force or changed condition").

4. The philosophical-political traditions of practical argumentation begun by Thucydides' pre-Socratic teachers and distilled in recent technical-philosophical literatures by Nicholas Rescher, Ronald Loui and Douglas Walton on practical and/or dialectical argumentation;

5. Derivation-dependent parsing, already clearly illustrated in Chomsky's *Syntactic Structures* and also visible in the context-sensitive rewrite rules of text linguistics;

6. The artificial intelligence literature on non-monotonic reasoning: non-monotonic reasoning has the historically suggestive properties: theses are tentative & reversible; axiomatic presumptions may change in the course of arguments; thus previously derived conclusions can be invalidated;

7. The self-compiling and self-modifying capacities of computer procedures or programs written in the lexically scoped SCHEME dialect of LISP, programs which have the additional property of "transparent historicity," process traceability back to original definitions and contexts of definition;

8. The ethnomethodological/phenomenological literature on scientific development and "members' time";

9. Hegel's phenomenologically inspired discussions of Reason and Spirit in History, Vico's and Marx's variants of historicism, and Heidigger and Marcuse's ontological discussions of historicity, from which Olafson's previously cited, analytically much clearer conception of historicity partly derives.

boundaries, parties, and issues making up some of the more complex wars of the present (and other) centuries. We need critically and constructively to rethink the bases for excluding from critical, comparative, scientific analyses ab initio certain nationalities, traditions or paradigms of research in the difficult, multi-disciplinary field of international relations research.

Part of the historical significance or noteworthiness of international events arises from the larger events, processes, histories or which they are seen to be part. Contemporaries can give significance to the events of their times in terms of larger (but debatable) historical constructs—Thucydides' account of Athens' imperial rise and tragic fall, Aristophanes proto-feminist indictments of the destructiveness of male Athenian economic greed come to mind. Historicist Soviet versions of the triumph of Socialism are now obviously bad history compared to those interpretations of specific recent events consistent with the large theme of the rise of global capitalism. But at what point, and why, should such internal, identity-constitutive connections to larger, debatable historical happenings be ignored?

In our scientific codifications of significance, we must remember that distances and historical projects are measured differently, with different degrees of universality and timelessness. From a multi-disciplinary perspective, is not the genre of classical authors' writings indicative of a multi-faceted approach to truths of various sorts? Aristophanes' entered his plays into the Athenian competition, presumably describing them as "comic fictions"; but they serve as evidence for feminists and Marxists of economic and gender differences neglected by "Realist" analyses. And although Thucydides' scientific "history" obviously can be distinguished from crowd-pleasing morality plays, that doesn't destroy Raymond Aron's claim that Thucydides wrote art and science simultaneously, or the Classical reading of this history as a tragic morality play about the arrogance of power.[16]

What "unbiased science" can legitimately discard the evidence presented by any of these perspectives? Ironic criticism has been a mainstay of progressive, critical, modern thought. Must we try to denude our language of its morally based critical power? Supposedly in the interests of analytical clarity, logical positivism tried to do so, but failed. Shouldn't a deeper appreciation of how language works be a better guide? The particular kind of event connectivity that most concerns us here was referred to above with terms like "socio-historical," "historical sociality," or the "historicity" of international events. Among philosophers of social science and historians, "historicity" has been a concept developed to delineate both a very precious, distinctive, and central feature of human socio-cultural evolution and of a set of humanistic disciplines (history, rhetoric and dialectic, etc.) substantively and methodologically distinctive from the natural sciences.

Admitting that further historical investigation of this argument is required, I suggest tentatively that the relative lack of attention to the conceptual and representational issues raised by this focus has several roots. It is linked both to the "logical positivist" or "behavioral scientific" origins of early events data research methodologies, to a resistant unfamiliarity of most International Relations researchers with these professional-identity-challenging issues, and/or to their lack of expert awareness of operationally relevant, but demanding, alternative representational approaches like those in Table 1. More will be said next about the paradoxical possibility that more technically sophisticated representational/codification practices—those described within a paradigm of "conversational computing"[17]—can give us more humanistically defensible empirical research practices.

The historicity of events takes place through what phenomenologists refer to as the intentional (in the double senses of "object-constituting" and pur- posive), the extensional (referential) and the intensional ("meaning constitu- tive") dimensions of meaning, and the interpretive ways groups of citizens and scholars recognize and define the events's existence. It takes place, one might say metaphorically, when a social group's "past" is born (i.e., it be- comes accessible to them in a temporal, but necessarily clock-like, fashion). Following Olafson, as articulated in Table 1, we defined "historicity" as the socially shared self-temporalization of their collective experiences among members of a continuous human society of some kind. Harold Lasswell, for example, clearly called for the empirical tracking of the demands, expectations and identifications that are part of these in such historicities. To summarize his views, for better or worse we are embedded in historical configurations which are characterized by the existence of a large number of comprehensive symbols in the name of which people kill or die.[18]

A second class of nationally and transnationally shaped historicities should also be mentioned: those of disciplinary societies of international relations scholars, including the overlapping professional groupings of historians, war researchers, and peace researchers. Among such "inter-disciplines," key symbol configurations, research-orienting concepts and their changing interpretations are central embodiments of professional "historicities."

The connections of socio-political and disciplinary historicities are complicated. Indeed, widely but incompletely shared concepts, paradigms of theory and practice, and specialized symbols and languages reflect and help constitute national, transnational and international self-identifications, understood both historically and in disciplinary ways. To cite a Communitarian, a Realist and a Radical/Marxist theorist, recall the notion of historicity implicit in Karl Deutsch's theory of pluralistic security communities, Hedley Bull's historical accounts of the expansion of the "anarchical society" around the globe, or Lenin's ideas about the revolutionary historicity of national Communist parties and Socialist Internationals in the age of imperialism[19].

When it is not practically or technically necessary to do so, to ignore the collaborative and/or antagonistic historicities just referred to is definitionally or methodologically to bias, to distort, to "silence" the multiple meanings imbedded within international historical reality. To codify or measure such events in a correspondingly partial, unconnected fashion is to sever, cut off, dismember or even "quantitatively butcher" essentially qualitative histories in the good name of science. It is to destroy the transnational and international historicities out of which international political community and world order might eventually grow.

Operationalizing Historicity in Event Data Research

Event data research attempts to apply scientifically justifiable and replicable procedures to the categorical or quantitative measurement of relevant newspaper accounts. It is a response, so far of limited but still urgent practical utility, to the need to address the great majority of historical materials, which are themselves qualitative in nature.[20] Having spent several decades researching the issues of humanistic interpretation and explanation of the practice and transcendence of "Power Politics," I believe that we need still further to develop much farther qualitative ways of modeling collective human intentions, interpretations, and differentially shared precedential memories.

A practical variant of Seki's ontological question still remains: How can international event data researchers be more deeply sensitive to the economic, cultural and political historicities in terms of which social groups give meaning to their collective experiences, in the name of which their typical members are willing to kill, to die, or to be killed? The regulative ideal I suggest for such work is develop computerized representations of socially significant events that simultaneously contain or reference most or all of their external and internal (identity constituting) relations, their inter- and inner-connections, and the cooperative and conflictful historicities giving them social and scholarly significance.

What are these relationships? Where can they be found? I have argued: search through human memories and their documentary external stabilizers, look at the constitutive conversations, the scholarly debates, the meaningful interactions, the social discourses and even the "negotiated silences" where the events become, remain, cease to be socially, culturally, economically or politically significant, either historically or scientifically. Because of the way it emphasizes historic interconnections, and includes the history of its generation, utilization and transformation, the relevant data set would look like a well organized, and transparent human memory. Additional research might try to fill in missing intentions, search for more holistic historical patterns, paralleling the ways that our own passionate or relatively detached intellects dissect and rewrite the past.

The very large role of natural language representations (which include and can generate quantifications where appropriate) is itself noteworthy. Data analyses according to different paradigmatic codifications and more richly comparable than mere numbers. Historical narratives written from different participant or scholarly perspectives provide levels of information and modalities of interpretive coherence not naturally representable as statistical coefficients or dynamically changing, differently colored, grid boundaries. When episode histories and codebooks can be treated as applicable precedents or case-redefining procedures, conversationally reflective modes of case- or explanation-based reasoning[21] and data analysis can more fully parallel the unsilenced conversational practices of emancipatory dialogical relations. The linking of freedom, critical rationality and the responsible pursuit of larger human goals goes back at least to Thucydides' history.

This idealized sketch shows several ways in which the historical context of particular events can be treated as part of that event, without the data analyst becoming, as Harold Guetzkow might say, "data bound." Histories of event citations in precedential scholar/practitioner texts or speeches would augment existing data sets. Evidence on the various ways in which practical historians or scholars construct their pasts would also grow. Evidence on multiple historical and scholarly temporalizations would allow empirically grounded, constructive characterizations of the shared historicity of social events and social scientific practice. Thus the sociality of shared, opposed, or coordinated perspectives and practices would be social facts within the data set, rather than statistically problematical realities.

Starting with work at MIT, and continuing at MIT and Syracuse, Gavan Duffy and John Mallery developed a RELATUS text analysis computer system for computationally parsing, storing, or retrieving, and analyzing different narrative accounts; they saw the need to extend these procedures to hermeneutic, conversational and historical contexts of application,[22] which can be organized in terms of different theoretical or socio-historical perspectives. Measurements corresponding to codebook definitions or revisions can be reconstituted into the descriptive sentences from which they were initially derived. Replicable, non-quantitative representations for catching elements of the past in the present are beginning to appear. Historicity, potentially, exists within a symbiotic network of human experts and their recursively structured computer programs.

Incorporating Political Histories into Adaptively Intelligent Multi-Agent Ecological Models

I have extended Seki's concern with the phenomenological and ontological dimensions of a deep commitment to the avoidance of nuclear war destruction like Hiroshima to include genocides like that exemplified by Auschwitz. And I have argued that such concerns can be treated as specific historicities. Can this way of thinking be scientifically extended to include the avoidance of ecological devastation? Can such precedential historicities be included at the foundational/ontological level in other research programs than those International Relations has normally concerned itself with?

Coincident with the age's concern with better understanding and promoting "sustainable development," I now want to discuss ecologically oriented models, and the need to put sharable human histories, with their trauma-avoiding lessons, into them. As Professor Seki would want us to do, I assert here, and try to exemplify, the continuing need for interdisciplinary researchers on war and peace to bridge gaps, to connect war and peace practices and possibilities, to the issues of contemporary concern. As the previous pages should have made apparent, the ontological and representational issues of putting shared human consciousness, memories and moral choices within ecological models is not a trivial one.

The need to historicize ecological modeling practices in a peace-relevant way arose in my mind at an exciting April 1994 workshop which I attended at the Santa Fe Institute in New Mexico (SFI).[23] There were at least three major thematic convergences, pregnant with further research implications, evident to me by the end of (or shortly after) my participation in the Crude Look at the Whole (CLAW) Workshop. Here is a brief sketch of them.

Lateral Pressure Theory Meets Adaptive Multi-Agent Modeling

The joint presentations of John Holland and Joshua Epstein were a wonderful kick-off for the seminar. As I soon learned, these were mere introductions to a style of adaptive, multi-agent, grid-based, ecologically inspired modeling that is a central thematic unity of the work at the SFI[24]. My background in elementary artificial life simulations and Holland's genetic algorithms meant that I was not totally surprised by either presentation, but the interdisciplinary synthesis of elements of geography, biology, demography, economics and sociology in Epstein's stunningly effective visual presentation was very impressive. The spatialization of social processes emergent from the interactions of autonomous, message passing agents recalled writings by Schelling, Bremer and Mihalka, Cusack and Stoll, and Duffy[25] on power political interactions on territorial grids. Some of this literature was unfamiliar to SFI scholars. And, driven by the concern for improving the peace relevance of the social ontologies used in inter-disciplinary futures oriented work, I engaged with these authors.

It was my impression that the Epstein-Axtell model had much simpler, but more social scientifically interesting bio-social foundations. But, I found Holland's ECHO system (with its evocations of Burks, Axelrod, Cohen and Holland—Michigan BACH) elegant and visually suggestive, with a deeper grounding in evolutionary ecology. The coloring of different Prisoner's Dilemma players on a spatial grid gave very nice "cooperative" results of the emergent sort one has come to expect from SFI. Holland's and Murray Gell-Mann's[26] emphasis on the minimally complex "cartoon-like" character of such formalizations/visualizations was entirely in the spirit of what I took to be a heuristic exercise. Holland's recognition of the modular character of genetic selection processes within selection processes recalled as well the Leibnizian ontology (monads within monads...) informing the Rapoport/DT

Campbell/Boulding/Simon hierarchies of knowing/adapting processes I learned from the *General Systems Yearbook* many years ago.[27]

The initial convergence of Epstein's artificial histories of life on his simulated sugarscape with Choucri-North lateral pressure accounts of the demographic-technological-resource-using growth, intersection and conflict of nations was stunning. Choucri and North's econometric analyses of processes leading up to World War I and their work on the imperialistic and nonimperialistic ways that Japan expressed its "lateral pressure" before and after World War II came immediately to mind.(Choucri & North, 1975; Choucri, North, & Yamakage, 1992). And the demographic-technological-territorial profiles in (Choucri, 1993)[28] (which correspond roughly to different population densities differently located on Epstein's sugarscapes) all fit Epstein-Axtell's story extremely well. The best evidence of a closeness of fit came when Robert North and Joshua Epstein started talking about a common problem: how to build hierarchical social structures into their expansionary stories. A kind of class structure seemed to appear on Epstein's video screen, as in North's sociologically and empirically grounded theorizing.

But there was a divergence, too, which I was puzzling about until I later heard Thomas Homer-Dixon speak at MIT in a seminar on environmental stress, migration and violence. Homer-Dixon has a chapter in *Global Accord*, a major research project underway, and considerable notoriety from Robert D. Kaplan's Malthusian look at Third World development prospects.(Kaplan, 1994) He passed out two papers, one summarizing his project's research findings, and the second discussing the "ingenuity" necessary to avoid the violence-provoking ecological disasters in the making reported on in that summary[29]. He is not the fatalistic pessimist Kaplan makes him out to be; on the other hand, he insists that real changes ("adaptations") have to be made if environmentally focused degenerations are not to occur with increased frequencies.

The first divergence troubling me was one of modeling styles. Unlike Epstein or Holland, Choucri has used either econometric modeling and nonlinear, feedback laden, Systems Dynamics formulations. Territorial concepts figure in Choucri-North theories, and data-based models for separate countries are the norm, but territory is not explicitly represented in her models. Structural adaptation and environmental degradation are nicely handled by her non-linear feedback loops (whose dynamics are so easily graphed by Systems Dynamics/STELLA software), but there are no message-passing autonomous agents in her models; she and Rothenberg and most other modelers in their style are using econometrics or Systems Dynamics, not object-oriented programming.

The missing link was migration! If Choucri and North were to model their processes of lateral expansion on territorial grids, and these territorial grids were to be like Epstein's sugarscapes, they would capture a new set of emergent interaction possibilities. Ironically, some of Homer-Dixon's best slides were of highly polluting sugar or prawn plantations located on low level flatlands at the foot of, or in between, Philippine mountains where much poorer farmers held on to their degraded, non-terraced, much less attractive production possibilities, or from which these farmers migrated to highly polluted city slums in increasing numbers. Obviously a later version of Epstein's software should have resource rich sugar spots on flatlands near the harbors, not way up in the mountains. Various groups could migrate, trade and talk among themselves and with others, not just view their unequally limited horizons, etc. Message passing could also be used as a control process, to calculate systems wide environmental limits processes as well (simulating global warming, nonrenewable resource elimination, etc.) The resource rich "high points" of his societies/civilizations would historically have been river basins. A real shift to a more socially complex, historically adaptive multi-agent simulation modeling style might well result.

Modeling Historicity on the Sugarscapes of Life

A growing impression throughout the meeting was that much of what I have been working on as a modeler over the last 20 years could conceptually and technically be fitted into what I called "volume 2" of Epstein-Axtell's project. Object-oriented LISP routines could be imbedded in Epstein's object-oriented PASCAL programs to explore new domains. This was a "pregnant convergence" of projects par excellence. It would also help improve upon Choucri style modeling, and transform it into the artificially intelligent SCHEME/LISP style of modeling that allows historicity-rich process representations[30].

Let me further try to set up this line of thought by first emphasizing a divergence. The mechanisms featured in Holland's genetic algorithms (reviewed in Mitchell, 1996) and Epstein's models are "low down" on the Lovejoy/ Boulding/Campbell Great Chain of Being/Acting/Knowing mentioned above. Specifically, collectively, socially, humans have evolved memory-rich, language-rich, imagination-rich, organization-rich modes of problem-solving—firms, universities, markets, nations, and even science itself—whose mechanisms/processes/ capacities/ tendencies are not well represented in either Holland's or Epstein-Axtell's models. To put it bluntly, there is some sociology, no cultural anthropology, no politics, no law, and no science in Epstein's models. There are blue-dot-consuming "fights" on his sugarscapes, but not the "games," and certainly none of the "debates" that Rapoport wrote so well about (Rapoport, 1960).

As previously explicated, I think of the discovery of historicity as the birth of the "time ordered, [collective] self-understanding of a continuing human society." Nations socialize their children into the exploits of their founding heroes and great transitional actors, and the evils of their age old enemies, with powerful effects: Le Pen is citing Joan of Arc to argue for throwing out the foreigners, the Bosnian Serbs are still throwing out the Turks! A lot of "projecting" of domestic enemies on to international antagonists relies on this shared kind of "mythical" understanding. And since Auschwitz and Hiroshima, many are trying to create a new, anti-nuclear-war and anti-genocidal historicity for world society.

Now the operational implication for Epstein, volume 2, of such kinds of thinking would be to allow each of his actors individually and collectively, to have memories of past interactions, so that the above kinds of historicity could be represented and their developments studied. There would be both forgetting, and sharing of such memories. The "middle classes" higher up on the sugarscapes could develop shared "understandings" of the kinds of interactions one typically has with those lower down the sugarscapes, or across the valleys. Color coding of actors in such memories could have emergent effects like Holland showed us. Even without mimicking complex natural language capabilities of the Chomskyan sort, ethnic groups, classes, and territorially structured states could be modeled, and their memories imperfectly shared. Cultures, stereotypes, histories would be part of the sugarscape world. Principles of political and territorial organization could be suggested, and the identities, loyalties, and understandings typically associated with them could be crudely, but suggestively modeled. A higher level of organizational/ jurisdictional/responsibility boundaries could be identified (in a LISP-like way on territorial grids) allowing for the "tragedies of the commons" style ecology/security dynamics mentioned in the Santa Fe discussions. Historical bases for imagining new collective responses to these challenges could also be represented, and searched for, if memories were allowed different kinds of empathetic, recreative ingenuity.

Obviously, the past paragraph requires much elaboration and much new research before it is filled out. But I would like to signal here a strong convergence between the programming styles of contemporary MIT artificial intelligence programming and that of Epstein, Holland, and other Santa Fe researchers. Together they suggest what a new generation of intelligent complex adaptive systems might look like. The key metaphor is the Piaget-Pappert-Minsky one: the society of mind works by having differently capable, nearly autonomous agents, which have their own computational capacities and also pass messages to each other. Hierarchical aspects of "thinking" abound as well, but in flexible and sometimes ad hoc ways. Memory ("k-lines") is also important, but limited. Minsky's (1996) book presciently and correctly conveys the programming style of some of his most illustrious students (Winston, Hewitt, Sussman, Winograd, Stallman, Haase, Mallery, etc.) The extension of this complex, merged style of modeling to the social domain is very incomplete, but nonetheless promising.[31]

Effective Scenario Making Need not be Model Based

A third convergence at Santa Fe was, I think, not fully anticipated. When I publicly repeated a private suggestion that our future thinking would be scenario based, not model generated, a problem arose. What was the point of modeling, anyway? One of our members correctly anticipated that scenario-based future explorations would themselves generate model-based exercises, not vice versa. With his own considerable experience in advising decision makers, Dr. Zhenghua Jiang's accounts of the ways he presented different scenarios in between best and worst possible cases generally supported the view that modeling and future thinking could be symbiotically related. But again we would not be able to derive the future from our models, or all relevant alternatives.[32]

The convergence of the practice of the workshop to such anticipations was nearly exact. Thus Brian Arthur's worries about North-South style class conflicts, or subnational/transnational dual economies focused our thinking nicely. Nathan Keyfitz has written about a global middle class—itself a model sketch developed in demographic, yet non-Malthusian, reaction to the limits to growth debate (Keyfitz, 1977). Murray Gell-Mann added brave new worlds style class/race politics to this scenario. We could add the increased or decreased legitimization of genocide and nuclear war. Nonetheless, the heuristic role of the sugarscapes models could clearly be seen. Alternatives to the Keyfitz-Arthur-Gell-Mann scenario developed further in the conversation; ideas for specialized, model-based research were generated. Even a range of possible actor classes in the scenarios explored in CLAW's final report were identified.

None of the previous convergences can be taken for granted. None of the ideas previously sketched is fully fleshed out. Each is somewhat dependent on the others. Nonetheless, I think these three convergences are sufficiently exciting to suggest that they imply new areas for future work, new areas of collaboration in the social sciences domain, new ways of moving intelligent complex adaptive systems research closer to the global realities of war and peace. This is a line of thinking which Professor Seki has already begun explore. I hope others will continue to do so, because I believe historicity-rich modeling traditions better allow global citizens to learn from, and teach about, the lessons of Hiroshima, Auschwitz, and Chernobyl as well.

Toward Better, Still Revisable, Ontologies

To help fulfill the emancipatory promise of research on achieving peace, the operational concepts embodied in our intelligent complex adaptive systems models need to be more intelligently constructed, working from richer ontologies of historical representational possibilities[33]. Simulations with affectively encoded, symbolically represented memories need to contain ways of recognizing the practices constituting such past realities while at the same time containing the possibility of transcending those realities through revisions in their reality-codifying practices. As Hiroharu Seki has argued concerning the significance of the end of the Cold War, we "should include our political will [,..our] moral leadership as one of the most significant variables....[W]ithout the preference of ontology to epistemology or without the preference of subjectivity to objectivity...we can not start the road towards solving any kind of the global problematique."(Seki, 1996) Our ontologies of the real, the possible, the desirable and the awful, the necessary and the impossible must be revised to make such progressive development possible. I see Professor Seki as someone trying to redress the balance in a world of social scientists too committed to less adequate naturalistic ontologies.

Up until this point, except concerning the meaning of historicity, I have used, but avoided detailed discussions of, ontological issues of primarily a philosophical or metaphysical sort.

Unfortunately, many social scientists are embroiled rather unprofitably in an epistemological/ ontological debate between materialistic "realists," "idealists," and "constructivists" regarding essences and phenomenal appearances, ontologies and epistemologies, natural and social realities. Some participants in such debates might attempt, with some success, philosophically to unravel and criticize the language of "ontologies" with which I have structured the present discussion. But my focus here has been more operational, pointed toward the design of historicity-friendly, war and peace relevant event representations and intelligent complex adaptive systems. Therefore, let me suggest briefly some exciting new directions in social scientific research grounded in more sophisticated conceptions of social reality than much of the existing literature of International Relations, ontological conceptions with which I feel positively identified. These were completed or published since the first version of this text was written, yet they speak directly to the main points I have made.

For example, Gavan Duffy has proposed reconstructing event data analysis using the philosophical insights from W. V. O. Quine, Nelson Goodman, and Hilary Putnam. He accepts Putnam's notion of "internal realism" as a preferred alternative to either a "copy" or a "correspondence" theory of truth, and rejects both a copy theory or a constructivist theory of world-making. Metaphorically, both the mind and the world jointly make up themselves. Each person cognitively encodes a version of the world, which no one can identify as "objective truth," in the copy theory sense. "For internal realists, we each believe our versions right only in the sense and to the extent that they cohere with our other ideas. These include our conceptual constructs, our internalized norms, our perceptual fields, our life-experiences, and even our mental models of the world versions that those with whom we sociate disclose to us in discursive and practical action" (Duffy, 1996, p. 148f). Duffy then goes on to suggest principals for a representationally sophisticated, yet scientifically replicable, computational hermeneutics, based significantly on his years working with John Mallery and others in the development of the RELATUS system.

In a remarkably similar vein, the philosophical computer scientist Brian Cantwell Smith has proposed a middle ground between materialist and idealist metaphysics, a ground conceived of at least partly in terms of revisable computational ontologies, the sustained metaphor of this present discussion. He suggests a philosophy of presence governed by:

symmetrical realism: a commitment to One world, a world with no other, a world in which both subjects and objects...are accorded appropriate place...[T]hat world is depicted as one of cosmic and ultimately ineffable particularity: a critically rich and all-enveloping deictic [situation referring] flux...[which] sustains complex processes of registration: a form of interaction, subsuming both representation and ontology...[But] registration [has] metaphysical zest: the fact that all distinctions and stabilities—empirical, conceptual, categorical, metaphysical, logical—are taken not, at least not necessarily, and not in the first instance, to be "clear and distinct," sharp, or in any other way formal, but instead to be, or at least potentially to be, wily, critical, obstreperous, contentious, and in general richly eruptive with fine structure (Smith, 1996, p. 347f).

Here is a world uniting phenomenologies and ontologies, with plenty of room for moral imperatives, political and ontological differences, and inter-subjectively shareable historical learning, a world that Smith is suggesting we replicably explore with computationally facilitated symbolic procedures.

Finally, I call to my reader's attention to an impressive (yet horror filled), phenomenologically sophisticated, LISP-encoded account of many the overlapping and intersecting political worlds of what Russians usually call "The Caribbean Crisis" and Americans call "The Cuban Missile Crisis." Schmalberger suggests that this crisis "was about humiliation, prestige and leadership. It was a drama played before the world in which deception commonly used to enhance one's own prestige at the expense of the other, threatened to destroy the face of the protagonists."(Schmalberger, 1998, p. 5) Without reducing these interactions to causal models, Schmalberger provides text-based, phenomenologically grounded reconstructions of 66 conversation-like "turns" in the crisis, and analyzes this sequence counterfactually, generating alternative possible scenarios which lead the historically minded to many sobering reflections about the rationalistic self-misunderstandings of the key players.

These counterfactual reconstructions of the political process help facilitate deep learning about what brought the world the closest it has come to nuclear war since Hiroshima and Nagasaki. They suggest ways of behaving that should become part of the historicities of international and world society. Social and scientific international learning regarding nuclear war avoidance requires such historicities. If the next generation of International Relations scholars and intelligent complex adaptive systems modelers can build further on these fine ontological contributions to an ecologically sustainable, nuclear-war avoiding future, Professor Seki and I should be content.

References

Alker, H. R. (1997). Putting historicity into adaptive, multi-agent simulations: So that Hiroshima and Auschwitz might be remembered but not repeated. *Ritsumeikan Journal of International Affairs*, *9*(4), 125-132.

Alker, H. R. (1996, digitally reprinted 2007). *Rediscoveries and reformulations: Humanistic methodologies for international studies*. New York: Cambridge.

Alker, H. R., & Frasier, S. (1996). *On modeling historical complexity: "Naturalistic" modeling approaches from the Santa Fe Institute*. Paper presented on August 31 at the American Political Science Association meeting.

Alker, H. R., Gurr, T. R., & Rupesinghe, K. (2001). *Journeys through conflict: Narratives and lessons*. Lanham, MD: Rowman & Littlefield.

Alker, Jr., H. R. (1966). The long road to international theory: Problems of statistical nonadditivity. *World Politics*, *18*(4), 623-655.

Alker, Jr., H. R. (1988). Bit flows, rewrites and social talk: Towards more adequate informational ontologies. *Todai Symposium '86, Information and its Functions*, Tokyo: Institute of Journalism and Communications Studies, University of Tokyo.

lker, Jr., H. R. (1987). *Against historical/disciplinary genocide as a prerequisite to history's scientific dissection: Putting historicity at the center of events data research*. Presented at the 1987 meeting of the American Political Science Association.

Alker, Jr., H. R., & Brunner, R. D. (1969). Simulating international conflict: A comparison of three approaches. *International Studies Quarterly*, *13*(1), 70-110.

Alker, Jr., H. R., Duffy, G., Hurwitz, R., & Mallery, J. C. (1991). Text modeling for international politics: A tourist's guide to RELATUS. (1991). In V. Hudson (Ed.), *Artificial intelligence and international politics* (pp. 97-126). Boulder, CO: Westview.

Axelrod, R. (1997). *The complexity of cooperation: Agent-based models of competition and collaboration.* Princeton, NJ: Princeton University Press.

Bennett, J. P., & Alker, Jr., H. R. (1977). When national security policies bred collective insecurity: The War of the Pacific in a world politics simulation. In Deutsch, Fritsch, Jaguaribe and Markovits (1977), 215-302.

Bremer, S. A., & Mihalka, M. (1977). Machiavelli in Machina: Or politics among hexagons. In Deutsch, Fritsch, Jaguaribe & Markovits (1977), 303-338.

Bull, H. (1977). *The anarchical society.* New York: Columbia University Press.

Buzan, B., & Waever, O. (2003). *Regions and powers: The structure of international security.* Cambridge: Cambridge University Press.

Cederman, L. E. (2001). Modeling the Democratic Peace as a Kantian Selection Process. *Journal of Conflict Resolution, 45*(4), 470-502.

Cederman, L. E. (1997). *Emergent actors in world politics: How states and nations develop and dissolve.* Princeton, NJ: Princeton University Press.

Cederman, L. E., & Daase, C. (2003). Endogenizing corporate identities: The next step in constructivist IR theory. *European Journal of International Relations, 9*(1), 5-35.

Choucri, N. (1993). *Global accord: Environmental challenges and international response.* Cambridge, MA: M.I.T. Press.

Choucri, N., & North, R. (1975). *Nations in conflict.* San Francisco: W. H. Freeman.

Choucri, N., North, R., & Yamakage, S. (1992). *The challenge of Japan: Before World War II and after.* London & New York; Routledge.

Cohen, P. R., Morgan, J., & Pollack, M. E. (1990*). Intentions in communication.* Cambridge: M.I.T. Press.

Cohen, P. R., Schrag R., Jones, E., Pease, A., Lin A., Starr, B., Gunning, D., & Burke, M. (1998). The DARPA [U.S. Defense Advanced Research

Projects Agency] high-performance knowledge bases project. *AI Magazine, 19*(4), 25-49.

Cusack, T. R., & Stoll, R. J. (1990). *Exploring Realpolitik: Probing international relations theory with computer simulation*. Boulder, CO: Lynne Rienner.

Cusack, T. R., & Stoll, R. J. (1994). Collective security and state survival in the interstate system. *International Studies Quarterly, 38*(1), 33-60.

Dallmayr, F. (1991). *Between Freiburg and Frankfurt: Toward a critical ontology*. Amherst: University of Massachusetts Press.

Der Derian, J. (1998). *The Virilio reader.* Oxford: Blackwell.

Der Derian, J. (1991). *Anti-diplomacy: Speed, spies, and terror in international relations.* Basil Oxford: Blackwell.

Der Derian, J., &. Shapiro, M. J. (1989). *International/intertextual relations: Postmodern readings of world politics.* Lexington, MA: Lexington Books.

Deutsch, K. W., Burrell, S. A., Kann, R. A., Lee, Jr.,, M., Lichterman, M., Lindgren, R. E., Loewenheim, F. L., & Van Wagenen, R. W. (1957). *Political community in the North Atlantic area.* Princeton, NJ: Princeton University Press.

Deutsch, K. W., Fritsch, B., Jaguaribe, H. & Markovits, A. S. (1977). *Problems of world modeling: Political and social implications*. Boston: Ballinger.

Duffy, G. (1994). Events and versions: Reconstructing event data analysis. In (Duffy, ed, 1996), 147-167.

Duffy, G., Guest Editor, (1994*). New directions in event data analysis. International Interactions, 20*(1- 2), 1-168.

Duffy, G. (1992). Concurrent interstate conflict simulations: testing the effects of the serial assumption (in Cusack-Stoll's model). *Mathematical and Computer Modelling, 16*(8/9), 241-270.

Duffy, G., Frederking, B. K., & Tucker, S. A. (1998). Language games: Dialogical analysis of INF negotiations. *International Studies Quarterly, 42*(2), 271-294.

Dunn, T. (1998). *Inventing international society: A history of the English school*. Houndmills and New York: Macmillan and St. Martins.

Epstein, J., & Axtell, R. (1996). Growing artificial societies: Social science from the bottom up. Washington, DC: Brookings.

Gell-Mann, M. (1994). The Quark and the Jaguar: Adventures in the simple and the complex. New York: W.H. Freeman.

George, J. (1996). Understanding international relations after the Cold War. In (Shapiro, M. J. & Alker, H. R., eds. (1996, 33-79).

Gerner, D. J., Schrodt, P. A., Francisco, R. A., & Weddle, J. L. (1994). Machine coding of event data using regional and international sources. *International Studies Quarterly, 38*(1), 91-120.

Gordon, A. (2004). *Strategy representation: An analysis of planning knowledge.* Mahwah, NJ: Lawrence Erlbaum.

Hammond, A. (1998). *Which world? Global destinies, regional choices.* Washington, DC: Island Press/Shearwater Books.

Holland, J. H. (1995). *Hidden order: How adaptation builds complexity.* Reading, MA: Addison Wesley.

Homer-Dixon, T. (2000). *The ingenuity gap.* New York: Knopf.

Homer-Dixon, T. (1995). The ingenuity gap: Can poor countries adapt to resource scarcity? *Population and Development Review, 21*(3), 587-612.

Homer-Dixon, T. (1994). Environmental scarcities and violent conflict: Evidence from cases. *International Security, 19*(1), 5-40.

Hopf, T. (1998). The promise of constructivism in international relations theory. *International Security, 23*(1), 171-200.

Kaplan, R. D. (1994). The coming anarchy. *Atlantic Monthly.* February 27 issue, 44-75.

Keyfitz, N. (1977). World resources and the world middle class. In (Deutsch, Fritsch, Jaguaribe & Markovitz, 1977), 97-116.

King, G., & Zeng, L. (2001). Improving forecasts of state failure. *World Politics, 53*(4), 623-658.

Lakoff, G., & Johnson, M. (1999). Philosophy in the flesh: The embodied mind and its challenge to western thought. New York: Basic Books.

Lasswell, H. (1950, originally 1934). *World politics and personal insecurity.* Reprinted in H. D. Lasswell, C. E. Merriam, & T. V. Smith (Eds.), *A study of power.* Glencoe, IL: Free Press.

Lustick, I. S. Miodownik, D., & Eidelson, R. J. (2004). Secessionism in multicultural states: Does sharing power present or encourage it? *American Political Science Review*, *98*(2), 209-230.

Lyotard, J. F. (1984). *The postmodern condition: A report on knowledge.* Minneapolis, MN: University of Minnesota Press.

Merritt, R. L., Muncaster, R. G., & Zinnes, D. A. (1993). International *event-data developments: DDIR Phase II.* Ann Arbor, MI: University of Michigan Press.

Minsky, M. (1987). *Society of mind.* New York: Simon and Schuster.

Mitchell, M. (1996). *An introduction to genetic algorithms.* Cambridge, MA: M.I.T. Press.

Olafson, F. (1977). *The dialectic of action: A philosophical interpretation of history and the humanities.* Chicago: University of Chicago Press.

Rapoport, A. (1960). *Fights, games, debates.* Ann Arbor, MI: University of Michigan Press.

Roig, C. (1980). *La grammaire politique de Lénine*, Lausanne: L'Age d'Homme.

Schelling, T. (2006). *Micromotives and macrobehavior.* New York: Norton.

Schmalberger, T. (1998). *Dangerous liaisons: A theory of threat relationships in international politics*, unpublished Ph.D. Thesis #581, Institut Universitaire de Hautes Études Internationales, Genève.

Seki, H. (1996). *How nuclear weapons were related to the end of the Cold War.* Paper presented on September 17 to the Hiroshima Symposium on "The Fifty Years of Nuclear Weapons," Hiroshima.

Shapiro, M. J., & Alker, H. R. (1996). *Challenging boundaries: Global flows, territorial identities.* Minneapolis, MN: University of Minnesota Press.

Smith, B. C. (1996). *On the origin of objects.* Cambridge, MA: M.I.T. Press.

Sylvan, D. A., Ostrom, T. M., & Gannon, K. (1994). Case-based, model-based, and explanation-based styles of reasoning in foreign policy. *International Studies Quarterly*, *38*(1), 61-90.

Sylvan, D., & Thorson, S. J. (1992). Ontologies, problem representation, and the Cuban Missile Crisis. *Journal of Conflict Resolution, 36*(4), 709-732.

Wight, C. (2006). *Agents, structures and international relations: Politics as ontology.* Cambridge: Cambridge University Press

Endnotes

[1]   I wish to dedicate this essay to the memory of Professor Hiroharu Seki, late of Ritsumeikan University. Without holding them responsible for their contents, I would like to acknowledge the contributions to these reflections of a sabbatical visit to the Santa Fe Institute (SFI), and related conversations with W. Brian Arthur, Robert Axelrod, Nazli Choucri, Joshua Epstein, Murray Gell-Mann, John Holland, Stuart Kauffman, Christopher Langton, George Lakoff, Melanie Mitchell, and Thomas Ray. Not at the SFI, Thomas Schmalberger has also been a great inspiration. An earlier version of this essay was SFI Working Paper 99-02-011, which in turn was an expanded rewrite of (Alker, 1997)

[2]   One of the broader and more thoughtful treatments of constructivism in the war/peace context is Hopf (1998). For a British variant of social constructivism, see Tim Dunne's excellent historical-analytical account (Dunn, 1998). For a continentally oriented discussion of ontological themes reminiscent of some of the issues raised during SFI workshops on economics and cognition see Dallmayr (1991). An excellent recent modeler's treatment of social constructivism, relying heavily on Georg Simmel, is Cederman and Daase (2003). The recent ontological turn in IR theory is best articulated in White (2006).

[3]   A relevant, simplified rehearsal of the classical plot structures in contemporary historical accounts is (Knutsen, 2002); on post-modern ironic sensibilities see especially (Lyotard, 1984). In a discussion of the corrupted, nightmarish consequences of the Enlightenment's "narrative of reason, knowledge and freedom," Jim George suggests we "connect the ascent of the modern, rational subject with the experiences of Hiroshima and Auschwitz." (George, 1996, p. 54) Without denying the connections—John von Neumann fits into both narratives—I should state my view that the Enlightenment's scientific and political contributions, although flawed, are far too important and valuable to be summarily dismissed.

[4] For example, I cite from an exemplary study by one of the best contemporary complex adaptive systems modelers in International Relations today: "...[A] variable-sized grid constitutes the core of the model... [T]he main simulation loop contains five phases...As in my previous models, the logic of execution is quasi-parallel with double buffering... To achieve quasi-parallel execution, the list of actors is scrambled each time structural change occurs. The actors keep a memory of one step and thus make up a very complex Markov-like process..." (Cederman, 2001, p. 493). A similar analysis could be made of the first complex adaptive systems model featured (a multi-colored rectangular checkerboard-like grid on the front cover, no less) in the *American Political Science Review*: (Lustick, Miodownik, & Eidelson, 2004).

[5] Event data are typically nominal, ordinal or interval scale "measurements" of the kind or degree of cooperation or conflict between two parties, based on media accounts. For a scientifically respectable review and extension of this literature see Merritt, Muncaster, and Zinnes (1993)

[6] "The first and most intellectually taxing task when building a large knowledge base is to design an ontology." From Cohen et al. (1998, p. 26). Sylvan and Thorson (1992) agree on the importance on ontological issues, arguing that different ontologies can be more important than "options analysis" in determining decision-making possibilities in the Cuban Missile Crisis.

[7] Adaptive, multi-agent modeling in International relations is usually said to start with Bremer and Mihalka (1977). But this book also contains a more intelligent, empirically corroborated, memory-rich, geographically structured, adaptive, multi-agent predecessor of Cederman's and Duffy's more recent work: Bennett & Alker (1977). This article, based on Bennett's prize-winning thesis, might be said to pioneer "intelligent complex adaptive systems" in International Relations. Robert Axelrod and his student Lars-Erik Cederman are also rightly seen as pioneers in this style of International Relations modeling. See Axelrod (1997) and Cederman (1997). The most important recent theoretical refinement of this literature, paralleling the Bennett-Alker chapter in several respects, is: Lars-Cederman and Daase (2003).

[8] Alker, Jr., H. R. & Brunner, R. D. (1969). More elaborated descriptions of, and bibliographic citations to, the TEMPER, INS and Political Military Exercise simulations are given in that article.

[9]   The "post-structuralist/post-modern" discussion of ambiguous, mis-leading, simulated international events by Baudrillard and Virilio was introduced into academic International Relations in Der Derian and Shapiro (1989) and Der Derian (1991, 1998).

[10] See the contributions to Merritt, Muncaster, and Zinnes, op. cit., and the historically enriched proposals in Alker, Gurr, and Rupesinghe (2001).

[11] This section presents, in abbreviated and revised form, the substance of my provocatively entitled memo (Alker, 1987). Because no direct acts of violence are committed by such deficient coding practices, and the premeditations involved are not usually murderous, I would now retitle that memo and here propose for such a retitling the terms: "Cliocide" (and a related adjective "Cliocidal)," etymological references to the killing of the mythical Goddess of History, Clio. See the text below for a fuller definition of the "silencing" or symbolic killing of collective historical-political or disciplinary identities and identifying practices by historical- or discipline- deficient "scientific" coding practices.

[12] See chapters 5 ("Can the end of Power Politics...") and 10 ("Emancipatory Empiricism") of (Alker, 1996).

[13] See Alker (1996, passim), Schmalberger (1998), and Alker, Gurr, and Rupesinghe (2001).

[14] The relevant citation for this conception of historicity is Olafson (1977), which also richly reviews alternative conceptions of what sometimes is called "the essence of history." Further discussion of this seminal, partly Heidiggerian, partly Marcusian reformulation is contained in Chapter 11 of Alker (1996).

[15] The importance of regional contexts of meanings—and the relevance of covariance and regional factor analyses for multiplicatively reformulating relevant operational hypotheses and conceptual indicators—is an often neglected component of contemporary statistical training in International Relations. See Alker (1966). The study of regional security complexes has recently been improved upon in Buzan and Waever (2003).

[16] Sources for these interpretations can be found in Alker (1996, Chapter 1).

[17] A clarification of this ontological perspective and some earlier thoughts on informational and historical ontologies are offered in Alker (1988). See also the pioneering discussions in (Duffy, 1994). Reconstructing the

metaphorical (and hence not metaphysically necessary) bases of much ontological thinking about human affairs is a principal achievement of Lakoff and Johnson (1999).

[18]   Although I can't find an exact source, this summarizing text is doubtless inspired by Harold Lasswell (1950). See especially his Chapter 1: The configurative analysis of the world value pyramids; Chapter 2: Nations and Classes: The symbols of identification; and Chapter 3: The Balancing of Power: The expectation of violence.

[19]   See Karl W. Deutsch et al. (1957), Bull (1977), and Roig (1980).

[20]   Besides the various articles in Duffy (1994), there are several practically oriented efforts within Political Science and International Relations to get increased purchase on the voluminous body of daily newspaper accounts. For a thoughtful but modest effort to use linguistically-informed methods of event characterization, see Gerner, Schrodt, Francisco, and Weddle (1994). More ambitiously, see the description and analysis of the U.S. Central Intelligence Agency's State Failures project published by its statistical critics: (King & Zeng, 2001).

[21]   An excellent, Artificial Intelligence-inspired paper on such conversational modalities of practical reasoning is Sylvan, Ostrom, and Gannon (1994).

[22]   The chapters by Mallery and Duffy in Duffy, ed., op. cit., are the most relevant discussions of related procedures. See also Alker, Duffy, Hurwitz, and Mallery (1991); and the more dialogically oriented Duffy, Frederking, and Tuckner (1998).

[23]   The rest of this section recasts a memo prepared originally in April 1994 for the "Crude Look at the Whole" project at the Santa Fe Institute, and reported on previously in Alker 1997. It's original title was "Some Pregnant Convergences Observed at the CLAW Workshop." Both its composition and my visit to SFI were centered around the working out of my concern with war-avoiding historicities, the most central "rediscovery" of my earlier research, as represented and further developed in Alker (1996) and Alker and Fraser (1996). The most relevant, accessible books of these speakers are Holland (1995) and Epstein and Axtell (1996).

[24]   If an ECHO model is completed through the use of the SWARM modeling platform developed at SFI by Christopher Langton and his associates, or the REPAST modeling platform Cederman now prefers,

this may argue for trying to introduce richer historical capacities into ECHO rather than the Epstein-Axtell "Sugarscape" model. See Alker and Fraser (1996) for more details.

[25] Besides the Bremer and Mihalka work cited in End Note 8, see Cusack and Stoll (1990, 1994) and Duffy (1994). Of course, also see the earlier versions of Schelling (2006).

[26] A good over all introduction to Gell-Mann's vision of SFI research is Gell-Mann (1994).

[27] See the discussion and references in Alker (1996, p. 98-100).

[28] Other relevant citations to Choucri and her collaborators are included in this volume's Bibliography.

[29] The book length development of this later argument is Homer-Dixon (2000).

[30] For example, see Schmalberger (1998). An overview and demonstrative run of this simulation is available on http://www.usc.edu/dept/LAS/ir/cis/cews/html_pages/Dangerous_Liaisons/index.html.

[31] At some levels of linguistic, social, and historical complexity, such mergers become too complex to handle. Then, moving to the intelligent, adaptive modeling of symbolic cognition becomes a possible alternative. In this regard Cohen, Morgan, and Pollack (1990) and Gordon (2004) come readily to mind. But also review Duffy and Mallery's M.I.T. work on RELATUS, Bennett's War of the Pacific simulation, and the Cusack-Stoll and Duffy remodelings of Bremer and Mihalka's early "Machiavelli in Machina."

[32] The related SFI sponsored volume is Hammond (1998).

[33] It is interesting in this regard that Cederman's excellent complex adaptive systems model of the coming of the democratic peace identified in End Note 5 does not explicitly model the more complex processes of community building and community disintegration, focusing rather on forceful conquests and calculated alliance behaviors.

Chapter XI

The Allocation of Complexity in Economic Systems[1]

Jason Potts, University of Queensland & Queensland University of Technology, Australia

Kate Morrison, Volterra Pacific Pty. Ltd., Australia

Joseph Clark, University of Queensland & Suncorp Pty. Ltd., Australia[2]

Abstract

This chapter isolates a classic allocation problem in the substitution relation between two primary carriers of complex rules—agents and institutions—as a function of the relative costs of embedding rules in these carriers, all subject to the constraint of maintaining overall system complexity. We call this generic model the allocation of complexity, which we propose as a bridge between neoclassical and complexity economics.

Introduction

The market economy is an excellent example of an intelligent complex adaptive system. Economists, however, have largely failed to develop theoretical frameworks based upon this insight and have instead persisted with a timeless equilibrium-based analysis. The exception to this has been the work of the Austrian economists (such as Friedrich Hayek) and evolutionary economists (such as Joseph Schumpeter). In this chapter, we propose a novel way of analyzing the complexity of self-organization in economic systems that draws upon the key model of the equilibrium-based neoclassical framework in terms of a comparative static framework for analysis of the allocation of rules between different classes of carrier. We start by *assuming complexity* (i.e., that evolutionary forces maintain complexity in open systems) and then analyze the distribution of state-space equilibria under different relative costs/prices of embedding rule-complexity in different carrier systems, such as agents or institutions.

The outcome is an *allocation of complexity*. Changes in relative prices, as caused by technological, institutional, or financial innovation, say, will effect the position of the equilibria in carrier-space. We may, therefore, study how change in the cost of embedding rules conditions the evolution of the complexity of an economic system. The upshot is a framework for arraying

Figure 1. The allocation of complexity model of rules in agents and institutional carriers as a function of the relative price of embedding isocomplexity

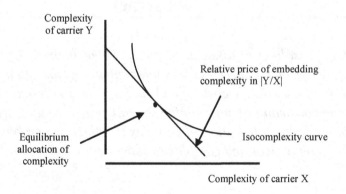

economic forces over the different dimensions of economic evolution. This enables us to study the effects of relative price changes on the dynamics of economic evolution. The use of complexity as a conservational concept (and its derivative, a convexity argument) may, we suggest, prove expedient for further theoretical and conceptual development of economic analysis. The generic graphical model, which we propose as a possible bridge between neoclassical and complexity economics is as such:

In modern evolutionary economics (Dopfer, Foster, & Potts, 2004a, Dopfer & Potts, 2007), an economic system is conceptualized as a system of meso units, with each meso unit the population of actualizations (or carriers) of a generic rule. Economic evolution is then defined as a process of change in the meso population of rules. The micro-meso-macro analytical framework reveals the underlying structure of economic evolution as a meso trajectory, and frames analysis of this process in terms of micro and macro domains. However, no account has yet been given of the economic nature of the complexity in this process, and, in particular, of the allocation problem of rules over carriers. What, in other words, are the "economics" of economic evolution? Evolutionary economists normally emphasize complementarity and connective structure (e.g., Potts, 2000). But here we propose that economic evolution can also be considered in terms of substitution and relative prices. This is achieved by recasting the prime dimensioning of analysis in terms of the comparative rule-complexity of agents and institutions, or, more generally, of "carriers."

The economic system is a rule-system and the economic process is a rule-process. From this premise, we may then isolate a classic allocation problem in the substitution relation between two primary carriers of complex rules—agents and institutions—as a function of the relative costs of embedding rules in these carriers, all subject to the constraint of maintaining overall system complexity. The allocation of complexity problem is, therefore, defined as analysis of changes in the relative costs of rule embedding in different carriers (agent and the environment) on the (allocative) distribution of complexity between them. Our fundamental premise is that complexity is carried in two fundamental classes of carrier—agents and institutions—and that difference in the cost of embedding rules in each determines the equilibrium allocation of complexity.

A framework of comparative statics, familiar to all students of economics, may thus be used to analyze the distribution of complexity carried by an economic system and how this changes as an evolutionary process. Section

2 introduces the relationship between rules and complex systems; Section 3 discusses the idea of complexity as a solution concept; Section 4 represents this in terms of the allocation of complexity problem; Section 5 completes the framework with the construct the relative price of complexity; Section 6 concludes.

Rules and Complex Systems

The economic system is a complex rule-system. The conceptualization of generic rule evolution is set out in Dopfer and Potts (2004b), and the micro-meso-macro framework is presented in Dopfer et al. (2004a) and Dopfer et al. (2007). A rule is a generic idea: a meso unit is then defined as a generic rule and the population of carriers of the rule. Beneath the surface phenomena of production and exchange, there lies the deep structure of *knowledge* as a complex system of generic rule populations; this is the abstract reality of the economic system as a complex structure of knowledge. Our question then arises: what determines the structure of this knowledge base of differentially embedded rules?

Economic evolution is the creative-destructive process of the origination and embedding of new rules and the displacement of others. This is analytically defined as a process of (generic) meso coordination and change along a "meso trajectory" of origination, adoption, and retention that occurs as a new technology (i.e., a generic rule) enters and changes the knowledge base of the economic order. The meso-centered analytical framework allows us to model economic evolution as the self-transformation of a complex rule-system. It links together evolutionary economic analysis of population dynamics and structural change—or agent learning and emergence of institutions—into a unified framework. By connecting population and statistical arguments together with arguments about complex structure, it provides a foundation for analysis of evolutionary processes as based on the coordination of complex systems. It is both ontologically and analytically coherent. Yet the generic meso-based model leaves the economics of this process unnecessarily, we think, unstated. Specifically, a basic assumption of the micro-meso-macro framework of economic evolution is that rules are embedded in the economic system in carriers. Yet Dopfer et al. make no attempt to tease out the specific form in which they are embedded, or to account for the operational economic forces that effect the allocation of rule complexity over different classes of carriers.

We propose, then, that the allocation of complexity framework can be used to analyze the rule substitution processes interior to a meso trajectory. A rule can be carried or, equivalently, embedded, in different ways: which is to say that the complexity of the economic system can manifest in various structural forms.[3] A technology, for example, could be embedded largely in the cognitive abilities of human agents, or largely in commodities or institutions. Smarter agents enable the same level of complexity to be achieved in a simpler environment, and a "smarter" environment may achieve the same with simpler agents. For example, the generic rules of bookkeeping and accounting could be embodied in accountant's heads, as it were, or in interactive software, or in some convex combination of the two carrier forms. But what determines the equilibrium allocation at a point in time, or the path an evolutionary trajectory of technology adoption will take? What determines this distribution, in other words, of rule complexity over classes of carrier?[4]

The *allocation of complexity problem* concerns the distribution of the population of a generic rule over different classes of carrier as a function of relative cost of adoption and embedding of the rule. Rules carried exclusively in one class of carrier are, obviously, not subject to the allocation of complexity problem. But, if carried in this way, they are also unlikely to be generic *economic* rules in the first place. Following Dopfer (2004) and Foster (2006), we plainly recognize that economic systems are human-centric (a methodologically individualist stance) in that they are composed of structures of knowledge (generic rules) that may be carried in agents or embedded in the institutional environment to which the agent is subject.

Economists, along with social scientists and philosophers, have traditionally drawn a sharp duality between rules carried in the mind or as behavior (by subjects) from rules carried in organizations of matter-energy (e.g., a physical technologies or commodities) or organizations of people (e.g., a firm or household). In the framework proposed here, these alternative carrier classes are conceptualized in a continuous substitution relation along the line of constant complexity (the isocomplexity function).

The agent-environment dichotomy is also a fundamental construct in complex systems analysis, including the definition of open and closed systems and of concepts such as feedback. But we suggest that an allocation problem—that is, an economic problem—emerges only when *choice* over where rules are embedded also exists. This is not the case for biological systems whose agents—genes, organs, butterflies, etc.—are constrained completely by their environment, precisely because these agents cannot exercise generic choice over the rule-composition of their environment. While it is plain that perhaps most organisms build some rules into their environment (e.g., bees nests, beaver dams, etc.), economic agents build complexity into their environment to an extent orders of magnitude greater (Raine, Foster, & Potts, 2006). Indeed, as Foster (2006) explains, such higher-order complexity is an effective definition of an economic system.

Although the science of economics relies fundamentally on the notion of human choice, we posit that the proper analysis of economic systems (or other human-based emergent complex systems, be they social, political or cultural) must rest on the recognition that human agents have the unique capacity to *externalize rules* by sometimes choosing to embed them in their environment.[5] It is the systemic consequences of such rule-embedding choices that we herein seek to illuminate. We suggest, in turn, that this hybrid methodology offers a useful way of unpacking a key mechanism in economic evolution. Our starting axiom, then, is that an economic system is a complex natural-artificial system of high-order complexity that is most immediately manifest in the variety of structural forms that a rule can be carried. The allocation of complexity problem thus arises as economic forces (and not just technological considerations) effect the equilibrium distribution of generic rules over classes of carriers.

Rules, in general, are fungible with respect to carriers, of which there are many types and classes. For ease of exposition and analytic parsimony, however, we shall presume just two classes of carrier: *agent* and *environment*. We shall assume that the complexity of a generic rule can be decomposed over these two carrier classes. Within this, and in order to allow dimensionality, each carrier class can assume varying levels of complexity. An agent, for instance, can be very simple or highly complex. The environment is also presumed to vary in complexity between states of being very simple and highly complex. While these two dimensions are clearly defined on a qualitative metric, we have in mind a quantitative metric based on an entropy measure of complexity in terms of energy or information processing as operationally "computed/processed" by the rule system (Raine et al., 2006). We thus infer (indeed axiomitize) a computational ontology of economic knowledge (Mirowski, 2007; Potts & Morrison, 2007).

The set of all combinations of a generic rule over carriers is mapped by what we call "carrier-space." The allocation of complexity is of a generic rule over carrier space. At a point in time, the complexity of a generic rule is carried in one part by the complexity of the agent in terms of its generic inheritance, generic learning, and operational acquisition, and in the other part by the complexity of the environment in terms of institutions, technology, and capital. Economic evolution is the process of change in the generic rules of the economic system: but where do these changes operationally manifest, and why? What, in other words, is the economic explanation for the allocation of the structure of knowledge over different carrier forms?

This question has general significance to the study of all intelligent complex adaptive systems, and we should not be at all surprised to find that economic systems, considered abstractly, offer insight into the nature of such systems. An economic system is a complex system of knowledge (or generic rules, in the language of our theory) composed of both rational and imaginative agents that live by and grow in wealth to the extent that they can off-load knowledge into the environment. Indeed, the nature and causes of the wealth of nations can reasonably be summarized as the extent to which we have been able to embed ideas and knowledge into the environment as technologies, capital, and institutions. Yet this is always an ongoing process from which every new idea (generic rule) begins as an idea in an individual's mind. A technology, indeed, is the name we give to such an idea that has completed the trajectory of adoption and retention into many agent carriers (as a meso trajectory). But this process has multiple equilibrium outcomes along a continuum of carrier configurations. Our question, thus, is on the determinants of this distribution.

Assume Complexity

Along with a specific understanding of the economic system as a rule-system, our theory is also based on a specific analytical assumption about the nature of complexity as a solution concept. Complexity is a partial region of the potential state-space of a system, and is therefore a property that a system may or may not have. A system may occupy one of many positions in the state-space continuum, yet only some of these states are complex. What is interesting about these states is that complexity seems to be an *attractor*. This point has been made by Kauffman (1993) and others (e.g., Potts, 2000, 2001) in relation to the balance of forces of variation and selection, and by

Prigogine (2005) and others (e.g., Allen, 1998; Foster, 2006; Schneider & Kay, 1994) in relation to the second law of thermodynamics. As the deep forces of energy mechanics in closed systems work to maintain an equilibrium state, the deep forces of open system thermodynamics and evolution seem to work to maintain complexity. The founders of the theory of fully connected market systems (e.g., Walras, Edgeworth et al.) saw fit to suppose the long-run state of the competitive economic system is general equilibrium, which became, in turn, the starting place for standard economic analysis. In contrast, we argue that the competitively maintained long-run state of a partially connected open-market economic system is general complexity, which is assumed to be a general solution concept for an open system.[6]

This is why we "assume complexity," and therefore allow a differential distribution of complexity over classes of carriers of a generic rule. Both Kauffman's hypothesis of "evolution toward complexity" and the Kay and Schneider hypothesis of "complex systems maximally degrading energy" both refer to deep forces that maintain a state of complexity in an open system process. There is mounting evidence that real world economic systems exhibit small world and scale-free properties,[7] which thus reinforces the role of complexity as a structural attractor in the state-space of a system. There are, of course, many reasons that a system will not be complex, such as to lock-in important structural features in the short run. But when this happens, flexibility or adaptive potential is lost somewhere, which tends to eventually impact on the long run prospects of the generic rule. In an open system, where there is always change in the flows of energy and information from the environment, and where the environment itself is subject to change, we should expect that the basic meso structure of an economic system will be structurally complex. Economic systems are complex because, in essence, they could not have evolved if composed otherwise (see Simon, 1969). The forces that determine the allocation of this complexity should be of significant concern not just to economists, but to all students of intelligent complex adaptive systems.

The Allocation of Complexity

In consequence, the embedding dimensions of generic rules (i.e. technology or knowledge) is a much neglected dimension of economic analysis. The allocation of complexity framework seeks then to fill this gap by proposing a decomposition of the distribution of rule complexity between rules embedded in agents and rules embedded in the institutional environment. Both agents and institutions are, in this sense, carriers of rules.

The complexity of an economic system C(R) is distributed across the complexity of agents $C(A_R)$ and the complexity of the environment of institutions $C(I_R)$ as such:

$$C(R) = C(A_R) + C(I_R)$$

Agent rules thus refers to the cognitive, behavioral, and interactive capabilities and actions of an economic agent. Economic agents are therefore *rule-using* and *rule-making* carriers (Dopfer, 2004; Potts, 2003). Examples of agent rules include skills, habits, routines, capabilities, and other instances of generic rule-behavior. These rules will have a measure of complexity.

Institutional rules, in turn, are the artificial (or artifactual) environment of the economic agent, and consist of the set of meso rules the agent is connected to. Examples include contracts, capital, commodities, organization, institutions, and so forth. These rules will also have a measure of complexity. Generic economic rules are therefore variously carried by agent and institutional rules in some convex combination. This maps the complexity measure we shall call an *isocomplexity function*, or *isocomp*.

The allocation of complexity across rule-carriers assumes a *2-d* rule-space we call *carrier space*. Any system of rules R will be distributed between agents (A_R) and institutional environment (I_R).[8] Consider Figure 2 in which the carrier dimensions of the agent and the environment are represented along orthogonal axes of increasing rule complexity. Each point in *generic carrier-space* represents a hybrid generic rule-system across agents and institutions at varying levels of carrier complexity.[9]

The generic nature of carrier-space is conceptualized as such. Point A has high complexity in the institutional environment and low complexity of agents. This might be an economic system in which there is a high degree of organization in the environment, with each agent specialized, but not very complex otherwise. A fascist or dictatorial state would be an example, as would a beehive. Point B has the same overall systemic complexity in the generic rule (i.e., has the same problem-solving capabilities—but this is achieved with less institutional complexity compensated for by greater com-

Figure 2. The carrying capacity of rule-systems by the complexity of agents and environment is mapped in meso space. ABC and FEG are a convex maps (isocomp curves) of constant complexity in meso rules C(R) and C(R') allocated over two classes of rule carriers C(I_R) and C(A_R). Isocomp curves have similar properties to indifference curves.

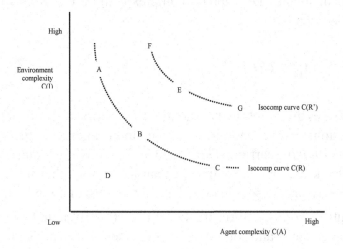

plexity in agents capabilities (learned rules)). This might be represented by a well-educated population in a more rudimentary environment (e.g., Japan after WWII, or Russia after the collapse of communism). Point C continues along this overall complexity invariance function, and might represent highly capable agents in a very primitive environment (as in the reality TV show Survivor, or Western businesses expanding into emerging markets). Point D corresponds to simple agents in a simple environment (human prehistory) and point E corresponds to complex agents in a complex environment (e.g., a modern first-world economy). Points F and G correspond to mostly uninhabited possibilities.

A map of complexity equivalent rule substitution in carrier space is called an isocomplexity function. For example, contour lines of isocomplexity are traced in meso space in the C(R) level of complexity in ABC and in the C(R') level of complexity in FEG in Figure 2. The same measure of aggregate complexity can be achieved in various ways: either with highly complex agents in a simple environment or simple agents in a highly complex environment; or some convex combination of the two. An isocomp represents the distribution of carrier-equivalent computational complexity about a meso unit that we presume to be convex in its equilibrium distribution. Convexity and complexity are thus aligned as equivalent statements of the same static/dynamic point.

A shift *along* an isocomp represents a change in the relative efficiency of carriers of a rule, and so leading to a rule being carried more by institutions rather than agents, as in Figure 2 with a shift from C to A, or E to F. This represents the process of institutional embedding. By substituting rule complexity from the agent to the environment enables simpler agents to solve the same problems as they embed rules deeper in the environment. The entrepreneur-led processes of market-making or infrastructure building are classic examples of this, as is the role of mass advertising or education. A shift along an isocomp is complexity invariant at the system level, but re-allocates complexity from one class of carrier to another. This will invariably be accompanied by structural change at the agent, firm, industry, and economy-wide level.

A shift *in* the isocomp, say from the locus of points though ABC to those running through FEG in Figure 2, represents an increase in the aggregate complexity of the rule-system. Such emergent complexity is, in fact, a necessary process in generic economic evolution as mandated by the second law of thermodynamics applied to an open system (Raine et al., 2006). Increased energy throughput is achieved through increased complexity. But there are many ways this can happen and without further consideration it is unclear what the distributive effect will actually be on the generic allocation of complexity between agents and institutions.

Three possibilities from point B are previously illustrated. An evolutionary meso trajectory B to E preserves the distribution of complexity, while a trajectory from B to F represents an institution-dominated growth of complexity, and one from B to G represents an agent-dominated growth of complexity. But what will happen is yet undetermined. All we can say is that a shift in an isocomp, say from $C(R) \to C(R')$, represents an increase in the complexity of the aggregate rule system in consequence of the growth of opportunities created by the growth of knowledge.

A shift along an isocomp curve is meso complexity preserving. A shift in the isocomp curve corresponds to increased overall energy-transformation and/or information processing or problem solving by an increase in the complexity of the generic rules of both agents and institutions. The growth of knowledge and the growth of economic systems are but two sides of the same problem of the allocation of complexity.[10] The normal direction of economic evolution is to increase both the complexity of institutions and agents as an overall increase in the energy or information throughput of the system. This will tend to correspond to an increase in the state of knowledge of the economic system. In general, the dynamical path of economic evolution can be traced out in this meso space.

But, without some notion of relative costs or prices of complexity under different allocative conditions, a generic trajectory is undetermined. The energy-complexity framework tells us the general direction upon which we should expect things to happen, but there is as yet no choice theory in this argument. For that, we need to consider the implications of a budget constraint on the allocation of complexity.

The Relative Price of Complexity

We may introduce relative prices, or relative costs,[11] into this framework by considering the relative price of carrying a generic rule as considered variously in terms of an agent or in terms of the agent's environment. As argued above, the existence condition of a generic rule is that it is always able to be substituted between agent and environment, and vice versa. We now suppose that the equilibrium outcome will be in proportion to the *cost* (relative generic and operational price) of embedding complexity in the agent or environment respectively.

The relative price of complexity between institutions and agents is given by the budget line C(I)–C(A). The slope of the budget line is given by the relative costs of carrying complexity (P_I/P_A). A steep budget line means that institutional carrier costs are relatively lower than agent carrier costs, making it better to carry complexity of rules in institutions rather than in agents. A flatter budget line means that agents carry the rule relatively more efficiently than institutions. A fall in the absolute cost of complexity, in both agents and institutions, shifts the budget line outward. An increase in the absolute cost of complexity shifts the budget line inwards. Figure 3 illustrates a shift in the carrying costs of complexity to make agent carriers relatively cheaper than institutions.

Figure 3. A shift in the budget line for carrying complexity. A fall in the complexity of institutions is compensated for by a rise in the complexity of agents

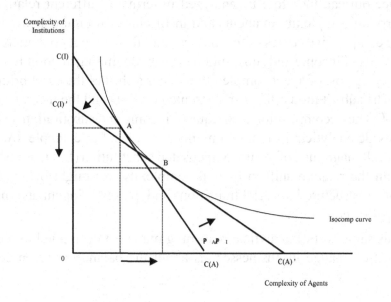

A pivot in the "budget line" as illustrated in Figure 3 might be caused by a change in the relative efficiency (or efficacy) of rule-carriers, but a shift outward of the budget line as in Figure 4 would be caused by an absolute change in the efficiency and efficacy of rule carriers. Both sorts of change are induced by new rules, and what specifically happens will depend on the particular character of the novel generic rule and its relation to other rules. For example, the introduction of a new generic rule in the form of an improvement in technology, or market infrastructure, or agent skills will probably change both the relative costs of embedding and the absolute costs of embedding.

Nevertheless, our analytical framework separates the two components of relative and absolute price changes. An absolute shift corresponds to a new rule enabling a higher level of aggregate complexity overall, and therefore energy throughput, but without changing the underlying carrying costs. This defines an outward shift of the budget constraint to a higher isocomp curve. A suitable example would be the introduction of PCs or mobile phones, both of which require more complex institutional support, and, in their early days at least, increased agent complexity.

The set of different possible trajectories an evolving economic system may trace out can therefore be analyzed in terms of different relative costs of carrying complexity in agents and institutions. In Figure 4, we decompose the comparative statics of this process into the conventional microeconomic notions of income and substitution effects. Beginning at point E, a fall in the carrying cost of agent complexity induces a shift of the equilibrium to point F. The substitution effect is represented by E–D and the income effect from D–F. The decomposition technique of income and substitution analysis may provide analytical insight in a number of ways. For example, by indicating the full magnitude of the uncompensated substitution (E–D) as distinguished from the relative shift in overall complexity, we might better understand how to structure industrial transitions and the sort of agent and institutional support required.

This same sort of analytical reasoning may also be applied to the management of change in businesses, as about the balance between centralizing

Figure 4. Income and substitution effects traced out by different relative costs of carrying complexity. A reduction in the relative carrying cost of complexity in agents induces a shift in overall complexity. This can be decomposed into an income effect and a substitution effect.

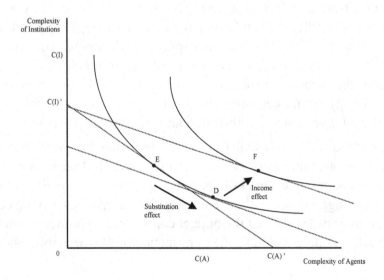

and decentralizing such a process of rule substitution, as say the process of adaptation to a new market or technology. Substitution effects therefore measure the *cost of change*, and income (or wealth) effects measure the *gain from change*. Of course, without formal elucidation of the analytical meaning of a complexity measure, these concepts are still somewhat conjectural. But they do hint at the possibility of a complexity-based welfare analysis of evolutionary economic processes.

There are other aspects of this framework we might explore. For example, Figure 5 illustrates how we may represent the dynamical path of a complex evolving system by constructing this as a meso trajectory of relatively constant complexity embedding. This forms, as mapped through 0BD, an evolutionary "contract curve" of system coordination.[12] The connection of this to the Schumpeterian notion of a trajectory should be obvious to scholars of evolutionary economics. Allocation of complexity theory therefore offers a method for analyzing evolutionary economic processes at the level of rule substitution between classes of carriers as a function of the relative price of doing so. In this way, rule complexity is allocated between carrier dimensions

Figure 5. A shift out in the budget line for carrying complexity along a meso trajectory. The introduction of a new meso rule that is agent-institution neutral corresponds to a shift out in the budget line and therefore to a new tangency condition on a higher isocomp (from B to D).

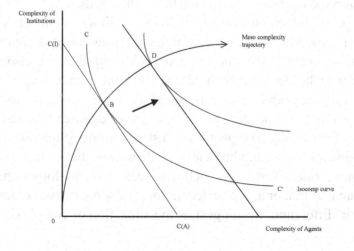

as a function of the relative price of embedding said rule complexity into each carrier dimension. Complexity goes where incentives tell it to go.

Conclusion

This chapter has sought to advance the theory of complex adaptive systems through consideration of a prime open-system economic dimension: namely, the allocation of generic rule complexity over different classes of carriers. What we argued was essentially that a standard neoclassical economic analysis of relative prices in the context of continuous substitution can provide a useful method for the analysis of an important economic dimension the behavior of an intelligent complex adaptive system, namely the allocation of generic complexity over carrier-space. We have proposed a comparative static methodology for analysis of economic evolution that, following Dopfer et al. (2004) and Dopfer et al. (2007), is conceptualized as a generic rule process. The basic ontological building block of this view is a meso unit: a generic rule and its population of carriers. Economic evolution is defined within this framework as an increase in the rule complexity of an economic system. But, in our view, the essential economic question is: complexity where? When knowledge grows, where does it accumulate?

Allocation of complexity theory is a way of analyzing the allocation problem inherent in this set-up, namely between changes in complexity in agents and changes in complexity in the economic environment in terms of continuous substitution along an isocomplexity function in terms of the relative price of adoption and retention. According to our theory, then, when the relative price of adoption and retention changes, so the equilibrium allocation of complexity will shift. And while we emphasize the foundational importance of this analytic concept to the study of economic evolution, we also wish to draw attention to the significance of this generic allocation concept in the evolution of all complex adaptive systems, intelligent ones especially: for what is intelligence, but the proper balance of dynamic engagement? Just as evolutionary biology foists a genotype/phenotype distinction on evolutionary social science, evolutionary economics has a generic distinction between classes of carriers of generic rules. Variously, each new idea or technology is best carried in the human mind, or as a pure technology, or some convex combination. The analytic difference, we suggest, is the allocation of complexity.

References

Allen, P. (1998). Evolving complexity in social science. In G. Altman, & W. Koch (Eds.), *Systems: New perspectives for the human sciences*. Berlin: Waltyer de Gruyter.

Dopfer, K. (2004). The economic agent as rule maker and rule user: Homo Sapiens Oeconomicus. *Journal of Evolutionary Economics, 14*, 177-195.

Dopfer, K., & Potts, J. (2007). *The general theory of economic evolution*. London: Routledge.

Dopfer, K., & Potts, J. (2004b). Evolutionary realism: A new ontology for economics. *Journal of Economic Methodology, 11*, 195-212.

Dopfer, K., Foster, J., & Potts, J. (2004a). Micro meso macro. *Journal of Evolutionary Economics, 14*, 263-79.

Earl, P. E, & Potts, J. (2004). Market for preferences. *Cambridge Journal of Economics, 28*, 619-33.

Earl, P. E., & Potts, J. (2001). Latent demand and the browsing shopper. *Managerial and Decision Economics, 21*, 111-22.

Foster, J. (2006). From simplistic to complex systems in economics. *Cambridge Journal of Economics, 29*(4), 873-92.

Foster, J., Ramlogan, R., & Metcalfe, J. S. (2006). Adaptive economic growth. *Cambridge Journal of Economics, 30*(1), 7-32.

Hayek, F. (1960). *The constitution of liberty*. Chicago: University of Chicago Press.

Loasby, B. (1999). *Knowledge, evolution, and institutions in economics*. Routledge: London.

Mirowski, P. (2007). Markets come to bits: Evolution, computation and markomata in economic science. *Journal of Economic Behavior and Organization, 63*(2), 209-42.

Ormerod, P. (2006). *Why most things fail: Evolution, extinction, and economics*. London: Faber and Faber.

Potts, J. (2003). Toward an evolutionary theory of homo economicus: The concept of universal nomadism. In J. Laurent (Ed.), *Evolutionary economics and human nature*. Edward Elgar: Cheltenham (ch 8).

Potts, J. (2001). Knowledge and markets. *Journal of Evolutionary Economics*, *11*, 413-31.

Potts, J. (2000). *The new evolutionary microeconomics: Complexity, competence, and adaptive behaviour*. Edward Elgar: Cheltenham

Potts, J., & Morrison, K. (2007). Meso comes to markets. *Journal of Economic Behavior and Organization*, *63*(2), 307-12.

Prigogine, I. (2005). The rediscovery of value and the opening of economics. In K. Dopfer (Ed.), *Evolutionary foundations of economics*. Cambridge: Cambridge University Press.

Raine, A., Foster, J., & Potts, J. (2006). The new entropy law and the economic process. *Ecological Complexity*, *3*(4), 354-60.

Schneider, E., & Kay, J. (1994). Life as a manifestation of the second law of thermodynamics. *Mathematical Computational Modeling*, *19*, 25-48.

Shackle, G. L. S. (1972). *Epistemics and economics: A critique of economic doctrines*. Cambridge: Cambridge University Press.

Simon, H. (1969). The architecture of complexity. *Proceedings of the American Philosophical Society* (Vol. 106, pp. 476-82).

Endnotes

[1]   Special thanks to participants at Organizations, innovation and complexity – New perspectives on the knowledge economy, NEXUS–CRIC Workshop, University of Manchester, 9–10 Sept 2004, and especially B Rosewell and P Ormerod, as well as those at Shifting boundaries: Governance, competence and economic organization in the knowledge economy, Bristol Business School, 2–3 Sept 2004, especially N Foss, N Kay and B Nooteboom. Also, special thanks to K Bruce, R Ramlogan, JS Metcalfe, K Dopfer, and J Foster.

[2]   The views expressed in this paper are his own and do not necessarily reflect the opinions of *Suncorp*.

[3]   Earl and Potts (2004) have recently illustrated how choice itself can be considered in this way when decision complexity leads boundedly rational consumers to outsource decision rules to market environments. Their 'market for preferences' concept can be viewed as an allocation

of rule complexity problem, when the rules are inputs into a decision heuristic conceived along an isocomp. See also Earl and Potts (2001) on the allocation of complexity with respect to the design of shopping environments.

[4] One might reasonably suppose that the answer to this question is transactions costs, in the Ronald Coase or Oliver Williamson. Isocomplexity theory is more aligned with Coase's original version about alternative coordinating institutions rather than Williamson's development of the idea into statements about bargaining games, etc. We suggest that isocomplexity theory provides a more general theory of this process, by taking into account the costs of embedding rules in a system, as well as the ongoing costs of using them. Isocomplexity theory deals with systems costs generally, an of which transaction costs are a subset.

[5] This is also called *exosomatic* evolution. It is a broader concept than what Richard Dawkin's calls *memes*. See Dopfer and Potts (2007) for general discussion.

[6] A further way of treating complexity, recently proposed by Foster (2006), is with the notion of an economic system as being 4th order complex (dissipative physiochemical systems are 1st order complex, biological systems are 2nd order complex, social systems are 3rd order complex). The emergence of higher order complexity turns on the emergence of new ways of acquiring and using energy through ever more complex systems of knowledge and interaction. An economic system is 4th order complex in that agents must not only form mental models of the environment (3rd order) but also of each other mental models. This is apparent in such things as contracts and other market institutions.

[7] See Ormerod (2006).

[8] The algebraic properties of meso space derive from the set-theoretic conception of the carrier dimensions. It is unclear to us whether it is reasonable to assume these to be real valued. It would certainly be convenient. At the risk of unhinging the analysis before it starts, let us make that a point for mooting.

[9] We immediately rule out corner solutions by assuming that there is no such thing as an economic system purely made of agents, and similarly, no such system purely made of environment. An economic system is a system of economic systems, and each economic system consists of a non-zero combination of both agents and institutions. All economic

rules are embedded in both agents and institutions and are fungible between.

[10]   See Hayek (1960), Shackle (1972), Loasby (1999).

[11]   Because each point on an isocomp corresponds to the steady state of a general equilibrium under competitive conditions (and so extensions to this framework arrive under conditions of imperfect competition), then each set of relative prices, under duality conditions, also corresponds to the set of relative costs.

[12]   This raises a number of analytic questions. What, for example, is the nature of the factors that determine relative cost of embedding, or the manner in which complexity is structured in an aggregate system? Does the network classification of the system matter (i.e., does the shape of the isocomp depend upon whether we are dealing with a small world or scale-free network?) Does the distribution of complexity over a population of agents matter?

About the Contributors

Ang Yang joined the Division of Land and Water at the Commonwealth Scientific and Industrial Research Organisation (CSIRO) in 2007. Yang holds a PhD in computer science (UNSW, Australia), a MInfoSc in information systems (Massey University, New Zealand), an MSc in environmental geography (Nanjing University, China), and a BSc in ecology & environmental biology (Ocean University of China, China). His current research interests include complex adaptive systems, multi-agent systems, modelling and simulation, evolutionary computation, network theory, and Web-based intelligent systems.

Yin Shan is with Medicare Australia as a senior review assessment officer working on data mining and machine learning applications on medical data. He previously worked as a scientific programmer in the Australian National University and a postdoctoral research fellow in the University of New South Wales, Australia. He received his PhD in computer science from the University of New South Wales (2005) and his MSc and BSc in computer science from Wuhan University, China (1999 and 1996, respectively). His main interests are evolutionary computation, in particular genetic programming and its applications.

* * *

Hayward R. Alker graduated in 1959 from M.I.T. in mathematics and received his PhD in political science from Yale University (1963). After serving on the Yale and M.I.T. faculties in political science, he is now a professor of international relations at the University of Southern California and an adjunct professor at the Watson Institute of International Studies, Brown University. He has served on the executive committee of the International Social Science Council as chair of the Mathematical Social Sciences Board and president of the International Studies Association.

Gordon L. Bonser obtained a bachelor of science degree in natural resource planning from Humboldt State University, Arcata, California (1974). Gordon taught geographic information systems (GIS) at Humboldt State University, Department of Natural Resources and Sciences (http://www.humboldt.edu/~cnrs/departments/enrs.html) His research specialized in the field of multi-spectral analysis of images acquired using space-based platforms such as LANDSAT for the purpose of ecosystem-level vegetation mapping and modeling. Projects included analysis of human impacts on salmon habitat in a large watershed in Northern California (1995) and an analysis of changes in fire frequency and intensity on the Snake Rive Plains of Idaho as a result of rainfall, introduced Asian plants, and land use (1996). Presently he is semi-retired.

Joseph Clark is a PhD candidate in the School of Economics at the University of Queensland. He is also a research economist at Suncorp Pty. Ltd. The views expressed in this chapter are his own and do not necessarily reflect the opinions of Suncorp.

David Cornforth is senior lecturer at the University of New South Wales. He has been an educator for twenty years, including teaching a variety of discipline areas at four different universities. He has worked as a programmer and data analyst in the automotive, tourist, financial, health, water supply, and electricity supply industries. He has been involved in research in complex systems for the last seven years, and has published a large number of research articles on this and related topics.

Jean-Louis Dessalles is associate professor at ParisTech, École Nationale Supérieure des Télécommunications. His domain of research is about the cognitive modelling of language and about the emergence of stable communication in a population of selfish agents. He authored a book on the emergence of language, now translated in English (*Why We Yalk*, Oxford University Press, 2007).

Guszti Eiben is professor and head of the computational intelligence group in the department of computer science at the Vrije Universiteit in Amsterdam, the Netherlands. His main research interest is evolutionary computation. Evolutionary computation is the binding theme in much of Guszti's academic research that can be catalogued under natural computing, or soft computing, with applications in optimization, data mining, artificial life, and artificial societies. Specific research subjects are multi-parent recombination, constraint handling and self-calibrating algorithms, the effect of communication in Artificial Life, and modeling evolving societies.

Jacques Ferber is professor of computer sciences at Montpellier. His domain of research is about multiagent systems (MAS), distributed systems, multiagent simulation, component-based and agent-based software engineering. He started to work in MAS in 1987 and is considered as a pioneer of this field in France. His introductory book on MAS and distributed artificial intelligence has been published in French, English, and German. Member of several editorial boards and program committee (conferences and workshops), Ferber is the co-author with Olivier Gutknecht and Fabien Michel of the MadKit multiagent platform.

David G. Green is professor of information technology at Monash University. In the course of thirty-five years of research on complexity he has investigated problems as diverse as forest ecology, proteins, and social networks. He proved the universality of networks in complex systems and is author of 9 books and more than 160 research articles on complexity theory, evolutionary computing, and multi-agent systems. An early pioneer of the World Wide Web as a distributed information resource, he also played a leading role in national and international efforts to create a coordinated Web of information sources about the world's biodiversity and environments.

Thomy Nilsson, a BSc '63 from Rensselaer, provided a physics background and, under Kandel, experimental psychology. At Columbia, Kietzman introduced the latest research technologies. For MSc '68 & PhD '72 with Thomas Nelson at Alberta, Thomy Nilsson developed vision laboratories and later as research associate expanded into ergonomics; Wilson introduced artificial intelligence. Bourassa at Portland's Neurophysiology Institute and Donchin at Illinois broadened Thomy Nilsson's technical and physiological skills. A professorship at UPEI added research on aging. Teaching inspired statistics and research methods books. Thomy Nilsson's vision research focuses on color, temporal factors, legibility, and memory; discovered visual temporal tuning, "cool effect," memory retrieval characteristics, pinhead mirror, and chromatic legibility. Thomy Nilsson is now an emeritus professor.

Geoff Nitschke is a research assistant working within the computational intelligence group in the department of computer science at the Vrije Universiteit in Amsterdam, the Netherlands. Nitschke's research interests include evolutionary computation, neural networks, artificial life, and collective behavior systems. The research issue being addressed is how concepts such as self-organization, evolution, and learning can be used in formulating biologically inspired design principles for collective behavior systems. The goal is to apply such biologically inspired design principles as problem solving methods in collective behavior systems. Examples of such collective behavior systems include collective gathering, reconnaissance, and construction in multi-robot systems.

Kate Morrison is director of Volterra Pacific Pty. Ltd., a Brisbane-based economics consultancy that specializes in complexity based analysis.

Pascal Perez is currently seconded by his French research agency CIRAD to the Australian National University (ANU) in Canberra (Australia). He is the convenor of the Human Ecosystems Modelling with Agents (HEMA) international network. Agronomist by training, his most recent work focuses on human ecosystems modelling. He has developed projects in northern Thailand, Indonesia, and Micronesia. He is currently teaching agent based modelling at the ANU.

Denis Phan is post and telecommunications administrator, doctor in economics, and senior researcher in economics and social sciences at the CNRS. His past research interests are in the economics of telecommunications, the software industry, and regulation. He has published papers and various books in this field. Since 2000, his main research interests have been cognitive and agent-based computational economics. He is the co-author with Antoine Beugnard of the *Moduleco simulation Framework*, now integrated into the Madkit Platform as a plug-in. He has organized several researcher schools on complex systems and MAS and published with Frederic Amblard an introductory book on MAS modeling and simulation for Human and Social Sciences in French, to be traduced in English for *The Bardwell Press*.

Jason Potts is senior lecturer at the School of Economics & ARC Centre for Complex Systems, University of Queensland, Australia. He is currently on secondment as principal research fellow at the ARC Centre of Excellence for Creative Industries and Innovation, Queensland University of Technology, Australia.

Grigorii S. Pushnoi has a master's degree in physics from the St. Petersburg State University, Russia. He is an investigator of Complex Evolving Systems. Working as a manager of business organizations in St. Petersburg, he observed the dynamics of those businesses' development: why some organizations are successful, while others fail or disintegrate. This valuable experience helped him to find a new vision of the evolutionary processes. He developed a unique "top-bottom" technique of the complex adaptive systems modeling: the Method of System's Potential: (MSP). His report for the 21st International Conference of the System Dynamics Society is included in the System Dynamics online course (Politechnic University of Catalonia; Terrassa, Spain). His papers dedicated to applications of MSP in Econophysics and Business Cycle Theory are published in the Proceedings of the International A.Bogdanov Institute in Russia. He moderates the interdisciplinary scientific forum: "Socintegrum," which is dedicated to the problems of civilization's development and their solutions.

Kurt A. Richardson is the associate director for the ISCE Group and is director of ISCE Publishing, a recently founded publishing house that specializes in complexity-related publications. He has a BSc(hons) in physics (1992), MSc in astronautics and space engineering (1993), and a PhD in applied physics (1996). Kurt's current research interests include the philosophical implications of assuming that everything we observe is the result of underlying complex processes, the relationship between structure and function, analytical frameworks for intervention design, and robust methods of reducing complexity, which have resulted in the publication of 25+ journal papers and book chapters. He is the managing/production editor for the *International Journal Emergence: Complexity & Organization* and is on the review board for the journals *Systemic Practice and Action Research*, and *Systems Research and Behavioral Science*, and has performed adhoc reviewing for *Journal of Artificial Societies and Social Simulation and*

Nonlinear Dynamics, Psychology, and the Life Sciences. Kurt is the editor of the recently published *Managing Organizational Complexity: Philosophy, Theory, Practice* (Information Age Publishing, 2005) and is co-editor of the forthcoming books *Complexity and Policy Analysis: Decision Making in an Interconnected World* (due August 2007) and *Complexity and Knowledge Management: Understanding the Role of Knowledge in the Management of Social Networks* (due December 2007).

Martijn Schut is an assistant professor working within the computational intelligence group in the department of computer science at the Vrije Universiteit in Amsterdam, the Netherlands. Martijn's research concerns the understanding of the behavior and self-organization of complex systems. That is, systems in which the interaction of the components is not simply reducible to the properties of the components. Martijn's research addresses how systems of very many independent computational agents should cooperate in order to process information and achieve their goals, in a way that is efficient, self-optimizing, adaptive, and robust in the face of damage or attack.

Russell Standish is a computational scientist and principal of High Performance Coders, a computational science consulting practice based in Sydney, Australia. He has extensive contacts with academia, with a visiting associate professorship at the University of New South Wales, and also an active research program in Complex Systems, focussing on evolutionary systems using artificial life techniques. He has recently published a book *"Theory of Nothing"* that applies the notions of complexity and information to tackle age-old ontological questions.

Hrafn Thorri Thórisson has been studying natural and artificial creative systems for several years. His research has earned significant recognition, including Iceland's National Young Scientists' Award and a nomination for the Icelandic Presidential Innovation Award. He studies computer science at Reykjavik University and is a member of the Center for Analysis and Design of Intelligent Agents. Thórisson is the founder of Iceland's first and only A.I. association, The Icelandic Society for Intelligence Research, and currently resides as its president.

Steven E. Wallis received his PhD from Fielding Graduate University in 2006. His academic work focuses on -Y´theory of theory¡ where he is developing insights and tools to support scholars as they create increasingly effective theory. Wallis's interdisciplinary approach spans the social sciences. In addition to complexity theory, a few of his interests include collaborative human systems, knowledge management, and organizational theory. Dr. Wallis has ten years of experience as an independent consultant in Northern California. There, in a variety of industries, he supports consultants, trainers, and leaders on issues related to collaboration, communication, succession planning, creativity, and knowledge management.

Index